Articles on Aristotle

Plato and Aristotle in dialectical debate, by Luca della Robbia, from the
Campanile del Duomo, Florence (photo Mansell Alinari)

Articles on Aristotle

2. Ethics and Politics

edited by

Jonathan Barnes
Malcolm Schofield
Richard Sorabji

St. Martin's Press · New York

Printed in Great Britain
Library of Congress Catalog Card Number 77-020604
· ISBN 0-312-05478-5
First published in the United States of America in 1978

CONTENTS

PREFACE

The excellences of Aristotle's ethical and political theories are both grand and familiar: few philosophers will be found to deny that the *Nicomachean Ethics* and the *Politics* are masterpieces of philosophy. One of the aims of the first volume in this series was to vindicate Aristotle's philosophy of science against the sweeping and contemptuous criticism with which it has often been assailed. The present volume has no need to take up the cudgels on Aristotle's behalf: its constituent papers (of which one is previously unpublished and four are newly translated into English) do, we think, cast a new light on old topics; but the importance and the value of what they illuminate has never been seriously in question. We do, however, hope to direct some fresh attention to the importance of the links between ethics and politics, subjects which Aristotle himself regarded as forming a single practical philosophy. Recent scholarship has often ignored this, treating the *Ethics* and the *Politics* separately from one another: we hope that the present volume, by uniting papers on ethics and papers on politics, will do something to compensate for that unhappy tendency.

In ethics as in science Aristotle's thought has firm roots in his intellectual past. In Chaper 1, Flashar examines some of the connections which link Aristotle to Plato. He analyses Aristotle's objections to Plato's attempt to ground moral philosophy on the metaphysical theory of Forms; and his analysis leads him to discuss the relationship between Aristotle's two treatises on morals, the *Nicomachean Ethics* and the less familiar *Eudemian Ethics*. Ackrill, in Chapter 2, considers in detail one of the arguments which Aristotle deploys against Plato. His paper brings out one of the ways in which Aristotle's own ethical thought rests upon logical and metaphysical doctrines.

Ethics is essentially practical philosophy: a chief task of Aristotle's *Ethics* is to guide us toward the best kind of life for man – a goal which Aristotle calls *eudaimonia*. A requisite for the attainment of *eudaimonia*, or 'happiness' as it is conventionally translated, is virtue (*aretē*). The Greek terms *eudaimonia* and *aretē* are notoriously tricky; and the notions of virtue and happiness to which they roughly – but only roughly – correspond, are philosophically elusive. In Chapter 3, Kenny offers a sympathetic analysis of Aristotle's main thesis, that *eudaimonia* is the 'good for man'; and he shows the impertinence of several of the commoner criticisms of Aristotle's eudaimonism. In Chapter 4, Hardie examines some central features of Aristotle's account of moral virtue; he anatomises the celebrated doctrine that moral virtue is a 'Mean'; and in a new appendix to his paper he scrutinises Aristotle's notion of an 'extraordinary' virtue.

An account of rational action must form part of any satisfactory moral theory. In the opinion of many philosophers, Aristotle's pages on this subject are among the sharpest and most stimulating in the *Ethics*. As a preliminary, Aristotle essays an analysis of voluntariness: Furley, in Chapter 5, places this analysis in its historical setting and expounds some of its more difficult aspects. Chapters 6 and 7 turn to rational action itself. Anscombe, in Chapter 6, provides a trenchant and subtle dissection of Aristotle's concept of rational choice (*prohairesis*); and she examines his difficult but rewarding remarks on practical reasoning and practical truth. Her paper is complemented by Allan's in Chapter 7; for Allan refurbishes the view that the task of practical wisdom (*phronêsis*) is not only to ensure that the means we adopt to a chosen end are satisfactory but also to give our choice of the end a foundation in reason. On this account, Aristotle stands in clear contrast to Hume and to a long tradition in modern moral philosophy: reason is not the slave of the passions but the author and director of practical thought and moral action.

If reason has such directive power, how can men fail to act as they think best? How is moral backsliding (*akrasia*) possible? Aristotle's attempt to answer this potentially embarrassing question is full of difficulties: in Chapter 8, Robinson offers a lucid exposition, and some close criticism, of his attempted solution. Pleasure will seem to be one potent inducement to backsliding; and pleasure is, in any case, one of the mainsprings of human action. Aristotle's twin accounts of pleasure in *Nicomachean Ethics* VII and X strike most readers as inconsistent: in Chapter 9, Owen presents a novel exegesis of those accounts; and he argues that Aristotle is striving towards a consistent and complex view of the several notions which we loosely conjoin under the title of pleasure.

An Aristotelian man, acting and thinking rationally, will aim at *eudaimonia*; and he will find it, according to the last pages of the *Nicomachean Ethics*, in a species of intellectual activity called *theôria* or contemplation. This thesis is further elaborated in the last tangled book of the *Eudemian Ethics*. Pierre Defourny, in Chapter 10, gives a detailed analysis of Aristotle's argument there, concluding that the rational contemplator will engage in a type of theology. This conclusion transports us from the *Ethics* to the *Metaphysics*; for theology and metaphysics are, in Aristotle's view, intimately connected. The topic will be taken up in our Volume 3.

Aristotelian men are not islands: man is a political animal, who can only live and live well in a society. The *Politics* opens with an account of the structure and purpose of political association. In this account the concept of nature (*phusis*) plays the leading part – indeed, it does so throughout the *Politics*. One of the features of Chapter 11, by von Fritz and Kapp, is a clear discussion of Aristotle's thesis that the state is a *natural* institution. In Chapter 12, Finley, whose paper carefully combines evidence from the *Politics* with evidence from the *Ethics*, is concerned, *inter alia*, with Aristotle's view on *natural* and *unnatural* uses of money. In Chapter 13, Fortenbaugh considers, with more care and sympathy than is customary, Aristotle's forthright judgments about the status of women and of slaves; he concerns himself with Aristotle's notorious thesis that some men are slaves by *nature*, and analyses Aristotle's attempt to connect the status of women with their *nature*.

More than any other branch of philosophy, political theory is determined by the historical circumstances of the theoriser. And Aristotle's theory is no exception: the type of society that he has in mind throughout the *Politics* is one we no longer know; and its internal structure, its characteristic problems, and its distinctive pursuits have no direct counterparts today. These facts emerge clearly from the papers by Kelsen (Chapter 14), Wheeler (Chapter 15) and Finley. One of Kelsen's main aims is to set firmly in their historical context Aristotle's views on the nature and merits of different forms of government. Both Wheeler and Finley compare and contrast Aristotle with Marx: Wheeler finds Aristotle aware of the importance of the class struggle between rich and poor, but even more impressed by the struggle between good and bad classes in the state; Finley refuses to see Marx's theory of exchange value, or any genuine economic analysis, in Aristotle's *Ethics*, and explains his opposition in the *Politics* to certain capitalistic practices in terms of the very different economic conditions of the time.

Yet the enormous difference in political background is in a way an asset: it forces us to recognise and reconsider some of our own presuppositions. We should be stimulated to think freshly not only by Aristotle's views on the status of women, on the use of money, and on the causes of civil strife, which are analysed by Fortenbaugh, Finley and Wheeler, but also by his ambivalent attitude to the rival charms of despotism and democracy, which is examined by Kelsen. Still more pertinent to contemporary problems is the subject-matter of Chapter 16, where Defourny considers Aristotle's views of the purpose of the state. The state is a natural institution which enables the individual to pursue his natural aim – *eudaimonia*. To further that aim, the primary objective of foreign policy must be peace, not war, since peace is a prerequisite of the goal of individual *eudaimonia*. Ethics and politics have, at bottom, this same goal. The fact has far-reaching implications: it connects, as our Volume 4 will indicate, with Aristotle's views on education and on aesthetics.

As a coda to this volume, Weil's essay assesses Aristotle's merits as an historian. Although Aristotle's historical researches, most of which have left no direct trace, were massive and influential, modern scholars have sometimes dismissed him as a blind or blinkered historian whose philosophical predilections overcame his desire for objectivity. Weil discusses the relation between philosophy and history in Aristotle's thought and practice; and he shows us a historian whose imperfections are outweighed by a scholarly seriousness and a philosophical vision of the nature of human history.

Once again, authors and publishers have not only granted us permission to use copyright material, but also viewed our requests with sympathy and interest and cooperated with us in every way. Acknowledgments are made as follows:

Chapter 1: Neske Verlag, Pfullingen.
Chapter 2: Bruno Cassirer Ltd., Oxford.
Chapters 3, 4, 9: The Editor, *Proceedings of the Aristotelian Society*.
Chaper 5: Princeton University Press.

Chapter 6: Routledge and Kegan Paul, and Humanities Press.
Chapter 7: North-Holland Publishing Co., Amsterdam.
Chapter 8: The Clarendon Press, Oxford.
Chapter 10: L'Institut Historique Belge de Rome.
Chapter 11: Macmillan Publishing Co. (Hafner Press).
Chapter 13: The Past and Present Society.
Chapter 14: Johns Hopkins University Press.
Chapter 15: The University of Chicago Press.
Chapter 16: Éditions Beauchesne, Rue de Rennes 117, Paris 6e.
Chapter 17: Fondation Hardt pour l'étude de l'antiquité classique.

The essays were originally published as follows:

Chapter 1   Hellmut Flashar   *The Critique of Plato's Theory of Ideas in Aristotle's Ethics*
Originally published in German in *Synusia: Festgabe für Wolfgang Schadewaldt*, ed. H. Flashar and K. Gaiser (Pfullingen, 1965). In this version, translated by Malcolm Schofield, the annotation has been greatly reduced.
Chapter 2   J.L. Ackrill   *Aristotle on 'Good' and the Categories*
Islamic Philosophy and the Classical Tradition: Essays Presented to Richard Walzer, ed. S.M. Stern, A. Hourani and V. Brown (Oxford, 1972).
Chapter 3   Anthony Kenny   *Aristotle on Happiness*
Proceedings of the Aristotelian Society 66 (1965-6), pp. 93-102. The revised version of the paper which is printed here has also been published in Kenny's *The Anatomy of the Soul*, to which the marginal pagination refers.
Chapter 4   W.F.R. Hardie   *Aristotle's Doctrine that Virtue is a 'Mean'*
Proceedings of the Aristotelian Society 65 (1964-5), pp. 183-204. The last eight pages, dealing with Aristotle's physical theories, have been replaced by a new appendix concerned with Aristotle's ethics.
Chapter 5   D.J. Furley   *Aristotle on the Voluntary*
Originally published as pp. 161-2, 184-95 and 216-26 of *Two Studies in the Greek Atomists* by D.J. Furley (Princeton University Press, 1967). Some text and notes relating primarily to Epicurus have been omitted, and the author has added some remarks to prepare the work for its altered setting.
Chapter 6   G.E.M. Anscombe   *Thought and Action in Aristotle*
New Essays in Plato and Aristotle, ed. R. Bambrough (London and New York, 1965).
Chapter 7   D.J. Allan   *Aristotle's Account of the Origin of Moral Principles*
Actes du XIe Congrès Internationale de Philosophie, Vol. XII, 1953, pp. 120-7.
Chapter 8   Richard Robinson   *Aristotle on Akrasia*
From his *Essays in Greek Philosophy* (London, 1969). The article was originally composed in French as 'L'acrasie selon Aristote', delivered as a lecture at the Sorbonne on 7 April 1954, and published in *Revue Philosophique*. The author translated it into English for this book.
Chapter 9   G.E.L. Owen   *Aristotelian Pleasures*
Proceedings of the Aristotelian Society 72 (1971-2), pp. 135-52.
Chapter 10   Pierre Defourny   *Contemplation in Aristotle's Ethics*
Originally published as 'L'activité de contemplation dans les morales d'Aristote', in *Bulletin de l'Institut Historique Belge de Rome* 18 (1937), pp.

89-101; translated by Jennifer and Jonathan Barnes.

Chapter 11   K. von Fritz and E. Kapp   *The 'Constitution of Athens' and Aristotle's Political Philosophy*

Originally published as Chapter III of the introduction to *Aristotle's Constitution of Athens and Related Texts* (New York, 1950).

Chapter 12   W.W. Fortenbaugh   *Aristotle on Slaves and Women*

Not previously published.

Chapter 13   M.I. Finley   *Aristotle and Economic Analysis*

This chapter is reprinted from *Past and Present, A Journal Of Historical Studies* 47 (May 1970), pp. 3-25. It has also been reprinted in *Studies in Ancient Society*, ed. M.I. Finley (London, 1974).

Chapter 14   Marcus Wheeler   *Aristotle's Analysis of the Nature of Political Struggle*

American Journal of Philology 72, no. 2 (1951), pp. 145-61.

Chapter 15   H. Kelsen   *Aristotle and Hellenic-Macedonian Policy*.

This is section III of the original article, which appeared in *Ethics* 48 (1937-8).

Chapter 16   Maurice Defourny   *The Aim of the State: Peace*

This chapter has been extracted from the author's *Aristote: Études sur la 'Politique'* (Éditions Beauchesne, Paris, 1932). It has been translated by Jennifer Barnes.

Chapter 17   Raymond Weil   *Aristotle's View of History*

Originally published as 'Philosophie et histoire: la vision de l'histoire chez Aristote', in Fondation Hardt, *Entretiens* XI (Vandoeuvres-Génève, 1964). It has been translated by Jennifer and Jonathan Barnes.

J.B., M.S., R.S.

ABBREVIATIONS

A.Pr.	*Analytica Priora*
A.Pst.	*Analytica Posteriora*
Ath. Resp.	*Atheniensium Respublica*
Cael.	*De Caelo*
Cat.	*Categoriae*
Col.	*De Coloribus*
De An.	*De Anima*
Div.	*De Divinatione per Somnum*
EE	*Ethica Eudemia*
EN	*Ethica Nicomachea*
Eud.	*Eudemus*
fr.	*Fragmenta*
GA	*De Generatione Animalium*
GC	*De Generatione et Corruptione*
HA	*Historia Animalium*
IA	*De Incessu Animalium*
Id.	*De Ideis*
Insom.	*De Insomniis*
Int.	*De Interpretatione*
Iuv.	*De Iuventute et Senectute,*
	De Vita et Morte
Lin. Insec.	*De Lineis Insecabilibus*
Long.	*De Longitudine et Brevitate Vitae*
MA	*De Motu Animalium*
Mech.	*Mechanica*
Mem.	*De Memoria et Reminiscentia*
Meta.	*Metaphysica*
Meteor.	*Meteorologica*
Mir.	*De Mirabilibus Auscultationibus*
MM	*Magna Moralia*
MXG	*De Melisso, Xenophane et Gorgia*
Oec.	*Oeconomica*
PA	*De Partibus Animalium*
Phys.	*Physica*
Plant.	*De Plantis*
Poet.	*Poetica*
Pol.	*Politica*
Probl.	*Problemata*
Protr.	*Protrepticus*

Resp.	*De Respiratione*
Rhet.	*Rhetorica*
Rhet.ad *Alex.*	*Rhetorica ad Alexandrum*
S.El. (or *Top. IX)*	*De Sophisticis Elenchis*
Sens.	*De Sensu*
Som.	*De Somno et Vigilia*
Spir.	*De Spiritu*
Top.	*Topica*
Virt.	*De Virtutibus et Vitiis*

We follow the book and chapter numbers used in the Oxford translation of Aristotle. Page, column and line numbers are based on Bekker's edition of 1831.

1
Hellmut Flashar
The Critique of Plato's Theory of Ideas in Aristotle's Ethics

1.

More than forty years have passed since the appearance of Werner Jaeger's
epoch-making book on Aristotle [25]. During that period research on
Aristotle has branched far and wide; and although the interpretations it has
thrown up have certainly differed widely on particular issues, their general
effect has been to shake Jaeger's basic theses at many points. Although
Jaeger was immediately criticised on individual points,[1] it was at first the
common opinion that the foundations of Jaeger's picture of Aristotle were
'built upon rock', to quote the characteristic judgment of Ernst Hoffmann.[2]
For by applying the notion of development (at that time a popular tool of
interpretation) to Aristotle, and by attributing to him a movement, affecting
the whole of his life and work, away from Plato's position to the stance of an
empirical scientist, Jaeger had made it possible to rescue Aristotle from the
confines of classical scholarship and bring him once more before the
attention of the educated public. So it is only natural that philosophers,
scientists and medical men who concern themselves with Aristotle should
have appealed – and should still appeal – to Jaeger, when they want the
backing of scholarship for their claims. It is only as the result of the research
of the last few years that a change in outlook has occurred. And it is again
Aristotle's relationship to Plato, so energetically thrust into the foreground
of our attention by Jaeger, which now begins to appear in a different light.

   The fresh stimuli come principally from three sources:

   (1) In his commentaries on the ethical treatises ascribed to Aristotle
[41], [42], [43], and in a series of shorter works,[3] Franz Dirlmeier has
conclusively shown, with a wealth of detailed observation, that Aristotle's
development cannot be understood as a progressive departure from Plato's
teaching. Argument with Plato extends through all Aristotle's writings; and
consequently if a particular notion is intimately connected with one of
Plato's, that is not in itself any evidence for the dating of one of Aristotle's
writings. Aristotle's 'development' is a matter of 'maturing in Plato's
company right to the end' ([41], p. 568).

---

1. cf. the review by H.-G. Gadamer, *Logos* 17 (1928), pp. 132ff; also E. Ivanka,
Scholastik 7 (1932), pp. 1 ff. and 9 (1934), pp. 520 ff.
   2. *Philol. Woch.* 44 (1924), p. 518.
   3. See especially 'Aristoteles', *Jahrbuch für das Bistum Mainz* 5 (1950), pp. 161 ff.;
'Zum gegenwärtigen Stand der Aristoteles – Forschung', *Wiener Studien* 76 (1963), pp.
52 ff.

224   (2) Ingemar Düring, by his critical edition of the ancient biographical material on Aristotle, has for the first time laid a proper foundation for any attempt to see his life and work in their mutual relation. The sifting and evaluation of the biographical material implies a wholly new picture of Aristotle. Düring has briefly sketched its main features.[4]

(3) Hans-Joachim Krämer has made us newly aware that the main concepts of Aristotle's philosophy, especially in metaphysics and ethics, themselves developed from Plato's theory of first principles ([95], especially Ch. VI, pp. 552 ff.). Aristotle's encounter with Plato's teaching in the inner circle of the Academy is studied in the light of the influence it had upon the formation of Aristotle's philosophy. That philosophy then presents itself as a dissolution of the Platonic system, as the disintegration of its unity into individual, self-sufficient disciplines, a process which Konrad Gaiser, who is associated in Krämer's investigations,[5] seeks to construe more specifically as a 'demathematisation'.

Through these researches, which converge at crucial points, it has become evident afresh that every interpretation of Aristotle is confronted by the question of his relationship to Plato. I propose in what follows to consider a text which has a central bearing on this question: the critique of Plato's theory of Ideas in Aristotle's *Ethics*. For while it is true that argument with Plato extends throughout the whole of Aristotle's work, it is only in a couple of passages (at any rate in the surviving writings) that Aristotle provides a continuous critique of Plato's theory of Ideas, i.e. to all intents and purposes only in the *Metaphysics* and the *Ethics*.

Jaeger made the critique of the Ideas in the *Metaphysics* (I 9 and XIII 4-5) the starting-point for his whole analysis of Aristotle. More specifically, his starting-point was a curious difference between the two otherwise almost identical versions of the critique of the Ideas: Aristotle six times uses the first-person plural in *Meta.* I in mentioning proofs for Ideas which he then goes on to criticise, whereas in *Meta* XIII the third-person plural stands in its place in every case (e.g. *we* say that the Ideas exist – *they* say that the Ideas exist). Jaeger inferred from this difference that in Book I Aristotle still felt that he belonged to the Academy, whereas Book XIII was written at a time when Aristotle, now head of his own school, had broken with the Academy openly. He saw confirmation of this hypothesis in the general construction of the two books of the *Metaphysics* in question. He took Book I as an expression of a new approach, adopted on Assos after Plato's death and Aristotle's departure from Athens, to the principal questions raised by Platonism. But in Book XIII, which is concerned with questions about intelligible substances in general, the critique of the theory of Ideas taken over from Book I is only (as it were) the base upon which a comprehensive treatment of number theory is built, with special attention to the opinions of Speusippus and in particular of Xenocrates, the main target of criticism here (as head of the Academy he was Aristotle's rival). Whatever view one

225   takes of Jaeger's position, there remains his observation that at some point

4. Düring [21]. He offers a sketch of the chronology of Aristotle's writing based on these researches in [48], pp. 287 ff.; also in his [14] and R.E. Suppl. XI (1968), cols. 330-5.

5. *Platons ungeschriebene Lehre* (Stuttgart 1963); esp. Ch. III 2, 'Die Auflösung des platonischen Systems bei Aristotles' (pp. 308 ff.).

or other Aristotle cited the Academic proofs for Ideas in the first-person plural form and that it was in all likelihood Aristotle himself, not an editor, who turned this into the third-person plural in Book XIII. Upon this observation Jaeger based the whole of his analysis of the strata of the *Metaphysics* (an analysis which, to be sure, is nowadays justly disputed). And on it he based his determination of the historical sequence of the treatises on ethics, too. He took the *Eudemian Ethics* (*EE*) to be the 'reformed Platonist stage', and he called it 'the original Ethics', supposing it to have been composed right after Plato's death, and so standing with *Meta* I in date and in character; whereas the *Nicomachean Ethics* (*EN*) is the late work, and so stands on a level with *Meta*. XIII.

Somewhat illogically, however, Jaeger did not set out this time from the critique of the Ideas contained in the two *Ethics*, as one would have expected him to do given his position on the *Metaphysics*. He rested his conclusion rather on other arguments, which have since then been shown to be by and large inconclusive.[6] Nor has Dirlmeier provided more than the briefest commentary on the chapter in *EN* which contains the critique of the Ideas (I 6, 1096a11-1097a14); and while admittedly he devotes a minute analysis of great erudition, occupying twenty-four pages of his commentary, to the relevant chapter of *EE* (I 8, 1217b1-1218b27), he has not really drawn any comparisons with *EN*. Precisely because Dirlmeier comes to the same conclusions as Jaeger about the relative chronology of *EE* and *EN*, but by a different route, it may be worth our while to pose afresh the question of Aristotle's relationship to Plato as it is expressed in the criticism of Plato in the *Ethics*. I propose to make the version in *EN* my main concern, drawing on *EE* for the sake of comparison only to supplement my account, and leaving the *Magna Moralia* (whose authenticity is disputed) to one side for our present purposes, if only because in that work one can speak only in a very limited sense of a properly worked out critique of the Ideas. We shall ask how the two versions are related and what relationship between Aristotle and Plato they allow us to recognise. We shall further enquire how and by what means Aristotle here accomplishes the momentous step of establishing ethics as an independent discipline, by severing the bonds by which it is tied in Plato to the first principles of an ontology conceived of as a science of value.

2.

In the first chapters of *EN*, on the pursuit of the highest good for man, Aristotle, in mentioning the natural and obvious goods, had already observed in passing that some people introduce another sort of good – good in itself – alongside these many goods, as cause of their being good (1095a26-8). After a brief reference to the various 'forms of life' whose goals might be thought to constitute a highest good, he turns to those who speak of the good in the sense of a universal essence (1096a11). He begins his

6. Jaeger had seen great significance in supposed divergences between *EE* and *EN* in the conception of ethical methodology and in the connotations of '*phronêsis*' (standardly translated 'practical wisdom' in *EN*). The divergences have proved either illusory (*phronêsis*) or not in all probability chronological (methodology).

226   discussion with some remarkable words: the enquiry, he says, is made
        difficult because those who have introduced the Ideas are his friends. But in
        order to recover the truth he intends to set aside even what is closest to him,
        especially since (he continues) 'we are philosophers; for while both
        [friendship and truth] are dear to us, we yet have a sacred duty to give the
        precedence to truth'. Thus at the beginning of his 'critique' Aristotle gives
        expression to the intimate bond which he feels with Plato in a manner
        unique in his writings. The only comparison can be with the elegy on an
        altar dedicated to Friendship composed by Aristotle and addressed to
        Eudemus, in honour of the man 'whom it is not permitted to the wicked
        even to praise'.[7] Just because of this strong personal avowal Jaeger ordains
        that the elegy was produced right after Plato's death; and the first thing one
        asks oneself is whether he ought not in that case to have made the same
        assumption for this passage of *EN*, too, since the expression of feelings of
        friendship and closeness to Plato fits perfectly with the 'we' style of *Meta.* I
        (i.e. the use of the first-person plural). No one will be so naive as to take
        these words as a first timorous introduction of criticism, or on the other
        hand to think it impossible that the expression of the feeling of an intimate
        bond with Plato could have occurred later on in Aristotle's life, in the
        wisdom of age, so to speak. But any interpreter with his feet on the ground
        will find Aristotle's statement that in the pursuit of the truth he must 'set
        aside what is closest to him *(ta oikeia)*' (whether one should take *ta oikeia* as
        referring to the doctrine itself, i.e. the theory of Ideas, or to the bonds of
        intimacy, as well as the more public ties, which bind him to the Academy)
        to be a clear sign that Aristotle belonged or was close to the Academy when
        he wrote it. This seems to be Dirlmeier's view, too, for he observes: 'It is
        usual to make Aristotle's membership of the Academy end with Plato's
        death in 347. But in view of a discovery made by Philip Merlan[8] Aristotle
        should be considered still a member of the Academy in 339'. That Aristotle
        must have been at the least very closely connected with the Academy when
        he wrote this sentence of *EN* is an inference which Dirlmeier does not draw
        explicitly, it is true. But his explanatory comment on the sentence clearly
        points to it. In any case, it is impossible to suppose that Aristotle would as
        head of his own school transpose the critique of the Ideas in the *Metaphysics*
        straight from the first to the third person, in a violent onslaught on the
        Academy, and yet at the same time in the *Ethics* protest feelings of closeness
        to advocates of the theory of Ideas in this way. Nor does it get us anywhere
        to take (with Gigon)[9] the line that our passage 'looks so out of place in the
        context of the treatise' that it has to be explained as taken over from an early
        exoteric work *(De Philosophia)*. For the very restrained tone of the actual
        critique in *EN*, which now begins, is in perfect harmony with the personal
        preamble. Aristotle, that is to say, generally advances his critical
        observations using the tentative potential construction (e.g. 'one might ask
        the question', 1096a34); and he begins his first argument with an
        observation in agreement with a line of thought accepted by his opponents.

227   In total contrast to this stands the beginning of the critique of Ideas in *EE*

---

7. Text in Diehl, *Anthologia Lyrica* I³, pp. 115 ff.; cf. Düring [21], pp. 316 ff.
8. cf. 'The successor of Speusippus', *Trans. Am. Philol. Ass.* 77 (1946), pp. 103 ff.
9. cf. 'Die Sokratesdoxographie bei Aristoteles', *Mus. Helv.* 16 (1959), p. 196.

(I 8, 1217b1-23). Aristotle does not aim here, as he does in *EN*, to interweave the line of thought explicitly with the preceding and succeeding chapters. Three doctrines already put forward about the highest good are announced (b1). The first relates to the Idea of the good, the second to the general concept of the good (both are targets of the critique which follows), and the third is the doctrine of Aristotle himself, which is not, as in *EN*, worked out *ab initio* in connexion with the critique, but is set over against the conception which is criticised, as something already in existence. One might almost say that Aristotle sees himself as a historical figure, inasmuch as he examines views of which his own is one. The whole chapter is in this way self-contained. The critique of the Ideas itself is introduced by a piece of doxography, in which Aristotle shows, with schoolmasterly clarity, what exactly has to be understood by 'Idea' (b2-15). Before he proceeds to employ his individual arguments, he rejects out of hand the hypothesis of Ideas summarily, once and for all (b20-1). Then he adds to this that he has already talked about the subject in various ways both in his exoteric and his strictly philosphical writings (b22-3). These cumulated references indicate unmistakably that there were already numerous investigations on the topic. It is curious that Jaeger, who otherwise lays the greatest stress on indications of this sort, has not discussed these statements, but sees in *EE* the reformed Platonist stage, when Aristotle had only just renounced the theory of Ideas.

When we come to the questions Aristotle actually raises in the critique itself, we observe that the presentation in *EN* plainly divides into two parts. In the first part (1096a17-b8) four arguments are adduced against the assumption of Ideas; they appear in similar form in *EE* too, but it is not possible in any of the four cases to determine with any real certainty that one version or the other is earlier. In *EN* there then follows an observation on the Pythagoreans and Speusippus (1096b5-8), which is missing in *EE* and does not have the character of a critical argument. In the second part (1096b8-1097a14) Aristotle deals in detail with two objections against his critique which he discusses and then refutes. This whole section has no counterpart in *EE*, which instead contains two additional arguments for Aristotle's thesis missing in *EN*.

In the detailed treatment of the arguments which are common to the two *Ethics* there turn out to be considerable differences, whose explanation is on occasion extraordinarily hard to discover. This becomes plain immediately in the *first argument*, the argument from the nature of an ordered series. Completely in the spirit of the personal introduction, Aristotle here first of all begins by agreeing with a point in his opponent's doctrine and from it develops his first critical argument, which amounts to the objection that   228
there is an inconsistency in the Platonic doctrine itself. For the view that no Ideas may be set up for elements which stand in the relation of 'prior' and 'posterior', and hence that no Idea of numbers may be posited, must strictly speaking on Plato's own principles (so Aristotle reasons) prohibit the assumption of a general Idea of the goods spoken of in the various categories. The good is predicated in a series which is ordered in the relation of 'prior' and 'posterior', viz. in the series of the categories. So Aristotle makes the criticism that Plato paid no attention to the argument from the nature of an ordered series in connexion with 'good'. In the parallel section

of *EE* (1218a1-9) the attempt to begin the critical argumentation in this way with Plato's doctrine is missing. Here the notion that there can be no general, separately existing Idea over above the elements of a series ordered in the relation of 'prior' and 'posterior' sounds like criticism; and no reader of *EE* would suspect that, according to the assertion of *EN*, this notion corresponds to the doctrine of Plato himself. This difference is so striking that people have questioned whether it is really the same thing that is intended in the two *Ethics*. However this difference be explained, it is in itself quite remarkable and is usually not taken into consideration in discussions of the much debated question of what is really meant by Plato's view, reported by Aristotle only in *EN*, that there are no Ideas in the realm of the 'prior' and 'posterior', and consequently that there is no Idea of numbers.[10] We must keep a firm hold on the main point, which is that at the beginning of the critique of the Ideas in *EN*, but not in *EE*, Aristotle argues on the basis of the very doctrine that he is criticising. This effort on Aristotle's part will prove, as we shall see, to be a characteristic feature of the discussion of Plato's doctrine in *EN*.

The *second argument* (1096a23-9) also starts from the categories, in which the good is said in just as many ways as is being itself. The fact that being is said in different ways according to the categories is thus introduced as an additional argument in favour of the thesis that there can be no common general concept over and above the categories. In *EE* (1217b25-35) the series of categories as it applies to being and good is made to yield a *single*, tighter, argument. There we find at the outset the observation that 'good is spoken of in many ways – in fact in just as many as being'; then the fact that being and good are said in different ways according to the categories is shown in detail; and finally, on the strength of the close parallel between being and good, it is concluded that 'there is not even a single science either of being or of good'. This conclusion is no doubt sharper and more radical than the observation in *EN* (put off until the third argument) that there is no single science of everything that is called good (1096a30f). But this difference between the two *Ethics* is a consequence of the difference in the construction of their respective arguments from the categories. Since in *EE* Aristotle consistently couples being and good whenever he is concerned with their articulation in the categories, he wants to draw the same conclusions for both terms. Consequently it seems hardly possible to interpret the difference between *EE* and *EN* at this point[11] as showing (a) that it was only later, viz. at the time of *EN* and after composing *EE*, that Aristotle (with the help of his theory of 'focal meaning', to use Owen's description) envisaged the possibility of creating a single science of being,

229

10. Cherniss, *Aristotle's Criticism of Plato and the Academy* I (Baltimore, 1944), Appendix VI (pp. 513 ff.), presents a review of the extensively ramified literature, which has concentrated rather one-sidedly on the question whether by 'numbers' (a19) Aristotle means Idea-Numbers or mathematical numbers.

11. As does G.E.L. Owen (with detailed arguments) in 'Logic and metaphysics in some earlier works of Aristotle', reprinted in vol. 3 of the present series; so more briefly Cherniss *ibid.*, pp. 238 f. and Dirlmeier [42], p. 201. *Contra* Theiler, *Mus. Helv.* 15 (1958), p. 91; the conception of being *qua* being accepted by Owen, Cherniss and Dirlmeier is questioned by Merlan, *From Platonism to Neoplatonism* (The Hague, 1960²), pp. 160ff.

viz. the science of being *qua* being, and (b) that at the time of writing *EE* he had not yet conceived of metaphysics in the sense of a science of being *qua* being.

The *third argument* (*EN* 1096a29-34, *EE* 1217b35-1218a1) is rendered in essentially the same terms in both *Ethics*: the good not only appears differently in the different categories – it appears in many different forms even within each individual category. But in *EN*, unlike *EE*, this argument is introduced by a hypothetical clause containing the specifically Platonic presupposition that a science attaches to every Idea, which, together with the assumption of an Idea of the good, must lead to the conclusion (in fact incorrect) that there is a single science of everything that is called good. Here again in *EN* we run up against the striking attempt to launch criticisms from ideas and presuppositions of Plato himself.

The *fourth argument* (*EN* 1096a34-b2) is directed against the separation of a 'good itself' from the particular goods, and against its hypostatisation by means of the prefix *auto* ('itself'). The treatment is fuller than in *EE*: first the idea is formulated absolutely generally (*autohekaston*, 'a thing itself'), then it is exemplified by the concept 'man himself' (*autoanthrôpos*), and only after that applied to the good. The following sentence (1096b3-5), introduced by the words 'but again' (*alla mên*), looks like an independent argument: there is no question of something being good in stronger measure by being eternal, for the intensity of a colour is not tied to its temporal duration. One can only gather what the actual connexion with the preceding argument is from *EE*, where it is expressly added that by 'itself' (*auto*) it is precisely the eternal which is meant (*EE* 1218a12). Only then does a clear line of thought emerge: the hypothesis of a 'thing itself' understood as an eternal Idea is quite useless, for a quality already in existence is not intensified by being eternal, and so (this inference one has to supply oneself) it is quite useless for the particular good to participate in an Idea of the good.

At the end of this whole series of arguments there stands the observation, belonging only to *EN*, not to *EE*, and hard to understand in its brevity, that the view of the Pythagoreans, who place the One on the side of the goods, is more persuasive (1096b5-8). The mention of Speusippus, as having followed this doctrine, is also striking (it too is absent from *EE*). The meaning is obviously this: the multifarious nature of goods cannot be subsumed under an Idea of the good. On the other hand, the view of the Pythagoreans and Speusippus is more convincing[12] – in the table of opposites[13] it is better to place the One on the side of the goods (i.e. the entire positive side of the table of opposites), not to reverse the position and subordinate all goods to a single good. Evidently this section ties up with the reasoning which ends at 1096a34 (i.e. with the third argument); the intervening section (the fourth

230

---

12. 'More convincing' does not mean that Aristotle shares this view, which he clearly rejects at *Meta.* XII 7, 1072b30-4; it means 'more convincing than the position we have so far been criticising'.

13. The table of opposites is presented at *Meta.* I 5, 986a22-7. On this topic cf. W. Burkert, *Lore and Science in Ancient Pythagoreanism* (Cambridge, Mass., 1972), pp. 51 f., who sets out the connexion with doctrines of the Academy, and shows that Aristotle has drawn the table of opposites from Academic tradition, probably from Speusippus.

argument, 1096a34-b5) correspondingly gains the character of an additional note of secondary importance.

This whole first part of the critique of the Ideas is concluded by a reference to an investigation of these questions in another place. The second part which now begins has no counterpart in *EE*. The train of thought which constitutes the first and longer section (1096b8-26) comes once more to the conclusion that 'the good, therefore, is not some common element answering to one Idea'. It is explicitly presented as the treatment of an objection (*amphisbêtêsis*) against 'what has been said', i.e. against Aristotle's critique of the Ideas. And the question raises itself whether we have to do here, as pretty well all interpreters assume, with an objection of Aristotle's own invention, or with an actual objection, i.e. with one originating from discussions within the Academy. In support of the latter interpretation one might cite the indicative *hypophainetai* ('comes to light', not 'may be discerned' (Ross), the verb used in the sentence introducing the objection), which contrasts with the optative normal in this chapter, and the style – somewhat intricate, emphatically lively, twice ending with a rhetorical question. The objection starts from the thesis that the theory of Ideas does not relate to every good, but only to those goods which are sought for their own sakes, and not the intermediate goods, which contribute to a goal and are only called good in a derivative sense. If this view is to present an objection to the critique of the Ideas, the objection in question must amount to the complaint that the critic's assertion, that the particular goods cannot be subsumed under an Idea of the good, is not valid, since the theory of Ideas is not concerned with these particular goods. Aristotle first gives an account of this objection, and then says in a rather involved way that he wants to separate things good in themselves from the goods which contribute to a goal, and to consider whether the former can be subordinated to an Idea.

As goods in themselves these are adduced: (1) understanding and seeing (*phronein kai horân*); (2) certain types of pleasure (*hêdonai tines*); (3) certain sorts of honour (*timai tines*). The distinction of goods into two classes, absolute and relative, that has just been made is then, however, rather obliterated again by the observation that these absolute goods may also be pursued for the sake of something else (1096b18), notwithstanding the fact that they can be reckoned among the absolute goods. But then the division of the absolute goods into the three groups mentioned above is dropped, and only the Idea (of the good) is accepted as an absolute good (in the sense of the objection). Thereupon Aristotle reduces the objection to absurdity: if the Idea of the good relates only to those goods pursued for their own sakes, and yet the only good pursued for its own sake is the Idea of the good, then the Idea relates to itself and is a form without content. Aristotle next discusses the first possibility, which he had dropped, and again the three values of honour, understanding and pleasure are named as goods in themselves. It is certainly no accident that he deals with the goals of the three forms of life treated in the preceding chapter (it is striking that Aristotle here uses the concept of *phronêsis* in a Platonic sense, as 'understanding'). But if these goods, too (so the argument runs), are goods in themselves, then they still cannot be subsumed under a single Idea, since they are good in different senses.

This whole train of thought, developed rather long-windedly, only becomes fully intelligible if one sets alongside it a section of Plato's *Republic* (II, 357B-D), to which Dirlmeier refers with the brief observation: 'The same division [of goods] at the beginning of Book II of Plato's *Republic*' ([41], p. 276). But the division of goods in Plato in not the same. As opposed to Aristotle's division into two classes, there stands here a division into three: (1) those goods which are pursued for their own sakes, such as enjoyment (*to chairein*) and such pleasures as are harmless (*hai hêdonai hosai ablabeis*); (2) those goods pursued not only for their own sakes but also for their useful consequences, such as understanding (*to phronein*), seeing (*to horân*), and being healthy (*to hugiainein*); (3) things which are only pursued for the sake of other goods. The verbal agreement with Aristotle is plain, and one can see how the concept of *phronêsis*, understanding, in Aristotle has been taken over directly from Plato here. But Plato's tripartite division is remodelled into a bipartite division by Aristotle ('clearly, then, goods must be spoken of in two ways', 1096b13), although in such a way that in the observation that the absolute goods are also pursued for the sake of something else (b18f.) the old tripartition still peeps through. In doing this Aristotle has combined 'understanding and seeing' from Plato's second group with 'certain pleasures' from Plato's first group in order to achieve a parallel with the goals of the three forms of life.

Now whether it be the case that Aristotle constructs a hypothetical objection by exploiting a text in Plato, or whether it is rather that he is refuting a Platonist who makes this objection by seizing on a Platonic division of goods, the objection itself, in any event, has its place within the context of Plato's Academy.[14] And it is curious that there is no trace of this detailed and lively discussion in *EE*.

The *last argument* (1096b32-1097a14),[15] too, has its place wholly within

14. We should accept that the objection, together with the notion that the Idea of the good relates only to those goods pursued for their own sakes, belongs with discussions in the Academy on the proper province of the Ideas: cf. *Meta.* I 9, 990b15 ff.

15. I shall do no more than mention the discussion set between this and the section 1096b8-26 of the sense in which we speak of 'good' (1096b26-31). Aristotle names and considers in succession three possible explanations of why different goods bear the same name 'good'. (1) By chance – an idea which is rejected as absurd. (2) Because everything tends towards one good or derives from one good. This possibility is considered, but dropped in favour of the third idea, which Aristotle endorses: (3) through analogy. cf. on this G.E.L. Owen, 'Logic and ...' [67], pp. 166 f. But I differ from Owen in thinking that Aristotle in the corresponding section of *EE* (I 8, 1218a30-2) in fact adopts the same standpoint, even if the word 'analogy' is missing. Explanation (1) of *EN* is not mentioned at all in *EE*; explanation (2) is signified by the words 'all the things that are desire some one good' (= 'all things tend towards one', *EN*), and is rejected still more decisively than in *EN*; Aristotle's view (3) is expressed in *EE* by the words 'for each thing desires its own proper good', and is identical with the analogy idea, as the examples which follow also show. But the examples are different: *EE* 'the eye sight, the body health', *EN* 'sight in the body, reason in the soul'. This difference, however, is in my view explained by the fact that *EN* is again trying to make a connexion with Plato, who at *Rep.* 508B-C conceives of the proportion 'in the intelligible world in relation to understanding and the things

the context of discussion in the Academic school. In it the existence of the Idea is first of all conceded for the sake of argument, but its usefulness, even supposing it existed, is impugned. This in turn yields another proof against the existence of the Idea. Aristotle here again discusses an objection against the application of the critique of the Ideas to the realm of ethics. The objection runs thus: even though the Idea of the good may not itself be attainable or accessible to action, it is none the less a pattern (*paradeigma*) to which people can look, and which then helps them to achieve the things that are good for men. Aristotle grants the argument – and this shows us something about the character of his own ethics – 'a certain persuasiveness' (1097a3f.); but then, all the same, he refutes it, resting his refutation on experience; the practical sciences do not in fact get their bearings from the Idea. What we here have before us is the reversal of a famous Academic proof for the existence of the Ideas, which Aristotle treats in his work *On the Ideas* (fr.3 Ross) and which as the 'proof from the sciences' was considered as an Academic commonplace. The idea was that scientific knowledge is in the last resort not concerned with the individual case, but with some general object separated from the empirical manifold, i.e. the Idea, which functions as a pattern when the sciences are applied to the individual case. In the Academic proof it was illustrated by the example of medicine, which as a general science aims at 'health itself' (*autohugieia*). Aristotle takes up the same example and turns it on its head: the doctor does not seek the Idea of health, but the health of the individual man. As one can see, this argument, too, has its place wholly within the context of discussion in the Academy. And it is very striking that this objection and its refutation are also not presented in *EE*.

Instead *EE* contains two additional arguments against the postulation of Ideas; they relate to number theory, which is not brought into play in *EN*.

(1) It is invalid to derive generally recognised goods – justice, health – from things which are not recognised as goods – numbers (1218a15-24). This argument is only conclusive within the context of a critique of the Ideas if it presupposes a view according to which numbers are considered as Ideas in which the goods of this world participate. The demonstration that these goods are goods rests on the hypothesis that they participate in the numbers, viewed as Ideas; and they in their turn derive their value from the One, set up as the supreme value. It is difficult to say whether it is Plato's doctrine of Idea-numbers, or Xenocrates' modification of them, or both, which Aristotle has in mind here. The way Aristotle formulates the doctrine makes one think of numbers in the simple sense as the things the goods are supposed to participate in. And that points rather to Xenocrates, who dropped the distinction between Idea-numbers and mathematical numbers, and construed the Ideas as mathematical numbers.

(2) It can be claimed with a higher degree of certainty that the argument which follows (1218a24-30) has Xenocrates for its target. For Aristotle turns to argue against the hypothesis that the numbers aim at the One, and a doctrine of such a striving (*ephesis*) on the part of the Ideas (=

---

understood: in the visible world in relation to sight and the things seen' as an analogy of the Good.

numbers) is attested precisely for Xenocrates.[16]

Both arguments relating to number theory in *EE* have the definite ring of actual debate. Methodological observations are at various points interspersed in the critique, such as: one has to proceed in a different way from that *now* customary (cf. 1218a15-18). The use of the word *nûn* ('now') twice at 1218a15-18 makes it especially plain that Aristotle is criticising a procedure actually employed in the Academy at the time *EE* was composed.

At this point we may break off our treatment of *EE* and summarise the conclusions to which comparison of the two versions of the critique of the Ideas has brought us:

(1) In *EN* Aristotle feels a personal bond between himself and the advocates of the theory of Ideas. In harmony with this the critique of the theory of Ideas is circumspect, governed throughout by the effort to begin with the presuppositions of the theory that is being criticised. Nowhere is   233 the tone of the argument particularly sharp. In *EE* one can recognise behind the critique a cool reserve.

(2) In *EE* Aristotle says that he has already frequently subjected the theory of Ideas to examination. So *EE* does not stand at the beginning of Aristotle's critical argument with Plato.

(3) In *EN* once more, the phrasing has not everywhere been pressed to the last degree of refinement. Much has been left standing in the style of notes. In *EE* many details have been rendered more clearly.

(4) Aristotle's essential position is the same in both cases. Neither of the two versions has grown out of the other.

(5) Consequently the two versions agree only in part. In both the *Ethics* the second part of the critique of the Ideas contains a pair of arguments, but one pair occurs only in *EN*, the other only in *EE*. These arguments originate from discussions within the Academic school. Yet in *EN* they relate purely to Plato's doctrine; but in *EE* they relate to the number theory not taken into consideration in *EN*, and are probably directed against Xenocrates in the first instance.

3.

If one wants to make use of these observations in assessing the relative chronology of the two *Ethics*, the most obvious move is to put them into relation with the two versions of the critique of the Ideas in the *Metaphysics*. Here the thought immediately occurs to one that Jaeger, had he followed his own position consistently, would strictly have had to set the critique of Plato in *EN* with the 'we' style of *Meta*. I, and the critique of the Ideas in *EE* with the 'they' style of *Meta*. XIII, where likewise the critique of Xenocrates stands in the foreground. But one would want to draw such a conclusion only if the starting-point and base of the argument were undisputed. But in this area the latest research has made the situation fluid in many ways. Consequently the course which recommends itself is to limit oneself at first to the requirement that it must be possible to fit our observations (in so far

---

16. Fr. 30 Heinze. This view is supported by H. von Arnim, *Eudemische Ethik und Metaphysik*, p. 62; it is rejected by J. Brunschwig, in [34].

as they are correct) organically into a total picture of Aristotle's life, work and doctrine.

But on the basis of the latest research it does seem possible to do that. At some points its results are in partial agreement, at others they supplement each other. And in consequence the contours of a new picture of Aristotle become visible, although its details admittedly still remain controversial here and there.

Of decisive importance, to begin with, is the realisation that in the twenty years in which Aristotle lived, during Plato's lifetime, in the Academy, he not only worked out the basic positions of his own philosophy by arguing things out with the Platonic theory of first principles[17] (and so had already dissociated himself from the Ideas very early).[18] He also presented this philosophy in teaching and writing, beginning with logical problems, but then turning to rhetoric, ethics, and the areas of physics and metaphysics as well.[19] But if Aristotle had already firmly sketched out his basic positions in the Academy, so too had Speusippus and Xenocrates, fellow members and later heads of the school, who were of course older than Aristotle. This explains the discussion of their doctrines, which in all probability did not first begin when they took over the headship of the Academy. In any event, it is not possible without further ado to consider polemic against Speusippus and Xenocrates in Aristotle's writings as chronological evidence that these writings were composed at the time of Speusippus' or Xenocrates' headship of the school. On the contrary, there is much reason to take their strongly polemical tone chiefly as evidence of discussions within the Academy, which did not, of course, lead to breaks either with Speusippus or with Xenocrates. It is in consequence perfectly possible to see the critique of the Ideas in *EE* as an expression of discussions of this same sort with Xenocrates which actually took place within the Academy. Moreover, even if one puts *EE* before Plato's death, Aristotle can already be looking back in that work on a series of critical utterances on the theory of Ideas.

Furthermore, Aristotle's departure from Athens in the year 347 does not signify any real break with the Academy. Notions of an 'academy in exile', understood as a protest against Athens, are gross exaggerations, just as it is also very questionable whether Aristotle at this time drafted the speculative foundations of his system in the style of a new policy. On the contrary, it has long been recognised that he devoted himself very strongly to scientific studies at this period; and indeed it was during these years that he met Theophrastus.

Nor yet is Aristotle's second period of residence in Athens to be understood as involving opposition to the Academy, as though the Peripatos

234

17. cf. H.J. Krämer [95], pp. 552 ff., esp. p. 561, n. 22.
18. There is no clear evidence that Aristotle at any time gave allegiance to the Platonic Ideas. On *Protrepticus*, fr. 13 (Ross), cf. Düring [48], pp. 213 ff., whose treatment admittedly leaves it doubtful whether and if so to what extent Aristotle's *Protrepticus* stands behind Iamblichus as his source in this passage. Further, the majority of the ancient biographical accounts speak of criticism of Plato by Aristotle during the former's lifetime. In the *Posterior Analytics*, which is quite early, Aristotle says: 'the Ideas may be dismissed' (83a32f.).
19. cf. the table in Düring [48], pp. 287 f., in essentials accepted by Dirlmeier, *Wiener Studien* 76 (1963), pp. 52 f.

and the Academy, with their respective heads, Aristotle and Xenocrates, stood confronting each other in rivalry or hostility. Aristotle came back to Athens, aged about fifty, as a regular member of the Academy, to which in a sense he belonged all his life, even though he did not join again in the tightly organised communal life. For it was only Theophrastus who founded the Peripatos as a school with its own buildings, as we know for sure.[20] Aristotle taught in the Lyceum, a public gymnasium, open to everyone. It remains uncertain how far the circle which gathered about him there was coordinated as a permanent working organisation.

There are good grounds for putting in this period a series of writings, such as the books of the *Metaphysics* on substance (viz. VII and VIII), *De Anima, Parva Naturalia*, etc., which are no longer sustained by the tone of aggressive polemic, but are phrased in a more mature style, though one sometimes more cautious and more aware of difficulties.[21] Within definite limits, they come closer to Plato again. These features are characteristic of *EN*, too. Its remarkable closeness to Plato in many stretches (cf. e.g. Book X) has been rightly stressed recently.[22] But we can now fit the critique of Plato in *EN*, too, in a context of this sort. For it now becomes evident that Aristotle's personal confession of attachment to Plato and his expression of feelings of closeness to the advocates of the theory of Ideas – unintelligible from a position of hostility, opposition or rivalry against the Academy – are not just born of the wisdom of age in general, but correspond more particularly to the situation in which Aristotle found himself living and teaching during his second period of residence in Athens. Beyond this, we are going to have to make the various external conditions of composition and presentation (differences of occasion and readership) responsible to a greater degree than hitherto for apparent substantial discrepancies between individual writings of Aristotle. Thus whereas the critique of the Ideas in *EE* constitutes evidence of discussions within the Academy, the critique of Plato in *EN* looks as if it is directed to an outside audience and is consequently introduced by a formal apology In this form – directed to an outside audience, much less a product of discussions which actually took place in the school, and in consequence doubtless of wider validity – the critique is principally dependent upon Plato himself, specifically upon the original form of the theory of Ideas, which according to the testimony of *Meta*. XIII, 1078b9-12, had nothing to do with number theory. Similarly,

235

20. Diog. Laert. V 39: 'He is said to have become the owner of a garden of his own after Aristotle's death, through the assistance of his friend Demetrius of Phalerum.' cf. C.O. Brink in Pauly-Wissowa, *RE* Suppl. VII (1940), col. 905: 'The view that he too (Aristotle) had already taught on the spot which later belonged to the school, and that his library and other teaching aids had been deposited there, is contradicted by the report [in Diog. Laert.]. Diogenes' mode of expression is so precise that we would be bound to expect *some* reference to Aristotle if the place in question was one which the founder of the school had already used for teaching'.

21. cf. the table in Düring [48], p. 289, convincing (to my mind) in all essentials. On *Meta*. IV, which Düring places in this period, see however the references in n. 11 above.

22. cf. especially Dirlmeier [41], *passim*; e.g. at p. 544 (on *EN* 1166a6 ff.): 'The conclusion is irresistible: the Aristotle of *EN* is here more of a "Platonist" than in *EE*'.

only what relates simply to Plato is borrowed from discussions within the Academic school. The two objections against the critique of the Ideas and their refutation in the second part of the chapter should be counted as belonging to this material. They certainly originated at an earlier time, but they are seized upon by Aristotle all the more readily because they were intended actually to defend the Ideas. By his detailed discussion of them, therefore, Aristotle is able to avoid giving an outside audience the impression that he is doing away with Plato's position too hastily. This is characteristic of the style of the critique of the Ideas in *EN* (in contrast to *EE*), and it is all of a piece with Aristotle's efforts, perceptible throughout, to launch his criticisms from Plato's own presuppositions, and to include them within his own train of thought. Plainly, the lectures which constitute *EN* were delivered outside the Academy before a wider audience: again, it is only here (1095a2-11), not in *EE*, that Aristotle expresses his opinion on the sort of group suited to listen to a lecture on ethics. So *EN* is a degree more exoteric than *EE*.

If this is how things are, then one will not cling to the idea that the change from the first to the third person in the critique of the Ideas in *Meta.* I and XIII must be the expression of a change of attitude to Plato, and consequently the foundation for a chronological assessment of the two books of the *Metaphysics*. The obvious move is to look for a solution in terms of theme and content here too, and to suggest that the critique of the Ideas in the two books has at times a different function.

So far as Aristotle's relationship to Plato is concerned, therefore, there is, in the nature of the case, little room for a genuine development. It was actually in the Academy that Aristotle succeeded in striking out a new line and differentiating his own position by criticism both of Plato and of Speusippus and Xenocrates. In the course of time he was able to define that position more sharply and to consolidate it, but at the same time by relaxing the polemics, he was able, while actually engaged in his criticism, to give stronger expression to the common ground to be found in the whole area of the problem (always within the limits he had drawn once and for all).

4.

236   It is characteristic of Aristotle that within the *Ethics* the critique of the hypothesis of an Idea of the Good, and consequently the separation of ethics from ontology, is not really achieved through argument with the fundamental principles of Plato's ontology. The question of the existence of the good appears, on the contrary, only on the horizon of the argument, in the sense that almost all Aristotle's critical arguments (especially in *EN*) are governed by the question of predicability (1096a12, 'how it is said'; a19, 'the good is said'; cf. a24, b10, 12, 14, 26 – 'but how is it said?'). Tied up with this is the issue of utility, which serves as a measuring stick with regard to the question of the principles of ethics. (Cf. *EN* 1096a34 ff., 1097a8; *EE* 1217b24f., 1218a35. Aristotle at *EE* 1217b16-19 makes the point particularly clearly that detailed refutation of the Ideas does not belong to ethics.)

If one asks how Aristotle's ethics in fact relate to the basic theses of this critique, one or two characteristics which Aristotle seems to have in common with the opponents he criticises stand out at once. For if it is said in the last argument of *EN* (1097a8-14) that science is concerned with the concrete individual case, Aristotle himself thinks this valid only in the realm of the practical, not absolutely (cf. *Meta.* I, 981a12 ff.; *EN* 1180b15-23). And if knowledge of an Idea of the good as a paradigm for human activity is rejected (1097a1-14), one should set against this the fact that Aristotle himself expressly characterises the supreme value, to which his own ethics leads through a hierarchical ordering of human values, goals, and activities, as a target for living of just such a sort (*EN* 1094a22-24). Nor does Aristotle fail to relate this supreme value, *eudaimonia*, to the highest level of being, i.e. to god conceived of as unmoved mover. While Aristotle decisively rejects the conception of the good shared by Speusippus and the Pythagoreans which he describes as 'more persuasive' in the critique of Plato in *EN*, not only is his own god characterised as mind, one, simple, changeless, eternal, but he is also given a specific way of life (*diagôgê*), which is described as most pleasurable and best and is treated as clearly analogous with the highest form of life attainable by man (*Meta.* XII 7, 1072b13ff.; cf. *EN* 1177a12ff.). And in another passage Aristotle speaks, in connexion with the unmoved mover, of the 'eternal beauty and the true and primary good', which he exalts in frankly Platonic tones (*MA* 6, 700b32-5; cf. Plato, *Symp.* 211A).

To show in detail how this connexion of being and value, so very much a Platonic inheritance, is all the same presented differently in Aristotle from the way Plato sets it forth, would take us too far afield here. In conclusion we may hint at the difference by considering an example, Aristotle's cave analogy, which is preserved by Cicero, *De Natura Deorum* II 95, and probably comes originally from the dialogue *De Philosophia* (fr. 13 Ross). Suppose, says Aristotle, that there were men who had always dwelt under the earth in beautiful and well-lit dwellings, decorated with pictures and statues and with all the good things enjoyed by those who are considered happy, and who had never yet come up to the earth's surface, but had had news of a divinity and its power only through hearsay. But if once they were given the possibility of coming to the place where *we* dwell, then if *suddenly* – that **237** characteristic 'suddenly', which in Plato describes the lightning flash of knowledge, is retained here – they saw earth, sea, and sky, if they observed the extent of the clouds and the force of the winds, if they gazed upon the sun in its size and splendour, and if, finally, when it became night, they followed the courses of the stars, then at the sight of these things they would think that there are gods and that all this is the work of gods.

What in Plato is an analogy of knowledge, in its progression by stages to the highest principle, becomes here a proof for the existence of god by an *argumentum e gradibus*. The figures in the cave symbolise for Aristotle not the human condition *tout court* (as in Plato): *we* live outside the cave. The transition from day to night at the end reverses Plato's presentation, in which the man who is led out of the cave sees things first in shadows and reflections, and is then led to ever greater brightness until he looks on the sun itself. Again, as there is no way back to the cave in Aristotle, so the discovery he depicts, that the cosmos is a work of gods, has no consequences for human life, apart from the realisation that the life devoted to *theôria*, in the sense of contemplation of the ordering of the cosmos, occupies the highest place among the various forms of human activity.

The difference between the ways in which the two philosophers develop the cave analogy is characteristic of the difference between Plato and Aristotle in general. If anyone was prepared to infer from the measuring sticks which Aristotle applies in his critique of Plato's ethics that his own ethics are pure situation ethics, without fixed norms, he would be mistaken. But on the other side, the connexion of Aristotle's principle of being with the good does not issue in any normative authority for ethical behaviour. So on one side the critique of the Ideas in the *Ethics* is the clearest possible expression of the dissolution of the inner unity of ethics and ontology; but on the other side this retrenchment and limitation of ethics means that it is now freshly constituted as an independent and self-contained department of philosophy.

2

J.L. Ackrill

Aristotle on 'Good' and the Categories

In the *Nicomachean Ethics* I 6, 1096a23-9, Aristotle argues that goodness is   17
not a single common universal: if it were it would be 'said' in only one
category, whereas in fact it is, like *being*, 'said' in all the categories. Aristotle
discusses in many places the transcategorial character of *being* and of *one*,
but most of his accounts of types of goodness or senses of 'good' do not rest
upon the point about categories – a point which is, however, taken up in the
traditional treatment of *bonum* along with *ens* and *unum* as categorially
unclassifiable. The *Ethics* passage is therefore of considerable interest, and it
has not, I think, received sufficient attention or final elucidation from the
commentators. The present discussion will be far from exhaustive, but it
may raise some questions worth further examination. It is perhaps a matter
for apology that in a paper written in honour of Dr. Walzer I have neglected
to consider the relevant passage of the *Eudemian Ethics* (I 8, 1217b25-34); but
since the argument there may be different from that in the Nicomachean
version, it seems safer to start by looking at the latter on its own.

Aristotle explains the statement that *good* is spoken of in as many ways as
being (i.e. in all the categories) in a parenthesis which translates as follows:
'for it is said both in the category of substance, as god and reason, and in
quality – the virtues, and in quantity – the moderate, and in relation – the
useful, and in time – the opportune, and in place – the locality, and so on'.
The central question is how to fill out the examples Aristotle here gives so
crisply. The most obvious way is to suppose that the terms listed are offered
as subjects of sentences in which the predicate is 'good', thus:

> god is good
> the virtues are good
> the moderate is good
> the useful is good.

I shall refer to this as interpretation *A*.

Most commentators seem to adopt *A*. It is not always clear how they   18
think that Aristotle's argument goes. The argument might be that simply
because the subject-terms in these sentences stand for items in different
categories, the common predicate 'good' must be being used in diverse
senses or ways. The sweeping principle here invoked would clearly be a very
powerful generator of multivocity, and perhaps too powerful. There seems
no obvious reason why one should accept it, or – what is more to the point –
why Aristotle should suppose or imply that the principle is an obvious part
or corollary of the doctrine of categories.

In *Aristotle's Ethical Theory* [58], Mr. W.F.R. Hardie has provided

Aristotle with a more persuasive argument. According to this the desired conclusion depends not simply on the fact that 'good' is predicated of such items. The examples Aristotle lists – virtues, the useful, and so on – are essentially good; and the principle on which the argument relies is that items in different categories cannot have some common element in their essences. By 'essentially' Hardie means more than 'necessarily'; the essence is what is expressed in the definition of the item. There can of course be necessary properties of a subject which are no part of its essence, and whose names do not therefore occur in its definition. The strict interpretation of 'essentially' is certainly called for if this account of the argument is to have a decisive advantage over the first. For the principle that any feature that attaches necessarily to an item in one category cannot attach necessarily to an item in another would seem hardly less arbitrary than the principle that any feature that attaches (whether necessarily or accidentally) to an item in one category cannot attach to an item in another. The argument looks very much better when it is supposed that the relevant predicate is part of the definition of the subject, gives (part of) its essence. We have now something approaching an identity-statement; and in such a statement the predicate-item cannot fail to be in the same category as the subject-item. It will follow that 'good' is being used in different ways, standing for items in different categories, when it is predicated essentially of the virtues on the one hand and of the useful on the other, since the virtues and the useful are themselves in different categories.

There seem to be two difficulties in this construal of Aristotle's argument. Firstly, it seems to require and rely upon the principle that the differentia of an item in a given category is itself in that category.[1] This principle goes far beyond the obvious fact that the two sides of an identity-statement (including one which gives a definition) cannot stand for items in different categories. Since Aristotle nowhere discusses adequately the status of differentiae in relation to the categorial scheme it is difficult to be sure whether he held this principle or, if so, why. His uncertain touch in the matter is exemplified in the passage of the *Categories* (3a21-8) where he distinguishes the differentia of substance from substance but says of it things which could not be said of qualities, quantities, etc. It would be unfortunate if the *Ethics* argument relied on a strict doctrine about differentiae which is not a clear and settled part of Aristotle's thought elsewhere.

It might be suggested that a rather different principle about the differentiae would suffice to justify Aristotle's argument, the principle, namely, that the differentia of an item in one category cannot be the differentia of an item in another. This rule guarantees that 'good' has different senses in our examples, if in them 'good' gives the differentia of the subject-term in each case. It is a rule that Aristotle formulates in various versions, and he relies on one of them in dealing with an important problem in *Metaphysics* VII 12. Yet he allows that it is not easy always to set up definitions that accord with the rule that the differentia introduces the genus; and his own practice often seems to break it. It would thus be somewhat arbitrary if he assumed its

1. I assume that, on Hardie's view, 'good' gives the differentia and not the genus of the subject; virtue, for example, is a *hexis* (state) of a certain kind, namely a good *hexis*.

universal validity in order to establish the multivocity of 'good'.[2]

A more fundamental difficulty concerns the propriety of applying doctrines about differentiae to the terms in question in the *Ethics* passage. Whether we think of the relatively simple scheme of the *Categories* or of the complex discussions in the *Metaphysics*, it is clear that there are severe restrictions on the terms which get places in the categorial scheme or which permit strict definition – have a *ti ên einai* (essence). Neither 'negro' nor 'doctor' stands for an item with a unique place in the categorial scheme: each is an abbreviation, and the items in question are man (a substance), black (a quality), and healing (an action) or the science of healing (a quality). Negroes and doctors are not species of man or of anything else (cf. *Meta*. VII 4 and X 2). Now is it to be supposed that terms like *to metrion* (the moderate) and *to chrêsimon* (the useful) figure as species in the genus-species pyramids falling under quantity and relation? The classification into moderate and immoderate, useful and useless, would seem to cut across any natural genus-species articulation of these categories. Yet unless *to metrion* and *to chrêsimon* sit squarely in such a classification, principles about differentiae cannot get to work. If we are reduced to saying that the *word* 'moderate' means 'good quantity' and the *word* 'useful' means 'good relation', the argument for the multivocity of 'good' will have to rest not on a principle about the differentiae of proper species but on the blanket thesis that no predicate attaching to items in one category can attach in the same sense to items in another. Suppose that some predicate '*f*' *could* attach in the same sense to *A* (a substance) and to *B* (a quality). We could then *invent* words '*a*' and '*b*' meaning '*A* that is *f*' and '*B* that is *f*' respectively. But we clearly could not now argue that '*f*' has two senses on the ground that '*a* is *f*' and '*b* is *f*' predicate '*f*' essentially of items in different categories. By inventing the words '*a*' and '*b*' we have not created two proper species; but unless *a* and *b* are proper species nothing can, strictly speaking, be predicated essentially of either – neither of them has an essence, any more than does *negro* or *doctor*. Thus the force of Hardie's appeal to a principle about differentiae is lost unless it can be shown that the terms in Aristotle's examples stand for genuine species and are not merely portmanteau words.

(*B*) I turn now to a quite different way of filling out Aristotle's examples. Perhaps the terms he lists are to be thought of not as subjects but as predicates of sentences:

.... is god
.... are the virtues
.... is the moderate
.... is the useful.

Gauthier and Jolif seem to adopt this view in one note, where they write: 'Si nous disons que le bien de Coriscos, c'est le dieu qui est en lui, c'est à dire l'intellect ... nous désignons son essence ... ; si nous disons que ce sont le vertus, nous désignons ses qualités; si nous disons que c'est la mesure, nous

20

2. A fuller study of the point here touched on would of course have to distinguish between: (a) if *f* is the differentia of an item in one category it cannot be the differentia of an item in another, and (b) if *f* is the differentia of an item in one category it cannot belong to an item in another.

désignons la quantité de nourriture ou la quantité d'effort ... qui lui convient ...' (*L'Ethique à Nicomaque*, II. i. 40). In their next note, however, they say: 'De même, lorsqu'on dit que l'intellect est le bien de l'homme et lorsqu'on dit que les vertus sont le bien de l'homme, le mot bien n'a pas le même sens, puisqu'il désigne ici l'essence et là la qualité'. It is not easy to see the precise form of the argument being attributed to Aristotle.

Interpretation *B* has been explicitly adopted and argued for in an interesting paper by L.A. Kosman in *Phronesis* [66]. According to him, the sentences Aristotle has in mind are not sentences which contain the word 'good' at all, but are sentences used to make disguised ascriptions of goodness. When we say that Socrates is courageous, we predicate in the category of quality – courage being a quality – but we also thereby predicate good of him. Similarly, to say that something is in the right amount is to predicate quantity, but also implicitly to say that it is good. 'The instances that Aristotle gives, then, are not the subjects of exemplary predicative statements, but rather the predicates of such statements. They make clear that the multivocity of 'good' is exhibited not only in the fact that many sorts of things may be said to be good, but more in the fact that predicates of radically different types are in fact disguised means of predicating the good in radically different senses' (p. 174).

The point that we praise or commend things by the use of diverse predicates is an important one, and very relevant to the question whether 'good' has a single meaning or stands for a single quality. But it does not seem easy to derive this point from Aristotle's text in the way Kosman suggests. It would be surprising if Aristotle were illustrating the diversity of senses of 'good' by allusion to examples that do not contain the word; this is not how he or anyone else normally proceeds when exhibiting any kind of ambiguity in a term. The context does not warn us that the rather sophisticated notion of a *disguised* predication of good is in play. Kosman suggests as a parallel a remark Aristotle makes in the course of his discussion of *on* (being) in *Metaphysics* V 7, where he points out that 'a man walks' is equivalent to 'a man is walking'. 'What this shows is that it is possible in Greek as in English to predicate being without explicitly using the verb *einai* or 'to be'' (Kosman, p. 173). So, Kosman argues, if categorially different forms of being can be ascribed without explicit use of the verb 'to be', categorially different forms of goodness can be ascribed without explicit use of the word 'good'. However, the straightforward grammatical fact that 'walks' and 'is walking' are equivalent is not quite on all fours with the rather more subtle point that to say 'X is brave' is a disguised way of predicating good of X; and even if the *Metaphysics* point about being can lead our minds to Kosman's point about good, it will be an ingenious reader of the *Ethics* who makes the connexion.

Moreover, and more important, the argument for multivocity will not work in the same way for goodness as for being. If 'is' in 'is walking' has a different sense from 'is' in 'is white', the reason is that walking and white are items (*onta* – beings) in different categories. The basic argument for the multivocity of *on* is that it means 'substance' in 'man is *on*', 'quality' in 'white is *on*', and so on (*Meta.* IV 2, VII 1); and there are familiar reasons why substance, quality, etc., cannot be treated as species of a single supreme genus *being*. If, however, we expand 'is brave' and 'is of the right amount' into 'is good (in the brave way)' and 'is good (in the right amount way)', what is the basic argument for the multivocity of 'good'? No doubt bravery is necessarily good, and the right amount is necessarily good; but the doctrine of categories that tells us that items in different categories are *onta* in different senses does not tell us that items in different categories cannot exemplify (even necessarily) one and the same property – that a predicate attaching (even necessarily) to items in different categories cannot be univocal. Thus, even if we allow the idea of a disguised predication of good, the actual argument for the multivocity of good is in effect an argument like that required by interpretation *A*; no term that applies (necessarily) to items in different categories is being used univocally. This argument, I have suggested, falls short of being evidently acceptable.

22

(*C*) Perhaps it is possible to reach a point similar to that which Kosman attributes to Aristotle, but by a rather different route. Suppose we take Aristotle's examples as follows:

> . . . . is good because (in that it is) god
> . . . . is good because (in that it is) virtuous
> . . . . is good because (in that it is) moderate
> . . . . is good because (in that it is) useful.

There is to be no implication that the subject-terms are in different categories. The point is that the ground for predicating 'good' in the different cases is radically different. If I say that Callias is good and am asked 'how do you mean, "good"?' or 'why do you call him good?', I answer 'he is brave and honest'. But other things may be commended as good for other reasons and indeed other sorts of reason – because they are of the right size or useful for some purpose. The criteria for commending different things as good are diverse and fall into different categories; and this is enough to show that 'good' does not stand for some single common quality.

This expansion of Aristotle's argument brings it into line with the way in which he typically shows a predicate not to be univocal. Thus in *Metaphysics* IV 2, he explains the multiple role of *on* by comparison with 'healthy' and 'medical'. One thing is healthy because it is productive of health (*tôi poiein*), another thing because it is receptive of it (*hoti dektikê*). Similarly, some items are *onta* because – or in that – they are substances (*hoti ousiai*), others in that they are attributes (*hoti pathê ousias*). Aristotle takes it that the phrases introduced by *tôi* or *hoti* (or sometimes *hôs*) give the sense of the predicate in the relevant example; they tell what it amounts to in each case to apply the predicate.

In Chapter 15 of *Topics* I Aristotle examines various ways of establishing homonymy. One passage deals with 'good' precisely in the way interpretation *C* suggests. 'One should examine also the genera of the predications corresponding to the word to see whether they are the same in all cases. For if they are not the same, what is said is clearly homonymous. Thus, for example, the good in food is the *productive* of pleasure but in medicine is the productive of health; while for a soul it is its being *qualified* (e.g. temperate or brave or just), and similarly for a man. But in some cases it is the *when*, i.e. the opportune; for the opportune is called good. And often the quantity, as

23

with the moderate; for the moderate too is called good. It follows that the good is homonymous' (107a3-12). It is clear in the earlier examples that Aristotle is contemplating sentences like 'this man is good', 'this food is good', and drawing attention to the categorially diverse grounds on which the predicate is assigned. The later examples are less fully given, but he doubtless means that sometimes something is called good because opportune, sometimes because moderate – and these grounds again differ radically from the relational and qualitative grounds appropriate to the previous cases.

This passage exhibits the diversity of meaning of 'good' by drawing attention to the categorial diversity of the features one would mention in explaining one's predicating 'good' of various items. This is precisely the line of thought which interpretation *C* finds in the *Ethics* passage. Though the two texts have not been brought together by modern commentators, the possible connexion between them has not escaped notice. Pacius remarks in his note on the *Topics* section: 'Ostendit boni homonymiam: quia refertur ad quatuor categorias; actionem, qualitatem, quando, et quantitatem. potest etiam ad alias categorias referri, ut ipse Aristoteles docet lib. I *Ethicorum* cap. 4. *ubi hoc loco utitur contra ideas Platonicas.*' Alexander in his commentary on the *Topics* follows up his (correct) elucidation of the passage quoted above by indicating examples taken from the other categories (including god and reason for substance); and it is fairly clear that he has the *Ethics* passage in mind.

The advantages of interpretation *C* are, then, that it gives Aristotle an excellent point, one that he certainly makes about 'good' elsewhere, and one that does not depend upon any arbitrary or esoteric doctrine (other than the general doctrine of categories); and that it assumes that the examples Aristotle has in mind in the *Ethics* are just the sort of examples he normally uses to exhibit multivocity, examples which all use the predicate in question but where the account (*logos*) of the predicate – the explanation of what in the different cases it conveys or what justifies its application – varies from example to example.

Can this interpretation be reconciled with the actual run of the words in the *Ethics*? Consider the sentence: 'for "good" is said ... in the category of quality: the virtues'. Interpretation *A* fills out with 'the virtues are good'; interpretation *B* with '... are virtues (or: is virtuous)'. Interpretation *C* does not take 'the virtues' as a part of the example Aristotle has in mind, but as a reference to what features are being assigned to, e.g., Callias when he is called good: that 'good' is here predicated 'in the category of quality' is shown by the fact that 'good' here refers to excellence in quality, virtues. The exceedingly compressed form of words is, I think, compatible with the expansions of both *A* and *B*; but is no less consistent with interpretation *C*. 'Good' is said in the category of quality when it is virtues that are being attributed, as when 'good' is said of Callias. It is true, of course, that to say 'Callias is good' is not to *say* 'Callias is brave and honest'; but it is such features of Callias that the speaker will have in mind, and the hearer will have to realise or discover this if he is fully to understand the speaker's remark.

The purpose of this brief discussion has been fulfilled if I have made interpretation *C* seem at least worth considering. Of the many difficulties

24

that need fuller examination I pick only two for comment. First, it may be said that the point being attributed to Aristotle has in fact no necessary connexion with the categories. If the fact that the criteria for calling different things good differ shows something important about 'good' (say, that it does not stand for a single simple characteristic), it shows this whether or not the various criteria are features in different categories. In other words, an argument from variety of criteria to multiplicity of sense will generate not ten but an indefinitely large number of senses of 'good'. There is of course no doubt that Aristotle recognises that 'good' is predicated of a man, a woman, and a slave on the basis of *different* qualities – though in each case on the basis of *qualities*. Why then should he speak as though the senses of 'good' like 'being' are ten and not very much more numerous? Perhaps the difficulty may be mitigated by noting a parallel in the case of 'being'. The doctrine is that there are ten senses of *on*. Yet in detailed consideration of what it is to be this, that, or the other thing in *Metaphysics* VIII 2, Aristotle implies a much greater variety of senses of 'is': 'Some things are characterised by the mode of composition, e.g. the things formed by blending, such as honey-water; and others by being bound together, e.g. a bundle; and others by being glued together, e.g. a book; and others by being nailed together, e.g. a casket; . . . Clearly then the word "is" has just as many meanings' (1042b15-26). So Aristotle's usual willingness to operate with just a few senses of 'is' (corresponding to the categories) does not preclude him from recognising finer distinctions when this serves his purpose. Similarly an insistence that features of things in virtue of which they are called good can be radically different, in different categories, is not incompatible with the recognition that in cases where the features in question are in the same category they may nevertheless be different. This would no doubt be a highly unsatisfactory position if the main objective were to settle precisely the rules for counting the number of senses of 'good'. It is less regrettable when the main point is to show against Plato that there are a number of different senses, or, better, that 'good' is not always applied for the same reason – goodness is not a single uniform property.

Secondly, it may be asked how interpretation *C* can accommodate an example in the category of substance. For the criteria for calling various things good are features of the things, features that fall under non-substance categories; and being a so-and-so, a substance of a certain kind, is not a feature of a thing. To meet this difficulty one must suppose that when Aristotle speaks of god and reason – or divine reason – he is not giving one among many possible examples for the predication of 'good' in the category of substance. God is just the one case of such predication, because the answer to the question 'why do you call god good?' is precisely 'because he is god': he provides in some way the ultimate standard by which other things are judged, the standard of perfection which other things can variously aspire to approach or imitate. Aristotle makes this sort of point with respect to *eudaimonia* (happiness) in *Nicomachean Ethics* I 12. *Eudaimonia* is above being praised as good, for it is that by reference to which other things are called good. Being the source and ground of goods we call it 'honoured and divine'. It is of course good, supremely so, but not through coming up to some standard (satisfying certain criteria) but by setting the standard. In '*eudaimonia* is good' 'is good' functions quite differently from the way it functions in, say, 'health is good'. The point Aristotle makes here about *eudaimonia* in connexion with human actions and virtues can be made at a different level about god or divine reason: it is towards this that the whole Aristotelian cosmos strives, each part in its own way. This account of the reference to god in the *Ethics* passage may seem rather forced, but the ideas on which it depends are not remote. *Nicomachean Ethics* I 12 gives the notion of a standard by which other things are called good, and the idea that god is the ultimate standard is central to Aristotle's whole account of the cosmos and its teleology. It is not only interpretation *C* that finds some difficulty in handling this example: it is after all not easy to understand the suggestion that in 'god is good' one is giving the *differentia* of the subject.

3

Anthony Kenny

Aristotle on Happiness

'From the dawn of philosophy,' wrote Mill, 'the question concerning the
summum bonum, or, what is the same thing, concerning the foundation of
morality, has been accounted the main problem in speculative thought and
has occupied the most gifted intellects.' For some time the most gifted
intellects have been averse to putting questions concerning the foundation of
morality in terms of the *summum bonum*. But recently there has been some
sign of a return of interest in the notion of a supreme good or happiness. We
might instance the chapter on 'The good of man' in von Wright's *Varieties of
Goodness* [74], B.A.O. Williams, 'Aristotle on the Good' [76], W.F.R. Hardie,
'The final good in Aristotle's *Ethics*' [73].

The notion of a supreme good is, I shall later argue, only one of the
elements which have contributed to the formation of our concept of
happiness. None the less, I shall follow the authors I have mentioned in
approaching the topic via Aristotle's discussion.

Aristotle defined the supreme good (*tagathon kai to ariston*) as 'an end of
action which is desired for its own sake, while everything else is desired for
the sake of it' (*EN* 1094a19). *Prima facie*, one can interpret the contention
that there is a supreme good in three ways. One may take it as a logical
truth, as an empirical observation, or as a moral imperative. Someone who
says that there is a supreme good, in Aristotle's sense, may mean that as a
matter of logical truth there is a single end which is aimed at in every choice
of a human being. He may mean, on the other hand, that every man does as a
matter of contingent fact have a single aim in every one of his choices. Or,
finally, he may mean that every man should, under pain of being
unreasonable or immoral, aim at a single end in each of his choices. Writers
on the *summum bonum* do not always make clear which of these alternatives
they have in mind.

Moreover, each of these alternatives is itself ambiguous. Is the 'single end'
in question an end which is, or ought to be, common to every choice of every
man? Or is it merely an end which governs every choice of each particular
man, but which perhaps differs from man to man? The first of the foregoing
alternatives, for instance, may be taken in two ways. It may be a strong
thesis to the effect that it is a logical truth that every man, in every choice,
aims at a single end which is common to all choices of all men. Or it may be
the weaker thesis that each man, in each of his choices, pursues a single end,
but one which is perhaps proper to himself.

Aristotle is sometimes thought to have presented the doctrine of the
supreme good in a form which is equivalent to the stronger of the two logical
theses just distinguished. It does seem to be a necessary truth that one

cannot choose everything for the sake of something else: chains of reasoning about means and ends must come to a halt somewhere. Aristotle alludes to this truth on the first page of the *Nicomachean Ethics* (1094a18).

> If, then, there is some end of the things we do, which we desire for its own sake (everything else being desired for the sake of this), and if we do not choose everything for the sake of something else (for at that rate the process would go on to infinity, so that our desire would be empty and vain), clearly this must be the good and the chief good. (tr. Ross)

This passage has been taken to contain a (fallacious) proof of the existence of a single supreme end of action. Thus Geach writes, 'It is clear that Aristotle thinks himself entitled to pass from "Every series whose successive terms stand in the relation *chosen for the sake of* has a last term" to "There is something that is the last term of every series whose successive terms stand in the relation *chosen for the sake of*"' (*Journal of the Philosophical Association* 5 (1958), p. 112). Such a transition is clearly fallacious. Every road leads somewhere: it does not follow that there is somewhere – e.g. Rome – to which all roads lead.

To convict Aristotle of this fallacy one must assume that he is offering the second if-clause 'we do not choose everything for the sake of something else' as a reason for the hypothesis in the first if-clause 'there is some end of the things we do which we desire for its own sake'. But this, Williams argues, it is not necessary to do: the second hypothesis may be a consequence of, not a reason for, the first. Von Wright and Hardie agree with Williams in acquitting Aristotle of the fallacy attributed to him by Geach. Von Wright points out that if Aristotle here accepts the conclusion that there is one and only one end of all chains of practical reasoning, then he contradicts himself. Clearly, happiness, for Aristotle, is at least *one* supreme end. But 'Aristotle also admits that there are ends, other than happiness, which we pursue for their own sake. He mentions pleasure and honour among them' ([74], p. 89, citing *EN* 1097b1-2). Aristotle seems, then, guiltless of the fallacy attributed to him, though it entrapped some of his followers, notably Aquinas (*Summa Theologie*, Ia IIae, I, 4-6).

It seems, in fact, to be false that it is logically necessary that there should be some one end which a man pursues in each of his choices. It might be thought that if we made our end vague and general enough, we might avoid this conclusion. To act voluntarily is to act because one wants to, either because one wants the action for its own sake, or because one wants something to be gained by the action. Therefore, it might be argued, there is some one end which we pursue whenever we act voluntarily, namely the satisfaction of our wants. But this argument is fallacious. If all that is being said is that when I act out of desire for x, then I am pursuing the satisfaction of my desire for x, it has not been established that I am pursuing a single end in all my actions; for there are as many different satisfactions as there are desires to satisfy. If, on the other hand, it is alleged that whenever a man acts he must be pursuing a goal which consists in the satisfaction of *all* his desires, then the theory, so far from being necessarily true, is not even empirically true. For it is perfectly possible not to have as a goal the satisfaction of all one's desires, and indeed positively to hope that not all one's desires will be satisfied. Russell, for instance, in *The Conquest of Happiness*, says 'to be without some of the things you want is an indispensable part of happiness'. In so far as Russell wants to be happy, he must, in conformity with his dictum, want to be without some of the things he wants.

There may seem to be a certain inconsistency here. It is akin to what logicians calls ω-inconsistency – the sort of inconsistency which is illustrated by the sentence 'he was wearing a glove on one hand, and he was not wearing a glove on his left hand, and he was not wearing a glove on his right hand'.[1] In persons, if not in systems, ω-inconsistent beliefs seem to me no bad thing. Modesty seems to demand that we should hold ω-inconsistent beliefs: e.g. that we should believe that some of our beliefs are false. Only a man who knows himself infallible could have reasonable confidence that all his beliefs were true. Similarly, patience seems to demand that we should have ω-inconsistent desires; at least, that we should be willing that some of our desires should be unsatisfied. But whether or not such ω-inconsistency in desires is desirable, it is certainly possible. If so, it cannot be a logical truth that in everything we do we seek a single aim of total satisfaction.

Williams has argued that Aristotle accepted the thesis that whatever is pursued is pursued for a single aim, not on the basis of the fallacious argument about chains of practical reasoning, but on the basis of the considerations about function in 1097b25ff. This account of Aristotle's argument seems to me mistaken. It is tendentious to translate '*ergon*' as *function*; we need not credit Aristotle with believing that men serve a purpose. If we translate '*ergon*' as *characteristic activity*, then the burden of the passage is as follows. Where an *F* has a characteristic activity, φ-ing, then a good *F* is an *F* which φs well. Different classes of men, and different parts of a man, each have their characteristic activity. Presumably, then, man has a characteristic activity: this must be an activity of the rational soul, else it would be common to animals and plants and so not characteristic of man as such. The characteristic activity of the good man, therefore, will be the good activity of the rational soul. Therefore, the good for man (*to anthrôpinon agathon*) will be the activity of the soul in accordance with excellence.

The surprising step in this argument is the identification of the good for man with the characteristic activity of the good man. Surely, we feel inclined to object, what is good for sculptors (e.g. adequate remuneration and good living conditions) is quite different from what the good sculptor does (e.g. sculpt well). But presumably Aristotle would reply that this merely showed the difference between what was good for sculptors *qua* men and what was good for them *qua* sculptors. What it is good for a man, *qua* man, to do is what the good man in fact does *qua* good man. But what the good man does is what all men *should* do: nothing follows about what all men *do*. The argument from the *ergon* of man, then, cannot show that, as a matter of fact or logic, all men pursue whatever they pursue for the sake of happiness.

Even as a matter of fact, Aristotle did not believe that men seek a single

---

1. Since the number of hands is finite this sentence is not itself ω-inconsistent.

end in all their actions.[2] The incontinent man who is described in Book VII, pursues pleasure in some of his actions, though the end he sets for his life is other than pleasure. However, we are told that the incontinent man does not *choose* to seek pleasure, so perhaps, it might be argued, Aristotle would support the weaker thesis that whatever is *chosen* is chosen for the sake of happiness. But even this thesis is ruled out by the passage at 1097a34 which Williams himself quotes. There we are told that while happiness is always chosen for its own sake and never for the sake of anything else, honour and pleasure and reason and virtue are chosen both for their own sake and for the sake of happiness. This seems to refute Williams' claim that Aristotle accepted the thesis $Ey\ Ax\ (Px{\rightarrow}Pxy)$ where 'Px' is to be interpreted as 'x is pursued' and 'Pxy' as 'x is pursued for the sake of y'. However, Williams' predicate letters are ambiguous, as he realises. He asks whether it is a sufficient condition of the truth of 'Pa' that a is at some time pursued by somebody. One might have thought it more natural to take 'Pa' to refer to some particular occasion of pursuit. Williams refuses to resolve the ambiguity. The difficulties, he says, 'lie not so much in the formalisation of Aristotle's discussion by means of the predicate "P" as in Aristotle's discussion itself' (p. 290). But Aristotle's text at this point does not appear ambiguous. He says that happiness is *never* chosen for anything but itself, whereas other things are chosen for the sake of happiness. It is clear that he means not that on some particular occasion honour and pleasure are chosen both for their own sakes and for the sake of happiness, but that on some occasions they are chosen for their own sakes, and on other occasions for the sake of happiness.

56   We can distinguish between two ways of taking Williams' formula. We may take it as saying that on each occasion when something is pursued, it is pursued for the sake of some one thing, namely, happiness. Or we may take it as saying that if something is ever pursued, then it is pursued on at least one occasion for the sake of happiness. Taken in the first way, the formula, as we have seen, would be rejected by Aristotle: pleasure is sometimes pursued for its own sake. I do not see that Aristotle gives us enough information for us to decide what truth-value he would assign to the formula taken in its second sense. Might there not be some things – perhaps, say, some of the perversions listed in Book VII, Ch. 5 – which were sometimes pursued for the sake of pleasure, and never pursued when pleasure was being pursued for the sake of happiness (as by the intemperate man) but only pursued when pleasure was being pursued for its own sake (as by the incontinent man)? There would then be some things which were pursued but never pursued for the sake of happiness. I do not see that Aristotle is committed to ruling out this possibility.

        The suggestion that all actions have a single end is one which Aristotle several times considers, but never opts for. At 1097b23 he says that if there is a single end of everything that is done, then this will be *to prakton agathon* (the practical good), but if there be more than one such end, then it will be these. He at once goes on to say 'there is obviously more than one end', and to exclude from consideration those ends which are not *teleia* (perfect), i.e. things such as flutes, wealth, etc., which are always sought in virtue of some

---

2. *EN* 1102a2 is as multiply ambiguous as 1094a19.

other end. But it is not even the case that there is only one *teleion* end: there are some things which are sought both for themselves, and for another end.

In the *Eudemian Ethics* Aristotle says, 'Everyone who has the power to live according to his own choice should dwell on these points and set up for himself some object for the good life to aim at, whether honour or reputation or wealth or culture, by reference to which he will do all that he does, since not to have one's life organised in view of some end is a sign of great folly' (1214b6ff., quoted Hardie [73], p. 277). The fact that this is made as a recommendation shows that what is recommended is not something that is already the case in the behaviour of all men.

It is not true, either in logic or in fact or in Aristotelian doctrine, that all men seek happiness in all they do. Is it even true that all men seek happiness? Here it is useful to follow Hardie in distinguishing between a dominant and an inclusive end. If happiness is thought of as a dominant end, then it is the object of a single prime desire: say, for money, or for philosophy. If it is thought of as an inclusive end, then the desire for happiness is the desire for the orderly and harmonious gratification of a number of independent desires. It seems clear that not everyone has a single dominant aim in life: it is surely possible to lead a life consisting of the successive pursuit of a number of unrelated aims of equal importance. If by happiness we mean something sought as a dominant aim, it seems to be untrue that all men seek happiness.

What of happiness considered as an inclusive aim? It may well be argued that a being who did not plan his life at all, and had absolutely no principles by which he ordered the pursuit of his desires, would be something less than human. But not every inclusive plan of life is a plan for the pursuit of happiness. A man may map out his life in the service of someone else's happiness or for the furtherance of some cause, perhaps devoting his efforts to the pursuit of some end which it may be possible to realise only after his death. Notoriously, such selfless dedication is sometimes the upshot of the wreck of a man's own hopes: he is crossed in love, or loses his family, or sees the collapse of the institutions for which he has worked. '*I* shall never be happy again', he may think, 'but at least I can work for the happiness of others, or seek truth, or help bring about the millennium'. Someone in such a position *has* sought happiness, and so would not be a counter-example to the thesis that all men (at some time or other) seek happiness. But selflessness is not always like this: people may be trained from childhood to pursue an ideal such as the service of the Party, or obedience to God, without this necessarily being presented to them as a means to their own happiness in this life or in another life. A daughter, from the first moment at which she is of an age to manage her own life, may forgo the prospect of marriage and congenial company and creative work in order to nurse a bedridden parent. It is unconvincing to say that such people are seeking their own happiness in so far as they are doing what they want to do. Happiness, considered as an inclusive goal, may include constitutive elements of many different kinds; but not *every* long-term goal consistently pursued is capable of constituting an ideal of happiness. In the cases I have considered happiness is renounced in favour of some other goal; but it is possible to renounce happiness for other reasons also, e.g. because the only possible way to achieve one's own happiness may involve the breaking of a

57

58

promise. In such a case, we might say, the agent must have the long-term goal of acting virtuously: but this would be a goal in a different way from happiness, a goal identified with a certain kind of action, and not a goal to be secured by action.

Aristotle, who considers happiness only in the dominant sense, does not make even the modest claim that everyone seeks happiness. He certainly says that all agree that happiness is the purpose of ethics, and that it is the highest of practical goods. But there is no reason why he should think that everybody practises ethics, or pursues the highest good. All he needs to presume, and all that he does presume, is that all of his lecture audiences are in search of happiness.

Later, Aristotle seeks to show that happiness is identical with philosophic contemplation. Even if he were right about this, it would not, of course, follow that all who seek happiness seek philosophic contemplation. Aquinas, adapting Aristotle, denied that the search for happiness involved any awareness of God. 'Admittedly, man is by nature aware of what by nature he desires, and he desires by nature a happiness which is to be found only in God. But this is not, simply speaking, awareness that there is a God, any more than to be aware of someone approaching is to be aware of Peter, even though it should be Peter approaching: many in fact believe the ultimate good which will make us happy to be riches or pleasure, or some such things.' This is the phenomenon familiar to logicians as referential opacity.

In Books I and X of the *Nicomachean Ethics* Aristotle behaves like the director of a marriage bureau, trying to match his client's description of his ideal partner. In the first book he lists the properties which men believe to be essential to happiness, and in the tenth book he seeks to show that philosophical contemplation, and it alone, possesses to the full these essential qualities. Aristotle's belief that the pursuit of happiness must be the pursuit of a single dominant aim, and his account of the nature of philosophy, seem to be both so seriously mistaken as to make unprofitable a discussion of his arguments that happiness consists in *theôria*. But the properties which he assigns to happiness in the first book are of great interest. They emerge largely negatively from his arguments against inadequate conceptions of happiness.

Aristotle starts from the traditional theme of the three ways of life – the apolaustic, the political, and the theoretic. It is wrong, he says, to think that the life of pleasure is the happy life, for this is brutish. Happiness, then, is to be regarded as a peculiarly human thing. Later on, he expressly denies that animals can be happy, and says that if children are called happy it is only for the hope of happiness which is in them. In English there are idioms in which it is natural to ascribe happiness to animals, but it seems clear that they do not pursue long-term, high-order goals of the kind we have been discussing. But there seems no reason why the pursuit of happiness might not include the pursuit of some things such as health and good food which are benefits which could be enjoyed also by irrational animals. Man differs from other animals in his concern for the absent and the future, and this naturally affects his enjoyment of and attitude to animal goods. Men, unlike animals, suffer from boredom, and human welfare must include some degree of intellectual stimulation and interest. Human happiness, therefore, could not consist wholly in participation of benefits which human beings have in common with non-human animals. But it does not follow, as Aristotle thought, that it must consist wholly in some activity which they do not share at all with other animals.

It seems odd to us that Aristotle should consider happiness an activity at all. He argues that happiness cannot be identical with virtue because it is possible for a man who has virtue to sleep or be idle throughout his whole life, or to suffer great misfortune, and no one would call such a man happy. But surely, if a man spends his whole life in bed and never does any virtuous actions, then it seems at least equally odd to call him virtuous. Happiness seems, like virtue, to be a long-term state rather than a particular activity or career; and if, unlike virtue, it is a state which is vulnerable to misfortune, this is not because it is an activity which is interrupted by misfortune.

Aristotle mentions two other properties of happiness: it must be perfect (*teleion*) and it must be self-sufficient (*autarkes*). Happiness is the most perfect thing: this is something we have already considered, namely, the fact that happiness, unlike wealth and pleasure and reason, is chosen only for its own sake. But there is a difficulty here, for when Aristotle speaks at 1097b2 of honour, pleasure and reason, it looks as if he has in mind once again the three kinds of life. But later he is to identify the life of happiness with the theoretic life. It is odd, then, that reason should appear here as something distinct from happiness, and therefore not most perfect, when in Book X the theoretic life is going to be praised as most perfect. Perhaps this is just an example of something familiar in recent philosophy, that what appears under one description as a means may appear under another description as an end; as the killing of an enemy may be done *for* revenge and yet be itself the revenge.

The self-sufficiency of happiness, Aristotle says, does not consist in its being a life for a hermit, but rather in its being an activity which by itself, and without anything else, makes life choice-worthy and complete. Of course, other goods added to· happiness will add up to something more choice-worthy. This last remark makes it clear that Aristotle did not consider happiness an inclusive state made up of independent goods.

So far we have considered happiness as a goal pursued. So considered, it appears as a long-term, inclusive, comparatively self-regarding goal. Happiness as a realised state cannot be simply identified with the achievement of such a goal; for notoriously a man in pursuit of happiness may realise all the specific goals he has planned and yet not be happy. Happiness as realised appears to be a state of mind, or perhaps rather a state of will: it appears to be akin to contentment and satisfaction, and might perhaps be described as an attitude, were it not that an attitude seems to be something which can be adopted at will in a way in which happiness cannot. Happiness in this sense might seem to be the satisfaction of one's major desires coupled with the belief that such satisfaction is likely to endure. The difficulty in such a definition arises with the word 'major': what is a major desire? It does not seem that we can say that every desire which occupies a great part of an agent's attention and efforts is a major desire in this context; for we might be reluctant to call a man happy whose only concern was to procure heroin, even if he was in a position to obtain regular and safe supplies. On the other hand it does not seem that we can decide *a priori* what a man's major desires must be by considerations of the major needs and concerns of human beings in general. For it seems that a man may be happy in sacrificing his own welfare: many martyrs have died proclaiming their happiness. The pursuit of altruistic goals, I have argued, cannot be called the pursuit of happiness; but the achievement of altruistic goals may bring happiness as a kind of epiphenomenon.

In assessing happiness we have regard not only to the satisfaction of desires, but also to the nature of the desires themselves. The notions of contentment and of richness of life are in part independent, and this leads to paradox in the concept of happiness, which involves both. Plato and Mill sought to combine the two notions, by claiming that those who had experience of both inferior and superior pleasures would be contented only with the superior pleasures of a rich intellectual life. This, if true, might show the felicity of Socrates satisfied, but will not prove that Socrates dissatisfied is happier than a fool satisfied. The greater a person's education and sensitivity, the greater his capacity for the 'higher' pleasures and therefore for a richer life; yet increase in education and sensitivity brings with it increase in the number of desires, and a corresponding lesser likelihood of their satisfaction. Instruction and emancipation in one way favour happiness, and in another militate against it. To increase a person's chances of happiness, in the sense of fullness of life, is *eo ipso* to decrease his chances of happiness, in the sense of satisfaction of desire. Thus in the pursuit of happiness, no less than in the creation of a world, there lurks a problem of evil.

4

W.F.R. Hardie

Aristotle's Doctrine that Virtue is a 'Mean'

'We must, however, not only describe virtue as a state of character, but also say what sort of state it is' (*poia tis*) (*EN* II 6, 1106a14-15). Aristotle's answer is that it is a state concerned with choice (*prohairetikê*), lying in a mean (*en mesotêti*) relative to us (*pros hêmâs*) and determined by a rational principle (*logôi*), the principle by which the man of practical wisdom (*ho phronimos*) would determine it (1106b36-1107a2). Each phrase in this statement of the differentia of virtue is difficult. We have to look further on in the *Nicomachean Ethics* for much of the explanation needed: Aristotle's account of choice is in Book III, his account of practical wisdom in Book VI. I shall consider now the statement that virtue is, or lies in, a mean.

Commentators and critics have had a great deal to say about and around this celebrated doctrine. Not surprisingly, Aristotle's view that moderation is good, and excess to be avoided, had been anticipated by popular morality and by poets as well as by Plato. Also not surprisingly, the concept of a mathematical mean, especially if allowed to expand to cover any sort of quantitative rule or formula, has many applications in the philosophy of Aristotle himself and of his predecessors: applications for the theory of what is good and bad in art and in the condition, healthy or unhealthy, of living bodies; applications, in Aristotle's works, to the physiology of perception and the constitution of physical bodies. Hence the student of the *EN* is bombarded with quotations from, and references to, the works of Plato and other works of Aristotle. The student is faced also by the widely ranging criticisms which have been directed against the doctrine of the mean. Aristotle is accused of spoiling Plato and of failing to anticipate Kant. All this comment and criticism is usually relevant and sometimes helpful. But it is not always needed to enable us to understand what Aristotle says in the *EN*, and it is sometimes only distantly relevant and sometimes confused. It is important, therefore, to start from what Aristotle says in the *EN*. If and so far as what he says can be understood, the pursuit and disentangling of similar and connected ideas in the works of Plato, and in other works of Aristotle, is not essential for the study of Aristotle's moral philosophy.

We have had a preliminary statement of the doctrine in *EN* II 2. Aristotle has just warned us that, in the sphere of action as in medicine or navigation, any general account must lack detail and precision (1103b34-1104a10). He then offers the generalisation that, as in the case of strength and health, it is 'the nature of such things to be destroyed by defect and excess' (1104a11-14). Thus, if an athlete takes either too much exercise or too little, he destroys his strength; similarly, health can be impaired by eating or drinking too much or too little, while that which is proportionate (*summetra*) both produces and increases and preserves it (1104a15-18). The same principle applies to the virtues of courage and temperance. To fear everything is to be a coward; to fear nothing is to be rash. It is self-indulgent to abstain from no pleasure, insensible to abstain from all. Thus, courage and temperance 'are destroyed by excess and defect, and preserved by the mean' (1104a18-27). Aristotle adds that the same kind of activity as produces a certain state, whether the strength of the athlete or an ethical virtue, is also the manifestation or actualisation of the state when it has been produced (1104a27-b3). Now in at least one obvious respect this statement of the doctrine does indeed lack detail and precision. A quantitative idea is applied to virtue and to vice with only a vague indication of how it can be applicable. Quantities of food and drink can be weighed and measured; exercise can be timed. But the quantities involved in virtuous and vicious action, which must at least be roughly measurable if the analogy with athletic training is to hold, are indicated only by reference to fearing everything or nothing, indulging in all pleasures or in none.

185 Chapter 6 gives a more explicit and definite answer to the question what, in relation to ethical virtue and vice, are the variable quantities excess or defect of which constitutes vice. The matter will become clear, Aristotle says, if we consider the specific nature of virtue. 'In everything that is continuous and divisible (*sunechei kai diairetôi*) it is possible to take more, less, or an equal amount, and that either in terms of the thing itself or relative to us; and the equal is an intermediate between excess and defect' (1106a26-29). Note first the precise meaning of the phrase 'continuous and divisible'. Quantity which is continuous is not merely divisible, but divisible *ad infinitum*: it has no indivisible, atomic, parts. This is the definition of continuous (*suneches*) in *De Caelo* 268a6 and *Physics* 231b16 (cf. 232b24, 233a25). Thus the sense conveyed by the whole phrase is that of 'continuous, i.e. divisible *ad infinitum*'. Grant and Stewart very strangely take the phrase to mean 'continuous and discrete'. Quantity which is discrete is quantity which is *not* divisible *ad infinitum*; and, if the number of indivisible units is odd, it cannot be divided at the half-way point. Having asked us to consider the nature of continuous quantity, Aristotle proceeds to try to explain the distinction between 'the intermediate in the object' (*tou pragmatos meson*) and 'the intermediate relative to us' (*pros hêmâs*) (1106a29-b7). Before we consider his explanation, it is desirable to see what answer Aristotle gives us, in this chapter, to the main question not so far answered, viz. what are the quantities with which virtue and vice are concerned.

 Ethical virtue 'is concerned with passions and actions, and in these there is excess, defect and the intermediate' (1106b16-18). It is a mean between two vices, and the vices 'respectively fall short of or exceed what is right in both passions and actions, while virtue both finds and chooses that which is intermediate' (1107a2-6). Similarly, in the summary of the doctrine at the beginning of chapter 9, virtue is said to be a mean 'because its character is to aim at what is intermediate (*stochastikê tou mesou*) in passions and in actions' (1109a20-4). The natural meaning of these statements is that in the case of *every* virtue, the virtuous man conforms to the mean, avoids excess and defect, in respect *both* of passions *and* of actions. This is asserted by Gauthier-Jolif: 'On peut donc tenir pour assuré que *toutes* les vertus, et pas seulement la justice, ont pour domaine les activités extérieures, en ce sens qu'elles assurent l'accomplissement d'oeuvres pourvues de certains qualités. Mais elles ne peuvent le faire sans modérer aussi les passions intérieures' ([35], pp. 141-2). But it is not clear how strictly this should be taken. As regards one important virtue, justice, Aristotle himself tells us that it is 'a kind of mean, but not in the same way as the other virtues' (V 5, 1133b32-3). We are not concerned at present with the meaning of this statement. The main point probably is that there is no single range of passions with which justice, in the sense in which justice is a particular virtue, is concerned. As regards the virtues generally, the following point is important. One of the ways in which an action can conform, or fail to conform, to the mean is in respect of the feeling or emotion which is expressed in it and accompanies it. Thus a brave man will go into battle feeling some fear, but not too much. A temperate man at a party will desire and enjoy the good things that are going round, but not too much. Two further points should be in our minds. In the case of some classes of virtuous actions, but not of all, quantitative variables, other than degrees of feeling, are involved. For the temperate man it may be a question of how much to eat or drink; for the liberal man of how much money to give away. But in the case of other virtues there may be no such quantitative aspect. A man is not called brave because he kills neither too many nor too few of the enemy. A man does not avoid the extremes of buffoonery (*bômolochia*) and boorishness (*agroikia*) by making neither too many jokes nor too few (IV 8). The second point is that all virtuous actions, including those in which external divisible objects are involved, can be right or wrong in respects which are not quantitative at all. They must be done, for example, 'at the right times, with reference to the right objects, towards the right people' (1106b21). Aristotle shows awareness of this in the very centre of his exposition of the doctrine of the mean (1106b21-4). There may be much that is unsatisfactory and unclear in Aristotle's doctrine that virtue lies in a mean. But it is wrong to criticise him in a way which would imply that this doctrine is the whole of what he has to say about virtue. What the doctrine does assert is that virtue is manifested in feelings and emotions, and also in actions, which avoid excess and defect, and that, where action is concerned with extensive quantities, virtue again shows itself in avoiding excess and defect. The second part of the doctrine as thus stated is comparatively trivial and obvious. But, in its application to 'passions' (*pathê*), the doctrine is important and an important *part* of the truth about moral goodness. As we shall find, not all of Aristotle's critics have seen this clearly or have given him the credit which is his due. I return now to Aristotle's exposition of his doctrine in II 6.

'Both fear and confidence and appetite and anger and pity, and in general, pleasure and pain may be felt both too much and too little, and in both cases not well; but to feel them at the right times, with reference to the right objects, towards the right people, with the right motive, and in the right way, is what is both intermediate and best (*meson kai ariston*), and this is characteristic of virtue. Similarly with regard to actions also there is excess, defect and the intermediate' (1106b18-24). In the application of the mean to athletic training the reference was to continuous extensive quanta, i.e. quanta with spatial or temporal dimensions. When two such quanta, i.e. extensive quanta, differ in size the lesser is equal to part of the greater. What is measured in the case of passions, at least in their psychical as opposed to physical aspect, is intensive quantity, degree of intensity. The assertion that quantity of this kind is continuous means, in the case of feelings, that there is no smallest interval between one degree of the feeling and another. Thus, if it is said that a pleasure or pain is becoming continuously more intense, this means that the change does not occur in jumps from one degree of intensity to the next: there is no next, any more than, if an extensive quantity is continuous, there is a next size. Having referred to degrees of the passions, Aristotle remarks that there is a mean, as well as excess and defect, 'similarly with regard to actions' (1106b23-4). This is not explained. It might, as we have seen, refer to the degree of the passion which is felt in the performance of the action. At least in some cases the reference might be to extensive quanta involved in the action as an external transaction, e.g. to the amount of food consumed or the amount of goods transferred from one owner to another. The parallel passage in the *EE* II 3 appears to offer an explanation in the remark that 'movement is continuous, and action is movement' (1220b26). But the explanation is surely not intelligible; it would·suggest that an action achieves the mean by being neither too fast nor too slow.

We return now to Aristotle's explanation, earlier in the chapter, of the distinction between the mean 'in terms of the thing itself' and the mean 'relative to us' (1106a28). The first point to notice is that the word which Aristotle starts by using, in his opening statement on continuous quantity, is not mean or intermediate (*meson*) but equal (*ison*). Equal to what? There can be no answer except 'equal to the amount which is right'. This at once gives rise to a puzzle. If we have to know what amount is right before we know that this is the amount which is intermediate, then surely the statement that it is of the essence of virtue to aim at and hit the intermediate does not tell us anything which has practical significance. We shall return to this question. In order to answer it we must decide how far Aristotle claims to find a resemblance between the ethical mean and the mean in the mathematical sense of a quantity intermediate between a larger and a smaller quantity and calculated from a prior knowledge of the extremes. The resemblance or analogy for which we might look is that knowledge of what is intermediate might be reached, though not strictly calculated, from a prior knowledge of what would be too much or too little. But, if Aristotle did mean to imply this, his use of the word equal instead of intermediate in 1106a27 would be misleading.

Aristotle now tells us that by the 'intermediate in the object' he means 'that which is equidistant from each of the extremes, which is one and the same for all men' (1106a29-31). By the 'intermediate relative to us' he means 'that which is neither too much nor too little'. This may well not be the half-way point between two extremes, and it is 'not one, nor the same for all' (1106a31-2). Aristotle illustrates again from the training of athletes. If a ration of ten pounds (of meat) is too much and two pounds too little, it does not follow that the trainer will order six pounds. This might be too much for the beginner, but too little for Milo, a wrestler of whom Athenaeus (X 412-13) tells us that he once ate a whole ox in the course of a day (1106a33-b5). Thus, a master of any art chooses 'the intermediate not in the object but relative to us' (1106b5-7).

There is nothing, so far as I can see, abstruse or elusive in the doctrine

188

conveyed by this passage: that the ethical mean must be appropriate to circumstances including facts about the agent himself. The mean is not 'one and the same' for all (1106a32). The mathematical terms in which Aristotle chooses to express himself need not, and indeed cannot, be taken very seriously. It is a lecturer's patter. Do not imagine, he is saying, that finding the mean is a matter of simply of 'splitting the difference' between opposing over- and under-estimates. It is not as easy as that. On the evidence of this passage, there is no suggestion of any quasi-mathematical derivation of the mean from prior knowledge of the extremes. This is made obvious by the fact that the extremes mentioned, ten pounds and two pounds of meat, are quite arbitrary. If the extremes named had been ten pounds and six pounds, the mean for the man beginning his training, a quantity less than six pounds, would not have been intermediate at all. 189

Since I find nothing either obscure or profound in Aristotle's distinction here between the 'mean in the object' and the 'mean relative to us', I do not agree with the commentators who make heavy weather of this passage. I have in mind Joachim in particular ([39], pp. 85-9). He extracts from the passage a 'geometrical proportion', i.e. an equation of the form $a:b::c:d$ of which the terms are the amount of a passion 'embodied in this act' by a given agent, the amount which the man of practical wisdom would embody, the nature of the agent and the nature of the wise man. The mean to be determined is 'the *meson* (mean) in a geometrical proportion, and therefore the range of its variations is determined by precise limits' (p. 87). I do not find any of this in the text. Moreover, I do not think that the expression 'mean in a geometrical proportion' is significant: as there are four terms in the proportion as formulated by Joachim there is no middle term (when $a:b::b:c$, b is the 'geometrical mean' between a and c). Aristotle is not saying that the ethical mean, while not an arithmetical mean ($a-b=b-c$), is some other kind of mathematical mean.

The next step in Aristotle's exposition of the doctrine is a suggestion that the principle of the mean is exemplified in the successful products of the acts. 'We often say of good works of art that it is not possible either to take away or to add anything, implying that excess and defect destroy the goodness of works of art, while the mean preserves it' (1106b8-14). This remark again is surely a popular illustration, a lecturer's aside, rather than an essential part of the exposition. The idea of spoiling a work of art by adding or removing a part is remote from the idea of excess and defect in action constituted by choosing too much or too little from a continuous range of quantities, whether extensive as amounts of food or intensive as 'amounts', in terms of degree, of a passion. Aristotle, in expounding the mean, allows himself to range over a wide territory. But for the student of the *Ethics* the important passages are those in which he formally and explicitly applies the doctrine to virtuous and vicious passions and actions. 190

There are two further passages which should be noticed in Aristotle's exposition of the mean in II 6. They are important not because they add any new points to the doctrine, or because they modify points which have been made, but rather because they indicate implications of the doctrine which have to be stated in order to anticipate or eliminate misunderstanding. The first is the statement that ethical virtue, while in its essence a mean, is an extreme 'with regard to what is best and right' (1107a6-8); cf. 1107a23:

'What is intermediate is in a sense an extreme' (*pôs akron*). Aristotle is pointing out that, on a scale of merit, a virtue is above both the corresponding vices and not between them. Thus to be in a state of excess or deficiency in relation to a virtue is to have a vice not to have a virtue but too much of it or too little of it. Similarly in IV 3 Aristotle says of the proud man that he is 'an extreme in respect of the greatness of his claims, but a mean in respect of the rightness of them' (1123b13-14). This point is closely connected with the point made in the second, and immediately following, passage which we have to consider.

'But not every action nor every passion admits of a mean; for some have names that already imply that badness is included in them (*euthus ônomastai suneilêmmena meta tês phaulotêtos*), e.g. spite, shamelessness, envy, and, in the case of actions, adultery, theft, murder; for all of these and such like things imply by their names that they are themselves bad, and not the excesses or deficiencies of them' (1107a9-14). The opening words of this passage might suggest that Aristotle was asserting or admitting that there are exceptions to the doctrine of the mean, ranges of actions or passions to which it does not apply. But he is making a purely logical point which arises from the fact that certain words are used to name not ranges of action or passion but determinations within a range with the implication, as part of the meaning of the word, that they are excessive or defective, and therefore wrong. Thus, envy is never right and proper because 'envy' conveys that it is wrong and improper. Again, it does not make sense to ask when murder is right because to call a killing 'murder' is to say that it is wrong. Most of the commentators get this point right, but Stewart at least is wrong or confused when he says: 'There are certain passions and actions which cannot be so modified as to form parts of an orderly character and life, but must be eradicated by education' ([37], I 120). This may be true, but it is not the point which Aristotle is making in this passage. There is a point about the vocabulary of the passage which should be noticed because of its significance for the doctrine. Aristotle says that some words name combinations of elements with the implication that badness is included. The word corresponding to 'combinations' is *suneilêmmena* (1107a10); cf. *EE* II 3, 1221b18-26. The word is applied in the *Metaphysics* to the combination of matter and form. Thus, in VII 10 he speaks of 'things in which the form and matter are taken together' (*suneilêmmena to eidos kai hê hulê*) (1035a25-6). The standard example of a term which refers to both form and matter is 'the snub' (*to simon*). ' "Snub" is bound up with matter' (*suneilêmmena meta tês hulês*) (for what is snub is a concave nose) (1025b32). We can now restate, making use of the Aristotelian expressions, form and matter, the point which Aristotle is making in the *EN*. In our vocabulary for referring to actions and passions there are words which name misformations; and, in such cases, there is no sense in asking what is the right formation of the object named. This, and no more than this, is what Aristotle means when he says that 'not every action nor every passion admits of a mean' (1107a8-9).

I have claimed that the doctrine of the mean states 'an important part of the truth about moral goodness' (p. 35). I wish now to amplify this statement and, in connexion with it, to comment on a criticism of Aristotle's doctrine made by Ross in his *Aristotle*. The discovery for which I wish to give

Aristotle credit is that of the distinction between two different kinds of moral goodness, the goodness of the man who does what is right in spite of desires which incline him strongly not to do it and the goodness of the man who does what is right without any resistance from unruly or discordant desires, the man whose inclinations are in harmony with his concept of the life he ought to lead. It would, perhaps, be more correct to speak of this as a distinction between classes of good actions than between men. For most men, sometimes at least, find that duty and inclination coincide; and most men, sometimes at least, find that they do not coincide. If we ask ourselves which of these two kinds of goodness is the better, we find ourselves distracted by a difficulty. In one way we admire the man who behaves well in a battle without undue distress more than the man who has to overcome obvious terror. In one way a man naturally moderate in his appetites is better than a man who has to struggle to control them. On the other hand, the merit of moral victory seems to be enhanced when there have been obstacles to overcome. Is the saint, or moral hero, the man who is not tempted or the man who struggles successfully with temptations?

The man who does what is right, in spite of opposing desires, is given by Aristotle the name conventionally translated 'continent' (*enkratês*). He is distinguished from the man who is temperate (*sôphrôn*), whose desires are in harmony with the right rule, being neither excessive nor defective. I quote from *EN* VII 9: 'for both the continent man and the temperate man are such as to do nothing contrary to the rule for the sake of the bodily pleasures, but the former has and the latter has not bad appetites, and the latter is such as not to feel pleasure contrary to the rule, while the former is such as to feel pleasure but not to be led by it' (1151b34-1152a3). To make this distinction so clearly was a major achievement in the reflective study of human conduct. If it has become a platitude, this is what happens to many discoveries in philosophy. As to the relative ranking of these two kinds of moral goodness, Aristotle, I think, takes it for granted that 'continence' is a second best to 'temperance' or virtue: it is better not to have bad or excessive desires. He does not formulate and face the problem, and there is still no agreed solution. But Aristotle's doctrine of the mean, taken along with his treatment in Book VII of continence (*enkrateia*) and incontinence (*akrasia*), brings the problem into the light.

Ross's chapter VII (Ethics) in his *Aristotle* has much that is interesting and suggestive to say on the doctrine of the mean (pp. 194, 196, and, with reference to particular virtues, pp. 202-8). But, in an important section of his criticism, he appears to take insufficient account of the distinction between virtue and continence, which I have held to be the vital centre of the doctrine. Ross writes: 'The essential thing is not that feelings should have some particular intensity, but that they should be thoroughly subjugated to the "right rule" or, as we might say, to the sense of duty' (p. 195). At this point Ross does not press his criticism; he points out that Aristotle's definition of virtue does include 'determined by a rational principle'. But he returns to the attack in a passage later in the chapter (p. 206) where he contends that 'the trinitarian scheme of virtues and vices is mistaken', and that 'each virtue has but one opposite vice'. 'Must not this be so from the nature of the distinction between virtue and vice? Vice is passive obedience to natural instinct, virtue the controlling of instinct by sense of

192

193

duty or by some other high motive – as Aristotle says, by the rule discerned
by reason. There can be too little of such control, but there cannot be too
much' (p. 206). It is clear that Aristotle has a reply to this criticism. The
criticism lumps together two states of character which Aristotle has been
anxious to distinguish, continence and virtue, both of which are manifested
in the control of natural instinct. In order to distinguish them it is essential,
as the doctrine of the mean affirms, 'that feelings should have some
particular intensity'.

Ross goes on to say that what Aristotle has seen, though he has not
expressed it very well, is that, in many cases at all events, 'natural reactions
to stimulus go in pairs of opposites' (p. 206). Thus, in Aristotle's account of
courage two types of feeling are involved, fear and 'cheer' or love of danger
(see J.L. Stocks in *Mind*, 1919). Both must be controlled. So, Ross suggests,
we must substitute for Aristotle's trinity 'not one duality but two'. Courage
is control of fear and cowardice the lack of control. Discretion is the control
of cheer and rashness the lack of control. Again the distinction between
virtue and continence disappears in this corrected version of Aristotle. The
distinction requires us, if there are two distinct ranges of feeling, to
recognise not two vices but four, and this is just what Aristotle does in his
treatment of courage in *EN* III 7. In principle at least, even if some types of
character are too rare to have been given a name, as in the case of the man
who has no fear (1115b24-8), there is excess and defect of both fear and its
opposite. It would be natural to suppose that this implies two virtues, even if
'courage' (*andreia*) is the name for both. But N. Hartmann, in his *Ethics*, Ch.
61, suggests that for Aristotle there is one virtue with two aspects, i.e.,
virtue, as he puts it, is a 'synthesis of values' (*Wertsynthese*) (pp. 517-18). In
this he seems to be right, Aristotle appears to hold that courage and
discretion, in the sense given to it by Ross, are aspects of a single virtue.

I have argued that Aristotle's 'trinitarian scheme' is a necessary
deduction from the important distinction which he makes between virtue
and continence. But Ross finds in Aristotle's treatment of temperance
(*sôphrosunê*) confirmation of the view that each virtue should be opposed to
only one vice. The vice which consists in the excessive indulgence of physical
appetites is profligacy (*akolasia*). Aristotle admits that the vice of defect has
no name. 'People who fall short with regard to pleasures and delight in
them less than they should are hardly found; for such insensibility
(*anaisthêsia*) is not human. Even the other animals distinguish kinds of food
and enjoy some and not others; and if there is anyone who finds nothing
pleasant and nothing more attractive than anything else, he must be
something quite different from a man; this sort of person has not received a
name because he hardly occurs' (*dia to mê panu ginesthai*) (III 11, 1119a5-11).
Ross is surely not justified in suggesting that, in this passage, we see 'the
breakdown of the doctrine of the mean' (p. 207). Even if complete
insensibility would be inhuman, it may be claimed that defective degrees of
sensibility are not uncommon. But is such a defect vicious? In the sense that
it is a deviation from a reasonable standard of human excellence it surely is.
Ross will not allow this. 'There is here no *vice* of defect; the "defect" can
only be either an innate insensibility for which one cannot be blamed, or
asceticism, which is not enslavement to instinct but subjugation of instinct
to a rule, though perhaps not to the "right rule"' (p. 207).

194

There are two comments to be made on these arguments. First, the suggestion that a man 'cannot be blamed' for 'innate insensibility' would, if pursued, have wide-ranging implications for Aristotle's whole theory of ethical virtue and vice. The profligate man might claim to be the victim of   **195** innate insensibility. Again, a similar argument might be used against the appropriateness of praising a man for courage and temperance, if these virtues can be developed only on the basis of normal and healthy innate tendencies. The argument might thus lead to the conclusion that, from a moral point of view, what should be blamed is incontinence not vice, and what should be praised is continence, control of 'instinct' when control is difficult, not effortless virtue. Secondly, Aristotle would not accept the descriptions which Ross gives of vice as 'passive obedience to natural instinct' (p. 206), or 'enslavement to instinct' (p. 207). According to Aristotle the vicious man deliberately pursues his ill-judged end. If, then, an ascetic is a man in whose 'end', or plan of life, there is no place, or not an adequate place, for bodily pleasures, Aristotle would surely reject Ross's assumption that asceticism is not a vice. The ascetic follows a rule which, as Ross says, is not the right rule. No doubt some deviations from right rules are much more serious than others. But the following of wrong rules is, in Aristotle's view, the essence of vice.

We have already seen, in considering Aristotle's doctrine that the mean is 'relative to us' (1106a29ff.), that he does not make clear how close an analogy he wishes to suggest between the ethical mean and the various types of mean in mathematics. Does the ethical doctrine assert only that deviations from what is right may be either excessive or defective, or does it assert also that, just as in mathematics, the extremes are data from which the mean is calculated, so, with due allowance for the fact that ethics is not mathematical, there is in moral thinking a movement of thought from the extremes to the mean? Aristotle does not explicitly make this second assertion, but Ross implies that it was in his mind. 'Even in the light of Aristotle's disclaimer of the suggestion that any mere arithmetical calculation will tell us what we should do, to describe virtue as essentially a mean suggests that we first know the extremes and from them infer the mean' (p. 195). Ross suggests that we do sometimes reach decisions in this way, e.g. in deciding how much to give to a charity we might start by thinking that £100 was too much and £5 too little, and then work inwards. In this way a man might 'finally decide what it would be right to give' (p. 196). But Ross thinks that normally 'we recognise what is too much and too little by recognising what is right'. Similarly, as Ross might have added, we   **196** recognise what is false by first finding what is true.

Have we any grounds for attributing to Aristotle the idea that, at least sometimes, we 'work inwards' from the extremes to the mean? I think that Ross could have put his case more strongly if he had connected the suggestion with Aristotle's doctrine that ethical knowledge is only approximate, that it lacks mathematical precision (*akribeia*) (I 7, 1098a26-32; cf. I 3, 1094b11-27). In the example of the subscription to charity we are, in fact, unlikely to decide that some determinate sum, say £25, is right. We are more likely to decide not to give more than £30 or less than £20, and then quite arbitrarily fix on £26 5s. 0d. The brackets are brought closer, but they remain separated. And so what is right is defined as coming between certain limits, and in this sense is a mean. The idea is expressed accurately by the words of Horace,

> sunt certi denique fines
> quos ultra citraque nequit consistere rectum.

In *EN* IX 10 Aristotle considers the question whether there is 'a limit to the number of one's friends, as there is to the size of a city'. 'You cannot make a city of ten men, and if there are a hundred thousand it is a city no longer. But the proper number is presumably not a single number, but anything that falls between certain fixed points' (1170b29-33). Similarly in X 3, in a discussion of the argument that pleasure cannot be good because it is indeterminate (*aoristos*), Aristotle points out that health, while determinate, nevertheless admits of greater and less. 'The same proportion (*summetria*) is not found in all things, nor a single proportion always in the same thing, but it may be relaxed and yet persist up to a point (*aniemenê diamenei heôs tinos*), and it may differ in degrees' (1173a23-8). Ethical virtue, like health, 'may be relaxed and yet persist'. In a given situation there is no precisely determinate intensity of feeling which is characteristic of courage or temperance. Any degree within a limited range is good enough to avoid the vices of excess and defect. It is not merely that we do not know which degree within that range is the right degree. There is no one right degree. Any degree within the range is right, just as any subscription between £20 and £30 would be right. I suggest that, in the passages to which I have referred, the doctrine of the approximateness of non-mathematical knowledge and the doctrine of the mean are interconnected and help each to elucidate the other.

197

APPENDIX
Continence, Virtue, Heroic Virtue

In the above account of the ethical mean, written about ten years ago, I argued that Aristotle should be given credit for discovering a 'distinction between two different kinds of moral goodness'. In support of this claim I quoted the passage in *EN* VII 9 where Aristotle defines the difference between continence (*enkrateia*) and the virtue of temperance (*sôphrosunê*) (1151b34-1152a3). I would still defend in general this interpretation and assessment of the doctrine. But what I then wrote was incomplete in at least two respects. First, I gave insufficient attention to the connexions between the goodness or badness of actions and the goodness or badness of ethical dispositions. Secondly I made no reference to Aristotle's assertion at the beginning of *EN* VII that there are three (not two) kinds of good ethical states (1145a15-b1). I am grateful to the editors for allowing me to explain, as briefly as I can, the ways in which I now think that, as a consequence of these omissions, my account of Aristotle's doctrine was misleading as well as incomplete.

In the opening sentence of VII Aristotle tells us that he must make a 'fresh start'. He proceeds to lay before us a division of ethical characters or states, three bad and three good. He starts from the bad states which are to be avoided (a16) and assigns to each an opposite to be pursued: bestiality (*thêriotês*) and the virtue which is beyond us heroic and divine, which are worst and best; standard vice (*kakia*) and standard virtue (*aretê*); incontinence (*akrasia*) and continence (*enkrateia*), less bad and less good than the corresponding standard states. A 'state' is a dispositional tendency, which may be more or less firmly established, to feel and act in certain ways; in the course of the passage Aristotle uses both *hexis* (a25, b1) and *diathesis* (a33).[1]

So far Aristotle's statements are clear. But there is one major respect in which his terminology in this division of states is irregular: *aretê* and *kakia* are general terms applicable to any virtue or vice or collectively embracing virtues or vices; *enkrateia* and *akrasia* are normally specific not general, having for their province the bodily pleasures and pains which are the province of the virtue of temperance (*sôphrosunê*) and the vice of intemperance (*akolasia*). But Aristotle allows that, on the basis of resemblance, the terms can refer analogically to desires and emotions which are the provinces of other specific virtues and vices.[2] In the present passage it is reasonable to suppose that *enkrateia* and *akrasia* are used in extended senses rather than that *aretê* is equivalent to *sôphrosunê* and *kakia* to *akolasia*. But, as we shall see, it would be wrong to assume that, when Aristotle uses the words *akrasia* and *enkrateia*, he is normally, if ever, deploying a concept which has the wide range and generality of expressions like 'moral weakness' and 'moral strength' or 'weakness (strength) of will'.[3]

Aristotle tells us that bestial or brutish appetites sometimes result from diseases and deformities (1145a31-2) but that the term is also used pejoratively of those who carry standard vice to an extraordinary pitch (1145a32-3). He promises to say more later about brutishness and, when he does (1148b15-1149a20), he distinguishes naturally brutish appetites, like varieties of cannibalism, from abnormalities due to disease (b24-5, a6). Nothing more is said explicitly about heroic virtue. Standard virtue and vice have been explained in earlier books. Thus Aristotle's main task in VII is to

---

1. 'A state (*hexis*) differs from a disposition (*diathesis*) in being more stable and lasting longer' (*Cat.* 7, 8b27-8).
2. 'Again, men are said to be incontinent with respect to anger and honour and gain' (1145b19-20; cf. 1148b9-14; 1149a1-4, b23-6).
3. Two further points may be mentioned here about Aristotle's use of the terms *akrasia* and *enkrateia*. (1) In VII 1 he introduces a second pair of terms, endurance (*karteria*) and softness (*malakia*). At the beginning of VII 3, when he is formulating questions to be considered, he asks whether the *enkratês* and the *karterikos* are the same or different (1146b11-13) and in VII 7 gives his answer, roughly that the continent man is undefeated by pleasure and the prospect of pleasure while the man of endurance holds out against pain and the prospect of pain (1150a11-15). (2) In one passage, described by Ross as an 'afterthought' ([15], p. 225), Aristotle distinguishes two varieties of incontinence, impetuosity (*propeteia*) and weakness (*astheneia*) (1150b19-22). The weak man fails to abide by (*emmenein*) the results of his deliberation; the impetuous man acts without having deliberated. Discussion of the questions raised by these elaborations of Aristotle's moral psychology would not be relevant to my main argument here.

define continence and incontinence and to explain how, as dispositions, they differ from virtue and vice.

The continent man and the temperate man are both such as to do nothing contrary to reason (*para ton logon*) on account of bodily pleasures, but the former has and the latter has not bad desires, unreasonable likings (*hêdesthai para ton logon*). The incontinent man and the intemperate man also resemble each other; they are different but both pursue bodily pleasures, the latter deliberately, the former not (1151b34-1152a6). The language of this passage shows that, as in VII 1, Aristotle is distinguishing one dispositional state from another. The 'bad desires' of the man who is intemperate or incontinent or continent are dispositions, e.g. to like and enjoy too much the pleasures of eating, drinking, sex. Bad desires can (sometimes) be corrected by right training, the object of which is to produce in us dispositions to like and dislike, neither more nor less than we ought, what we ought to like and dislike (1104b11-13).

The description of continence, in a generalised sense, conveyed by the passage can now be stated: it is a disposition such that there are classes of actions which the owner of the disposition, because he has bad desires, performs only with effort but which for a virtuous man would be effortless and pleasant (cf. 1099a11-21). A desire is bad if it is one concerning which a man of practical wisdom would rule that it should be eliminated or changed in some respect. An action is effortful if it involves the kind of struggle which Aristotle describes when speaking of actions which manifest continence.[4] It is important to keep clear about what are and are not the implications of this account. In distinguishing between dispositions at different levels of goodness Aristotle attempts to analyse what it is to fail, or to succeed only with effort and difficulty, in doing (refraining from doing) what is taken to be right (wrong). This analysis of acts is what most interests many readers; they are less interested in the precise description of dispositions. It is easy to slip into attributing to Aristotle the view that an action manifests continence not virtue (1) if it is both right and effortful, and (2) only if it is both right and effortful. It is important to notice that neither of these propositions is asserted, and that neither is implied by what is asserted, in the passage we have been considering (1151b34-1152a6). For (1) to say that certain sorts of behaviour, e.g. moderation at feasts, which are made difficult for the merely continent by their bad desires, are second nature to the virtuous is not to say that no virtuous actions are effortful. And (2) to say that the continent man's bad desires are liable to make difficult for him actions which the virtuous man would perform without effort is not to say that for the continent man rectitude is never effortless: he may find it difficult to avoid excess at feasts but quite easy on ordinary occasions. We can go further. Both (1) and (2) are contradicted not only by common sense, for Aristotle an important witness, but by what Aristotle says elsewhere in the *Ethics*.

(1) The idea that effortful rectitude necessarily manifests a disposition inferior to virtue requires the assumption that only bad desires can make right action difficult. But Aristotle is clearly aware that, when desires conflict, both adversaries in the conflict may be normal and good. The propensities which make it difficult, perhaps more than difficult, to hold out

---

4. e.g. 1150b22-5 and by implication in his treatment of incontinence in VII 3.

against the threats of a tyrant are constitutive of normal human nature
(1110a25), aversion from pain and love of parents or children (1110a4-31).
This example is in line with Aristotle's account of courage (1117a33-b20):
'the more he is possessed of virtue in its entirety and the happier he is, the
more he will be pained at the thought of death'; virtue itself, faced by the
loss of the 'greatest goods', aggravates the difficulty of facing self-sacrificial
death (b9-15). It may be suggested that, while these and other passages
show Aristotle's awareness, when he wrote them, that virtue is sometimes
an affair of blood, sweat and tears, this is not to say that the passages are
consistent with his view, when he expounds the mean, that the virtuous
man's feelings not only are within the right range of intensity but are
manifested at the right times (*hote dei*), towards the right people ... etc.
(1106b18-24). The temperate man does not desire sensual pleasures more
than he ought and such desires are not manifested at the wrong times or
when they are 'contrary to what is noble or beyond his means' (1119a14-
18). Thus, in his case at least, the harmony between desire and reason
shows itself in the latency of desire when its promptings, if present, would
conflict with reason (1119b15-18). But what Aristotle has in mind here is
surely that, in the normal circumstances of an organised life, desires to eat
and drink, for example, have their times and places; they do not trouble us
between meals. So understood the passage has no application to situations
in which it is 'difficult to determine what should be chosen at what cost, or
endured for what gain, and yet more difficult to abide by (*emmeinai*) our
decisions' (1110a29-31).[5]

(2) Aristotle lays down conditions which must be satisfied if an action is
to count as virtuous. It must be chosen by the agent and chosen with
knowledge of what is being done; but it must also be the expression of a
disposition which is 'firm and stable' (1105a28-33). An action which is right
and done without effort may express a disposition below virtue because it
does not satisfy the last condition. The merely continent man may have no
difficulty in refusing another glass early in the party but later on may do so
only effortfully or not at all. Thus Aristotle would have been inconsistent if he
had said or implied that an action is one which proceeds from continence only
if it is effortful.

We are now in a position to comment on Aristotle's doctrine in VII 1 that,
above the level of ordinary ethical virtue, there is a virtue 'heroic and divine'
but nevertheless found, although rarely, 'in men'. The commentators have
little to say, and in particular little to say that is positive, about this
doctrine. Grant identifies heroic virtue with 'divine virtue or pure reason',
which would mean that it was not a quality found 'in men'. Stewart and

---

5. Note that the same verb (*emmenein*) which is used of the success of the virtuous
man in 'abiding by' his decision that some action is right is also used to describe the
success of the continent man in resisting bad desires (1150b19-21). An action which is
difficult at the higher level does not manifest *enkrateia*, as Aristotle defines it, because
the propensities which make it difficult are not 'bad'. To speak of difficult actions as
continent actions is to slide into the mistake of which I have offered a diagnosis: as
Aristotle defines continence, some right actions done by continent persons are not
effortful and some right actions which are effortful are not done by continent (but by
virtuous) persons.

Burnet, and most recently Dirlmeier, do not say what they think Aristotle
had in mind. Gauthier-Jolif say in effect that heroic virtue is merely posited
as the counterpart of brutishness: 'the whole passage, far from being an
appeal in favour of heroic virtue, on the contrary invites man to be truly
himself'. Ross is even more explicitly negative: Aristotle's doctrine as
worked out 'leaves no room for anything higher than "virtue"'; temperance,
which is a virtue on the human level, is 'described as involving the entire
absence of bad desires and there is no room for a superhuman virtue beyond
this' ([15], p. 222). Here Ross seems to be assuming, on the basis of
Aristotle's distinction between virtue and continence, that a man reaches
the summit of virtue when he does effortlessly what he knows to be right. I
have argued that this is a misinterpretation. If it is a misinterpretation, the
alleged difficulty of finding room at the top for extraordinary virtue does not
arise. The hero must, of course, have the attributes which are essential in
Aristotle's account of standard practical virtue: he must be free from bad
desires, from excess and defect in feeling and action, and he must have the
opportunities for great action conferred by the possession of external goods,
political power and money. So we ask what can raise a man above this level.
What possible opposite is there to the man who goes beyond all ordinary
levels of vice, one kind of bestiality (1145. 32-3)? The obvious answer is that
it is shown by those who abide by the rulings of right reason in
circumstances which 'overstrain human nature'. Aristotle refers more than
once to such persons and in terms which make it difficult to suppose that he
was not 'in favour of heroic virtue'.[6]

6. 1110a4-8, 9-31; 1117a33-b16; 1124b8-9; 1169a18-26. Cf. 1100b22-1101a8.
Aristotle turns to Homer for examples, the valour of a Hector (1145a20-2) or the
endurance of a Priam (1101a6-8; cf. 1100b30-3). But when he speaks of the tyrant's
prisoner he might have in his mind an example nearer home. Hermias, the ruler of
Atarneus, who was Aristotle's fellow student as well as the uncle and guardian of his
wife Pythias, was put to death in Susa, 'having done nothing weak or unworthy of
philosophy', when he refused to betray the secrets of his Macedonian ally. Aristotle
wrote in honour of Hermias a hymn in which Virtue is addressed as 'toilsome to
mortal race, fairest prize in life'. On Hermias and Aristotle's hymn see C.M. Bowra,
Classical Quarterly, 1938 (with references to earlier discussions); During [21].

5

D.J. Furley

Aristotle on the Voluntary

What follows was originally published as two essays, forming part of an attempt to elicidate the historical background of the Epicurean theory which introduced an unpredictable swerve of atoms as a necessary condition for morally responsible human action.

When the philosophers discussed the subject of moral judgment, they 161 found they had to separate human misdemeanours into two classes: those for which the alleged culprit had an adequate excuse and for which he could not therefore reasonably be blamed, and those for which he had no excuse and for which he was therefore responsible. They had to draw up a list of criteria for placing any given action into one class or the other. Difficulties arose when certain criteria were proposed which seemed to imply that *all* actions were excused from blame, and were correspondingly exempt from praise also. Epicurus' philosophical system led to a difficulty of this kind. One of the obvious criteria for classifying actions as culpable or not was the question of whether or not they were the result of merely physical or corporeal interactions. Thus a man cannot reasonably be blamed for being over six feet tall, or for getting his clothes dirty if he is beaten up by thugs. But the Epicurean system was one which allowed *only* physical interactions: the one possible interaction was the collision of atoms with each other. This applied to the human *psuchê* as much as to any other compound in the 162 world. Epicurus was therefore required to show that morality was not meaningless in such a system: he had to find criteria for distinguishing actions which are, and actions which are not, liable to praise and blame.

The main evidence for his handling of the problem is a passage of Lucretius, *De Rerum Natura* II 251-93. The theory of the swerve is not mentioned at all in the extant writings of Epicurus. There is general agreement that it was in fact an original Epicurean theory; but there is no agreement on how it was supposed to work. In order to understand the problem-situation in which Epicurus worked it out, I examined Aristotle's treatment of the distinction between actions that are voluntary and those that are not....

1.

Epicurus believed that he had to save the human mind from fate in order to 184 give meaning to the concepts of morality. 'That which is in our power is free', he says, 'and blame and its opposite are applicable to this' (*Letter to Menoeceus* 133). The same point is made and elaborated in the first five chapters of Aristotle's *Nicomachean Ethics,* Book III:

Virtue, then, is a matter of feelings and actions. Since praise and blame are attached to what is voluntary, while what is involuntary receives forgiveness, or sometimes even pity, those who study virtue must obviously establish the distinction between the voluntary and the involuntary[1]. (III 1, 1109b30-4)

There is no need here to repeat the details of Aristotle's distinction. He treats the involuntary first, and thus arrives at a definition of the voluntary.[2] Things are involuntary if they are brought about through external force, or through ignorance. Hence, the voluntary must be 'that of which the source is in the agent himself, provided that he knows the particular circumstances in which the action takes place' (III 1, 1111a23).

185

Now Epicurus, as we know, thought he had to refute a theory according to which there would be no place at all for voluntary action. Aristotle, too, mentions one such theory, and rejects it, in the course of his discussions of the involuntary:

> Suppose someone says that pleasant and good objects are compulsive, since they exercise force upon us and are external to us. Then (1) everything would be compulsive on such a theory, since these are the objects for which everyone does everything. Moreover (2) people who act because they are forced, involuntarily, do so with pain, whereas those who act because of anything pleasant and good do so with pleasure. But (3) it is absurd to blame external objects, rather than oneself as being too easily caught by such attractions, and to take the credit oneself for one's good behaviour but blame pleasant objects for one's bad behaviour. (III 1, 1110b9-15)

It is important to observe both the nature of the suggestion here rejected by Aristotle and the means by which he demolishes it. The suggestion follows a discussion of some borderline cases, which cannot be placed at once in the category of the voluntary or the involuntary. Some actions may be in themselves involuntary, because they are in some way disadvantageous to the agent, and yet in certain circumstances they may be preferable to all other possible courses of action, and therefore voluntary. It is hard, Aristotle says, to lay down general principles, because circumstances alter cases; but it may *not* be held that actions can be involuntary simply because they are stimulated by pleasant objects which are external to us. Such is the context of the passage we are considering.

Aristotle gives three reasons for rejecting this suggestion (or so I think; by punctuating differently it is possible to set out the argument differently). The first is simply to point out that it would destroy altogether the distinction between the voluntary and the involuntary; so in this context at least Aristotle assumes what Epicurus had to prove. The second again fails

---

1. I am of course aware of the difficulties which arise from this or any other English translation of *hekousion* and *akousion*. See Gauthier and Jolif [35], II 1, 169-70. I hope this translation will not be misleading.

2. A significant point incidentally. Cf. J.L. Austin [127], p. 6.

to answer the question which Epicurus put to himself, since a pleasant **186** action *may* be forced. The third is a more interesting one. It asserts (without proof) that the proper target for blame is the deficiency of one's own character, not the external object which stimulates the action. If the suggestion is pressed in spite of Aristotle's insistence that there *is* a distinction between the voluntary and the involuntary, the third reason is the only one which will bear any weight.

But it may be suggested, by someone determined to break down the **187** distinction between the voluntary and the involuntary, that character after all may be 'out of our power', in the sense that it is given by nature. Aristotle considers such a suggestion, in a passage that may be worth quoting at length.

He has already established the distinction between the voluntary and the involuntary, and analysed the concepts of choice (*prohairesis*), deliberation (*bouleusis*) and wish (*boulêsis*). It follows from this analysis, he says, that virtue and vice are 'in our power'; for virtue and vice are simply enduring **188** dispositions which are produced by performing actions of the voluntary kind. So to say, with Socrates, that no one is voluntarily wicked, or unwillingly good, is partly true and partly false; it is true that no one is unwillingly good, but wickedness is a voluntary thing.

> Or else we must dispute what has just been said, and deny that a man is the source and orginator of his actions as he is of his children. But if we approve what has been said and cannot go back to sources beyond those which are in us, then those actions will be in our power, and voluntary, whose sources are in us. This seems to be confirmed both in the sphere of private life and in public legislation too. People impose punishment and retribution on those who do wicked things (provided that they do not do them either through force or through ignorance for which they are not themselves responsible), and they give honour to those who do good, with the purpose of encouraging the latter and restraining the former. On the other hand, no one is encouraged to do the kind of thing that is not in our power or voluntary, since there is no point in being persuaded (for example) not to get hot or suffer pain or hunger, etc. etc.; we shall not thereby suffer any less. (III 5, 1113b17ff.)

Aristotle continues with the defence of his thesis that virtue and vice are 'in our power'.

> Punishment is imposed for ignorance itself, too, if the man seems to be responsible for his ignorance; for example, penalties are doubled **189** in cases of drunkenness, since the source of action is in the man himself – for he was in a position *not* to get drunk, and his getting drunk was the cause of his ignorance. Punishments are imposed, too, on those who are ignorant of anything in the law which it is their duty to know and which is not difficult to learn. Similarly in other cases, people are punished for ignorance which seems to result from lack of care, on the ground that this ignorance is in their power, since they were in a position to take care. (III 5, 1113b30ff.)

It is from this part of his argument that Aristotle develops a line of thought which is of great importance for understanding both his own and Epicurus' theories.

> But perhaps he is the kind of man *not* to take care. No; people are themselves responsible for having become men of this kind, by living in a slack way. They are responsible for being unjust or overindulgent, by cheating, or by spending their lives drinking and so on. In every field of ·action, actions of a certain kind make a corresponding kind of man. This is clear from the case of people who practise for any sort of contest or similar activity – they practise by continually repeating the action. (III 5, 1114a3ff.)

The reader will see that the suggestion considered here by Aristotle, that 'perhaps he is the kind of man not to take care', follows on, in a sense, from the suggestion he considered and rejected in the first chapter of *Nicomachean Ethics* III (see pp. 48-9). There he rejected the suggestion that actions are compelled by external attractions, by insisting that the blame belongs to *character*. Here he takes up the possibility that character itself is something given, something out of our power. He rejects this by insisting that character is not given, but grows from our actions.

190 We seem to have a distinction between two periods of a man's life, in Aristotle's theory – before and after the formation of his character. Or rather, before and after the formation of each particular disposition (*hexis*); for character (I am assuming) is simply the sum of a man's dispositions, and some dispositions (those connected with food and drink, some physical skills, etc.) may develop before others (skill in driving a car, attitudes to bringing up children). Before a man's disposition is formed, he is apparently 'in a position' (*kurios*) to act in different ways. Once it is formed, however, this is no longer true. But nothing is said about the first stage. Aristotle continues his exposition with some notes on the second stage, after first ruling out one particular plea of ignorance: one cannot plead ignorance of the fact that actions do establish corresponding dispositions. He goes on:

> If a man does the things that will make him unjust, and is not ignorant of this, then he must be *voluntarily* unjust. But nevertheless he will not cease to be unjust and become just, whenever he wishes. For the sick man does not return to health whenever he wishes, although (it may be) he is *voluntarily* sick through living an undisciplined life and disobeying the doctors. *Then* it was possible for him not to fall sick, but once he has let things go it is no longer possible; just as a man who has thrown a stone cannot get it back again, in spite of the fact that the throwing of it was in his power, since the source of the action was in himself. It is the same with the unjust man and the overindulgent man: in the beginning it was possible for them not to become men of this kind, and so they are *voluntarily* men of this kind; but once they have become so, it is no longer possible for them not to be so. (III 5, 1114a12ff.)

I am not sure whether Aristotle would stand by the letter of this pessimistic passage, if pressed. It implies, if taken literally, that men become, after a certain degree of development, incorrigible. Evidently, however, he did not think that many men become incorrigible soon, since the *Ethics* is explicitly designed to make men better, and is not directed at the young.[3] On the other hand, he does repeat the same point in another context, when he is making a distinction between 'intemperance' (*akolasia*) **191** and 'incontinence' (*akrasia*). The man who is merely incontinent is one who knows what is right (the precise sense of 'know' here is discussed at length by Aristotle), but is led by passion to do the opposite. The man who is viciously intemperate, on the other hands, does *not* know what is right. He chooses, deliberately, and with full consciousness, a bad course of action, believing it to be right. Hence, Aristotle adds, he is incurable. 'If we make the comparison with diseases, vice is like dropsy or consumption, whereas incontinence is like epilepsy, since the former is uninterrupted wickedness, whereas the latter is not'.[4] It seems that he seriously believed in the incorrigible wickedness of those who had grown up, through bad habits, into bad dispositions.

The significant thing is that Aristotle does not seek a criterion of what is voluntary or involuntary in whether or not a man may act otherwise *now*, or in whether or not his behaviour can be accurately predicted. He does not say or imply that an act is voluntary only because it is 'freely chosen', or because it is preceded by 'a free act of will'. If we imagine his unjust man confronted with a temptation to gain something for himself by cheating, we can predict his response to this temptation; in a sense he may be on this occasion 'unable to do otherwise' than cheat – for what else does it mean to say 'he will not cease to be unjust and become just, whenever he wishes'? In fact, Aristotle might not wish to go so far as to say that he was *unable* to do otherwise; he might not wish to say that a certain disposition *necessarily* brings about actions of a certain type. But this point does not seem to be relevant to his doctrine of the voluntary and the involuntary. From the moral point of view, an act is voluntary if it proceeds from a disposition which is voluntary.

Aristotle observes that, as well as states of the *psuchê*, some physical conditions fall into the category of what can be morally appraised, for some physical conditions are the result, not of nature, but of behaviour. He **192** continues then to raise and answer another objection that may be brought against his belief in the voluntariness of virtue and vice:

> Suppose someone were to say that everybody desires what *appears* good; but we are not masters of what appears to us – the goal appears to each man in accordance with the kind of man he is. But (against this) if each of us *is* somehow responsible for his disposition, he will be somehow responsible for this appearance; otherwise no one is himself responsible for acting badly, but does these things through ignorance of the goal, believing that he will achieve what is best for himself by these means. And the desire for the goal is not a matter of choice, but

3. *Nicomachean Ethics* I 3, 1095a2-11.
4. *ibid.* VII 8, 1150b32-5.

it is necessary to be born with a natural faculty of sight, as it were, by which one will judge well and choose what is really and truly good; in that case, to be well born will be to have a good natural faculty of this kind. For it will be the greatest and best thing, and one which a man cannot get or learn from someone else but will possess or not according to his nature at birth; so to have such a good and fine nature would be the perfect and genuine 'good birth'.

Well,[5] if this is true, how will virtue be any more voluntary than vice? To both alike, the good man and the bad man, the goal is presented and established by nature or however else it may be; and they both act in whatever way they do act by referring all the rest to this. So, whether the goal is presented to each man in whatever form it may be presented not by nature but with some dependence on the man himself, or the goal is natural but virtue is voluntary because the good man performs the actions leading to the good voluntarily, in either case vice must be no less voluntary than virtue. For the bad man also has this property of doing something by himself, in his actions even if not in his goal. So if the virtues are voluntary, as we say (because we are somehow responsible in part for our dispositions, and we establish such and such a goal for ourselves by being people of such and such a kind), then the vice must be voluntary too, since the cases are similar. (III 5, 1114a31-b25)

193   Here we have a suggestion that moral character is determined at birth. It may be regarded as a development of the suggestion already considered at 1114a3 (see p. 50) that 'perhaps he is the kind of man not to take care'. In both passages, the essence of the suggestion is that behaviour is the outcome of character – i.e. of a man's fixed dispositions – and that character is 'out of our power'. In the later passage Aristotle makes more precise the sense in which character may be out of our power. It is because character may be just a matter of one's constitution at birth; the causes of his genetic constitution cannot be 'in the man himself', and therefore character must be involuntary, according to the definition laid down at the beginning of the book.

In the later passage, just quoted, it will be obvious that Aristotle gives an unsatisfactory answer. He merely points out that if character is a matter of genetic constitution, then virtue is out of our power, as well as vice. The reason for this is that the whole passage – and no doubt the whole of Aristotle's thinking on the subject – starts from the famous Socratic paradox 'no one is voluntarily wicked' (1113b14). By this Socrates meant – or, what is more significant, Plato said that he meant – that men only stray from the right course through some kind of ignorance. That is why Aristotle is more concerned with defining the relations between *ignorance* and voluntary action than those between *compulsion* and voluntary action.

The fact that Aristotle's argument is to a great extent *ad hominem* (a fact excellently brought out by Gauthier and Jolif [35]), accounts for some differences between himself and Epicurus. It was enough for Aristotle to show

194   that the Socratic paradox, unqualified, would exempt *good* behaviour, as well

5. For this translation of *dè* see Denniston, *The Greek Particles* (1954), pp. 238-9.

as bad, from moral appraisal; for this would be fatal to the teaching of Socrates and Plato. But it was not enough for Epicurus, who had to defend himself against arguments which would remove all actions from the realm of moral appraisal.

However, although it is true that Aristotle is largely content to reply *ad hominem*, we can find in the text the outline of a more general reply. It lies of course in his insistence that a man's dispositions are established by nothing but his own actions, the source of which is certainly 'in himself' and cannot be traced back any further. It is odd that Aristotle never (to my knowledge) asks himself why the discipline of parents and teachers is not to be taken as an external cause of a man's dispositions. Our own experience of 'juvenile delinquency', and the generally held belief that young people's crimes may be due not to wickedness but to faulty environment, raise this question at once. But Aristotle seems never to have considered this point....

2.

The criterion of the voluntary is that the source of the action is to be found in the agent himself and not wholly in things that are external to him. If it appears that we can find all the causes of his action in his environment, then his action cannot qualify as voluntary. Christian thinkers tried to break the causal chain by introducing an undetermined act of will, Epicurus by introducing the swerve. But where exactly in the agent's psycho-history is the causal chain broken by a swerve? According to the orthodox interpretation (that of Cyril Bailey in his influential books on Epicureanism), the theory holds that for every 'free' action a swerve must occur in the soul-atoms of the agent between the stimulus provided by the environment and his response to it.

But there are serious objections to this view of Epicurean theory, and an examination of passages of Lucretius suggests that the swerve might be located at a different point: namely at the stage of habit formation. This idea receives support from the following study of the Aristotelian theory of action, which seeks to show that Aristotle, too, assumes a discontinuity in the causal chain, not between stimulus and response, but between the influence of heredity and environment and the formation of habits.

The things which move an animal, says Aristotle,[6] are thought, **216** imagination, choice, wish, and appetite; but since imagination and sense perception can be classified as 'mind', and wish and temper and appetite are all forms of desire (*orexis*), and choice is something which shares in both thought and desire, it follows that all the motives of animals can be attributed to two things alone – thought and desire. After further discussion of these two, Aristotle sums up:

> The animal moves and walks through desire or choice, because some change has been caused as a result of sense perception or imagination. (*MA* 701a4-6)

The 'change' or 'alteration' mentioned here is described in more detail

6. *De Motu Animalium* 6.

later on after some examples of the practical syllogism which do not seem to add much of importance to our subject. Aristotle compares the movement of animals with the movement of *automata* – that is, semi-automatic marionettes – and with the movement of a toy cart with wheels of unequal size. The point of comparison is a little obscure, but I think it is supposed to show that one small and simple movement can by purely automatic means bring about a complex series of *different* movements. A simple turning of a cylinder on which strings are wound causes the puppet to perform complex movements with its limbs, and the end of one movement brings about the beginning of another. A simple push on the cart drives it straight forward for a while; then it loses equilibrium, heels over on to a smaller wheel, and so begins to move in a circle. (I am not sure of the details of either of these illustrations, but this must be approximately right.) In marionettes and toy carts, Aristotle notes, no change of size takes place, though if it did the effect would be similar. But in animals there *is* change:

217

> In the animal the same part can become larger and smaller and change its shape, as the tissues become swollen with heat and contract again with cold and so change. The causes of change are acts of imagination and sense perception and thought. Sense perceptions are themselves changes of a kind, and imagination and thought have the same force as their objects have. For in a way, the mental image of what is hot or cold or pleasant or terrifying is the same sort of thing as its object. That is why people shiver and are afraid simply as a result of a thought. (*MA* 701b13-22)

> The cause of movement, then, as I have said, is the object of pursuit or avoidance in the sphere of what is practical. The thought or imagination of these objects is *necessarily* followed by heating or cooling. For anything painful is an object of avoidance and anything pleasant is an object of pursuit (though in small instances we don't notice this), and anything painful or pleasant is normally accompanied by some cooling or heating. (*MA* 701b33-702a1)

Aristotle gives a few examples: confidence, fear, and lust have the sort of effect he has described, and the same effect is produced in some degree by memories and anticipations of these feelings. The human body, he says, is suitably arranged, in that the regions near the origin of motion in the limbs are able to change, from pliant to rigid, from soft to hard, and vice-versa. He goes on:

218

> Since these parts are affected as described, and since, furthermore, there is that connexion between the active and the passive which we have often spoken of, whenever it happens that there *is* an active and a passive, both of them perfectly fulfilling the definition, then immediately the one acts and the other is acted on. That is why a man sees that he must walk, and pretty well instantly walks, so long as nothing prevents him. For the organic parts are brought into the right condition by the feelings, the feelings by desire, desire by the mental picture; and this last is produced either by thought or by

sense perception. The immediacy and speed of the reaction is due to the natural connexion between the active and the passive. (*MA* 702 a10-21)

Lucretius' discussion of voluntary movement (IV 876-90) is an Atomist's commentary on this passage, or at least on the doctrine contained in it. His example – walking – is the same as Aristotle's. Both of them stress the mental picture which starts off the reaction: Lucretius speaks of the *imago*, Aristotle of *phantasia*. Aristotle observes that the mental pictures may be caused either by thinking (i.e. imagination, in the usual modern sense of the word) or by sense perception. Lucretius, being committed to the theory of *simulacra* (images), says that the mind must already have been in contact with *simulacra* of walking – which is true for him whether it is a case of imagination or sense perception. The mental picture stimulates desire, says Aristotle. This corresponds to Lucretius' statement: 'The mind moves itself so as to want to go'. This is the sentence in which the editors have most plausibly sought for the 'spontaneous movement of the mind which constitutes free choice'. The close correspondence of Lucretius' account with Aristotle's, however, makes this much less plausible.

The rest of this passage of Lucretius is closely related to Aristotle's *De Motu Animalium* 10. Lucretius describes how the mind operates on the limbs through the 'force of the *anima* dispersed through the limbs'. This force is the Atomists' version of the Aristotelian *pneuma*, which is introduced and explained in the chapter just mentioned. There is no need to go into this more fully now; but one further point of similarity should be briefly mentioned. Aristotle stresses the part played in the physiology of movement by expansion and contraction. This concept had to be modified by the Atomists, since matter cannot in their theory precisely expand, but can only become more dispersed, with larger interstices between the atoms. So Lucretius says the body becomes less dense when the *anima* operates on it (he does not say why), and admits particles of air. And he uses this thought, with some cunning, to explain another of Aristotle's points – how such tiny movements in the parts where motion originates can produce large movements in the heavy limbs. The air, says Lucretius, gets inside and works as it does on the sail of a boat.

Now in the whole section of *De Motu Animalium* devoted to voluntary movement Aristotle never states that there must be some 'free' movement of the mind between stimulus and response; nor has anyone, so far as I know, tried to find room for one in his theory. He does not say that at the time when the external object stimulated the man's desire and provoked a movement, the man 'could have chosen otherwise', but as a matter of fact chose *this* course. He arouses an expectation in the modern reader, at one point, that he is about to discuss this, when he says at the beginning of chapter 7: 'How is it that when one thinks, one sometimes acts and sometimes does not?' (This comes immediately after he has said that thinking – or, more precisely, the mental picture caused by imagination or sense perception – is the cause of motion.) But the reader's expectation is disappointed. Aristotle's point is simply that *some* thinking is concerned with reaching theoretical conclusions only, and this kind of thinking does not produce movement.

219

The section of *De Motu Animalium* which I have just outlined may be compared with the discussion of *akrasia* (incontinence) in the *Nicomachean Ethics*. In dealing with this topic, if nowhere else, we might expect to find a discussion of 'will'. For Aristotle attributed to Socrates the doctrine that there is no such thing as *akrasia*, on the ground that 'no one acts contrary to what is best, supposing that that is what he is doing, but (only) through ignorance'.[7] Aristotle found this doctrine contrary to the facts. How could he refute
220   Socrates, we may wonder, without saying that *akrasia* is not a matter of a failure in knowledge, but of a failure of *will*?

But Aristotle does refute him without saying this. The relevant chapters of *Nicomachean Ethics* are difficult, and much discussed,[8] but fortunately we can deal with them briefly here. Aristotle's analysis depends on the distinction between *prohairesis* (rational choice) and *epithumia* (appetite) or *thumos* (anger or passion). The actions of the incontinent man do not result from his choice; but they do result from his appetites or passions, and we have already learned[9] that such actions are to be classed as voluntary rather than involuntary. Hence we must not after all expect to find any important contribution to the question of what makes actions voluntary in this context.

Aristotle's solution depends, not on the concept of *will*, but on the concept of *knowing*. He finds that the incontinent man acts in one sense knowingly and in another sense unknowingly. His position is after all not very far from that of Socrates. His analysis of the psychological processes which produce actions is perfectly consistent with the analysis given in *De Motu Animalium*. Again he stresses that given the premises of the practical syllogism, the conclusion, which is an action, follows 'immediately' and 'necessarily'.[10]

Even in Aristotle's treatment of *akrasia*, then, we find the same picture of the voluntary as in the earlier book of the *Nicomachean Ethics*: the criterion of the voluntary act is not that it is 'spontaneous' or 'freely chosen' or that 'he could have chosen otherwise', but that the source of the action cannot be traced back to something outside the agent. The criterion is still a negative one.

It has been maintained, however, that a more positive criterion can be found in Aristotle in the operations of the *mind*, and it may be useful to look briefly at some texts which appear to confirm this.

It may be suggested that a positive criterion is indicated in the last chapter of *De Motu Animalium*. Aristotle begins it by remarking that he has now discussed the voluntary movement of animals and will turn to involuntary or non-voluntary movements (this last distinction is explained in *EN* III 1, and depends on whether or not the action in question is regretted afterwards – though this criterion cannot perhaps be applied very literally here):

7. 1145b26.

8. See most recently Gauthier and Jolif [35] II, 579-654, and Walsh [152].

9. *Nicomachean Ethics* III 1, 1111a24-b3. Cf. *Eudemian Ethics* 1224b26-36, where Aristotle remarks that the *parts* of the soul in *akrasia* may be said to act by compulsion, and hence involuntarily, but as a whole the soul acts voluntarily.

10. *euthus* 1147a28, *anankê ... prattein* a 30.

I mean by 'involuntary' such movements as that of the heart and the **221**
penis (which often move when some mental image is present *but no
command is given by the mind*); and by 'non-voluntary' such as sleeping
and waking and breathing and so on. Strictly speaking, neither
imagination nor desire is master of any of these movements. The fact
is rather that animals must *necessarily* undergo physical change, and
when the tissues change some parts swell and some contract, and so
they move immediately and undergo the changes which are naturally
in sequence one with another (the causes of these motions are heating
and cooling, either external or internal and natural). Hence even
those movements of the parts mentioned above which are contrary to
reason occur when there is a change. For thinking and imagination,
as has been said before, bring with them the things which produce
feelings, in that they bring with them the *forms* of these things. (*MA*
703b5-20)

There is certainly a hint here that an involuntary movement is one which
is not 'commanded by the mind', and hence that a voluntary movement is
one which *is* commanded. Does Aristotle then envisage another more
positive criterion of the voluntary? The same idea is repeated in *De Anima* III
9.

But what causes movement is not the reasoning faculty or what is
called 'mind'. For the speculative mind does not think of what is
practical and says nothing about what is to be avoided or pursued,
and movement is always a matter of avoiding or pursuing something.
Even when the mind *does* think of a practical object, it does not at
once give orders to avoid or pursue. For instance, it often thinks of
something that provokes fear or pleasure, but does not give the
command to be afraid – though the heart moves, or if it is a case of
pleasure, some other part. (*De An.* III 9, 432b26-433a1)

The involuntary leap of the heart in the presence of some terrifying object **222**
(real or imagined), and the involuntary movement of the penis in the
presence of an erotic object, are contrasted with voluntary reactions to these
stimuli. Both the brave man's and the coward's heart beats faster when the
enemy's tanks begin to move forward, but only the coward deserts his post
on the gun. Why? The heartbeat is apparently caused by a natural sequence
of changes: the chill of fear is an inevitable result of seeing the enemy's
tanks, and the chill causes some physical part to contract, and this causes
the heart to thump. But how does this differ from Aristotle's account of the
coward's running away, as we can infer it from the discussion of *voluntary*
movement in *De Motu Animalium*? We find there the same sort of talk about
heating and cooling, expansion and contraction, caused by the mental
image of an object seen as terrifying.

I am not sure that Aristotle has worked out a clear and consistent solution
of this problem; but there seems to be a hint in the passage just quoted from
De Anima. The mind, he says, 'often thinks of something that provokes fear
or pleasure, but does not give the command *to be afraid* – though the heart
moves'. That is to say, the terrifying mental image necessarily produces a

primary reaction – the chill of fear which makes the heart jump; but the secondary reaction, 'being afraid', depends on the 'command' given by the mind. To some extent this outline can be filled in from other sources. The feelings which cause physical heating and cooling are ultimately reducible to pleasure and pain (*De Motu Animalium* 701b34ff.). But these feelings are a matter of *training* (*Nicomachean Ethics* II 3):

> For a sign of what our dispositions really are we must look to the pleasure or pain which accompanies our actions. For the man who abstains from physical pleasures and takes pleasure in his abstinence itself is a temperate man, and the one who feels pain about it is an intemperate man; the one who stands fast in the face of danger and feels pleasure or at any rate no pain in doing so is a brave man, and the one who feels pain is a coward. For moral virtue is a matter of pleasures and pains; it is for the sake of pleasure that we do what is bad, and because of pain we fail to do what is good. Hence we must be brought up from youth, as Plato says, to feel pleasure and pain about the right objects; that is right education. (1104b3-13)

223

We may take it, then, as Aristotle's doctrine, that moral training is not merely a matter of practice in *doing* the right things, but also involves, as an essential and perhaps even the most important ingredient, having the right feelings about the action. Thus the brave man cannot avoid the primary chill of fear at the sight of danger; but *because of his training* he has no further painful feeling. By definition, the brave man is one who has a fixed disposition to stand fast in the face of danger. His mind is trained, by practice, in checking the primary reaction and so checking the spread of painful feelings; his mind does not 'give the command to be afraid'.

It will be seen that this 'command' of the mind is still consistent with the account of voluntary action I have given above. In Aristotle's theory the mind gives its commands *according to its disposition*. It is nowhere implied, so far as I have discovered, that its commands are 'spontaneous' and 'free', in the sense of 'uncaused' or 'unpredictable' – or at any rate this is true once the mind has acquired fixed dispositions. The actions it commands are voluntary, because dispositions are voluntary, in the sense already explained.[11]

The same point may be made more directly by referring to Aristotle's definition of moral virtue[12] as a disposition to *choose* in a certain way, rather

---

11. See also *Eudemian Ethics* II 7, 1223a23-8, 1224a7. The relation between Aristotle's two *Ethics* on this problem is particularly interesting, but a thorough examination of it would take too long here. My own view is that the treatment in the *Eudemian Ethics* is consistent with its being intermediate between Plato's theory and that of the *Nicomachean Ethics*, and that *Nicomachean Ethics* (including the controversial books V-VII), rather than *Eudemian Ethics*, is likely to have influenced Epicurus.

On the important issue now being discussed – that of a negative or positive criterion for distinguishing a voluntary action – *Eudemian Ethics* seems to be more positive than *Nicomachean Ethics* in concluding that 'the voluntary is a matter of acting with some kind of thought' (1224a7). For a discussion of this, see Adkins [120], Ch. 15.

12. 1106b36f.

than a disposition to *act* in a certain way. It may be a typical characteristic of a voluntary action that it should proceed from a 'command of the mind'; usually this command will be classifiable as a *choice* (*prohairesis*), in Aristotle's use of the term, though this need not always be so.[13] But it is not part of Aristotle's criterion of a voluntary action that this choice (or whatever else it may be) is 'spontaneous', if by 'spontaneous' we mean uncaused by previous events. Choice is determined by disposition; once the disposition is fixed, a stimulus of a certain type will produce a *characteristic* reaction, not a random one.[14]   224

Before leaving Aristotle's ideas on the Voluntary, we must look at a passage of the *Ethics* which may seem at first sight to be somewhat inconsistent with the rest. This is part of his discussion of Justice. An act of injustice, he says first, must be voluntary; and he offers a definition of the voluntary which accords well enough with the definition of Book III.[15] But later there comes this curious argument:

> People think that it is in their power to act unjustly, and therefore that it is easy to be a just man. But it isn't. It *is* easy, and in their power, to go to bed with their neighbour's wife or to strike the man next door or to pass money across the table. But to do these things *in a certain manner* is neither easy nor in their power . . . And they think the just man is none the less able to act unjustly, because the just man is equally or even more able than others to commit acts of this kind – I mean, go to bed with his neighbour's wife, or strike someone. The brave man, too, can throw away his shield and turn and run in any direction. But being a coward and being unjust are not a matter of doing these things, except incidentally, but of doing them *in a certain manner*. (*EN* V 9, 1137a4-9; 17-23)

This is of course an application of Aristotle's doctrine that virtue is not defined merely by performing acts of a given kind, but by performing them in a certain way, or more precisely by performing them from a certain state of mind.[16] A just man is not merely one who performs a number of actions of the kind we recognise as just, but one who performs these actions in the way a just man performs them. To that extent this passage is perfectly consistent with the rest. What may seem inconsistent is the suggestion that anyone can perfectly easily commit an *act* of injustice. This seems to imply that *acts* are detached from dispositions, in such a way that everyone – whether his disposition is just, unjust or neither – may at anytime commit an injustice.   225

13. cf. 1135b8-11.

14. I have said little about the role of mind in Aristotle's psychology of action and this may give the false impression that I intend to attribute a sort of behaviourism to him. The role of mind is important and complex, and not easily summarised (see especially *De Anima* III 7-11). Mind is of course involved in knowing the major premise of the practical syllogism, and also in appreciating the particular circumstances within which any choice is made.

My aim in this chapter is not to deny the role of mind in Aristotle's psychology of action, but rather to show that his theory of responsibility does not involve any 'free' or 'uncaused' motion of the mind.

15. *Nicomachean Ethics* V 8, 1135a23ff.   16. *ibid.* II 4, 1105b2-18.

But I think we need not trouble seriously about this. Aristotle rejects the suggestion that the just man will also excel at injustice, or the brave man at running away. He says firmly that dispositions are *not* productive of opposites.[17]

What we find in Aristotle, then, is first an insistence that there is a real distinction between voluntary and involuntary actions, such that moral categories are relevant to the former but not to the latter; and secondly a theory of the psychology of action which locates this distinction not in the individual actions of the adult but in the way in which his habits of behaviour are formed. It has been my purpose in this chapter to stress the latter point: we do not find in Aristotle the 'free volitions' dear to later ethical philosophers.[18]

17. *Nicomachean Ethics* V 1, 1129a11-16. I may have overstated the degree to which a fixed disposition of the mind *determines* a man's actions in Aristotle's theory. He allowed that a just man could (in some sense of 'could') commit an unjust act. But this does not weaken the force of my main contention, that the 'freedom' of an action, for Aristotle, does not depend on his being able to choose otherwise at the time of the action. The act might still be liable to praise or blame, even though his character were so rigidly fixed that he could not possibly in the circumstances choose otherwise. Dispositions (*hexeis*) obviously vary in the degree of their fixity. Man's responsibility for his actions depends on the claim that his dispositions are created *by himself*, not on the degree to which his dispositions are now unfixed.

18. If anyone still doubts this, let him read the spirited Chapter 18 'Angebliche Willensfreiheit' in Loening [61], and D.J. Allan's quieter but equally compelling article [130].

6

G.E.M. Anscombe

Thought and Action in Aristotle

Is Aristotle inconsistent in the different things he says about *prohairesis*, mostly translated 'choice', in the different parts of the *Ethics*? The following seems to be a striking inconsistency. In Book III (1113a4) he says that what is 'decided by deliberation' is chosen (*prohaireton*), but he also often insists that the uncontrolled man, the *akratês*, does not *choose* to do what he does; that is to say, what he does in doing the kind of thing that he disapproves of, is not what Aristotle will call exercising choice; the uncontrolled man does not act from choice, *ek prohaireseôs*, or choosing, *prohairoumenos*. However, in Book VI (1142b18) he mentions the possibility of a calculating uncontrolled man who will get what he arrived at by calculation and so will have deliberated correctly. Thus we have the three theses: (*a*) choice is what is determined by deliberation; (*b*) what the uncontrolled man does *qua* uncontrolled, he does not choose to do; (*c*) the uncontrolled man, even when acting against his convictions, does on occasion determine what to do by deliberation.

Without a doubt the set of passages is inconsistent if we are to understand that any case of something being determined by deliberation at all is a case of choice, as seems to be suggested by the formulation 'what is decided by deliberation is chosen'.

If, then, Aristotle is consistent, perhaps his 'choice' is not *simply* determination by calculating or deliberating. There is some reason to think this; though he says that what is determined by deliberation *is* chosen, we may say that the *context* shows that he himself has in mind a deliberation what to do with a view to one's ends, and that ends are things like being honoured, health, the life of virtue, or material prosperity, or enjoyment of knowledge, or sensual pleasure. The uncontrolled man, the *akratês*, is not one whose general object is, say, enjoying a life of sensual pleasure; he simply has the *particular* purpose of seducing his neighbour's wife.

On this view, we remove the inconsistency by saying that 'choice' is of something determined not just by any deliberation, but by deliberation how to obtain an object of one's *will* (*boulêsis*) rather than merely of one's *desire* (*epithumia*): there will be a contrast here even for the *akolastos*, the licentious man. For *his* will is *to satisfy his desires, his sensual appetites*; and his decision to seduce his neighbour's wife, say, is a 'choice', as well as being an expression of his lusts, just because his end in life *is* to satisfy his lusts; this has to be shown before one can say that a man who is going after objects of 'desire' evilly, has a bad 'choice'.

Now – though I think this does represent Aristotle's view – an objection that strikes one is that people's 'ends' aren't in general nearly as definitely one thing or another as Aristotle makes out. *If* 'will' (*boulêsis*) is simply the type of wanting (*orexis*) that one has in relation to one's final objective *in* what one is deliberately doing at any time, then there seems no objection to saying that the weak man at 1151a2 (the uncontrolled man who calculates how to get what tempts him, for he is surely a man of the weak rather than the impulsive type) has a *will* to seduce his neighbour's wife, or a will for the pleasure of it, at the time when he is cleverly reckoning how to do it. The fact that he has a bad conscience about it doesn't seem to be either here or there *for determining whether he is making that his aim* for the time being; but this fact, that he has a bad conscience about it, *is* just what makes him uncontrolled rather than licentious, *akratês* rather than *akolastos*.

There is, however, another defence against the charge of inconsistency, which perhaps is not open to the objection that it requires an unrealistic idea of the clear-cutness of people's ends. Not all deliberation is with a view to making a 'choice', forming a *prohairesis*, where none has yet been made; some deliberation is with a view to executing a 'choice'. This is made clear at 145 1144a20; 'Virtue makes one's choice (*prohairesin*) right, but as for what has to be done for the sake of it (*ekeinês heneka*), that doesn't belong to virtue but to another power – cleverness.'

But also in Book III Aristotle speaks of *trying* to do the thing that a deliberation has terminated in: 'If it seems possible, they try to do it. Possible things are the things that *might* come about through us' (1112b26). So we might say that something that seems to be a way of achieving your end and to be possible may be decided upon; *that* you will do this (or at least will try) is a 'choice'; and now there may be further deliberation just how to manage that possible-seeming thing. Now in Book III there is no suggestion that wanting (*orexis* of) the more immediate means (adopted to execute the remoter means that have already been decided on) is not itself *also* a 'choice', *prohairesis*. But if we are to reconcile the denial (which *also* occurs in Book III, 1111b14) that the uncontrolled man acts *choosing* so to act (*prohairoumenos*) with the account in Book VI of a calculating uncontrolled man, then we must say that when deliberation how to execute a decision terminates in an action – the man contrives a skilful approach to the woman – this will not be a case of 'choice' if the decision was not reached by deliberation.

Thus the passages in which Aristotle describes deliberation as going on till we have reached something we can do here and now, and decribes 'choice' as being of what deliberation has reached, must not lead us to think that matter for a 'choice' has *only* been reached when there is no more room for deliberation of any kind.

On the other hand, just as the first defence left us wondering what Aristotle supposed a *boulêsis*, a case of 'will', to be, since apparently the pleasure sought by the uncontrolled man who calculates is not an object of his will; so this defence leaves us in the dark as to what a 'choice' is. We may well have thought we knew this; for 'what you can do here and now, which you have reached as a result of deliberating how to achieve an end' – the first cause, the last thing in analysis and first in execution – did seem a relatively clear notion. But if, as must be admitted on the basis of the text, there is room for calculating how to execute a 'choice', then just where in the chain of deliberations from an end to the immediate thing that I can do without 146 having to consider *how* to do it – just where in this chain does the first 'choice' come?

It must be admitted that Aristotle's account of deliberation often seems to fit deliberation about how to execute a decision, and in particular to fit technical deliberation, better than deliberation which is about the means here and now to 'living well in general'. It seems at its clearest when he is describing the doctor deliberating how to restore health by reducing the imbalance of humours by . . . , etc. But this is a piece of technical deliberation.

I am not saying that Aristotle so uses '*prohairesis*' ('choice') that the termination of a piece of technical deliberation is not a 'choice'. On the contrary; that would, I think, be quite inconsistent with the treatment in Book III. But Book VI teaches us, as I think we might not have realised from Book III, that there is no such thing as a 'choice' which is *only* technical (I use 'technical' to cover practical cleverness in bringing particular situations about, even when it is not strictly a technique that is in question). There is always, on Aristotle's view, another 'choice' behind a technical or purely executive one (1139b1-3). That is why he denies the name of '*prohairesis*', 'choice', to the technical or executive decision, even though this is the fruit of deliberation, if that particular thing for the sake of which this decision is being made is not *itself* decided upon by deliberation.

To return to the weak, calculating, uncontrolled man, who disapproves of adultery but is tempted about his neighbour's wife: he gives way to the temptation and sets out to seduce her; then he calculates how best to do this and shows plenty of cleverness in his calculations. If he had been a licentious man, an *akolastos*, the decision to seduce her would have been a 'choice', and the volition to perform each of the steps that he reckoned would enable him to succeed would in turn each have been a 'choice' too. For the decision to seduce this woman was simply the particular application of his general policy of pursuing sensual enjoyment. But although the uncontrolled man perhaps reckons how to proceed – once he has given way to the temptation to go after this woman – in exactly the same way as the licentious man, his volitions in performing the steps that he calculates will enable him to succeed are not 'choices'. (Aristotle, of course, does not set up a word for 'volition' as I have been using it.) So we have to say that the uncontrolled man carries out a deliberation how to execute what would have been a 'choice' if he had been an *akolastos*; this, however, is something for which Aristotle has no regular name – for he has no general use of a psychological verb or abstract noun corresponding to '*hekousion*' (usually translated 'voluntary') as '*prohaireisthai*' ('choose'), '*prohairesis*' ('choice'), correspond to '*prohaireton*' ('chosen'). Of course he regards the uncontrolled man as acting voluntarily. When he describes this man as calculating cleverly, he says he will get what he 'proposes' (*protithetai*); and this verb expresses a volition, or perhaps rather an intention. Aristotle ought, we may say, to have seen that he was here employing a key concept in the theory of action, but he did not do so; the innocent unnoticeable verb he uses receives no attention from him.

Let us return to the point that a technical 'choice' is never the only 'choice' that is made by the man who makes it. The definition of 'choice' as deliberative wanting (*orexis*) would not at first sight seem to justify this. The calculating uncontrolled man choosing means of seduction – he wants them, surely, i.e. has an *orexis* for them, and this is a result of deliberation. However, there is – what may give us pause in making this criticism – a puzzling remark in that passage in Book VI (1139a17-b13) where Aristotle devotes most

147

discussion to this definition of 'choice'. He says '. . . choice does not exist
without intellect and judgment, *nor yet without* moral character' (*êthikês hexeôs*).
That sentence, in fact, starts with the word '*diho*' – 'That is why'. It is
puzzling, because while the previous sentences give ample grounds for saying
that choice involves intelligence, they don't seem to give any ground for
saying that it involves moral character. However, the succeeding sentence
starts 'For' – so perhaps we should look for the explanation there first. 'For
doing well (*eupraxia*), and its opposite, does not exist without judgment and
character (*éthous*)'. That does not seem to help us much. A little farther on,
however, he tells us 'The end, absolutely speaking, is not anything one *makes*,
but something one *does*. For doing well is the end, and that is the object of the
wanting (*orexis*). That is why choice is appetitive (*orektikê*) intelligence or
intelligent wanting'.

148   This brings us back to our first defence; namely, that something is only a
'choice' if it is of means to the objects of a man's 'will' (*boulêsis*); hence,
however much calculation may have gone into determining it, if it is of what is
only a means to the objects of a man's *epithumiai*, his 'desires', then unless his
'will' in life *is* to satisfy these desires (as holds of the licentious man) it is not a
'choice'. Thus the second defence resolves into the first. The second defence
was that since some deliberation is done with a view to executing a 'choice',
something may be reached as a result of deliberation even when the
significant decision what to do has already been made; and if this has *not* been
made by deliberation, then it was not a 'choice', and the results of
deliberations how to execute it won't be 'choices' either. Well, the question
whether the significant decision is reached by deliberation seems to reduce to
the question whether it is made with a view to the objects of the man's 'will'
(*boulêsis*). Now our question about this was: what does Aristotle suppose 'will'
(*boulêsis*) to be? Why, we asked, shouldn't we say that the uncontrolled man
has a 'will' for the pleasure he hopes to obtain from seducing his neighbour's
wife? The answer we get suggested by the passage in Book VI is: the
uncontrolled man is not prepared to say: 'This is my idea of good work
(*eupraxia*), this is the kind of life I want.' Whereas, of course, that is the
attitude of the licentious man, the *akolastos*: a life spent doing such things is his
idea of a well-spent life – and a fig for moral virtue. It is not that the licentious
man thinks licentiousness is moral virtue; what he thinks is rather that this is
a good way to carry on. 'One should pursue the present pleasure' doesn't
mean: it's virtuous, or morally obligatory, to do that – but: that's the thing to
do!

    Now, why can't one have 'choice' without moral character of some sort? I
think Aristotle does not explain this, beyond saying that 'doing well', 'a good
way of carrying on' is the end of any 'choice'; i.e. any sort of decision which
does not have in view what one thinks of as a good way of proceeding in one's
life, does *not* qualify to be a 'choice'.

    His thesis, then, clearly is that there is no such thing as your acting with
eupraxia, 'doing well', in view unless you have some sort of moral character,
virtuous or vicious. Now, how is this? Let us imagine some cases.

149   Someone thinks that it is a good sort of life always to get the better of people
by tricking them, taking them in, defrauding them; to do that is to be strong
and not soft and not a sucker oneself, and to get the best of whatever's going;
whereas the honest man is weak and soft and a fool, and always gets the worst

of things. A particular decision to cheat X will be a 'choice' of something here and now which he makes for the sake of doing well as he conceives it.

Another case: Someone thinks that he will do well if he spends his life in scientific research; to do this he must have leisure; to get the money for his living expenses he does a disgraceful but not time-consuming thing: one great fraud.

These are two rather different types of case; however, in both of them it would be natural enough to say that the man is described as having a sort of moral character. On Aristotle's view, a character exists only when there is a habitual performance of the typical acts of that character. Now I have described the cases so that the men's ends are clear, but I have put in only one act for each. The first case is not credibly described on the supposition that there is only one such act. This one act with a view to this sort of 'doing well' – what is supposed to have preceded it? Has he done things of the same sort, but not done them under any such conception? under what conception, then? – say in obedience to a mentor, or attracted by the particular gains of each action? Very well; but what is to make us call this the first act done with a view to that sort of 'doing well'? It is not enough for the agent to have those thoughts; suppose he had them on just one occasion – that would not show that he was acting so as to 'do well' in that kind of way, only that he had indulged in a certain picture of his actions. Only if they are the thoughts which come to habitually inspire those actions shall we be able to say: that is his end, that is his idea of a good way of going on. If, on the other hand, he had not done any actions of the sort before, then still more one would want plenty of actions performed under the influence of his new thoughts before one could recognise one as done with a view to this sort of 'doing well' rather than as, say, an experiment in wrongdoing.

The other case is different; here the single act which is to be the object of a choice is not the kind of act which the agent supposes to be the way to spend his life well. If the agent had never done any scientific research or study at all, then the description of the case would be suspect. Either it would be nonsense, or it would be a description of someone under a fantastic illusion. Perhaps it is possible to conceive something as the activity you aim to spend your life at even though you never do it at all, even in a feeble and elementary fashion. But then either it would have to be something you could understand without doing it (like riding horses, say), or you could only want the name, no doubt with some piece of imagination attached – as if, e.g., someone who had never learnt any mathematics wanted to become a mathematician because of the expression on the face of a mathematician he knew, and had no other conception of a good way of spending his life: that was it, for him. This would rather be a lunatic obsession than a conception of a certain sort of doing well as the end.

If, then, 'choice' is only of those things which are done as means to 'doing well', we may concede that Aristotle is right in saying that it does not occur without moral character, i.e. without good or bad habitual action. But there is no reason to say that the action which is the subject of 'choice' must itself be the act of a virtue or a vice. That will only be so where the objects of 'choice' are (in Greenwood's phrase) constitutive means towards the (putative) good way of going on. In the second case I described, the fraudulent act was a productive means; and if the man did not perform other fraudulent acts, this act would not mean that he was a fraudulent man – i.e. that he had the vice of being fraudulent.

The notion of 'choice' as conceived by Aristotle, his *prohairesis*, is a very peculiar one. I used to think it spurious. If it had been a winner, like some other Aristotelian concepts, would not 'proheretic' be a word as familiar to us as 'practical' is?

At any rate, 'choice' cannot do all the work Aristotle wants to make it do. The uncontrolled man who has further intentions in doing what he does, whose actions are deliberate, although the deliberation is in the interest of a desire which conflicts with what he regards as doing well – to describe his action we need a concept (our 'intention') having to do with will or appetition: not just *epithumia*, 'desire', for that may be only a feeling.

Aristotle talks as if 'desire' were a force (1147a34), but this is only a metaphor. He will have it that if one acts against one's convictions, one's judgment has always failed in some way under the influence of 'desire' or
151   some other passion. One fails to know or remember either the last premiss or, possibly, the conclusion. There are such cases. For example, a man who disapproves of adultery may fail to find out something which he easily could have found out, and so may commit adultery through culpable ignorance of a particular premiss: 'This woman, whom I have picked up at a party, is someone's wife' – his failure to find out being explained by his passion. And similarly for failure to get or keep clear before one's mind already known facts, with their implications for action in view of one's ends; and for lies one may tell inwardly or outwardly when one wants to do wrong. But Aristotle writes as if these were the only cases of doing what you believe is wrong. He apparently cannot admit the case where a person forms a perfectly clear-headed intention of acting contrary to his convictions. On one interpretation the trouble always concerns one of the particular premises; on another, Aristotle allows a case where the sinner is clear about all these, but then fails to draw the conclusion; at most he draws it verbally, without knowledge of what he is saying.

The usual explanations of this are that Aristotle was a Greek, that he was still under Plato's influence, etc. No doubt there is something in that; particularly when he restricts the explanation 'he repeats the thing, but it's just babble like a drunk man reciting Empedocles' to the particular premiss: or possibly to that and the conclusion. It is, surely, an explanation far better suited to enunciation of the universal premise, say: 'No one should commit adultery' or 'It is disgraceful to get very drunk', by the man who is about to do it. Aristotle explicitly wants to exempt the universal sort of knowledge from 'being dragged about like a slave'.

However, I suspect that he was also influenced by his own conception of practical reasoning. To set out the form of practical reasoning is to set out the form of deliberation. If it is all made explicit (as of course it hardly would be in real life, since one does not need to advert to the obvious) its formal character becomes quite clear. You have a set of premises starting with a universal one to the effect that a kind of thing A is, say, profitable for a kind of being B, and proceeding through intermediate premises like 'C's are A's' and 'a C can be obtained by a procedure D' and 'a procedure D can be carried out by doing E', together with another premiss to the effect that you are, or someone whose
152   profit is your concern is, a B; and if the action E is something that you can do,

then it is clear that the conclusion of this reasoning is for you to do E. But let us consider what this means. Does it mean that if you have embarked on the reasoning you *must* do E? Aristotle seems to have thought so. At least he thought you must do E unless something prevented you – the something might be the drive of 'desire', *epithumia, against* doing E. When making this point, he often gave examples of practical syllogisms in which there is a certain necessity about the conclusion – 'It is necessary to taste everything sweet, and this is sweet' (1147a29); 'Every man must walk, and I am a man'; 'Now no man must walk, and I am a man'. The last two examples come from the *Movement of Animals*, Chapter VII. The man does the thing in question (walks or halts) at once, if not prevented from walking in the one case, or forced to walk in the other. There are two features suggesting the necessity of the conclusion – the gerundive form, and the type of universality in the premiss.

> Every man has got to walk
> I am a man
> I have got to walk

is a formally valid deductive argument – I will call such an argument a proof-syllogism. I mean that is a proof of the conclusion, if only the premisses are true. Now Aristotle had special ideas about proof, so he would not have agreed to say what I have just said. 'Every man has got to walk' is not a changeless truth, so he would have said this is not apodeictic (see, e.g., 1140a33-5). Disregarding this let us merely note the formal validity of the reasoning as a deduction. Further, let us grant that if I agreed to the premises and therefore to the conclusion, and say 'I have got to walk', speaking quite seriously, it would be queer of me not to walk, if nothing prevented me.

Now let us look at another example:

> I need a covering,
> A cloak is a covering,
> I need a cloak;
> I must make what I need,
> I need a cloak,
> I must make a cloak.

The conclusion, that a cloak must be made, Aristotle says, *is* an action. So here is a 'choice'. But, he goes on, action has a starting-point – and so he sketches the reasoning with a view to execution of the 'choice': 'If there's to be a cloak, first such and such is needed, and if such and such, so and so', and this last the man does at once. Now it is hard to tell whether Aristotle reflected that 'I need a cloak' is not a formally valid deductive conclusion from 'I need a covering and a cloak is a covering'. The fact that it is not, is, I should contend, no criticism of the syllogism as a piece of practical reasoning. But it is possible that if he had been challenged about this, he would have said one could amend the syllogism by putting in that a cloak was the best covering or the easist to make or something of that sort (cf. *Nicomachean Ethics* 1112b16). For he is marked by an anxiety to make practical reasoning out to be as like as possible to speculative reasoning. 'They work just the same', he says in the

153

Movement of Animals, and seems to be referring to a necessitation of the conclusion. But you do not get this where various ways of obtaining the end are possible.

A further sign is that when he is looking at practical syllogism in this light – as necessarily yielding the conclusion – his examples of the first universal premisses always go 'It's needed', 'It's expedient', 'such and such a kind of being ought to do such and such a kind of thing'. He wants a 'must' in the conclusion in the verbalised form in which he gives it in the *Movement of Animals*, though each time he gives the conclusion he adds – 'and that's an action'. But when he is not talking about this automatic-machine aspect of the practical syllogism – which he is keen on because he thinks it helps to make it clear how the syllogism *kinei*, how it sets the human animal in motion – then we have such a universal premiss as 'Heavy waters are unwholesome'. Here the *De Anima* formulation (of a doctrine also expressed in the *Nicomachean Ethics* at 1140b16, though not so clearly) that the starting-point of the whole business is what you want (the *orekton*) can come into play. And we may remark that there are two possible conclusions of the reasoning about heavy waters, according as you want to be healthy or not. That, of course, sounds absurd; but let the universal be 'Strong alkalis are deadly poison', and it is easy to spell out the practical reasoning of the suicide. Aristotle recognises this two-way possibility at *Metaphysics* IX, 1046b5-7.

154   It looks as if, in his enthusiasm for making practical reasoning like theoretical and explaining its power to set one in motion (aided, no doubt, by his own picture of proof and by the Platonic conception of sin as error, which he did not entirely shake off), Aristotle did not notice some significant features of his discovery; the fact that though it is perfectly correct to call practical reasoning 'reasoning', and though some practical syllogisms are also (in my sense) proof-syllogisms, i.e. are entailments, in general practical syllogisms have a different form from proof-syllogisms.

Consider:

Owning a Launderette would make me wealthy.
There is scope for opening a Launderette on such-and-such premises

and so on down to where I might get going. This is practical reasoning, and given all the premisses it is a formal matter what the conclusion is, in the form 'so I'll ...' Whether, if it is I who have put out the syllogism, I *draw* the conclusion, depends on whether I actively want to be wealthy and am working out this one of the many possibilities with a view to action – I might be doing it idly, or as an academic example. If by a practical syllogism you mean – as Aristotle did (*De Anima* 433a15) – one that terminates in action, and the purpose of which is to act, then this won't be practical; but if you mean a *type* of reasoning – i.e. reasoning reaching from a general sort of objective to something one can choose to do here and now – then it will be practical. St. Thomas would call it 'theoretical *de practicis*' (*Summa Theologica* I, 14, art. 16c). In general, people would not trouble to work such things out except with a view to action.

We have seen two strands in Aristotle's thought. First there is the explanation of how the human being is set in motion by thought, and second there is the idea of the thing wanted as the starting-point for such thought. For the first he seems to have wanted, not only a necessity in the connexions which is not always present in practical reasonings, but also a compulsiveness about the universal premiss, a 'must' about it: that is, it seems he wanted a universal premiss acceptance of which implies intellectual acknowledgment of it as the guide to action. The need for necessity in the connexions can fairly be discounted. Then we can happily combine the two strands by postulating at the back of all these premisses a first premiss to the effect that only such- **155** and-such is doing well, is happiness or blessedness, 'the good for man'. Aristotle's grand universal premiss is that blessedness is activity in accordance with virtue, especially intellectual virtue. The argument for this as the true premiss is the *Nicomachean Ethics* itself. If the truth of this premiss is acknowledged, then it is itself acknowledged as the ultimate guide to action. For blessedness, or doing well, it is the end that anyone must have so far as he has a rational end, that is to say so far as he has 'will', i.e. the kind of wanting that belongs in the rational part, at all (cf. *De Anima* 432b5-7.)

Here we touch on the difference between Aristotle and Hume. Hume's doctrine that reason is inert, that for considerations to lead to any action a sentiment, a passion, is required may be compared to Aristotle's 'It is not reason as such that sets in motion; but reason which is with a view to something and is practical' (1139a36). Aristotle's 'will' will then be a 'calm passion' in Hume's terminology. But they disagree about the applicability of the descriptions 'in accordance with reason' and 'not in accordance with reason' to actions and wants.

I suggest that the idea of rational wanting should be explained in terms of what is wanted being wanted *qua* conducive to or part of 'doing well', or blessedness. If one admits that what one wants is no good, but still one wants it, it is, in Aristotle's conception, merely the object of a passion; when the thing that one so wants is a pleasure, though it is no good (like smoking in some people's view) then one is being led simply by 'desire', *epithumia*. For though what constitutes blessedness is necessarily utterly pleasant, it is not something one wants because it is a pleasure even though it should be no good; on the contrary, it is the object of will as the best possible thing for a human being, being the activity of his rational part and the activity that is an end, not a means.

For as seeing can be seen to be what the eye is for, so understanding – the enjoyment of the truth – can be seen to be what the mind is for. But here we must note a certain split in Aristotle's thought. For the highest blessedness he thought of as something divine, which we should grasp at to the poor extent that we can – taking the side of and imitating the immortal. He coins a word for what we should do, namely 'to immortalise' (*athanatizein* 1177b33), sounding like an echo of 'to Medise' which means to be on the side of and **156** imitate the Persian. But he acknowledges that in the ordinary course of life for most people 'doing well' amounts to something more mundane: a successful and honourable conduct of life, the heart of which is, if one judges rightly, action in accordance with *moral* virtue.

Apart from being ruled by passion (this is what I want, even if it is no good), 'doing well' is what anyone wants in some obscure and indeterminate way. One could call it that part of blessedness for which one's own action is essential. Aristotle's unrealistic conception of the clear-cutness of people's ends seems on investigation not to be so bad as it looked. For the many objectives that are no good are allowed for in his thought. The assumption of clear-cutness is the assumption that people generally know what they count as 'doing well' – i.e. that they definitely so count being rich or being famous or the life of knowledge.

My eventual goal has been to expound the concept of 'practical truth' and the discussion of *Nicomachean Ethics* Book VI, Chapter II on 'choice'. I will start from 1139a21. 'What affirmation and negation are in judgment, pursuit and avoidance are in desire.' That is, one can say 'yes' or 'no' both to a statement and to a proposal. Suppose, then, that the statement should say that doing such and such is 'doing well'. There is the 'yes' in judgment and the 'yes' in the will, meaning that one wants to do that sort of thing. For to characterise it as 'doing well' is *eo ipso* to propose it as an object of 'will' – to put it up as a candidate for 'will', *boulêsis*.

'So,' Aristotle goes on, 'since moral virtue is a disposition of one's choice, while choice is deliberated wanting, these things show that the judgment must be true and the wanting right, if the choice is to be sound, and the one must say and the other pursue the same thing.' We may remark that the one must say and the other pursue the same thing if there is to be any 'choice' at all, sound or unsound. So far we have only mentioned the judgment on what *eupraxia*, doing well, is. A false judgment on this necessarily means that if there is a 'choice' at all the wanting in it is wrong. To make this clear, imagine a worldling's idea of doing well. If the worldly man has any wants that are right, they don't occur in his 'choices'. Any 'choice' that he makes, since in 'choice' the wanting goes after what the judgment declares to be doing well, must involve wrong wanting.

157   Can the judgment be false at a lower level than one's idea of doing well, without the wanting being wrong if they are in accord? Suppose the man has judged truly, as Aristotle would say and as I want to say, that to act justly is necessary for doing well, but falsely that justice would be done by dividing all the goods available in the country into equal shares according to the number of the population and assigning each share to one person by picking name and number of share out of a hat; or that it is justice for a poor man to be punished for assaulting a rich one, but not vice versa. I am not speaking of particular procedures, but of judgments about what *sort* of procedures are just.

It appears to me that only when we get to questions where it is difficult to know the truth, or questions as to facts which the agent can't be expected to have found out, is there any chance for the wanting of what is judged a means to doing well to be right when the judgment itself is wrong. This then will be why Aristotle said in Book III (1110b31) that ignorance in choice is the cause not of involuntariness but of scoundrelism. He himself laid down the rule about difficulty at 1113b33-1114a2.

We now approach the great question: what does Aristotle mean by 'practical truth'? He calls it the good working, or the work, of practical judgment; and practical judgment is judgment of the kind described, terminating in action. It is practical truth when the judgments involved in the formation of the 'choice' leading to the action are all true; but the practical truth is not the truth of those *judgments*. For it is clearly that 'truth in agreement with right desire (*orexei*)' (1139a30), which is spoken of as the good working, or the work, of practical intelligence. That is brought about – i.e. made true – by action (since the description of what he does is made true by his doing it), provided that a man forms and executes a good 'choice'. The man who forms and executes an evil 'choice' will also make true *some* description of what he does. He will secure, say, if he is competent, that such-and-such a man has his eyes put out or his hands cut off, that being his judgment of what it is just to do. But his description 'justice performed' of what he has done will be a lie. He, then, will have produced practical falsehood.

'Since everything that is done about them is false, how should these be gods?' – The notion of *truth or falsehood in action* would quite generally be countered by the objection that 'true' and 'false' are senseless predicates as applied to what is done. If I am right there is philosophy to the contrary in Aristotle. And if, as I should maintain, the idea of the *description under which* what is done is done is integral to the notion of action, then these predicates apply to actions strictly and properly, and not merely by an extension and in a way that ought to be explained away.

7

D.J. Allan

Aristotle's Account of the Origin of Moral Principles

120   A few words must be said in defence of the title chosen for this essay, and in explanation of its scope. It is true, in the first place, that Aristotle does not assume a plurality of independent moral principles, but only a supreme end or good, and a number of rules which can be said either to express the nature of this end, or to provide or suggest the means of its realisation. I have spoken of moral *principles* partly because we ought not to exaggerate the importance, for Aristotle, of the means – end distinction, and partly because it is in these terms that the equivalent problem presents itself to the modern mind.

    Secondly, in one sense the question how we obtain our knowledge of such principles is easy. As far as their genesis in the individual mind is concerned, Aristotle undoubtedly traces it to induction and teaching, accompanied by a training of the emotions. He gives admirable advice to the politician or parent who wishes to achieve this result. But this answer is not very informative, and can only lead on to the question, whence does the teacher who directs the process of induction derive his own knowledge of the principles? how, when they have been acquired, does Aristotle suppose that we can assure ourselves of their authority and validity? and, in particular, what, in his system, is the part played respectively by *reason* and *desire* in the formulation of the end or good for man? Needless to say, it is with the question understood in this sense that the present essay is concerned. It may be observed here that knowledge of the way in which an individual has acquired his knowledge of the principles, or even of the way in which this knowledge is normally acquired, will not by itself furnish an answer to the question in *this* sense.

    In order to attend satisfactorily to this problem, I must exclude from the discussion two closely related topics, both of which are of interest to the student of the *Ethics*: (1) Aristotle's original and illuminating account of the way in which such principles, once acquired, are brought to bear upon a particular case. I cannot here offer a full account of the psychology of action as conceived by him. (2) I must also leave aside the question, in what manner and to what extent the practical life and the moral virtues are in Aristotle's system subordinated to the life of contemplation.

    At a time when there is great interest in theories according to which
121 moral judgments do not so much describe actions as express or evince an attitude towards them, it is well worth while to consider Aristotle's pronouncements upon the questions I have mentioned; not, I must add, because he himself held a theory of that subjectivist type, but because he seems to have grasped the problem more fully than any thinker before the

eighteenth century or perhaps down to the present day. I shall not pretend that a constructive answer to the problem posed by contemporary thinkers can be derived from him; but his reserve and caution are always significant, and, in a case like this, are a better proof of his acuteness than a glib answer would have been; and I wish to show that, contrary to what some scholars have maintained, a consistent doctrine is presented in the *Ethics*, and amplified in the psychological treatises.

Among the nineteenth-century Aristotelian scholars, there were some who held that it is the function of practical reason to ascertain, formulate and posit the end or good for man, in addition to discovering the means by deliberation, in the manner outlined in Book III, Ch. 3 of the Nicomachean version. The intuitive judgment of the proposed action, upon which Aristotle lays so much stress, was also naturally ascribed to practical reason, but it was maintained that this was not meant to be its only function.

But Julius Walter of Jena, in a work exclusively devoted to this problem [139], launched an attack on the above view as expounded by Teichmüller, Trendelenburg and Zeller in the first two editions of his history. Walter asserted that *EN* VI, 1143b1-5 should not be taken to mean that there is a practical reason which intuitively grasps the true end of human action, in the same way as theoretical reason perceives the ultimate first principles of the sciences. So far, he was probably on firm ground. But he further denied that *phronêsis* has anything to do with the apprehension of the end, pointing to those passages in which Aristotle says that moral virtue makes the aim right, whereas the means are found by *phronêsis*. He maintained that, according to the true account of Aristotle's doctrine, the first principle or end of conduct is determined by moral virtue, which is a habitual state of the *appetitive* faculty (*orexis*). Practical reason and *phronêsis* are *deliberative*, and all deliberation is a discovery of means to an end already established.

Since in his treatises Aristotle himself evidently does discuss and define the end, and refute false views of its nature, Walter was induced also to deny that Aristotle's own discussions of ethics and politics were regarded by him as exhibitions of practical reason; and to claim that the division of philosophy itself into a theoretical and a practical branch was due to the later Peripatetics, and is untrue to the spirit of the founder's doctrine. This facet of Walter's thesis does not concern us here. **122**

In reply to Walter's criticism, Teichmüller wrote a defence of his original position; but Walter seems to have carried many scholars with him, including Zeller, who in the third edition of his history, and in his *Grundriß*, modified his exposition and acknowledged that he had been mistaken. In the English translation made from this edition, vol. 2, pp. 182-3, the passage runs:

The ultimate aims of action are determined, according to Aristotle, not by deliberation but by the character of the will; or, as he would explain it, while all aim at happiness, it depends upon the moral character of each individual wherein he seeks it. Practical deliberation is the only sphere of the exercise of insight [German *Einsicht = phronêsis*], and since this has to do not with universal propositions, but with their application to given cases, knowledge of the particular is more indispensable to it than knowledge of the universal. It is this application to particular aims and to particular given cases that distinguishes insight both from science and from theoretic reason.

Zeller's change of view is important because he, in turn, deeply influenced the exposition of the *Ethics* in other countries; for example, by Burnet in his commentary published in 1900 [38]. Thus, in consequence of Zeller's submission to Walter, a false doctrine has, since the beginning of this century, to a great extent invaded the Oxford schools, and Aristotle, whose ethic is really of a rationalist type, is brought into connexion with Hume, and with the modern subjectivists and 'emotivists'.

The situation was changed once more by the appearance in 1903 of a work on *Die Zurechnungslehre des Aristoteles*, by Richard Loening, a professor of jurisprudence at Jena. The author showed that the problem itself had been inadequately and falsely formulated by his predecessors; that it was beyond dispute Aristotle's doctrine that practical reason leads the way, in the sense that it provides the first apprehension of the end or good, though it is desire (and moral virtue, which is the formed habit of right desire), which actually *posits* the end, and converts the judgment of practical reason into a command; that the same account of the collaboration of practical reason and desire is given in the psychological writings of Aristotle; and that apparent exceptions to it in the *Ethics* can be explained away. Loening therefore reproached Zeller for his surrender to the arguments of Walter, but he found fault to an almost equal extent with the manner in which Trendelenburg and others had stated the thesis that reason formulates the end.

123 Loening also gave a clear-headed and interesting account of Aristotle's views on freedom and responsibility, that being the main theme of his work.

Of the influence of Loening, in general, I am unable to speak; his work is seldom cited, yet his exposition appears to me to be correct in every essential point; and my principal purpose here is to repeat and reinforce his arguments. The question whether practical reason does or does not determine (*bestimmen*) the end, has been, he says, a source of confusion. One must distinguish two acts, bringing into play different psychological faculties, the positing or determining of the end, and the knowledge what the end is, and in virtue of what qualities it is the end. The latter is a *judgment* of value, an act of thinking, and must belong to practical reason. On the other hand, the promotion of the thing thus judged desirable into an actual object of desire or pursuit – this is in no way different from the desire or pursuit itself, and is something which *must* proceed from the appetitive faculty (*orexis*). It is not by their object, but by the performance of different functions in regard to the same object, that practical reason and *orexis* differ.

This is a cardinal point, and perhaps the reason why I have, in the title, spoken vaguely of 'the origin of moral principles', is now apparent, but I should prefer to avoid altogether the word 'determine', firstly, because it is ambiguous and is not used only in the way which Leoning indicates; and secondly because the Greek equivalent is not, *in this context*, used by Aristotle. The first and proper sense of the word 'determine' is, to give fixity to a variable quantity by reference to a standard (*terminus, horos*). Thus, it might be said that the Minister of Food determines the price of bacon, assuming that his decision is not a matter of caprice. But the word is also constantly used by scientists and others when nothing more is involved than the accurate measurement of something which is *not* variable; for instance 'to determine the distance of the earth from the sun'. In asking whether it is practical reason or virtue which, for Aristotle, *determines* the end, commentators have been at cross-purposes with one another, and have been perplexed by what they find in the text, because they have not agreed what kind of act it is that is described by the word '*determine*'. It should be noticed that Aristotle himself used the word only in the former, the stronger sense, and thus speaks in II 6-7 and VI 1 of the determination of the mean, which is variable, by the wise man, with reference to the good. But you will not find in the Ethics such an expression as *horizesthai ton skopon* or *to agathon* or ('determine the end' or 'the good').

With this obscurity cleared away, we can briefly state the position maintained in *De Anima* III 7 and in the sixth and seventh books of the Ethics. Practical reason 'differs from theoretical reason by its end'; i.e. its aim is *action*, not knowledge of the truth. But, 'practical' though it may be, it cannot achieve this aim by itself alone. The order of events is somewhat as follows. From practical reason we derive the conception of something as good (*phainomenon agathon*). Until such a conception is present, desire will have no object. On the other hand, it is desire which, by its propulsive force, converts judgment into wish (*boulêsis*) and the knowledge of the good into the actual pursuit of an end or aim (*telos, skopos*). One might say, in parody of Kant, that reason without desire is powerless, while desire without reason is blind. Reason, then, can issue a *command* to the appetitive faculty; the words *epitattei* and *keleuei* are repeatedly used in this connexion. If this command is obeyed (but, of course, there may be contrary forces at work), an actual desire for the good will ensue, and an end will have been established.

Even now, though the motive for action is present, we may not immediately proceed to act; for the good propounded may be (a) distant, or (b) general. Thus there is fresh work for practical reason to perform. In the former case, we have first to calculate the means which will, in due course, achieve the end. In the latter, we have to subsume the particular case under a general rule. Both these processes are analysed by Aristotle, in a masterly fashion, in different parts of his work, the former in the third book of the Ethics, the latter in Books VI and VII and in his psychological writings. Either process must terminate in the perception that a particular action, which is either a means to the good or an exemplification of it, can be done *now*. Then, at last, desire, again assuming that no contrary forces are at work, will prompt us to the action. As is well known, Aristotle appropriates the name *prohairesis* to such desire, but tends also to use this word in a broader sense.

A few comments on this doctrine may now be offered. Although Aristotle certainly thinks, and says, that the judgment of the good emanates from practical reason, he does not enter into the question *how* it is formed, or show what weight is to be assigned to philosophical views on the one hand, and uninstructed opinion on the other. Perhaps he thought that his own mode of argument in the *Ethics* made the procedure sufficiently clear. Secondly, since he definitely makes the judgment of the good *precede* desire,

124

it can hardly have been his view that reason merely lights up the scene in order to reveal an end which has already been effectively, though blindly and instinctively, chosen be desire. Thirdly, his remark that 'thought itself moves nothing', *Ethics* VI 2, is sometimes misquoted, and used in a way which would 125 not have met with his approval. The sentence does not continue 'but it is desire which moves'; had it done so, Aristotle would here have been false to his whole psychological doctrine. The next words are, 'but *practical* thinking can do do'; and this makes it clear that by 'thought itself' he means scientific or contemplative thought.

What is it, then, which has led some scholars to suppose that for Aristotle it is the moral character which 'determines' the end, in the sense of providing not only the impulse towards the good, but a judgment of its nature, towards which reason can make no contribution? The fact is that he makes some statements which, to a superficial view, imply that practical reason – or what comes to the same thing, *phronêsis* – deliberates about means *and does nothing more.*

That practical reason formulates the good is the doctrine of the *De Anima*, and appears beyond doubt from the following passages of the *Ethics:*

VI, 1139a21. Pursuit and avoidance are, to desire, what assertion and denial are to thinking. Hence, since we regard moral virtue as a settled disposition of choice, and define choice as deliberative desire, it follows that choice can only be good where there is both true reasoning and right desire; and that the object which reason asserts and desire pursues must be the same. This, then, is practical thinking and practical truth.

VI, 1142b31. If excellence in deliberation (*euboulia*) is one of the traits of men of practical wisdom, we may regard this excellence as correct perception of that which conduces to the end, whereof practical wisdom is a true judgment. [Walter and Burnet have here proposed to regard *to sumpheron*, not *to telos*, as the antecedent of *hou*, because they mistakenly suppose that the statement is inconsistent with the normal doctrine of Aristotle.]

VII, 1152b1. The consideration of pleasure and pain belongs to the political philosopher. For he is the architect of the end, with reference to which we call this or that thing, without qualification, good or evil.

On the same side, it may be urged that if practical wisdom does not furnish or help to furnish its own conception of the good, but merely chooses means, it would no longer correspond to the practical arts with which Aristotle obviously intends to compare it. For the medical man does start from his own notion of the general nature of health, etc.

Now in Books VI and VII, which should be read as a continuous passage, Aristotle maintains that moral virtue, and particularly *sôphrosunê*, which is most concerned with pleasure and pain, is a necessary *condition* of true judgment about the good. Not only is *sôphrosunê* necessary if a man is always to be guided by his knowledge, but in its absence a man drifts into a state in 126 which no general principle at all is recognised. *Phronêsis* and moral virtue are mutually necessary; neither can be fully developed in the absence of the other. This is the answer to the question 'Of what use is *phronêsis*? Why is it not enough if a few selected persons acquire it?'

It is therefore possible, and sometimes convenient, to speak of *sôphrosunê* as preserving a true opinion about the good, without suggesting for a moment that virtue can, from its own resources, provide a conception of the good. (How could it do so, since (a) it is not an intellectual state, but a disposition towards pleasure and pain, and (b) it is by definition a 'right rule' imposed upon the passions, and can have no content prior to the ascertainment, by *phronêsis*, of this rule?)

It is in this sense that the following passages should be read:

> VI, 1140b11. Hence also is derived the name *sôphrosunê*, which we apply to the virtue which preserves *phronêsis*; for it is a judgment of the aforesaid kind which it preserves. For not all opinions are liable to be corrupted or distorted by pleasure and pain, e.g. whether the angles of a triangle are, or are not, equal to two right angles, but only judgments concerned with action. The principles of action are the *ends* for which actions are done. But a person corrupted through pleasure and pain simply does not recognise any principle, or think that there is an end which should govern all his choice and action.
>
> VII, 1151a15. Virtue and vice preserve and corrupt the principle, and in actions the end is the principle, occupying a place like that of the hypotheses in mathematical proof. Neither in that case nor in this is reasoning able to teach the first principles, but virtue, either a natural gift [in the former case] or habitual [in the latter] having for its effect a true opinion about the principle. (Compare *EE* 1227b12ff.)

In Book VI, however, we do find a passage which at first seems to confirm Walter's exposition:

> VI, 1144a6. [The question has been raised why the average man needs *phronêsis*.] Moreover, the function of man is jointly achieved by *phronêsis* and moral virtue; for virtue makes the aim right, while *phronêsis* ensures the correct means . . .
>
> [a23] There is a faculty which men term cleverness, and this shows itself in ability to perform the acts which lead to a proposed end, and so achieve the end. If the aim is honourable, this is worthy of praise, if disgraceful, it is villainy. This is why cleverness is ascribed both to wise men and to villains. [Read *kai tous panourgous*]. Now *phronêsis* is not this faculty, but presupposes its existence . . . Syllogisms of action start from a judgment of the form 'since such is the end and the highest good'. Its nature need not here be specified. This premiss does not appear at all except to the man of good character, for vice warps the judgment, and causes us to be deluded about the principles of action. From this it plainly follows that it is impossible to have practical wisdom without being a good man.

127

Even in this place it is not said that moral virtue, unassisted by wisdom, furnishes a *judgment* about the good; but only that virtue 'makes the aim *right*'. 'Right' here is synonymous with 'sound' or 'upright', and does not connote reflection. There is no formal contradiction between these words and the statement, already cited, according to which we owe to *phronêsis* the *hupolêpsis* of the end. It is not even necessary to say, with Joachim, that the statement represents a lapse from the truer view of the function of thought in conduct which Aristotle has elsewhere expressed. And in proving to a hypothetical objector that *phronêsis* is not a luxury, he is surely entitled to point to a task, viz. the choice of means, which *must* be performed by *phronêsis*, without intending to imply that it is not competent to do any other work. Suppose I make the statement that 'the nurse prepares the instruments and the surgeon operates', or 'the driver drives the bus, and the conductor issues the tickets'. If it should subsequently appear that the surgeon *also* tells the nurse which instruments to prepare, and that it is the business of the ticket-collector to inform the driver of the destination of the bus, you might feel that you had been given a wrong impression, but would have no right to say that you had been *deceived*, unless I had plainly implied that I was offering an *exhaustive* account of their work. And, to quote Joachim again, Aristotle does not really think that in the good life end and means fall apart in this mechanical fashion.

Practical reason, then, is for Aristotle not a reasoning process which precedes action, but rather thought expressed in action and controlling it. F.H. Bradley wrote in 1884 that practical reason 'has been placed on the shelf of interesting illusions' (*Collected Essays*, vol. I, p. 142). Has not the time come to take it down again? Finally, although I have emphasised the rationalist and objectivist strain in Aristotle's thought, I do not think he would be entirely out of sympathy with those recent writers who hold moral judgments to be expressive of an emotion or attitude; he might think their views interesting. Incredible as it may seem, there is much also in his discussion which might be interesting and even instructive to them.

8

Richard Robinson

Aristotle on Akrasia

Aristotle asks himself in Book VII of his *Nicomachean Ethics* how a man can do what he knows to be wrong. Doing what one knows to be wrong is what he calls *akrasia*. On the one hand, it seems evident that *akrasia* occurs from time to time. On the other hand, Socrates declared that knowledge ought to rule in the soul and not be dragged about like a slave. He concluded from this authority of knowledge that in reality *akrasia* never occurs. Whenever we seem to see a man doing what he knows to be wrong, the truth is that the man does not know that his act is wrong; he is in error about the right and the wrong. This constitutes a difficulty or *aporia*. The common-sense view that we sometimes do what we know to be wrong appears to contradict the Socratic view, itself also very convincing, that knowledge is commanding.

How does Aristotle resolve this problem? Evidently he did not write nearly a whole book on *akrasia* in order to deny that it ever occurs. On the contrary, he always retained the common view that we sometimes do what we know to be wrong. This is probably what he is saying, though not without a certain ambiguity, in the passage where he first introduces the Socratic thesis, when he writes (1145b28) that this doctrine obviously goes against appearances and that the acratic clearly does not think so until he is in the passion – meaning, I suppose, that the acratic does not think that his act is permissible until he is in the passion.

But what is the meaning of the mysterious words that come between the two phrases which I have just translated: 'it being necessary to ask about the passion, if it comes about from ignorance, what sort of ignorance is involved'? Are they to be interpreted by reference to the Socratic thesis or by reference to the explanation of *akrasia* which Aristotle is going to develop in what follows? If we refer them to the Socratic thesis, we suppose that Aristotle is meaning to say to Socrates: 'Since you hold that what we call *akrasia* is really ignorance, you ought to have told us what kind of ignorance we have here.' If we refer them to the view which Aristotle is about to set out we suppose that Aristotle is here saying, though so succinctly as to be almost incomprehensible, that he is going to satisfy Socrates by saying that there is a certain ignorance in *akrasia*, but at the same time he is going to distinguish the nature of this ignorance so as to preserve the doctrine that the acratic knows that his act is wrong.

Aristotle rejects as unacceptable that solution of the difficulty which consists in saying that the acratic does not *know* that his act is wrong but only *believes* that it is (1145b31ff.). Aristotle takes this to mean that belief involves a less strong and sure conviction than does knowledge and that it is the weakness of the acratic's conviction which makes it possible for him to

disobey it. Aristotle rejects this solution on the ground that the man whose
conviction is weak is pardoned, whereas the acratic is blameworthy. He
seems to think that this solution amounts to another way of denying that
akrasia in the proper sense can occur.

In Chapter 3, Aristotle returns to this supposed solution and rejects it
again, but now for a different reason. He now declares (1146b24ff.) that the
distinction between knowledge and belief does not necessarily involve any
difference of certainty or conviction. Some who only believe are as certain as
some others who know. With the humour that occasionally lightens the
141   sombre theme of this book, Aristotle instances Heraclitus as a man who was
perfectly certain although he did not know.

These two ways of rejecting the solution are consistent with each other.
One of them attacks the premiss. The other attacks the inference, implying
that it is an *ignoratio elenchi.*

Finally Aristotle gives us the four solutions which he considers correct.
The first depends on distinguishing the time when we possess a certain
piece of knowledge but are not using it from the time when we both possess
and are using it. The latter is also called *theôrounta*, contemplating. Aristotle
gives no example of what he has in mind; but no doubt he would have
accepted the following. As I begin this sentence, you possess but are not
using the knowledge that Greece is an arid land; as I end it, you are using it
as well as possessing it, because I have recalled it to your minds. This is part
of his great doctrine of potentiality and act, although he uses the word
energei only twice in this chapter. To say that a man knows something is not
to say that he is always thinking of it, nor that he is thinking of it now.
Aristotle appears to mean that the acratic knows that his act is wrong in
that he *possesses* this knowledge, but he can do the act because he is not at
the time *using* this knowledge, not contemplating it. I hold that Aristotle
accepts this solution and believes it to contain virtually everything necessary
for the explanation of *akrasia*, since it shows how the acratic both knows and
does not know that his act is wrong. He knows it, in that it is part of his
permanent and general intellectual equipment. He does not know it, in that
he does not use or contemplate it at the moment when he needs to do so, the
moment of his acratic act. However, Aristotle adds three more solutions.

The second of these four solutions consists in introducing his doctrine of
the practical syllogism. According to Aristotle the motion of the human
animal is sometimes governed by a syllogism. When such a motion
constitutes a *praxis*, that is an action in the proper sense, it is perhaps always
142   governed by a syllogism. Aristotle is never very precise in explaining this
syllogism. For example, its conclusion sometimes seems to be an action, but
at other times a statement. It is certain enough, however, that the premiss
has two parts, one of which is *katholou* or universal and the other *kath'
hekaston* or particular. The universal premiss gives us a practical principle,
such as 'Every sweet thing should be tasted'. It is expressed sometimes by
means of the verb *dei* or the verbal adjective in -*teon*, but sometimes also by a
simple descriptive phrase such as 'Dry things are good for every man', or
even 'Everything sweet is pleasant'.

Aristotle's second solution consists in pointing out that it is possible for
an agent, while *possessing* both premisses, to *use* only the universal premiss.
Such an agent may do an act forbidden by the syllogism. Yet he possesses

the forbidding principle, and therefore it is correct to say that he knows that the act is wrong.

Aristotle adds that one can distinguish even more finely. Since the universal premiss will often contain two terms, such as, for example, 'man' and 'dry' in the premiss that 'Dry things are good for every man', it will need as it were two particular premisses to particularise each of these universal terms. Hence it can happen that an agent particularises one of these terms but not the other. This agent will use both the universal premiss and a part of the particular premiss, and still not do the act which the syllogism prescribes.

We see that the second solution as well as the first consists in showing that the acratic both knows and does not know that his act is wrong. He knows it in that he possesses the principle in virtue of which his act is wrong. He does not know it in that he does not use this principle, or he does use it but he does not use the particular premiss that would put the principle into action, or he even uses part of the particular premiss but not the whole of it.

Let us pass to the third solution. It is again a distinction, a subdivision. **143** Aristotle now subdivides his 'possessing but not using'. A sleeping man and a waking man may both possess the practical principle. But, says Aristotle, the sleeping man possesses it 'in a manner other than those just mentioned' (1147a10); he 'both possesses and does not possess it in a way'. Aristotle adds that such is the condition not merely of the sleeping but also of the mad and the drunk and the acratic. He assimilates *akrasia* to medical cases. (His ethics has a tendency to turn into medicine.) The acratic can even utter the words which express the knowledge and yet not be using it. For a moment Aristotle almost seems to want to say that during his act the acratic simply does not know; for he uses the expression *isasi d' oupô* ('they do not yet know'). At any rate, this third solution amounts to saying that during his act the acratic possesses the knowledge that it is wrong only in a most attenuated way.

Thus we find Aristotle tending for the third time to deny that the acratic fully knows the nature of his act while he is committing it. He seems to tend to believe with Socrates that knowledge cannot be outraged, and that it can be disobeyed only when it is not fully present. If we think, as some interpreters do, that in the end Aristotle is going to present *akrasia* as involving throughout perfect knowledge that the act is wrong, then this third solution at any rate is absolutely absurd and irrelevant. There remains, however, the following substantial difference between Socrates and Aristotle, that Socrates, as far as we know, never entertained the idea that the acratic's state of knowledge might change importantly during the course of the transaction, in that he knew the nature of his act perfectly both before and after but not during the commission of it.

Let us turn to the fourth and last solution. Here is no further distinction of senses of the word 'know'. Aristotle begins by expanding somewhat the nature of the practical syllogism. He brings out now the aspect of necessity in this syllogism. Once the premisses have become one, he says, it is necessary, *anankê*, to act, to realise the conclusion at once. What a **144** paradoxical thesis! And what a very Socratic thesis! I think it the most Socratic sentence in this fundamentally Socratic chapter. Even if we add, as Aristotle does not, that the agent knows the two premisses and is thoroughly convinced of them, the sentence remains extraordinary. In proceeding to illustrate it he greatly weakens it, for he says now that the act is necessary 'if one has the ability and is not prevented'ʻ(1147a30); but it remains pretty Socratic and pretty extreme.

What was his purpose in introducing it? Surely not in order to go on to say that one can do an act while possessing and fully using a syllogism that forbids that act. It is now very improbable that the fourth solution is finally going to reject the Socratic doctrine. I believe on the contrary that he introduces this practical necessity in order to prove that the acratic must do the wrong act because of a syllogism which imposes this wrong act upon him. For he speaks now of the complicated case where four things are present at once in the soul. (1) First, there is in the soul a universal premiss which forbids the man to 'taste', where to 'taste' is probably to commit the acratic act, while the phrase, 'there is in the soul', *enêi* (1147a32), probably means that he possesses this premiss but is not using it. (2) Second, there is also in the soul another universal premiss to the effect that everything sweet is pleàsant; and this premiss is actual, *energei*. (3) Third, there is also the particular premiss that this thing is sweet, a premiss which can set the second universal premiss into action. (4) Fourth, there happens to be a desire, *epithumia*, in the soul.

What according to Aristotle is the result of this combination of four things in the soul? He seems to indicate three consequences. First, the first universal premiss orders the man to shun this thing; second, desire carries him away; and, third, it thus results that the acratic act accords in a way with a *logos* and an opinion being opposed to the correct *logos* only accidentally, and not in itself.

145   This short and vague account makes us ask the following questions. What exactly does the first universal premiss say (for Aristotle does not tell us)? What is the particular premiss belonging to this first universal premiss (for he does not say that either)? And is the first and right syllogism completely actual in the soul of the acratic at the time of his act, or is it not?

I answer as follows. In the other three solutions, and also in the early sentences of this fourth solution, it seemed clear enough that Aristotle was thinking that at the time of his act the acratic is not using in complete actuality every part of the right syllogism. I will suppose, therefore, that here too he thinks that the acratic is not using every part of the right syllogism, provided that the text allows me to do so. Does the text allow me? I see only one phrase that has any appearance of forbidding it, namely the phrase *hê men oun legei pheugein touto*, 'the [first universal premiss] tells [him] to shun this' (1147a34). But it is not necessary to hold that by these words Aristotle intends to tell us that he is now supposing the right syllogism to be completely actual. The word *legei* is vague enough to mean no more than that the right universal premiss *tends* to forbid the act, and *would* forbid it if joined to its own particular premiss in actuality.

It follows from this interpretation that the particular premiss belonging to the right universal premiss is not the same as the one belonging to the wrong universal premiss. For the latter particular premiss is actual in the acratic's soul. Hence, if the two particular premisses were the same, the right syllogism would be actual in his soul, which on this interpretation it is not.

The particular premiss of the right syllogism is not the same as the particular premiss of the wrong syllogism. What then, is the particular premiss of the right syllogism? We cannot tell. We can only conjecture. Similarly, therefore, we can only conjecture what is the universal premiss of the right syllogism, which also Aristotle does not tell us.

The fourth solution continues with a remark about animals, and why **146** they cannot be acratic (1147b4). I confess that I do not see the relevance of this. Possibly there is something hidden in this sentence which would disprove my interpretation if it were revealed.

However that may be, my interpretation is strongly supported by the next phrase, 'how the ignorance is dissipated and the acratic resumes his knowledge' (1147b6). For this phrase undoubtedly implies that some kind of ignorance exists during the acratic act; and one can hardly suppose that it refers merely to the first three solutions. It must imply that this ignorance also occurs in the circumstances supposed in the solution which stands nearest to it in the text, and that is the fourth solution.

The next sentence begins with the words 'Since the last premiss' (1147b9). It seems a little odd to talk of a last premiss when there are only two. Perhaps Aristotle is thinking of a sorites or chain of syllogisms, such as could easily be constructed out of examples which he gave earlier (1147a6-7). In such a chain there would be more than two premisses altogether. In any case this 'last' premiss would be a particular premiss; and Aristotle now tells us that the acratic while 'in the passion' either does not have this premiss or has it only as the drunk has the verses of Empedocles. This is another affirmation of the Socratic thesis that some kind of ignorance occurs during the acratic act; but it is not a strong piece of evidence for the interpretation of the fourth solution, because now, by mentioning the drunken man reciting Empedocles, Aristotle refers us back to the third solution; and he could have forgotten by now the intervening fourth solution.

Aristotle does not say explicitly what the man will do if he has both syllogisms completely actual in his mind, nor whether such a state of mind is possible.

Before beginning his discussion of *akrasia*, Aristotle had made some remarks on the character that the discussion ought to have (1145b2-7). **147** These five lines are neither the only nor the longest passage in the *Nicomachean Ethics* where Aristotle teaches us what sorts of study ethics and politics are or ought to be. But they illuminate best the method that he tried to follow and the result that he wished to attain. He wishes to establish, if possible, all received opinions, *endoxa*. If that is not possible, he wishes to establish as many as he can of the more important received opinions. He limits himself to the removal of difficulties, and leaves standing every opinion that he is not compelled to reject. He will accomplish this design in three stages. First, he will list the opinions. That is to 'posit the appearances' (1145b3); and he performs it in the last part of the first chapter of Book VII. Secondly he will raise the difficulties, *tas aporias*. He does that in the second chapter. Finally, he will resolve these difficulties, if possible without rejecting any received opinion; in any case he will reject as few of these opinions as he can. He does this in Chapters 3 to 10, which constitute the whole of the rest of his discussion of *akrasia*, and by far the largest part of it.

It is a very modest programme. No grandiose construction. No metaphysic of morals. Aristotle does not look down on common sense. On the contrary, he subjects himself to common sense almost entirely. He thinks of his work as justifying rather than as superseding common sense. He ventures only to raise certain 'unpleasantnesses', *duscherê*, and to make a few alterations in order to remove them.

He carries out this programme in regard to *akrasia*. He notes and accepts the common opinion that *akrasia* occurs from time to time. That is to say, from time to time men do acts which they know to be wrong, owing to some passion. Then they are 'ecstatic of reason', as he puts it once; and this is a blameworthy state. But he notes also the opinion, maintained in the most striking way by Socrates, that the knowledge a man possesses cannot be overcome, or dragged about like a slave, by anything else in his soul. The words in which he here reports Socrates (1145b24) remind us strongly of the thesis that *epistêmê* (knowledge) is something that leads (*hêgemonikon*) and rules (*archikon*), which Plato had made his 'Socrates' maintain. in his *Protagoras*, 352 B. Aristotle accepts this opinion too. What he does not accept is the view that the Socratic thesis is inconsistent with the ordinary opinion that *akrasia* occurs from time to time. He confines himself to showing, by means of his doctrines of potentiality and of the syllogism, that the two propositions are consistent, so that we are not obliged to reject either of them. He removes the difficulty and leaves the received opinions standing. That is in his view a sufficient demonstration (1145b7). For the solution of the difficulty is a discovery (1146b7). No more extraordinary discovery is to be looked for in this matter.

Objections to this interpretation

Several objections have been made against this interpretation. In the first place, it is objected that, if Aristotle had explained *akrasia* as I have said he did, he would have left unexplained the most essential and most paradoxical kind of *akrasia*. For pure. essential *akrasia* occurs, it is said, when a man does wrong although he understands perfectly and completely, at the very moment of doing the act, that it is wrong. That, precisely, is the essence of *akrasia*, and also the only kind of *akrasia* that needs explaining. But on my interpretation it appears that the only kind of *akrasia* that needs explaining is precisely the only kind that Aristotle does not explain. For on my view every one of the four solutions amounts to saying that the acratic, at the time of his act, does not have fully in mind all the parts of the practical syllogism that ought to govern it. And, it is said, one cannot believe that Aristotle was so stupid.

My answer consists of two remarks. I remark first that everyone agrees that the first three solutions consist in saying that, in one way or another, the acratic does not keep all the parts of the syllogism active in his mind throughout. If then it is true, as the objection declares, that this sort of *akrasia* does not need to be explained, Aristotle has been in any case pretty stupid in introducing these three solutions. In fact, these interpreters are embarrassed by these three solutions, because in their opinion they do not bear on the real question. They are obliged to use the word 'dialectically', and to declare that Aristotle is here speaking dialectically and when he speaks dialectically he is not serious. But what good reason could Aristotle have had to introduce into his discussion a page that was not serious? I think we do better to suppose that Aristotle is serious in his first three solutions as well as in his last. And from this supposition it follows that Aristotle himself did not consider it superfluous to explain the case in which the practical syllogism is wholly present in the mind of the man who does a wrong act. I believe on the contrary that he would rather have been stupid if he had tried to do that, because this case does not occur. It is a wholly imaginary case, whereas Aristotle wished to explain realities. It does not happen that a man sets himself to consider, in its totality and all its parts, an argument forbidding him to do a certain act, while at the same time he yields to a strong desire and does as the desire wishes. The human mind is not adapted to do two things at the same time while giving full attention to each. During the crisis of his passion the acratic can hardly even remember the words that would express the argument. If by exception he does still remember the words, he does so only like a drunken man reciting verses by Empedocles without understanding them, as Aristotle remarks.

I turn to the second objection to my interpretation. It is in a way an attempt to revive part of the first objection, by saying that, however absurd it may seem to us to set out three solutions that are not serious, Aristotle himself tells us that he has done this, when he introduces his fourth solution with the word *phusikôs*. The fourth solution is indeed described as *phusikôs*. We are told that this implies that the first three failed to reach the nature or *phusis* of the thing. And this in turn implies that we must not interpret the fourth solution as introducing once more the feeble idea that the acratic does not have the syllogism wholly present in his mind. **150**

I reply as follows. When we read in the works of Aristotle the eleven cases of *phusikôs theôrein* etc. listed by Bonitz [9], we find that a paragraph or a thought is sometimes called *phusikôs* by Aristotle in order to mark some very general difference between this thought and the preceding ones, although it concerns the same topic. The preceding thoughts are sometimes contrasted as *logikôs* or *katholou*, though not in our chapter. We find also, I admit, that Aristotle sometimes seems to be suggesting that the *phusikôs* thought is a better thought and provides a point of view from which the topic appears more distinctly. But I do not find that *phusikôs* thought is *always* better than *logikôs* thought according to Aristotle. I find rather that he meant that *phusikôs* thought is better when one is dealing with physics, and that he sometimes wished to reproach certain philosophers for having treated physics rather as philosophers than as physicists, a criticism which his own eminence as a physicist gave him the right to make. I do not find him thinking that *phusikôs* thought is also the best in inquiries other than physical. It seems probable to me that Aristotle would have held that, just as it can be dangerous to trust to *logikôs* thinking in physics, so it can be dangerous to trust to *phusikôs* thinking in logic.

In our chapter the first three solutions are *logikôs*, though Aristotle does not say so. They give us no information about nature (though the third has much appearance of doing so). Instead of this, they offer us logical distinctions, between having and using, between the two premises, and finally between two levels of having. And that is what counts in this matter. **151**

To explain how a man can do what he knows to be wrong, although knowledge is powerful or even omnipotent, we need, not facts about human nature, but a logical division of the sense of the word 'know'.

Aristotle adds a *phusikôs* explanation, not in order to get down at last to the question, but rather to satisfy those unfortunate persons who cannot distinguish philosophy from psychology. If you ask me, he says in effect, for information about the acratic's state of mind, I will give you some: the acratic often has in mind a kind of *logos*, a syllogism of sorts, not indeed the one he ought to have, but another one, favourable to his act. Though Aristotle does not say so, I think I hear him adding under his breath: 'But this pretty psychological story has nothing to do with our question, the answer to which still resides in the logical distinctions I have drawn between the different kinds of knowing.' We note that a little later he refers us to 'the physiologers', if we wish to know 'how the ignorance is dissipated and the acratic resumes his knowledge' (1147b6-9). That is physics, not ethics.

I pass to the third objection. We have been told in Book III, chapter 1, that an act is involuntary, *akôn*, if the agent does not know all the particulars of his act. Let us take the case of Oedipus. Aristotle seems to be telling us here that Oedipus killed his father *akôn*, in that he did not know that the man he killed was his father. The objector infers from this that on my interpretation the acratic act is involuntary, because the absence of the minor premiss is the absence of the knowledge of a necessary particular. But an involuntary act is innocent, whereas the acratic act is blameworthy. A contradiction! The objector proposes to remove the contradiction by denying my view that Aristotle maintains throughout that in *akrasia* the important syllogism is not fully present.

152   I reply as follows. Oedipus' ignorance about the man he killed was not the ignorance of a moment or merely of the last degree. Oedipus did not, as soon as the man was dead, come to his senses and exclaim: 'I have killed my father'. It was not until many years afterwards that he learned for the first time that the man was his father. Thus his parricide was genuinely involuntary. He had never known the important fact. The acratic, on the contrary, knows the important fact perfectly well before he commits his act, and he will know it again as soon as the act is done and the desire assuaged. He *has* this essential knowledge, in the technical sense that Aristotle gives to *echein*, throughout the duration of his act, and before it, and after it. He also *uses* it, *chrêtai*, before and after his act. During his act he does not use it. He is blameworthy nevertheless, because he *has* the knowledge all the time.

I pass to the fourth objection, the last objection against my view that I shall mention. This is drawn from the words which Bywater gives us as follows: *ou gar tês kuriôs epistêmês einai dokousês parousês ginetai to pathos, oud' hautê perielketai dia to pathos, alla tês aisthêtikês* (1147b15-17). Bywater mentions no other importantly different reading. *Tês aisthêtikês* what? *Tês aisthêtikês* [*epistêmês*], undoubtedly, although this phrase never occurs and virtually contradicts Aristotle's epistemology. Also without doubt, this 'aesthetic' or perceptual knowledge is what the minor premiss gives us. The sentence opposes this perceptual knowledge to some other knowledge which is *kuriôs*. Apparently we must conclude that *kuriôs* knowledge is what is given in the major premiss, that is to say, the moral principle which the acratic disobeys. It follows that the first part of the sentence tells us that 'the passion', that is the acratic act, does not occur in the presence of the major premiss. Hence it occurs only when the major is absent. Hence it is the absence of the *major* premiss which explains *akrasia* and makes it possible, not the absence of the *minor* as my interpretation maintains.

I reply that the reasoning is correct; but I conclude, not that on account 153 of this one strange sentence we should abandon the view we have collected in reading the whole of the rest of the chapter, but that the text of these strange lines is corrupt and requires emendation. There are two further reasons for thinking that this text is corrupt. (1) The words *dokousês parousês* have a suspicious sound. (2) The sentence as it stands contradicts itself. We have seen that its first part means that *akrasia* is caused by the absence of the major premiss. But its second part denies this: *oud' hautê perielketai dia to pathos*. That is, *akrasia* does not cause absence of the major premiss. It cannot achieve that. It can only render the minor premiss inactive. The major, which is the real knowledge, remains unmoved during the acratic act.

How are we to emend? I know nothing better than Stewart's *periginetai: ou gar tês kuriôs epistêmês einai dokousês periginetai to pathos*. 'The passion does not overcome what seems to be the real knowledge; it is not this which is dragged about by the passion but the perceptual knowledge.' With this emendation the sentence no longer conflicts with my interpretation but confirms it.

Criticism of Aristotle on akrasia

It has been objected to Aristotle that his account of *akrasia* tells us nothing about the moral struggle, the struggle that a man wages sometimes against a desire and for a moral principle. This is true. But it was not the intention of Aristotle to do so. What he wished to do here was to analyse how one can act contrary to one's principles, whether this act occurs after a struggle or not. He notices elsewhere that such a struggle is possible (1102b17).

A second objection is that this account explains only one of the two forms of *akrasia*. Aristotle says later (1150b19 ff.) that there are two sorts of acratic 154 men, the impetuous, who are carried away by the passion because they have not deliberated, and the weak, who deliberate but, owing to the passion, do not abide by the result of their deliberation. My teacher, Sir David Ross, has written that Aristotle's account of *akrasia* explains at best only the *akrasia* of impetuous men, not also that of weak men. I take him to imply that, whereas according to Aristotle one commits an acratic act only when some part of the relevant practical syllogism is not completely actual in the mind, in weak *akrasia* everything is perfectly actual because the man has deliberated.

I think that this objection fails. The weak acratic has indeed deliberated about everything; but it does not follow that the passion cannot still drive out of his mind the premiss which was in it for a time. Aristotle's view is, I think, as follows. The weak acratic deliberates and actualises the whole of the practical syllogism. But his passion, when it becomes strong, drives some part of the syllogism out of his mind for a moment; and during that moment the acratic commits his act. As to the impetuous acratic, since he never has deliberated, the question how he can do an act that he knows to be wrong does not arise in his case. He has never known that the act is wrong, because he has never realised the minor premiss, because he has not reflected. He is acratic nevertheless, provided that he knows the major premiss, the moral principle, that ought to have operated here.

A third objection, also to be found in Sir David Ross' book ([15], p. 224), is that the cause of *akrasia* lies not in lack of knowledge but in weakness of will. It is held sometimes that the Greeks could not explain *akrasia* because they lacked the concept of the will. In rejecting this objection, I make use of an idea drawn from Gilbert Ryle's *The Concept of Mind*, namely that weakness of will is not the cause but the form of *akrasia*. *Akrasia* is not the effect of weakness of will; it is one of the kinds of weakness of will. To say that *akrasia* is a weakness of will is to explain it neither more nor less than one explains a crow by saying that it is a bird. Such an explanation is certainly worth giving; but this does not entail that the sort of explanation given by Aristotle is either false or superfluous or even inferior. The same thing admits of several kinds of explanation.

A fourth objection seems better founded. It is necessary to criticise questions beginning with the word 'How?' or '*Pôs*'; 'How does a man with the right view act acratically?' (1145b21). The question 'How?' is perfectly proper in practice. 'How can I get to Lyons? – By taking a train or a plane, sir.' 'How do you do that conjuring trick, sir? – Excuse me, madam; it is a secret.' These 'Hows?' are perfectly correct. They are requests to be told the means which someone uses to achieve a certain end. But in intellectual enquiries, for example when one asks how a man can act contrary to the right, it is a different matter. Here we are not supposing that the acratic possesses some wonderful secret which we want to extract from him. We are not supposing that the acratic has at his disposal some superior means of doing wrong. We are simply supposing that the acratic cannot do wrong. 'How can he?' is a way of saying 'He cannot'.

I suggest that this expression is ill conceived, and that it is a somewhat insincere way of maintaining that *akrasia* cannot occur. If someone asks you how a man can do what he knows to be wrong, I suggest that you had better reply as follows: 'Experience shows clearly that it is possible to do what one knows to be wrong; so why do you suppose that it is impossible?' By this manoeuvre you will make it clear that it is not you but he who ought to give an explanation. For it is he and not you who has asserted a thesis that contradicts experience. Therefore it is he who ought to justify himself. He ought to give you some reason to believe his paradox. If he does not, there is no reason in the world why you should accept it. But he does not. On the contrary, by disguising his thesis as a question beginning with 'How can?', he succeeds in making you think that it is you who are the debtor and the unreasonable man.

Had Aristotle any reason to believe the paradox that a man cannot do what he knows to be wrong? Yes: he believed, like Socrates, that knowledge is stronger than anything else in the mind of a man. 'When knowledge is present, thought Socrates, it is an awful thing that anything else should master it and drag it about like a slave' (1145b23). Like Socrates, Aristotle believed that knowledge is always commanding. Socrates concluded that *akrasia* does not occur. Aristotle tries to show that *akrasia* can nevertheless occur, not without raising certain suspicions. But this is too troublesome a way of attaining the end. The simple and good way is to deny the thesis that knowledge is always commanding. It is evident in our experience that it is not always so. If we do this, we no longer need any question beginning with 'How can?' We need this kind of question only when we deny some fact of experience.

Perhaps you will agree with what I have just said and still demand some explanation of *akrasia*. For perhaps you will say that it is not enough to submit to experience and recognise the fact of *akrasia*; we must also understand this strange and repellent fact; we must see something of its place in the totality of human nature. You are right. We must do so; and it will probably be an endless task. For the present, however, I offer you only one thought, a thought which, if true, must help us a little to understand *akrasia*. It is the thought that moral principles are not discoveries but resolutions. When we adopt a moral principle, we are not deciding how the world is made, but how we are going to act. The principle that one ought not to kill, for example, does not reveal the composition of the world, nor the orders of a god. It takes a stand with regard to the world. The adoption of it 157 constitutes a sort of generalised choice.

If this is so, it follows that when a man acts acratically he acts not contrary to a known fact, so to speak, but contrary to a decision he has taken. *Akrasia* is not like going through a wall by means of a door which one knows does not exist. It is more like visiting Cologne after having decided not to visit Germany.

These considerations make *akrasia* more intelligible by putting it into that huge class of contradictions, hesitations, vacillations, incoherences, and absurdities of every kind, which composes a large part of our practical life. *Akrasia* seemed more mysterious than it is to Aristotle because he assimilated morality to science, in that he regarded the principles of morality as statements of fact, which it would be as impossible to disregard as to disregard a wall that barred our path.

Criticism of Aristotle on akolasia

Who is this acolastic man of whom Aristotle speaks in Book VII? I doubt whether such a person exists. He is not the acolastic of whom Aristotle spoke in Books II and III. In those books *akolasia* was not contrasted with *akrasia*, for Aristotle did not mention *akrasia*; it was opposed to temperance, and consisted in pursuing a certain kind of pleasure excessively because one was led on by desire. The acolastic had no principle or *logos*; he was simply led on by desire. And Aristotle did not say whether he afterwards regretted his actions.

In Book VII, on the contrary, the acolastic is contrasted with the acratic rather than with the temperate man; and he appears as a man of principle. He possesses a *logos*; he obeys his *logos*; and he does not regret having obeyed his *logos*.

What is the *logos* of the acolastic? It can hardly be the *logos* that 'I ought to pursue excessive pleasures'. For if he used the word 'excessive' he would be 158 condemning himself; and I think Aristotle would have recognised this. But if he condemned himself he would be acratic and not acolastic. It is the acratic who condemns himself. The acolastic has a clear conscience about himself.

We find in the text the principle that 'everything sweet should be tasted' (1147a29). Is this one of the acolastic's principles? If it were the acolastic would certainly be a mythical person; for there has never been anybody who adopted the principle that everything sweet should be tasted. But I think that Aristotle is not here intending to tell us one of the acolastic's principles. I think rather that he is giving us one of those inappropriate and even absurd examples which unfortunately are not rare in his work.

We read also that the acratic is not persuaded 'that he ought to pursue such pleasures unrestrainedly' (1151a23). Are we to understand that the acolastic, on the contrary, adopts precisely the principle 'that he ought to pursue such pleasures unrestrainedly'? The answer, I believe, is more or less yes.

But to answer the question what principle Aristotle attributes to his acolastic the safest passage is 1146b22, where he expressly says that the acolastic 'is led on intentionally, holding that one ought always to pursue the present pleasure'.

This principle is a bad one according to Aristotle. For the badness of the acolastic consists in his principle's being bad. It does not consist in his disobeying his principle; for on the contrary he obeys it.

Does Aristotle think that the acolastic himself considers his principle bad? He does not explicitly answer this question. But I think he would answer no. For it seems that, if the acolastic himself considered his principle bad, he would thereby too much resemble the acratic, though in a strange and obscure way. So it is only Aristotle who considers the principle bad. The acolastic considers it good.

159   And which of them is right, the acolastic or Aristotle? If we insist on the 'always', it is evidently Aristotle who is right. There is, unfortunately, no practical principle that one can always follow without ever being in the wrong. But, just because this is too obvious, we ought to doubt whether an acolastic of this sort ever occurs. If, on the contrary, in order to avoid making the acolastic into a man of straw, we do not emphasise the 'always', it becomes much less certain that it is Aristotle who is right. It seems to me that there are fewer men who on principle seek the present pleasure too much than there are men who on principle seek the present pleasure too little. Against puritanism we need to insist that 'we ought to pursue the present pleasure'. This is a duty deriving necessarily from our great duty to alleviate human misery. The duty to restrain our appetite, which of course is often incumbent on us too, also derives from some moral rule justified by the same end, that is, the diminution of human misery.

Aristotle does not discuss the principle with the acolastic. He does not discuss practical principles at all. He hardly even expresses them. I venture to say that this is the greatest defect in his ethics, which nevertheless are magnificent. He did not grasp the fact of moral relativity, the fact, I mean, that sometimes two men, though equally serious and conscientious and obedient to their consciences, nevertheless find their consciences uttering opposed principles. Owing to this fact, we ought to debate moral principles, to discuss them, to defend them, and not to reject other people's principles as evidently false because they do not harmonise with ours. Once we have realised that, among the men who act in ways we disapprove, there are some who do so not because they have no conscience, nor because they flout their own conscience, but because they obey their own conscience and their conscience tells them to act so – once we have realised that, what are we to do? We must not use disapproving words like 'acolastic'. Nor must we use the medical metaphor, as Aristotle too often does, and regard these men as patients to be cured, and even to be cured against their will. The man whose moral principles conflict with mine is to be neither cured nor insulted, but persuaded. I must reason with him and try to convince him; and I must always admit the possibility that in the end it will be I, and not he, who ought to change.

But Aristotle denies the possibility of a rational discussion of the principles of morality. He declares that there is no *logos* to teach the principles: 'neither there nor here can the *logos* teach the principles', where 'here' refers to practice (1151a18). He recognises only nature and habituation as teachers of morality. That seems to me a great despair. If one day Aristotle happened to think that perhaps he himself had been ill endowed by nature, or ill trained by his teachers, what would he do to reassure himself, either by confirming his principles or by exchanging them for better ones? According to his own theory he could do nothing at all. He says that the bad man does not know he is bad (1150b36); what if one day he overheard this 'bad' man saying to a friend: 'Aristotle does not know that he is bad'?

I believe that we ought to confess our moral principles, and try to make them probable (not to prove them; one cannot prove practical principles), and seek also the reasons against them, and listen to and weigh the principles and reasons of others. By this method we may hope to be always purifying our principles and making them more serviceable for their end, which is the diminution of human misery. It is more or less the same method of approximation as we also follow in the pursuit of the truth about nature. If we adopt this method we continually progress a little towards the end. If we adopt the method of Aristotle we never progress at all, so that, unless we have had the extraordinary luck to be established right on the end by our teachers, we shall never get any nearer to it.

160

9

G. E. L. Owen

Aristotelian Pleasures

135   Aristotle's discussions of pleasure have figured largely in recent philosophical writing on the topic. Ryle, I think, showed English philosophers a way in; Kenny [161], Urmson [160], and many others have carried the explorations forward. But there has been an air of piecemeal raiding about the enterprise rather than of connected exploration, for Aristotle seems to have no consistent account of pleasure to offer. I do not mean that the *Rhetoric* (1369b33-5, 1371a25-6, 33-4) and *Magna Moralia* (1205b7-8) repeat the Academic view of pleasure as a process of restoration which Aristotle rebuts in the *Eudemian* and *Nicomachean Ethics*. Both are in different ways *argumenta ad homines*, soon modified in the *Rhetoric* (1370a4-9) and directly rebutted in the *Magna Moralia*. I have in mind the more baffling inconsistency that seems to lie at the heart of the discussions of pleasure on which philosophers have chiefly drawn, the studies that now appear in the seventh and tenth books of the *Nicomachean Ethics*. This has exercised critics from the Greek commentators on. It led Miss Anscombe to say that the difficulty of the concept of pleasure, 'astonishingly, reduced Aristotle to babble, since for good reasons he both wanted pleasure to be identical with and to be different from the activity that it is pleasure in' (*Intention*, p. 76). My first interest is to propose a different approach to this puzzle. My second is to discuss some arguments whose form will, I hope, be made clearer by such an approach. I shall end by confessing some residual puzzles, but their interest will be more historical than philosophical.

The mismatch of A and B

136   In a study of pleasure which is common to our texts of the *Eudemian* and *Nicomachean Ethics* Aristotle says that pleasures are *energeiai* (*EN* VII (= *EE* VI) 1153a9-15); in a second study which is found only in the *Nicomachean* he says that pleasures complete or perfect *energeiai*, but must not be identified with them (1174b14-1175b1, 1175b32-5). I shall follow Festugière [158] and distinguish the two studies, *EN* VII 11-14 and X 1-5, as '*A*' and '*B*' respectively. For '*energeia*' I shall use, pending later discussion, the conventional translation 'activity'. What *A* says, and *B* appears to deny, is that pleasures are just the unhindered activities of our natural faculties. In both contexts the activities are such basic ingredients of a man's life as the exercises of his intelligence.[1] By identifying pleasures with such activities *A*

---

1. In *A* 1153a1 (retaining the *energeia* or *energeiai* of the MSS. with Festugière and

can argue that the best life for man may simply be some pleasure or class of pleasures (1153b7-13). By distinguishing them *B* can leave it an open question whether we choose the life for the sake of the pleasure or *vice versa* (1175a18-21).

Traditionally the question has been whether the two accounts are too divergent to be compatible. I hope to show that they are too divergent to be incompatible. They are neither competing nor cooperating answers to one question, but answers to two quite different questions.

Since the ancient commentators the tendency has been to play the discrepancy down in the hope of finding Aristotle a unified thesis.[2] Commonly it is excused as the difference between an early draft and a finished version, *A* being the hastier and more polemical, *B* showing signs of refinement at leisure (e.g., Festugière [158], p. xxiv; Gauthier-Jolif [35], p. 783; Dirlmeier [41], pp. 567, 580-1). Stewart ([37], pp. 221-2, n. 1) dismissed it as 'of trifling and merely scholastic significance'. Hardie ([58], p. 304) conflates *A* and *B* in speaking of *B* as propounding 'the view held by Aristotle, that it (sc. pleasure) is an activity (*energeia*) or the completion of an activity'. Sometimes the suggestion that *A* is rougher because more polemical is exaggerated into the claim that *A* is merely negative: Ross wrote ([15], p. 228) that 'where there is contradiction, the preference must be given to Book X, for here Aristotle not only criticises the views of others but states his own position positively'. But in both accounts a positive view is produced (Aristotle claims to be saying what pleasure is at 1154b33, 1174a13, and does so at 1152b33-1153a17, 1173a29-b20, 1174a13-1175a3). And in both it is reached by rebutting others. So another reason for assimilating them suggests itself: the positive account of pleasure in *A* and *B* must be essentially the same, since it is Aristotle's reply to the same mistaken view of pleasure. What he rejects in both contexts is the thesis that pleasure is a *genesis* or *kînêsis*, a process towards some state in which it terminates, as convalescence is a process to health.[3] On the strength of this Stewart ([37], p. 223) proposed a single Aristotelian 'formula', that pleasure 'is inseparable from *energeia*, enhances *energeia*, is *energeia*', and found the 'true significance' of this

137

Gauthier-Jolif against Bywater, who was probably mistaken to say that Aspasius did not have this reading (*in EN* 145.16-17, 20-1)). In *B* 1174b21.

2. Gauthier-Jolif misrepresent the Ĝreek commentators here ([35], p. 780). Pseudo-Alexander (*Apor.* 143.9-46.12) does not hold that *A* commits Aristotle to equating pleasure with enjoyed activities. If a good life consists in the latter, still if pleasure is *unhindered* activity the real source of happy living will be the virtue that ensures the unhinderedness. Nor does Aspasius (*in EN* 150.31-152.3) hold this view. He says that, if *A* is indeed by Aristotle, the argument is dialectical, *ad homines* (151.21, 26). So Dirlmeier ([41], p. 567).

3. The possible objection that the polemic in *A* concentrates on *genesis* (e.g. 1152b13,23) and that in *B* on *kînêsis* (1174a19-b9) would not show a substantial division between them. *Genesis* and *kînêsis* are coupled at 1152b28, 1173a29-30 (though the subsequent argument distinguishes them, 1173a31-b4, 1173b4-7), 1174b10 and 12-13, just as they are coupled in the specimen argument about pleasure at *A.Pr.* 48b30-2. Building is an example of *genesis* in *A* (1152b13-14) and of *kînêsis* in *B* (1174a19-29). Lieberg ([159], p. 104, n. 1) thought the difference showed that after *A* Aristotle has reached some distinctions recorded in *Phys.* V 1, but he too thought the same form of thesis was under attack in both contexts.

concoction in the fact that 'it asserts the opposite of "Pleasure is *genesis* or *anaplêrôsis*" '. ('*Anaplêrôsis*' or 'filling-up' is the less general but more vivid expression for a restorative process that Aristotle occasionally borrows from the opposition.)

This argument will not do. One reply is too obvious to spend time on. If a philosopher twice rebuts a given thesis and offers a substitute, that is not the least guarantee that he offers the same alternative on both occasions. The range of alternative options may be wide and his own view of it may be wider. But this reply does not find the root of the trouble. The root of it is the assumption that, when Aristotle argues that pleasure is not a *genesis* (coming into being) or *kînêsis* (change), he must have the same target in his sights on both occasions.

138   '*Hêdonê*', like its English counterpart 'pleasure', has at least two distinct though related uses. We can say 'Gaming is one of my pleasures' or, alternatively, 'Gaming gives me pleasure' or 'I get pleasure from (take pleasure in) gaming'. In the first use the pleasure is identified with the enjoyed activity, in the second the two are distinct and their relationship is problematic. Philosophers have sometimes concentrated on one of these uses to the near-exclusion of the other. Aristotle puts almost exclusive emphasis on the first in *A* and on the second in *B*. Thus what he takes himself to be rejecting in *A* is a thesis about what is *enjoyed* or *enjoyable* (in English, *a* pleasure): he wants to deny that what we enjoy is ever, in some last analysis, a process such as convalescing or relieving our hunger. But what he takes himself to be rejecting in *B* is a mistake about the character of *enjoying* or *taking pleasure*: he denies that the Greek equivalents of these verbs have the logic of process-verbs such as *building* something or *walking* somewhere. Neither rejection implies the other. Each determines the form of the positive thesis it introduces.

The distinction I have invoked is put by Kenny ([161], p. 128) in this way: 'We get pleasure out of pleasures, and derive enjoyment from enjoyments'. But I doubt that the logic of his two plurals is the same. Given that I enjoy smoking and play-going, I can certainly say that among my pleasures is the pleasure of smoking and among my enjoyments the enjoyment of play-going. But the first 'of' seems identificatory ('the pleasure which consists in smoking', as in 'the honour of being your Mayor'), while the second marks a verb-object relation (as in 'the murder of Smith'). Pleasures are enjoyed activities (or feelings, etc.); enjoyments are enjoyings. Now the Greek plural '*hêdonai*' can be rendered either by 'pleasures' or by 'enjoyments'. *A* will normally require the first sense, *B* (e.g. 1176a22-9) the second.

The consistency of A

At the end of *A* (1154b32-3) Aristotle claims to have said what pleasure is. He evidently refers to his thesis (let us call it '*T*', for brevity) that pleasure is *anempodistos energeia tês kata phusin hexeôs* or, as Ross and others translate it, 'unimpeded activity of the natural state' (1153a14-15). *Hexis* or 'state' is
139   Aristotle's word for any settled condition or propensity of the agent that is exhibited in characteristic performances, and *energeia* or 'activity' is his word for the performances that exhibit it; or, more narrowly, when *energeia* is

contrasted with *kînêsis* or *genesis* as it is here, it is his word for those performances which are not end-directed processes like convalescence but self-contained activities like the exercise of a healthy body. Aristotle wants to connect pleasure with the second, not the first. But what is the connexion? To sharpen the question, what does he mean here by 'the natural state'? Joachim described *A* as concerned with 'pleasure – the *feeling pleased*'. Is Aristotle speaking of some natural pleasure-faculty issuing, perhaps, in pleasure-feelings?

Emphatically he is not. He means that a pleasure is the unimpeded activity of *any* natural state. Any such exercise of our natural faculties or propensities *is* (and not: is accompanied by) pleasure. Let me try to clinch this as briefly as possible, before turning to some more interesting issues that arise. Consider first how the thesis *T* is put to work, then how it is reached.

(1) It is put to work in 1153b9-13. 'Given that there are unimpeded activities belonging to every state, it arguably follows that the activity either of all the states or of one of them – depending on which of these alternatives constitutes happiness – must, provided it is unimpeded, be the activity worthiest of choice. *And this is* (or, *is a*) *pleasure*. Consequently, even if most pleasures turned out to be unqualifiedly bad, the highest good would still be *some* pleasure'. One phrase deserves explanation. Aristotle is answering the thesis that the best life cannot be a pursuit of pleasure. He is presupposing an analysis of the good life which appears earlier in the *Nicomachean Ethics*: either happiness is made up of all the best activities or it is just one, the very best of these (1099a29-31), that which exhibits the 'best and completest excellence' (1098a16-18). This last option is what he means to leave open in speaking of 'the activity of all the states or of one of them'; he is looking forward to his thesis that happiness consists in the exercise of one superhuman faculty, pure intelligence (1177a12-1178a8). But on either alternative he takes one plain conclusion to follow from *T*. It is that such activities, when they proceed unhindered,[4] are pleasures, not that they give rise to pleasure. Otherwise he could not, as he does, envisage the good life as consisting in some pleasure or pleasures, or rebuff the opposition by allowing the good and rational man to aim at *some* pleasures even if not at all.

(2) There is the same use of 'pleasure' in the arguments leading to *T*. Aristotle lists three views about pleasure (1152b8-12) of which he wants to dismiss two. One of these is that no pleasure is good either intrinsically or even derivatively, the other is that even if all pleasures were good the greatest good could not be a pleasure. The two seem to him to share one principal argument: that pleasure is always a *genesis* or end-directed process and never the end-state of such a process (1152b22-3) – or, more specifically, that all pleasures are perceptible processes towards some

140

---

4. Elsewhere Aristotle says something of hindrances to activity. (a) Misfortune may block our activities (1100b22-30) but so may too much good fortune (1153b17-25), too many friends (1170b26-9); note the asceticism of 1178b3-7. (b) The pleasure of one activity will interfere with another: people who enjoy fluteplaying cannot attend to arguments while a flute is being played (1175b1-22, cf. 1153a20-3; more on this later).

natural or normal condition (1152b13-14). As Aristotle's reply shows, his opponents would have approved the obituarist who wrote 'Dining was among his pleasures; he valued the repleteness that resulted'. The pleasure, they held, was never 'in the same class' (1152b14) as its desirable outcome. Depending on the intransigence of the opponent this had been taken to show either that the pleasure had no value at all (cf. Plato *Philebus* 54C9-D12) or that it had the lesser value.

The point comes out sharply in the example Aristotle chooses to discuss, that of convalescence. We notice that we are getting better, and enjoy this (it is a *perceptible* process to a natural state); but what we want and value is ordinary health, which we scarcely notice but would not trade for any convalescence, however enjoyable. It is into this argument that Joachim introduced his identification of pleasure with 'feeling pleased'. But Aristotle is quite clear what the opposition intend: for them the pleasure is the convalescing. For him, as his reply will show, it is the activity of a healthy body. These are the only alternatives in the case that he considers.

141   At first, without directly challenging the assumption that pleasures consist in processes towards some desirable state, he tries a Platonic reply. Some such processes at least are not the pleasures they seem to be, namely those that involve discomfort for the sake of a cure – those that occur in the sick, for example. He is reminding his hearers of *Republic* 583B-586C, *Philebus* 51A. But then he turns to reject the assumption. He keeps another part of the opposition's case: in their view the valuable part of our lives is always some state or activity (1152b33), never the process leading to such a state or activity. Very well, even in convalescence there is a pleasure which is valuable by their standards, for the real pleasure is, as he will shortly put it (1153a14), 'an activity of the natural state'; not the trudge back to health but the exercise of actual health. But where is this healthy activity to be found in convalescence? 'The activity shown in the desires', he explains, 'is the activity of the state which still survives in us, our natural consititution' (or perhaps 'The activity is found in the desires of the state . . .'; 1152b35-6, cf. 1154b18-20). He is claiming, I take it, that any actual pleasure associated with convalescence consists in the proper functioning of the healthy residue of the patient; without this the sick man would not want to get better.

That this is his point becomes clear in his summing-up (1153a7-12). Our pleasures are not to be contrasted as end-directed processes with their desirable ends. Pleasures are not such processes, they do not even all come hand in hand with such processes (those which occur in convalescence do; theorising is one that does not). They are all activities constituting an end in themselves; in them we are not becoming so-and-so (healthy, say) but using the faculties we have. The only pleasures that have some further justification beyond themselves are those found in men who are being 'brought to the perfecting of their nature'; thus (as I gloss it) the functioning of the healthy parts in convalescence has a further point, that of promoting total health, but their comparable functioning in a wholly healthy man has no such further point. And Aristotle ends by rejecting the thesis that pleasure is a perceptible *genesis* and replacing it with *T*. The sense of 'pleasure' that was required to explain Aristotle's application of *T* is the sense needed to explain the steps by which it is introduced. In these contexts

Aristotle's question 'What is pleasure?' means 'What is the character of a   **142**
pleasure, what ingredients of a life are enjoyable in themselves?' The nature
of enjoying does not come into question in *A*. If we are asked what is
admirable about politics or detestable about beagling, we do not stop to
ponder what admiring or detesting is before embracing the question.

Other evidence for the dominant use of 'pleasure' in *A* could be adduced.
Is there evidence for a different use, in which the pleasure is a concomitant
or consequence of some enjoyed activity? Not in 1153a6-7, where the
'pleasant things' contrasted with the 'pleasures' are not the enjoyed
activities but their objects. But in 1153a20-3 there seems to be a sketch of
the contrast we are after. Yet the point – that the enjoyment of an activity
stimulates it and inhibits others – is made with nothing like the detail and
perspicuousness of the comparable argument in *B*, 1175a29-b24. The
conclusion remains that the central arguments of *A*, those which import and
then apply *T*, are controlled by that first sense of 'pleasure'; and it is quite
otherwise in *B*.

Corollaries

But the argument of *A* is too curious to put aside without more comment,
particularly since *B* has had the lion's share of other discussions. How, to
begin with, does Aristotle assure himself that he can identify the
convalescent's pleasure with the activity of his healthy parts? His immediate
argument (1152b36-1153a2) is that there are pleasures which do *not* involve
wants and discomforts and which *are* the proper functioning of a natural
faculty, such as the activities of theorising or rational contemplation. So he
is looking for some common feature in all pleasures, some necessary and
sufficient condition for anything to be enjoyable; and he uses something like
a method of concomitant variations to isolate it. And his critics have long
complained that this search for the unit is a delusion. Working at a cross-
word puzzle is surely an end-directed process, yet why should this not be
more enjoyable than rationally contemplating the solution?

One more move is open to him. He has grasped, and never forgets, the
essential point that pleasures are 'ends', that to enjoy *X*-ing is a reason for
X-ing or for taking steps to bring *X*-ing about. True, this suggests that the   **143**
X-ing I enjoy is always something I can choose to do (this seems to be
Aristotle's view in *B*) or else can try to bring about (the healthy functioning
in *A*). But I can enjoy receiving unexpected letters; in that case my
enjoyment is a reason for others to send me letters. I can enjoy the
knowledge that my horse has won; and if you think I shall enjoy that
knowledge, that is a reason for imparting it to me, for making or letting me
know. But I cannot make myself know that something is the case, as I can
make myself go gardening or become a licensed plumber. And there are
more teasing questions: can I claim without paradox to enjoy *believing* that
my horse won? (Perhaps the oddity is that this could only be a reason for
the ministrations of flatterers.) But these refinements do not touch
Aristotle's clarity on the main issue, that a pleasure is or can be satisfying in
itself. So if I find working at cross-word puzzles more enjoyable than
contemplating their solutions, that is surely because for me the puzzling has
the form of a self-contained activity like juggling, not that of an end-directed

operation like recovering one's stamina or building a house. At any moment that I say I am working at such a puzzle I can say I have worked at it (cf. *Meta.* 1048b18-35), and that use of the perfect would not be open to me if I described myself as solving the puzzle.

But there is a larger curiosity in Aristotle's argument. He seems to claim that we can misidentify the object of our enjoyment, and misidentify it systematically. When we say we enjoy convalescence we are always wrong about what we really enjoy. To find out what we are really enjoying we must resort to a curious induction – as though an enjoyment turned up and it had to be settled on some generalisation from other cases what it was an enjoyment of. But Aristotle cannot mean this absurdity. In *B* the complaint would be easily settled, for there Aristotle maintains, in Urmson's admirable summary ([160], p. 324), that 'different activities are differently enjoyable. Just as perception and thought are different species of activity, so the pleasures of perception are different in species from the pleasures of thought. Every activity has its own 'proper' (*oikeia*) pleasure; one could not chance to get the pleasure of, say, reading poetry from stamp collecting'. But that is *B*, not *A*. *A* is not concerned (save perhaps in 1153a20-3) with the relation between the enjoying and what is enjoyed. And *B* is not concerned with the misidentifying of the activity enjoyed.

Now in *A* Aristotle prefaces his own account of pleasure with the comment that the processes[5] which restore us to a natural state are only *incidentally, kata sumbebêkos,* pleasant (1152b34-5). Commonly he explains this expression by saying that an *A* is incidentally *B* when its being so is an exception (we should prefer to say, when under that description it is an exception): *A*s are not always or necessarily, or even usually, *B*s (cf. *Top.* I 5; *Meta.* V 30 and VI 2 with Kirwan's commentary). But he cannot be concerned here to point out that convalescence is not always or usually a pleasure; his thesis is plainly much stronger than that. There is a more basic suggestion that seems often to underlie his accounts of *to kata sumbebêkos.* Statements which hold good only 'incidentally' are formally misleading, suggesting a mistaken analysis or explanation of the fact they convey, and calling for rewriting or expansion into some unmisleading canonical form. This I suppose is the sense of Waitz's note (*Aristotelis Organon* I, p. 443) that '*kata sumbebêkos* dicitur quod non nisi cum abusu quodam vocabuli dicitur', and it is the point of Aristotle's dictum that an *A* which is *B* is only incidentally so when it is not the *nature* of *A*s to be *B* or it is not *qua A* that this one is *B* (e.g. 1026b37-1027a8, 1025a28-9). 'A baker made this statue' is an example. Aristotle holds that the fact is better displayed by saying that what made the statue was a sculptor who happened to be (but for this purpose need not have been) a baker. Similarly with 'convalescence is a pleasure': the pleasure is the operation of the healthy parts which happens to occur in a process of convalescence but might have occurred apart from any such process.

Now this seems to give Aristotle a reply to the objection. The

144

---

5. Understanding '*kînêseis kai geneseis*' at 1152b34 with Grant, Stewart, Ross, Dirlmeier, Gauthier. Rackham and Festugière understand '*hêdonai*'. Gauthier agrees with Ramsauer that this comes to the same thing, but the first reading is the more perspicuous.

convalescent was wrong, we may say, not about the activity he was enjoying, but about the description under which it was enjoyable to him. For the functioning of the healthy residue does in this case happen to be also a process of convalescence. The baker who makes the statue *is* a baker; only it is not as a baker that he can be clarifyingly treated as responsible for the statue. And thus, it seems, the mistake that Aristotle claims to detect can be assimilated to one that has recently exercised philosophers, in which a subject, while enjoying X, rejects or overlooks the appropriate description of the X he is enjoying: the familiar schoolboy at the dormitory feast, who thinks he is enjoying eating cold bacon when he is really enjoying breaking the rules.   145

But this reply should give us qualms. It might indeed seem an anachronism. Aristotle does not speak unambiguously of identifying even a substance under different descriptions, let alone those intractable items, events. He does indeed speak of a thing as being 'one in number but two in *logos*', as the same mid-point of a line can be called both the end-point of one line and the beginning of another (*Phys.* 262a19-21, 263b12-14). But when he uses the same idiom to express the identity of a body with its matter (*GG* 320b14) we should cavil at the glib translation 'one thing under different descriptions'; the identity in question is too problematic. And it is worth recalling that Aristotle is prone to think of 'the sculptor is incidentally a baker' as importing two things which somehow combine into a unity (*Meta.* 1015b16-36, cf. 1017b33 and Kirwan's notes). Yet his discussion of the 'mixed' action at *EN* 1110a4-b17 is surely a treatment of one action under different descriptions: the jettisoning of the cargo which is *a priori* irrational, the jettisoning to save the ship which represents the rational choice. But those who distrust such aids in our context will prefer to say that Plato had after all argued that we can be mistaken about our real pleasures, and that Aristotle in A is still within that tradition. In B he is his own man, and there is no further hint that we may systematically misidentify what we enjoy.

The verb takes the stage

In B, as I have said, it is quite otherwise. Given any faculty of perception or intellect, Aristotle says, the exercise of that faculty will be best, and so most complete and pleasant, when the faculty is at its best and exercised on the finest kind of object. But the exercise of the faculty is not itself the pleasure; the pleasure comes to complete or perfect the activity (1174b14-23). Aristotle tells us something of what this means. The pleasure, he says, augments the activity, in that people who engage in the activity with pleasure are more exact and discriminating (1175a30-b1); the stronger it is the more it prevents them from attending to other activities (1175b1-13), and the longer and better the activity goes on (1175b14-16). But its contribution to the completeness or perfection of the activity is not the same as that of the well-conditioned faculty or the fine object. It is more like the health the doctor produces than like such pre-existing contributing factors as the doctor (1174b23-6, taking '*kai ho iatros*' to follow and be governed by '*homoiôs*') or the health already in the patient (31-2). In brief it is an end in itself, something that gives the action a point different from that of exercising a good faculty on a good object. Enjoyment inevitably marks such exercises (1174b29-31) but it is still not, as we may put it, merely   146 entailed by satisfying the conditions (1174a6-8). To say that Smith is using his excellent eyesight on some comely object is not to say, or say .what entails, that he enjoys doing this, any more than to say that he is physically at his prime is to call him beautiful, though the beauty inevitably follows (1174b32-3). Yet the beauty and the enjoyment are not merely contingent benefits that might have been got otherwise. The beauty is that of a man in his prime, the pleasure can only be identified by reference to the activity it promotes.

Plainly Aristotle is refusing to identify the pleasure with the enjoyed activity. A little later he says so flatly. Unlike desires, pleasures are so bound up with the activities they complete that there is disagreement on whether the pleasure is simply identical with the activity. But it doesn't look as though the pleasure *is* just thinking or perceiving; *for that would be absurd* (1175b32-5).

There is the difference between *A* and *B*. How to explain it? Well, perhaps it occurred to Aristotle that the activities of the natural states which served as *A*'s paradigms of pleasure need not be enjoyable at all. Smith is exercising his wits on an argument; but his wits are blunt, he is tired, the argument is tangled. So *B* is spelling out the further conditions that are requisite for pleasure – sharp wits, impeccable object. But this does not explain the difference. For one thing, such conditions might be covered by *A*'s requirement that the activity proceed unhindered. For another, *B* does not conclude that when such conditions are satisfied the activity *is* a pleasure, only that pleasure inevitably ensues. And for a third, *B* seems curiously unaware of the central claim of *A* that only self-contained activities and not end-directed processes are enjoyable. I shall take up the argument in 1173b9-15 later; meanwhile notice the kinds of activity that are promoted by their proper enjoyments in 1175a34-5. One is house-building, a paradigm of an end-directed process in both *A* and *B*. It is even odd that the senses, which provide a model of enjoyable activity in *B*, are so readily dismissed in *A*, in deference to convention, as neutral or a source of discomfort (1154b4-9).

Let us leave the attempt to build a bridge from *A* to *B* and consider a declaration of independence. I suggested that in asking what pleasure is, and concluding that it is not a process, *B* is engaged in a quite different sort of enquiry from *A*. It is concerned to say, not what is enjoyable, but what enjoying is. It is interested in the logic of the verb or verbs we translate by 'enjoying' and 'being pleased', and in the associated nouns just in so far as these go proxy for the verbs.

Notice first the quite different emphasis that *A* and *B* put on verbs connoting pleasure. Aristotle's standard noun for 'pleasure' is '*hêdonê*' (elsewhere, but not in *A* or *B*, he also uses '*apolausis*' and '*terpsis*'). The verbs he associates with it are *chairein, hêdesthai, areskein, terpein, agapân*. The difference is not just that in *B* the use of the verbs increases noticeably in proportion to that of the noun proper (from 8:47 in *A* to 23:83 in *B*). Nor is it only that the range of such verbs deployed in *B* is very much widened, though this deserves comment in view of Urmson's generalisation that 'the verb *hêdesthai* is far less common in the *EN* than *chairein*' ([160], p. 333). The fact is that in *A* only *chairein* occurs (8 times), whereas in *B* it is easily overtaken by *hêdesthai* (12 to *chairein* 7) as well as being joined by *terpein* (2),

147

agapân (1) and *areskesthai* (1). This in itself is some evidence of the perfunctory treatment of the notion of enjoying in *A*, by contrast with the new sensitivity to it in *B*. But the most significant difference is that at various cardinal points in *B*, but never in *A*, the argument turns directly on an appeal to the behaviour of the verb. It will be worth reviewing the cases.

(1) 1173a15-22. Some hold that pleasure cannot be good, since pleasure is a matter of degree and goodness is not. But (objects Aristotle) if they base this conclusion on *being pleased*, the same difference of degree can be found in *being just* or *brave, acting justly* or *temperately* (the last expressions being single   148
verbs in the Greek); so the supposed contrast with goodness is not there. Translators commonly render the pleasure-verb here in terms of 'feelings of pleasure', *Lustempfindung*, but Aristotle says nothing of feelings; he is recognising and finding parallels for one feature of the logic of pleasure-verbs, namely that we can say 'He is more pleased than I am', 'I enjoy it less than I used to'. Only the form of the argument matters for us, though there will be one implication to notice later.

Subsequently he turns to the more important business of collecting features of the logic of pleasure-verbs which show that pleasure is not a *kînêsis*, a process from some state to another.

(2) 1173a31-b4. Pleasure cannot be a process like walking (some distance) or growing (to some size), for these can be done quickly or slowly but one can't be pleased or enjoy something either quickly or slowly. One can of course *get* to be pleased as one can get angry quickly; but one can't be so. This mark of process-verbs, that they collect adverbs of relative speed, is of the first importance for Aristotle, as Penner has pointed out ([166], pp. 411-14). It is a corollary of his constant claim that any process must be such as to cover some distance in some time – the distance being either spatial, between two places, or an analogous stretch between different qualities, sizes, etc. This is why he subsequently says (1174b5) that 'the whither and whence make the form' of the process; the criteria of its identity must include the limits of the distance it covers. Now (to pursue the point) it is true that an enjoyment may have to be specified by some object of enjoyment – say the First Rasumovsky – which itself has a beginning and end and intermediate stages. The quartet may accordingly be played quickly or slowly. But if it is played quickly it does not follow that I enjoy it (or hear it) quickly. If it is left half-played then, in the sense of 'pleasure' appropriate to *A*, I have an unfinished pleasure; but, in the sense appropriate to *B*, I have not half-enjoyed something. (There is another sense, suggested by the argument under (1) above, in which I may only half-enjoy what I hear.)

(3) 1173b7-13. This passage may suggest that after all *B* does share *A*'s   149
interpretation of the theory that pleasure is a *kînêsis*, for what Aristotle rejects here, as he does in 1153a2-4, is the claim that pleasure is 'a replenishment of nature'. But notice the radically different treatment of the thesis. In *A* he argued that not the process of replenishment but the resultant activity of the natural state was the pleasure, i.e. the proper functioning of the 'established nature'. This evidently allows the pleasure to be identified with the behaviour of the healthy body. But in *B* he argues the enjoyment-verbs cannot have 'my body' as subject. It is the body that is replenished, so if '. . . is replenished' is treated as equivalent to or as a specification of '. . . is pleased', the subject-gap in the second should also be

fillable by 'my body'; but we jib at this (*ou dokei de*). Rather, one (a person, *tis*) can be pleased when his body is being replenished. So once more, *A* asks what is enjoyed or enjoyable, and is accordingly ready to argue: a bodily function. But *B* asks what enjoying is, and by considering the logical requirements on subjects for enjoyment-verbs replies: not a bodily function.

(4) 1174b7-9. A process (Aristotle's examples have included building a temple, going for a walk) always takes time, but being pleased can be whole in an instant. Of course Aristotle does not mean that I can be pleased but pleased for no time; his point is rather that if I am enjoying doing something which takes time to complete, the construction appropriate to the subordinate verb does not transfer to the verb of enjoyment.

(5) 1174a14-b7. I shall not dwell on this text, possibly the most-discussed in *B*. Aristotle compares pleasure with seeing and contrasts it with processes such as temple-building, traversing a distance and other motions represented by verbal nouns. All these latter have stages and at any intermediate stage are still unfinished; one can't find a process complete of its kind at any arbitrary time in its progress. None of this holds good of enjoying or seeing (though, to be sure, it can hold good of what is enjoyed).

That Aristotle is concerned here still with the logic of enjoyment-verbs is, I think, clear. Conventionally he is represented as noticing that, if I say 'I am enjoying the First Rasumovsky', it would be bizarre to reply 'I am sorry you have not yet enjoyed it', while the same form of reply to 'I am making myself a winter coat' would be wholly in order. But he does not expressly import these familiar and debatable connexions between present- and perfect-tense utterances into this passage (and indeed the verb '*hēdesthai*' had no known perfect tense). What he insists on is the unfinishedness of processes if we consider them stage by stage. They are complete, if at all, only in the whole time they take (1174a27-9 – but the 'if at all', '*eiper*', may mean only 'doubtless'). So it is natural to think that he is calling attention to the possibility that the building of a temple, unlike enjoyment, may be interrupted or remain unachieved. Now this could not be his point if some remarks of Vendler, which have been quoted as throwing light on Aristotle's analysis, give a correct account of the matter. Vendler wrote: 'If I say of a person that he is running a mile or of someone else that he is drawing a circle, then I do claim that the first one will keep running until he has covered the mile and that the second will keep drawing until he has drawn the circle. If they do not complete their activities, my statement will turn out to be false' ([168], p. 145). But suppose you interrupt me when I am drawing a circle and the circle is never finished; it cannot follow that I was not drawing a circle. For if what I was drawing was not a circle but the circle-fragment left on my paper, you did not interrupt my drawing. If Aristotle's view were Vendler's, he could not accept the possibility of any process such as the building of a house or walking to London remaining finally incomplete. But there seems to be no ground for fathering this unsatisfactory view upon Aristotle.

(Indeed, I suspect that in *Metaphysics* VII 7-9 Aristotle runs into paradox concerning the role of 'a statue' in 'I am making a statue' partly because the truth of that statement does not require an actual statue to emerge. But that is another matter.)

You may indeed feel qualms at the suggestion that the world contains unfinished processes – as though there could be journeys from Oxford to London that ended at Reading. But that would mistake the point. If my journey to London remains incomplete I shall not be entitled subsequently to say that I *did go* or *have gone* to London on that occasion, only that I was going there; but that leaves the truth of my present claim 'I am going to London' untouched. When Aristotle uses a present tense to describe a process he standardly has in mind the imperfective sense represented by the continuous form in English; that is why he is unwilling to use that tense to say that something comes to have a certain character at some instant, and prefers to say that from that first instant it *has* come to have the character (*Phys.* 263b21-264a6). Nor, as his example of an object changing colour shows (*ibid.*), are such uses of the tense confined to contexts where the idea of intention need figure in the analysis.

151

So the point holds firm. There is no reason to deny that Aristotle is interested in the possibility of interrupting some process without falsifying the natural description of what is interrupted. And 'enjoying' can never stand for such a process.

Conclusions

There the case may rest. When Aristotle rejects the thesis that pleasure is a process in *A*, he is offering to tell us what our real pleasures are, what is really enjoyed or enjoyable. When he rejects a thesis in the same form of words in *B*, he is offering to tell us what the nature of enjoying is by reviewing the logical characteristics of pleasure-verbs. In *B* he moves naturally to the question what the enjoying contributes to the enjoyed activity, and apart from one peripheral hint there is no sign of that question in *A*.

No doubt the arguments of *B* suggest one explanation of the shift. What persuades him to decide there that it is 'absurd' to say the pleasure is the thinking or perceiving? He has noticed, we may guess, that many epithets of the thinking do not transfer to the pleasure, however much that pleasure may be the pleasure of that thinking. Circular or syllogistic thinking cannot without joking be called a circular or syllogistic pleasure. And the point comes out more sharply when processes are allowed to be enjoyable, as they are in *B*. If I enjoy building or dining quickly I do not quickly enjoy building or dining. So the question becomes: what can be said about enjoying *X*-ing that cannot be said about *X*-ing, and the converse? Verbs and their adverbs, and then their other logical features, take the centre of the enquiry; and for the philosophically suspect enterprise of *A* are substituted the admirable studies of *B*.

But the residual problem remains unresolved. It is not enough to say that Aristotle shifts his interest, so that what he says in *A* is broadly compatible with what he says in *B*. The rub is that he uses the same expressions to identify the theories he rejects in *A* and *B*, and these are theories of quite different types. In both contexts he claims to be explaining *what pleasure is*. That remarkable and, I think, unremarked ambiguity I can only commend to your curiosity. But it is not clear that we need expect a philosophical explanation for it; and what had to be removed was a block to the philosophical assessment of Aristotle's arguments.

152

10

Pierre Defourny

Contemplation in Aristotle's Ethics[1]

89 This article aims at a precise definition of the object of that supreme activity which the *Ethics* presents as both the ultimate norm of action and the source of happiness. Jaeger's *Aristotle* is, as so often, the starting-point. Leaving on one side the *Magna Moralia*, I shall examine in turn Chapter 3 of the last book of the *Eudemian Ethics* (VIII 3, 1249a21-b23) and Chapters 7 and 8 of the tenth book of the *Nicomachean Ethics* (X7, 1177a12-8, 1178b32).

In planning his moral life, man finds himself in a position of choice between a large number of goods, devoid in themselves of any moral property. He then has to decide to what extent he should enjoy these goods; for wealth, fame, and popularity, excellent in themselves, engender moral evil if they become the tools of an evil man, and even if they are heaped too generously in the lap of a good man. Morality should therefore lay down an ultimate 90 criterion to determine the proper balance, the mean, of permissible external goods. This is the problem Aristotle seeks to solve at the end of the *Eudemian Ethics*.

> But since the doctor has a standard (*horos*) by reference to which he distinguishes the healthy from the unhealthy body, and with reference to which each thing up to a certain point ought to be done and is wholesome, while if less or more is done health is the result no longer, so in regard to actions and choice of what is naturally good but not praiseworthy, the good man should have a standard both of disposition and of choice, and similarly in regard to avoidance of excess or deficiency of wealth and good fortune. (1249a21-b3)

The solution which suggests reason as the answer is too general: 'The standard being – as above said – 'as reason (*logos*) directs'; this corresponds to saying in regard to diet that the standard should be medical science and its principles. But this, though true, is not clear' (1249b3-6). In the whole of his treatise the only criterion that Aristotle has used to establish the mean is *logos* or *orthos logos*, reason or right reason. We should therefore remember that our final criterion will go further than this; for it is too vague, just as the advice to eat scientifically fails to explain to the patient which foods he should avoid.

1. As a scholar on the Viscountess Adolphe de Spoelberch foundation, the author benefited from a stay in Rome to complete a study of Aristotle's religious philosophy; this article is a part of that work.

In his inquiry Aristotle relies on the maxim of the subordination of a function or its exercise to its principle, a maxim which he immediately applies to man's psychological make-up. From this starting-point, two steps will lead him to the *horos* he is seeking.

(1) 'One must, then, here as elsewhere, live with reference to the ruling principle (*pros to archon*) and with reference to the formed habit (*hexis*) and the activity of the ruling principle, as the slave must live with reference to that of the master, and each of us by the rule proper to him (*pros tên hekastou kathêkousan archên*). But since man is by nature composed of a ruling (*archontos*) and a subject (*archomenou*) part, each of us should live according to the governing element within himself' (1249b6-11). These two parts are the only ones so far recognised in the *Eudemian Ethics* which distinguishes between the rational soul (*logon echôn*) which commands (*epitattein*), and the irrational soul (*alogos*) which obeys (*peithesthai, akouein*) the other, or which follows it (*akolouthêtikos*) (1219b26-31; 1220a8-11). It is obvious that the irrational part of the soul has its principle in the rational soul, and must obey it. In spite of this we cannot accept the latter as the *horos* of action. Reason characterises it as *archon*; but reason, like the art of medicine, in itself tells us nothing about what we should or should not do. The first step in the analysis only raises our new point of view to the level already occupied by the account at the beginning of the discussion.

(2) In a more thorough investigation of the theory of the guiding principle, Aristotle reaches the *horos*. 'But this is ambiguous, for medical science governs ·in one sense, health in another, the former existing for the latter' (1249b12-13). This distinction is suggestive; it invites us to look for the *end* which lies behind what first appears as the principle. Reason, and the part of the soul possessing reason, were both principles in the way medicine is. Is there, in the soul, another principle which, like health, is the ultimate end, the norm? 'And so it is with the theoretic faculty (*kata to theôrêtikon*)', answers Aristotle (1249b14). He has let fall the great word. What does it mean?

(A) It implies a psychological theory which is totally absent from the main part of the *Eudemian Ethics*. It reminds us, indeed, of the famous distinction within the rational soul between a *praktikos logos* and a *theôrêtikos logos*, between a *logistikon meros* and an *epistêmonikon*.[2] *Theôrêtikos logos* and the *epistêmonikon* are certainly identical; they both refer to the power of contemplation in the soul. The *theôrêtikon* in our *Ethics* is precisely this.

(B) To dispel any uncertainty, the *Nicomachean Ethics*[3] returns to the simile of health and medicine, in order to establish the connexion between the two parts of the rational soul; it compares wisdom, a virtue of the theoretic soul, to health, and describes it as the goal, *hou heneka*, of lower activities (*EN* VI 13, 1145a6-9).

(C) Lastly, the further depiction of the *theôrêtikon* as an ultimate principle

2. See *EN* VI 1, 1139a5-15; *Pol.* VII 14, 1333a16-30, where the distinction is clearly explained.

3. The expression '*Nicomachean Ethics*' is incorrect, since Book VI, to which I frequently refer, also forms part of the *Eudemian Ethics*. By *Nicomachean Ethics* I therefore mean its ten books, which include Books IV-VI of the *Eudemian Ethics*; by *Eudemian Ethics* I mean the books which are peculiar to it, namely I-III and VII-VIII.

92   shows convincingly that Aristotle is already thinking in terms of the *Nicomachean Ethics*: 'For God is not an imperative ruler (*epitaktikôs archôn*), but is the end with a view to which prudence (*phronêsis*) issues its commands (*epitattei*)' (1249b13-15). The text needs a twofold explanation.

   (a) First, God (*ho theos*) suddenly supersedes the *theôrêtikon*. Further on, however, *hê tou theou theôria* (1249b17) and *ton theon . . . theôrein* (b20) occur as synonymous expressions. This proves that the ultimate norm is a very specific kind of contemplation: the study of God. Compared with less elevated activities, the faculty of contemplation (*theôrêtikon*), the study of God (*theôria tou theou*), and the object of contemplation (*ho theos*), merge in the perspective of a single goal.[4] There is no need to invoke the deity in person and so to imbue the close of the *Eudemian Ethics* with a religious intensity.[5] Here, as in the *Nicomachean Ethics*, it is the study of the divine which crowns the hierarchy of human activities, and which they should all seek to further.

   (b) In *epitattein*, forbidden to contemplation and reserved for *phronêsis*, we discover again the more developed ideas of the *Nicomachean Ethics*. There 'commanding' is the proper function of *phronêsis*, which, drawing its inspiration from *sophia*, dictates to practical action what acts it should perform.[6] I shall later have occasion to show that *sophia* (wisdom) corresponds exactly to *theôria tou theou* (see below, p. 109).

   Comparison with these sections of the *Nicomachean Ethics* makes the end of
93 the *Eudemian Ethics* perfectly clear. All Aristotle's argument manifests a fourfold parallelism of ideas: in his most general remarks he speaks of the subordinate object, of its immediately superior guiding principle, and of its ultimate aim; he compares the three links to the diet that should be followed and to the medical skill that gives concrete instructions as to the patient's health. With the moral question in mind, he seeks the *horos* which will inspire reason, in an attempt to determine exactly how external goods should be used; and at last the definitive solution is provided by the hierarchy of the faculties: the irrational soul is guided by *phronêsis*, which is sovereign in its own domain while obeying the demands of a supreme activity, *theôria tou theou*.[7]

---

   4. There is another example of the same grouping in *De Anima* III 10-11, where Aristotle is seeking the cause of bodily movements, and finds it in the *orektikon* (faculty), as well as in *orexis* (activity) and in the *orekton* (object desired).

   5. Fritzsche, in his *Aristotelis Ethica Eudemia* (1851), has this translation: 'Sed non verbis conceptis mandata dat et imperat Deus, qui ille princeps et gubernator est, sed ob eundem finem praecepta dat, ob quem prudentia.' Von Arnim, *Die drei aristotelischen Ethiken* (*Akad. d. Wiss. in Wien, Philos.-histor.Klasse Sitzungsber.*, Bd. 202, 2 Abh.) felt so strongly the impossibility of taking *ho theos* as a personal god that he suggested the emendation *ho nous*. Jaeger, *op. cit.*, insists on the religious nature of the passage. See the texts quoted below on p. 107.

   6. *EN* VI 13, 1145a6-9: '<*phronêsis*> *epitattei* for the sake of <*sophia*>'; 10, 1143a8: 'for *phronêsis* is *epitaktikê*'.

   7. Von Arnim suggests equating the soul's *archon* at 1249b10 with the principle which in the health analogy corresponds to *nous* (*ho theos*). Similarly, he forms the equation: *archomenon* = *iatrikê* = *phronêsis*. Von Arnim fails to grasp that if the *archon* is the rational soul, then the aim of the health analogy is precisely to find a principle superior to the *archon*. In von Arnim's terms we must form three equations: on the

Whatever choice, then, or possession of the natural goods – whether bodily goods, wealth, friends, or other things – will most produce the contemplation of God (*theôria tou theou*), that choice or possession is best; this is the noblest standard (*horos*), but any that through deficiency or excess hinders one from the contemplation (*theôrein*) and service of God is bad; this man possesses in his soul, and this is the best standard for the soul – to perceive the irrational part of the soul, as such, as little as possible. (1249b16-23)

We must devote a moment's thought more to *phronêsis*, on account of the important role assigned to it by Jaeger: 'By *phronêsis* the *Eudemian Ethics* understands, like Plato and the *Protrepticus*, the philosophical faculty that beholds the highest real value, God, in transcendental contemplation, and makes this contemplation the standard of will and action; it is still both theoretical knowledge of supersensible being and practical moral insight'. Directed both to the world of speculation and to the world of morality, it is 'the transformer' which converts knowledge of the divine *archê* into an intention that can guide action. Thus 'ethical action is striving towards God' ([25], pp. 239-40). Again: 'The conclusion of the *Eudemian Ethics* is the *locus classicus* for theonomic ethics as taught by Plato in his later days. God is the measure of all things' (*ibid.*, p. 243).

Behind Jaeger's description lurks a theory: the *Eudemian Ethics*, in accordance with Jaeger's general account of Aristotle's development, represents the *Urethik*. *Phronêsis* is evidence of the development of Aristotle's thought. Here, as in the *Protrepticus* (Aristotle's Platonising dialogue), it is the activity of understanding which is both immersed in study of the divine and simultaneously the guiding principle of moral action. Later, when Aristotle is freed from the Platonic tyranny, it will lose its ascendency: a new function of the soul will account for contemplation, and *phronêsis*, transformed into prudence, will become its slave, directing only the less exalted of the soul's activities.

My interpretation of the end of the *Eudemian Ethics* suggests, on the contrary, a conception of *phronêsis* identical with the *phronêsis* of the *Nicomachean Ethics;* there are clear indications that it is subordinate to, rather than identical with, the *theôrêtikon*. It is, however, certain that the earlier *Ethics* recognises a *phronêsis* which is a supreme speculative faculty. In the description of one of the kinds of life that men generally accept as happy, the phrases 'contemplative life', 'philosopher's life', and 'life of *phronêsis*' are used indiscriminately[8]; Anaxagoras, who regularly appears as an advocate of this life, portrays the wise man as 'engaged in some divine contemplation' (*EE* I 4, 1215b12), or again as wishing to live 'in order to contemplate the

94

lowest level, *archomenon* = what *phronêsis* commands; in the rational soul, *archon* = *iatrikê* = *phronêsis*; crowning the hierarchy, *hugieia* = *to theôrêtikon* = *ho theos* (*nous* in von Arnim).

Von Arnim's ideas on the passage in question are to be found in *Die drei aristotelischen Ethiken*, pp. 67 ff.; *Eudemische Ethik und Metaphysik*, pp. 25ff.; *Das Ethische in Aristoteles Topik*, pp. 35ff. (*Akad.d. Wiss. in Wien, Philos.-histor. Klasse, Sitzungsber.*, Bd. 202, 2 Abh.; Bd. 207, 5 Abh.; Bd. 205, 4 Abh.).

8. *EE* I 1, 1214a32; 4, 1215a34,b1; 5, 1216a19, 29, 38.

heavens and the order of the universe' (*EE* I 5, 1216a13). Only the vocabulary is rejected; Aristotle returns to ideas which he has already expressed, but which are now no more than an introduction to new analyses in which the function of *phronêsis* has passed to the *theôrêtikon*.

95   We are speedily convinced by the first book of the *Nicomachean Ethics* that happiness is the goal towards which men direct all their energies and also the principle which rightly governs their moral life.[9] However, it is not until the last book of the *Ethics* that we discover the nature of the activity which must supply that happiness.[10] The section dealing with happiness is unique in Aristotle's work, both for its lyrical style and for the richness of its thought; it finds in the speculative life all the characteristics of happiness:

> So if among virtuous actions political and military actions are distinguished by nobility and greatness, and these are unleisurely and aim at an end and are not desirable for their own sake, but the activity of reason (*hê tou nou energeia*), which is contemplative, seems both to be superior in serious worth and to aim at no end beyond itself, and to have its pleasure proper to itself (and this augments the activity), and the self-sufficiency, leisureliness, unweariedness (so far as this is possible for man), and all the other attributes ascribed to the supremely happy man are evidently those connected with this activity, it follows that this will be the complete happiness of man, if it be allowed a complete term of life (for none of the attributes of happiness is *in*complete). But such a life would be too high for man; for it is not in so far as he is man that he will live so, but in so far as something divine is present in him (*hêi theion ti en autôi huparchei*); and by so much as this is superior to our composite nature is its activity superior to that which is the exercise of the other kind of virtue. If, then, reason is divine (*ei dê theion ho nous*) in comparison with man, the life according to it is divine (*ho kata touton <noun> bios theios*) in comparison with human life. But we must not follow those who advise us, being men, to think of human things, and, being mortal, of mortal things, but must, so far as we can, make ourselves immortal (*<chrê> eph'hoson endechetai athanatizein*), and strain every nerve to live in accordance with the best thing in us; for even if it be small in bulk,
96   much more does it in power and worth surpass everything. (*EN* X 7, 1177b16-1178a2).

Such a life promises men the special protection of the gods:

> Now he who exercises his reason and cultivates it seems to be both in the best state of mind and most dear to the gods. For if the gods have any care for human affairs, as they are thought to have, it would be

---

9. The terms *archê, telos, horos* and *tês aretês athlon kai telos* often refer to happiness.
10. Margueritte has attempted to find a closer link between the first and the tenth books. He believes that X, 1178a23-1179a32, was once part of Book I, coming at the end of Chapter 8 between 1099b8 and b9 ('Une lacune dans le livre I de l'Éthique à Nicomaque', *Revue d'hist. de la philos.* 1930, pp. 176-88).

reasonable both that they should delight in that which was best and most akin to them (i.e. reason), and that they should reward those who love and honour this most, as caring for the things that are dear to them and acting both rightly and nobly. (*EN* X 8, 1179a22-9)

Happiness is reduced to three main characteristics:
(1) It is identical with a speculative activity of the mind.
(2) It is linked to *nous*, our most divine attribute, as its source.
(3) Happiness transcends man and immortalises him.

(1) While Aristotle is usually content to describe happiness as a speculative activity, can we say that happiness and speculation are exactly coextensive? A close examination suggests not. Aristotle also uses the terms *sophia* and *sophos* to identify happiness and the happy man.[11] Now wisdom (*sophia*) occupies a strictly limited area of theoretical activity: that of beauty and divinity (*EN* X 7, 1177a15); it is the knowledge of the noblest goods (*EN* VI 7, 1141b3). The wise man, according to Thales and Anaxagoras, contemplates things which are 'excellent, admirable, difficult, and divine' (*EN* VI 7, 1141b6-7). The *Magna Moralia*, which often explains the *Nicomachean Ethics*, also defines the object of wisdom as the eternal and the divine (*MM* I 35, 1197b7-8). Hence, the science which makes men happy seems to be that branch of theoretical knowledge which centres round God and everything connected with him, a branch which the *Metaphysics* describes as first philosophy or theology, though sometimes adopting the less technical terminology of the *Ethics*.[12]

Ross, however, believes that it is the practice of theoretical knowledge in all its three forms that constitutes happiness: philosophy, mathematics, and physics ([15], p. 234). One text in particular seems to support his view. Aristotle is trying to prove that happiness is a theoretical activity. He begins by explaining how ridiculous it would be to see the gods' happiness as anything other than a speculative activity. And he continues:

of human activities, therefore, that which is most akin to this must be most of the nature of happiness. This is indicated too by that fact that the other animals have no share in happiness; being completely deprived of such activity. For while the whole life of the gods is blessed, and that of men too in so far as some likeness of such activity belongs to them, none of the other animals is happy, since they in no way share in contemplation. Happiness extends, then, just so far as contemplation does, and those to whom contemplation more fully belongs are more truly happy, not as a mere concomitant but in virtue of the contemplation, for this is in itself precious. Happiness, therefore, must be some form of contemplation. (*EN* X 8, 1178b23-32)

This is more than a straightforward identification of contemplation and happiness.

11. *EN* X 7, 1177a24-5 (*sophia, philosophia*), 32-3 (*sophos*); 8, 1179a30, 32 (*sophos*).
12. *Meta.* I 1, 981b28, 982a2; 2, 982a6, 17 (*sophia*). *Sophos* also occurs, e.g., at I 2, 982a9.

(a) Aristotle does not define happiness as contemplation. Assuming that we already have the notion of happiness, he insists on its contemplative nature. The first and last sentences of the extract exactly define the limits of the discussion; further, they suggest that happiness is not *theôria tout court*, but *theôria tis* – a certain sort of contemplation (twice, in lines 8 and 32); we should take this as the *theôria* of the divine.

(b) When Aristotle equates happiness and contemplation, does he not simply mean that where one is possible so is the other? He is thinking of three classes of beings: god, man, and animal. Contemplation is sufficient to establish the same similarity between man and god, and the same separation between man and animals, as were set up by happiness. It is in this sense that the two concepts are coextensive, and there is now nothing to prevent us from specifying happiness as theological contemplation.

(2) *Nous*, the faculty which is the source of the happy life, is man's divine element (*EN* X 7, 1177b27, 30; a15). What does this mean? Zeller hopes to explain its divine character by taking *nous* to be the active intellect of the *De Anima*, which he equates with the mind of God.[13] Boutroux and Hamelin also find the active intellect present in the *nous* of the *Ethics*.[14] The active intellect is divine, and that provides a neat justification of Aristotle's remarks; it is, however, invalidated by a number of objections. (i) The assimilation, loose or strict, of active intellect and divine understanding is not a formal doctrine of the *De Anima* but an interpretation of the commentators. (ii) The *Nicomachean Ethics* makes no distinction between the two intellects and no reference to this psychological problem. (iii) Appeal to the active intellect fails to explain why happiness should exist only in philosophical activity. For it is plain that the soul also moves from potentiality to actuality when the intellect indulges in mathematical and physical speculation. (iv) A final objection: how can the active intellect, which in the *De Anima* seems to be impersonal thought, always actual, and transcendent, be that understanding which is immanent in us and constitutes our very selves?[15]

We must, then, stay within the confines of the *Ethics*. Now here *nous* sometimes has the extended sense which is normal elsewhere in Aristotle – the sense of understanding or reason, a faculty opposed to perception and to desire, whether rational or instinctive.[16] This is the sense that Heliodorus gives to *nous* in Book X of the *Ethics*.[17] We must still explain the divine character, so heavily stressed by Aristotle, which *nous*, if it be human reason,

13. 'Was zunächst die thätige Vernunft betrifft, so könnte es scheinen, sie sei nicht allein das göttliche im Menschen (X 7, 1177a15), sondern von dem göttlichen Geist selbst nicht verschieden' (Zeller, *Philos. der Griechen*, II 2 (Leipzig, 1879), p. 572; also p. 372, n. 6).

14. E. Boutroux's article 'Aristote' in the *Grande Encyclopédie*, vol. 3, p. 346A; O. Hamelin, 'La Morale d'Aristote' (posthumous), *Revue de Métaph.*, 30, 1923, pp. 503-4.

15. *EN* X 7, 1178a7: 'if this especially is what a man is'; 1177b34: 'the most powerful element in us'; 1178a5: 'what is by nature most proper to each of us'.

16. There is no need here to raise issue with *nous* as an intellectual virtue, since we are looking for a faculty. *Nous*, as a virtue, is the intuitive understanding of first principles, and as such is also an element in *sophia* (*EN* VI 7, 1141a19).

17. *Nous* in the sense of reason is frequent, e.g. IX 8, 1169a17-18, referred to by Heliodorus in connexion with X 7, 1177a20-1: 'For as was said in the account of

does not particularly deserve. The introduction to Aristotle's account of happiness contains this suggestive remark:

> If happiness is activity in accordance with virtue, it is reasonable that
> it should be in accordance with the highest virtue; and this will be
> that of the best thing in us. Whether it be reason or something else
> that is this element which is thought to be our natural ruler and guide
> and to take thought of things noble and divine, whether it be itself
> also divine or only the most divine element in us, the activity of this in
> accordance with its proper virtue will be perfect happiness. (X 7,
> 1177a12-17)

It emerges that on the one hand activity – virtue – plainly is a determinant of happiness, and that all doubts centre round the faculty in question and the exact nature of its divine being. Surely this is an invitation to look for the origin of the epithet *divine* in this activity? The right of this latter to be called divine is expressly allowed by Aristotle in the *Metaphysics*: knowledge is divine only under two conditions: (i) it must deal with things divine; (ii) it must be worthy of God's possession. Philosophy alone satisfies both these conditions. (i) It is a science that studies the divine. This is obvious for the theoretical science described above, and it also holds for philosophy as Aristotle sees it in the *Metaphysics*, the study of the most general causes; for 'God seems the cause and principle of all things'. (ii) 'God alone, or at any rate God above all others, may possess it'.[18] Thus if Aristotle, having registered his reluctance to allow *nous* divine characteristics, describes it without more ado as divine, may we not say that the adjective proper to the philosophical activity has been transferred to the faculty? The word *theios* (divine) will thus have more than a purely metaphorical value: a study wherein men may discover a perfect life has a real connexion with divinity, in virtue of which it may itself be called divine; and by extension everything associated with it – the understanding that nurtures it (*nous*), the life that it controls (*bios*), the happiness it inspires,[19] and even the man who devotes himself to it[20] – may share the same epithet.

Perhaps it is possible to find out why Aristotle insists more on the divinity of *nous* than on that of its activity. There was a philosophical tradition

100

---

friendship (i.e. IX 8), *nous* is what it is to be us, and for that reason its activity is best' (*Comm. in Arist. Graeca*, XIX, pp. 221, 38-222, 2).

18. *Meta.* I 2, 983a5-10. Ross, fearing that a philosophical god may not know the world, assumes that Aristotle is not speaking precisely (*Aristotle's Metaphysics*, I, p. 123). The assumption is unfounded, since Aristotle, following up Simonides' view, cannot be accused of negligence; and the fear is unjustified since God, knowing himself, knows also the most perfect of causes and hence has a high degree of philosophical knowledge without bending his mind to anything other than his own nature. Hence we can account for the passage.

19. In the very first book of the *Ethics*, happiness is depicted as divine (I 1, 1094b7-10); in respect of the deference with which men treat it, it is on the same level as the gods (I 12, 1101b18-30).

20. *EN* I 12, 1101b23-5: 'For we call the gods blessed and happy, and of men we call blessed the most divine (*theiotatos*)'.

asserting the presence of a divine element in men, or the ontological participation of the intellectual soul in divine Being, a tradition that Aristotle had accepted in the early dialogues;[21] he was still under its influence in those sections of the *Eudemian Ethics* dealing with chance;[22] he alludes to it again when he asks whether *nous* may not be divine in itself, and, by showering *nous* with divine epithets, he remains linguistically faithful to this tradition without parading the basic incompatibility between his new theory and his previous views.

(3) Lastly, we should not be misled by the description of happiness as superhuman, transcending the powers of the composite man. We only have to state what in this context Aristotle means by the higher life and human life. Aristotle contrasts the happiness of a speculative life with a secondary happiness resulting from practising the moral virtues. These are the 'properly human virtues', the 'virtues of the composite', because body and soul collaborate organically in order to practise them.[23] Doubtless intellectual virtues need the body to a certain extent; but for them it is at best a *sine qua non*, at worst an obstacle.[24] Primary happiness is therefore superhuman and a thing apart, not because it implies a divine intervention transcendent over men, but because the purity of its practice elevates it above all inferior powers.

After this twofold examination, it is easy to see that at bottom the activity put forward in the *Eudemian Ethics* as the *horos* of action is identical with that advanced in the *Nicomachean Ethics* as the source of happiness. The difference of emphasis that Jaeger sees does not exist; you cannot set off the religious inspiration of the one against the rationalism of the other ([25], p. 243). In both works, Aristotle envisaged only *theôria tou theou*; the two differ only in this, that whereas the end of the *Eudemian Ethics* describes the object of contemplation, God, and leaves us to discover the human faculty in question, the *Nicomachean Ethics* describes the speculative activity of *nous* and leaves us to find its divine object. The true difference between the two works is quite other: it concerns the part which *theôria* has to play in life as a whole. Without doubt, in the *Nicomachean Ethics* it is the supreme end of all action, giving men simultaneously both happiness and moral perfection. In the *Eudemian Ethics*, although the first books give promise of a *horos* which establishes a mean for *virtue*, the conclusion ignores the virtues and considers the *horos* only in connexion with external goods. This problem remains unsolved: the *Nicomachean Ethics* appears to have expanded the role of *theôria tou theou* to include the whole moral order.

21. See the dialogues *Eudemus, Protrepticus*, and *On Philosophy*; these fragments have been most thoroughly collated by Walzer, *Aristotelis dialogorum Fragmenta* (Florence, 1934).

22. The *Eudemian Ethics* examines divine fortune, which appears to be caused by *to en hêmin theion* (1248a27), taken to mean a divine presence in the soul.

23. *EN* X 8, 1178a9-14: 'And secondly a life in accordance with the other virtue; for activities in accordance with this are human; for they are just and courageous and the rest; ... and all these seem to be human'. 1178a20-1; 'The virtues of the composite are human.'

24. *EN* X 9, 1178b3-5: 'But in general they are actually impediments, to contemplation at least.'

11

K. von Fritz and E. Kapp

The Development of Aristotle's Political Philosophy and the Concept of Nature

In one of Aristotle's early works, the *Protrepticus*, which, in all likelihood, was written and published when Aristotle was still a member of Plato's Academy,[1] we find the following passage:

> Just as he will not be a good builder who does not use the rule or the other instruments of this kind,[2] but takes his measure from other buildings; so he will not be a good lawmaker or a serious statesman who gives his laws or administers the affairs of the state with a view to, or in imitation of, the actions of others or of the consitutions of actual human communities as, for instance, those of the Lacedaemonians or of the Cretans. For a copy of that which is not beautiful itself cannot be beautiful, nor can the nature of that which is not divine and stable be imperishable and stable. (frag. 13 in Ross)

From this statement, it seems a far cry to the last sentences of Aristotle's *Nicomachean Ethics*, which lead over to the latest version of his *Politics*. For here he emphasises the importance of experience for the lawmaker and the statesman and then concludes with the following words:

> First, then, we shall try to review whatever valuable suggestions have been made by earlier writers [namely, in regard to the different problems of political philosophy]; then we shall attempt, on the basis of our collections of constitutions, to find out what things contribute to the preservation or the destruction of states in general and what things help to preserve or to destroy particular types of constitutions, and finally also, for what reasons some states are well governed and others the opposite. For once we have considered these problems, we shall, perhaps, be better able to discern what the best state must be like, and also how each given type of state must be ordered, and what laws and customs it should have in order to function as well as possible. (1181b15-22)

1. Aristotle entered the Academy in 368/7 at the age of seventeen while Plato was absent in Sicily, and remained in the Academy until after Plato's death in 348/7. He left only after Plato's nephew Spcusippus had been elected head of the Academy.
2. Namely the plummet, the compass, etc.

Yet the two points of view are by no means so far apart as it may seem at first sight, and it would be quite misleading to say that in the *Protrepticus* Aristotle speaks as a 'rationalist' pure and simple, while in the *Nicomachean Ethics* he speaks as an 'empiricist' pure and simple. To determine as exactly as possible in what respects the Aristotle of the *Protrepticus* agrees and in what respects he disagrees with the Aristotle of the *Nicomachean Ethics* is most important for a full understanding of the relation between Aristotle's historical studies and his final political theory.

The *Protrepticus* was an exhortation to the study of philosophy addressed to Themison, the king of Cyprus. Not only this fact in itself but the whole content of the treatise, of which a very considerable part has come down to us, proves beyond doubt that, at the time when Aristotle wrote it, he still believed in Plato's famous doctrine that kings should become philosophers or philosophers kings. Some years later, in his treatise on kingship which he addressed to his former pupil, Alexander the Great, he wrote that not only was it not necessary for a king to become a philosopher but it was a positive hindrance in his work; instead, a good king should listen to the true philosophers and be agreeable to their advice.[3] In regard to this point, then, undoubtedly Aristotle in the *Protrepticus* was still a Platonist while later he disagreed with his former master. Yet the *Protrepticus*, though unquestionably written under the strong influence of Plato and the Academy, is by no means entirely Platonic. In fact, even the mere extracts of the work that have come down to us contain an amazing number of ideas and statements which, in a slightly different wording, recur in the most fundamental sections of the theoretical works of Aristotle's most mature period.

The sentence from the *Protrepticus* quoted at the beginning of the present chapter seems to reveal Aristotle as essentially still a Platonist, since it appears to contain a direct application to lawmaking and political activity of Plato's contention (*Rep.* VI, 500B-D) that only the philosopher, who looks at eternal ideas and not at things in space and time, which are but imperfect 'imitations' of ideas, can know the truth and guide himself and others according to the truth.[4] But the question is much more complicated.

Plato, in the beginning of Book X of the *Republic*, speaks of the craftsman who makes a couch or a table not by looking at and slavishly imitating another couch or another table, but by looking at the idea of a couch or a table and so producing something which may be different from any existing real couch or table but which is still a good couch or table, fulfilling the function or purpose of a couch or a table. Certainly, instead of speaking of these pieces of household furniture, Plato in this connexion might just as well have spoken of a house. This, however, only makes it clearer that Aristotle in the *Protrepticus* did not use the theory of ideas in this form. For, if this had been the case, the sentence quoted at the beginning would have been formulated as follows: 'Just as he will not be a good architect who does

---

3. It need hardly be mentioned that this sentence is almost identical with part of Kant's famous statement on the relation of kings and philosophers in *Zum ewigen Frieden, Zweiter Zusatz zum Zweiten Abschnitt.*

4. The sentence is actually interpreted in this way by W.W. Jaeger [25], pp. 90ff. But cf. W. Theiler, *Zur Geschichte der teleologischen Naturbetrachtung bis auf Aristoteles* (Zürich, 1925), pp. 87ff. and E. Kapp, *Mnemosyne* 6 (1939), pp. 185ff.

not look at the idea of a house and at its purpose, but imitates actually existing buildings; so he will not be a good lawmaker who takes actually existing constitutions as his models instead of looking at the idea of a state.' Instead of mentioning the idea of the house, however, Aristotle refers to the use by the builder of exact tools, as, for instance, the plummet, the rule, and the compass; and, in the second half of the sentence, which is not very clearly formulated in Iamblichus' extract from Aristotle's *Protrepticus*, reference is made to nature rather than to the idea of the state. What does this mean? What is the meaning of 'nature' in this context, and what, in the activity of the lawmaker and the serious statesman, according to Aristotle, corresponds to the exact tools of the builder?

In order to find an answer, it must first be pointed out that Plato himself never speaks of an idea of the state and that, in fact, such a concept never enters into his political philosophy. Plato does speak on various occasions of the truly wise statesman, especially in his *Politicus* (292Dff., 300C-E), which probably was written not very long before Aristotle wrote his *Protrepticus*. This truly wise statesman – one might also say the ideal statesman, though the word 'ideal' is not found in Plato's terminology – according to Plato, is superior to the laws. For the laws[5] are, of necessity, always general rules which set down what should be done in certain types of cases. Since the incidents of human life, however, are infinitely varied, even the best laws are too rigid to deal adequately with this infinite variety. In order to illustrate further the relation between the truly wise statesman and the laws, Plato uses the analogy of the doctor (*Pol.* 295 C). Since the doctor cannot always be   36 around the patient, he will prescribe the rules for the latter's treatment. The rules have to be followed strictly by the friends and relatives of the patient, as they are intelligent enough to apply the rules but do not have the doctor's true insight into the nature of the disease. The doctor himself, on the contrary, is not bound by his own prescriptions, which, like the laws, are always of a general nature and therefore hardly ever totally adequate to the infinite variety of incidents that may occur in the development of a disease. Hence, when he comes back to visit the patient, he, with deeper insight, may change the treatment in accordance with the state in which he finds him. In like manner, the truly wise statesman, who is the rarest of human beings and who, even when and where such a man may be found, cannot attend to all matters personally, will set down laws which should be strictly adhered to by those who are able to apply them and who administer the state but who do not share his deeper insight. But he himself must be free to deviate from them whenever the inevitable rigidity of the law does injustice to the claims of the individual case.

There is no room here for a discussion of the implications, the merits and demerits, of Plato's lofty and perhaps somewhat unrealistic theory of the truly wise statesman.[6] But it is necessary for the present purpose to clarify the relation of this Platonic concept to Aristotle's concept of the activity of the true lawgiver and the serious statesman as they are found in the *Protrepticus*. Plato's truly wise statesman is above the law. But he, too, both

---

5. For this and what follows cf. *Politicus* 294Aff.

6. It should, however, be noted that in the *Politicus* the 'truly wise statesman' is considered as so rare an exception that he seems to be introduced to elucidate a point

when making laws and when deviating from them, must have a criterion for
his action. This criterion, however, is not the idea of the state, but the idea
of the just and of the good.

Aristotle, as is known, later rejected Plato's theory of ideas. It is possible
37   that in the period in which he wrote the *Protrepticus* he was still an adherent
of this Platonic theory as Jaeger tried to demonstrate.[7] But in all the rather
extensive extracts from the *Protrepticus* which have come down to us, there is
no direct reference to it; and, in the section on the true lawgiver and the
serious statesman, we find instead the concept of *phusis* or 'nature'.

The term *phusis* is not unfamiliar to Plato, especially in his later writings,
and it is also true that it sometimes occurs in close connexion with the
theory of ideas. But it is never identical with 'idea'. The fact, therefore, that
Plato's truly wise statesman orients himself by looking at the idea of the just
and the good, while Aristotle's true lawgiver and serious statesman derives
his measure from 'nature', is certainly significant.

The Greek concept of *phusis* has a long history which cannot be discussed
in detail in the present context.[8] One very important element in this concept
was developed in early Greek medicine. In medicine, *phusis* is that which
keeps the world in motion and makes things grow, and, more specifically,
that which makes the human body grow and function and restores or tries
to restore it to its normal strength and functions when these have been
impaired or weakened by external injuries or by sickness and disease. The
doctor must study nature in all its manifestations, both in the human body
and in the surrounding world, in order to be able to support it in its struggle
for restoration of the body and its functions against inimical influences.[9]
38   The investigation of 'nature' in this sense certainly contains a strong
element of empiricism, since it is largely based on empirical observation.
Nevertheless, it seems to contain also an element which, in a way,
transcends empirical observation, pure and simple. For the assumption is
always made that 'nature' *aims* at something, namely, perfect health, a
perfect harmony and functioning of the body which is but scarcely, if ever,
realised. This concept of 'nature' is frequently found in Aristotle's writings
and most clearly illustrated by those passages in which he says that 'nature
wishes to do something but cannot quite do it' (cf. e.g. *Pol.* 1255b3).

---

of theory rather than to imply the possibility of his actual appearance on the political
scene.

7. In actual fact, the problem is probably a good deal more complex. There are
strong indications to show that Aristotle at a rather early time and long before Plato's
death began to entertain doubts concerning the validity of the theory of ideas in its
Platonic form, though it was evidently much later that he freed himself completely
from it and definitely attempted to refute it.

8. For special phases of this history, cf. W. Heidel, '*Peri phuseôs*; A study of the
conception of nature in the pre-Socratics', *Proceedings of the Am. Acad. of Arts and
Sciences* 45 (1910), pp. 77-133, and W. Theiler, *op. cit.*

9. The role of the study of nature in medicine is also discussed by Plato in the
Phaedrus 270Bff. In the same context, Plato speaks also of the 'nature' of the soul,
which must be studied by the true orator. Here too, however, nature is not identical
with 'idea'. There is no 'idea' of the soul anywhere in Plato's writings. For the
concept of 'nature' in Greek medicine cf. W. Jaeger, *Paideia*, III, p. 28.

Another element in the complex concept of 'nature' found in Aristotle and other philosophers was developed in the course of what may be called the *nomos-phusis* controversy. This controversy arose from the observation made by the.Greeks in their contact with other nations with different cultural traditions, that what in one country was the most sacred law or custom might be abhorred as impious in another country, and that, nevertheless, there appeared to exist certain moral principles which, though not identically formulated or always applied in all respects in the same fashion, yet, in a general way, seemed to be acknowledged as valid everywhere. From this observation the conclusion was drawn that the laws, rules, or customs of the first kind were man-made and owed their existence to mere 'convention',[10] while the principles of the second type were in some way based on nature, or, as the Greeks said, existed *phusei*, by nature.[11] It was further observed that these latter principles were only partly incorporated, and, within the various nations or political communities, in very different degrees, in the positive or 'written' laws, so that, for instance, in the famous funeral speech which Thucydides attributes to Pericles (II, 37, 3), the greatest moral glory of the Athenians can be found in their obedience to these 'unwritten laws', the violation of which brings shame upon the transgressor but is not punished by a law court.

39

In this form, the theory of the contrast between the conventional and the natural law or laws obviously does not preclude the possibility that the natural law could be completely and adequately incorporated in a written code, though this has never been done. Yet it is not a very far step from the theory in this form to the Platonic view that the incidents of human life are of such an infinite variety that the just and the equitable can never be formulated in general rules or laws in such a way that strict or literal application of the written law will never lead to a violation of true justice or equitableness. Plato's conclusion is that the laws of existing states are doubly imperfect; namely, both for the general reason that a formulated law is always somewhat imperfect because it is too rigid, and for the particular reason that they deviate from the ideal even more than necessary. It is then the test of the truly wise statesman as a lawgiver to make laws which come as near as possible to true justice and equity; but when called upon and able to deal with special situations and individual cases, he will still have to deviate from his own laws, on occasion, because of their inevitable imperfection.

In a way, then, it may be said that Plato continues in the tradition of the theory of natural law.[12] Yet there is a difference which is essential for a full understanding of Aristotle's position in respect to Plato, both in his

10. The word used for 'convention' is the same as the word which means 'law': *nomos*. The difference, then, is that between laws which have merely been set down as laws by human beings and laws or rules which have a foundation in 'nature'.

11. It need hardly be pointed out that there was also a theory according to which the 'natural law' was the rule of the stronger over the weaker. But it is not necessary to discuss this theory in the present chapter.

12. For an excellent discussion of this aspect of Plato's philosophy cf. the article by Joseph P. Maguire, 'Plato's theory of natural law' in *Yale Classical Studies* 10 (1947), pp. 151-78.

Protrepticus and in his later writings, inasmuch as in the early beginnings of a theory of natural law, just as again later in Aristotle's *Protrepticus*, the fundamental concept is 'nature', while Plato speaks of the 'idea' of the just
40   and the good. Plato's ideas are definitely beyond the world in space and time. The wise men must try to see them in all their purity. 'Nature', on the other hand, in the early beginnings of a theory of natural law, just as in early Greek medicine, is something which is common to all human beings, but it is also characterised by its quality of always aiming at something which is rarely, if ever, realised. Like the investigation into 'nature' in early Greek medicine, so also the investigation of 'natural' law is at the same time empirical and in a way transcendent of empirical observation pure and simple. It is quite true that Aristotle in the *Protrepticus* uses terms which are characteristic of Plato's theory of ideas and which Aristotle later does not use any longer in the same context. It is also true that he uses 'nature' in *almost* exactly the same way as Plato uses the idea of the just and the good. The ambiguity of his position between Plato and his own later philosophy is illustrated by the fact that, according to one decisive passage of the *Protrepticus*, the wise statesman must take his criteria of what is just and useful (in an individual case) from nature itself *and from truth*. One may even have different opinions as to how far Aristotle himself, when he wrote the *Protrepticus*, was aware that he was on a road that led away from Platonic philosophy. Yet, with all this, the fact that he did *not* speak of ideas but of nature is certainly highly significant. For this deviation from Platonic philosophy,[13] or at least from Platonic terminology, brought him nearer to the pre-Platonic beginnings of a theory of natural law and to early Greek medicine and medical anthropology. It made it possible for him later to abandon Plato's theory of ideas completely and yet to retain the fundamental principles on which his political philosophy in the *Protrepticus* was based. Above all, it opened to him the road to the historical and
41   empirical exploration of political problems which he later was to undertake on so large a scale, though, at the time when he wrote the *Protrepticus*, he was obviously not yet fully aware of the usefulness of such an undertaking.

If, then, it has been shown that the step from the fundamental principles of the *Protrepticus* to the 'empiricism' of the last paragraphs of the *Nicomachean Ethics* is not so great as it may seem at first sight, it can also be shown that the empiricism of the *Nicomachean Ethics* itself does not go quite so far as a superficial perusal of the sentences quoted at the beginning may lead the reader to expect.

At the end of the tenth book of the *Nicomachean Ethics* (1179a33ff.), Aristotle extemporises a transition from his Ethics, that is, his theory of human happiness, to his Politics, that is, political science in the narrower sense. Stated in the briefest possible way, the idea is this: the mere theory of happiness is not sufficient to make the average human being qualified for happiness. What is needed are good laws providing the right kind of

---

13. It is true that Plato himself, in the *Republic*, when discussing the happiness or blessedness of the just man, also analyses in a way the 'nature' of the human soul, as J.P. Maguire, *op. cit.*, has pointed out. Yet there remains the fact that Aristotle uses the concept of nature in a somewhat different way and in a context in which Plato would not speak simply of nature, but of the idea of the just and the good.

public education for the young and enforcement of right behaviour for those who are grown up. But such laws exist for the time being only in theory, namely, in the new political science as established by Plato[14] and continued and perfected in Aristotle's school. Hence, there is the necessity – even in regard to private education (*EN* 1180a30ff.) – of turning now to the theory of legislation and to political science in general (*EN* 1181b13ff.) Although it is expressly conceded that, in special circumstances, experience alone, without a general scientific foundation, gets excellent results, nevertheless, the superiority of theory over mere experience even for practical results is as strongly emphasised as it had been emphasised in the *Protrepticus*;[15] and the **42** example of the scientifically trained doctor is, at this point, used in the same way in which it is used at the beginning of the *Metaphysics*.[16] There is no indication that, in this respect, Aristotle ever changed his convictions fundamentally. Yet there is a remarkable change in tone. Whereas every line of the chapter from Aristotle's *Protrepticus* seems to express an ethusiastic belief that theory, accessible to none but the philosopher, can and will be the source of all that is truly good in practice, the *Nicomachean Ethics* states in a tone of resignation:

> In the Spartan state alone, or almost alone, the legislator seems to have paid attention to questions of nurture and occupations; in most states such matters have been neglected, and each man lives as he pleases, Cyclops-fashion, 'to his own wife and children dealing law' [Homer, *Od.* IX 114f.]. Now it is best that there should be a public and proper care for such matters; but if they are neglected by the community it would seem right for each man to help his children and friends towards virtue, and that they should have the power, or at least the will, to do this. It would seem from what has been said that he can do this better if he makes himself capable of legislating. (*EN* 1180a25-33)

In other words: even if political theory is not carried into practice by the existing states according to its original meaning, it is still most essential and, under the conditions now prevailing, will have to serve as a guide for educational practice in private circles.

One of the characteristics of a theoretical science is that it can be taught

14. Plato's name does not occur, but his views on education as a major if not the main objective of the art of the wise statesman and legislator are presupposed from the beginning of this whole section. It is less important, though still worth mentioning, that in 1180a5ff. the requirement of 'preambles to laws', of which Plato's *Laws* had made so much (719E and *passim*), is directly referred to and adapted to Aristotle's argument.

15. *EN* 1180b7-28; for the *Protrepticus* see the following note.

16. *EN* 1180b8ff., *Meta.* 981a7-b9. In the *Protrepticus* Aristotle had introduced the geometrician as compared with the practical land-surveyor, the theorist in the field of music as compared with the practical musician, the astronomer as compared with the navigator (fr. 52 in V. Rose's *Aristotelis qui ferebantur liborum Fragmenta*, Leipzig, 1886). But what we have is, unfortunately, only the negative part of the argument, namely, Aristotle's report of how opponents of theory and philosophy use examples like these. In his view, the case of the doctor may have been different.

(*EN* 1180b35ff.; *Meta.* 981b7-9). Who is able to teach political theory? The
43   way in which Aristotle raises and answers this question makes it quite clear
that in his mind political science was taught adequately only in his own
school. He does not consider at all any kind of philosophical competition in
this field, and he disposes of the possible claims of practical politicians and
of the 'sophists' on the political art in the orthodox Platonic way: the
politicians do not teach, because they are guided by experience (*empeiria*)
rather than by thought (*dianoia*); and the 'sophists', who profess the political
art without practising it, simply prove to be absolutely ignorant of what it
takes to teach politics. Aristotle must, of course, have been fully conscious of
the fact that, with regard to the claims of philosophy on political science, he
was taking Plato's position; and, although he does not name Plato (but cf.
n. 14 above), it is unthinkable that he intended to disregard his master in
this field. But when he sums up: 'Now since earlier generations have left the
subject of legislation unexamined, it is perhaps best that we should
ourselves study this, and the problems of political life and constitution in
general, in order to complete, to the best of our ability, the philosophy of
human affairs' (*EN* 1181b13-16), it would seem as if at the time when this
was written he considered himself as the only legitimate follower of Plato in
this field.

So far the trend of the argument is understandable without difficulty;
there is scarcely anything in it that Plato could not have said or had not
actually said. Only in the concluding sentences which outline the contents
of the *Politics* do we find the emphasis already mentioned (above, p. 113) on
the importance of historical and empirical studies, not only for a philosophy
of the political world as it actually is, but even for an understanding of the
problems concerning the 'best constitution'.

If from here we look backwards, we must admit that Aristotle has
managed somehow to prepare us for this turn of thought. When he dealt
with the practical politicians, he had remarked: 'Still, experience seems to
contribute not a little; else they could not have become politicians by
44   familiarity with politics; and so it seems that those who aim at knowing
about the art of politics need experience as well' (*EN* 1181a9-12). Much
more interesting, however, is his section about the 'sophists'. He replaces
the great old sophists, with whom Plato had dealt in his *Protagoras* and in
other dialogues and passages (see especially *Republic* 492A-493D), by
Isocrates, not naming him, but making him the representative of the
'sophists' by an unmistakable quotation.[17]

> Those of the sophists who profess the art [of politics] seem to be very
> far from teaching it. For they do not even know what kind of thing it is
> nor what kinds of things it is about; otherwise they would not have
> classed it as identical with rhetoric or even inferior to it, nor have

17. Isocrates had stuck his neck out by a foolish remark about legislating. In early
times, according to Isocrates (XV, 79ff.), when the first states were founded, it was a
great thing indeed to give laws, but now it has become quite easy for anyone. After
history has produced laws by the ten-thousand, a would-be lawgiver does not need
any creative thinking of his own; all he has to do is to collect out of this vast number
those laws which are favourably known from elsewhere. How much more difficult and
important the task of Isocratean oratory!

thought it easy to legislate by collecting the laws that are thought
well of; they say it is possible to select the best laws, as though even
the selection did not demand intelligence and as though right
judgment were not the greatest thing . . . (*EN* 1181a12-18)

In his attempt to elucidate this point further, Aristotle comes for a second
time to the example of medicine and points out that, in medicine also, the
study of handbooks, however detailed their descriptions of treatments may
be, is not sufficient to produce a doctor, and that, in fact, only the expert
doctor, and not he who lacks his training,[18] can make use of medical books.
Then he goes on (*EN* 1181b6-12):

> Now perhaps also the collections of laws and of constitutions[19] can be   45
> of good use to men capable of theory and capable of judgment
> concerning what is commendable or the opposite and what kinds of
> things are consistent with each other; on the other hand, those who
> go through such collections without firm training cannot possibly
> have sound judgment, unless they have it from nowhere [or: have it as
> a 'gift'], but they will perhaps become better prepared, in this field, to
> understand [what another man says].[20]

Aristotle's words leave no doubt that in the field of political science, just as
in medicine, one has to be an 'expert' first, before one can make appropriate
use of the written material of the collections; not a word is said about how
the expert comes to be an expert. The example of the doctor is here used
only to point out, in an extreme case, that the study of books, or written
material of any kind, will *not* make an expert. But while, in the case of
medicine, the books had been called useless for the non-expert, Aristotle
finally modifies the implications of his example with respect to beginners in
the study of political science. For them a certain familiarity with the
collected material is obviously considered desirable if they are to follow the
lectures on 'Politics' which Aristotle is going to announce.

This is important, because it is the main connecting link between the
preceding discussion and the emphasis on empirical research in the
announcement itself. For if we read in this announcement: '. . . then we

18. Readers of the Greek text should not allow themselves to be confused by the
fact that in 1180b16ff. the man who cures himself or others *di'empeirian* (through mere
experience) was supposed to be *anepistêmôn* ('an unscientific person' in the Oxford
translation), whereas now (1181b6) the *empeiroi* are *opposed* to the *anepistêmones* (those
who lack scientific training). The exact meaning of the words *empeiria, empeiros*
depends entirely on the context.

19. It is clear that Aristotle is now thinking of his own collections of constitutions,
an undertaking which, of course, could not be known to Isocrates, who wrote his
speech XV 'On the Antidosis' in 354 B.C., when Plato was still alive and Aristotle
was still a member of the Academy.

20. *eusunetôteroi* i.e. 'of better understanding'. This kind of 'understanding' or 'good
understanding' is defined in *EN* VI as 'the exercise of the faculty of opinion for the
purpose of judging *of what someone else* says about matters with which practical wisdom
is concerned – and of judging soundly; for 'well' [*eu*] and 'soundly' [*kalôs*] are the
same thing' (1143a13-15, Oxford translation).

shall attempt, on the basis of our collections of constitutions, to find out . . .;
for once we have considered these problems, we shall perhaps be better able
46   to discern what the best state must be like ... ,' etc. (fully quoted above, p.
113), it is clear that Aristotle is not talking of his own way to mastership, but
that he simply presupposes his own qualification to deal with the historical
material as an expert; actually, he is concerned with a prospectus for his
students, and what he promises is that if they have a certain preliminary
acquaintance with this material *and* follow his own guidance, *they* 'shall
perhaps be better able to discern . . .'[21]

For us it is very fortunate that we have such a revealing description of the
part that the collections of constitutions played in Aristotle's school; and we
should be careful not to misinterpret the evidence, which plainly shows so
much – no more and no less – namely, that, without having become an
empiricist pure and simple, Aristotle was by now thoroughly convinced of
the importance of intensive and extensive historical studies.

At the same time, it cannot be denied that the whole transition from the
Nicomachean Ethics to the contents of the *Politics* is of a rather provisional
character. The need for a political theory in the narrower sense is one-
sidedly derived from the fact that average human nature yields only to some
kind of coercion; and the amusing but almost vicious attack on one single
passage from one of Isocrates' speeches can hardly claim to give a complete
solution of the whole problem. We may, therefore, ask why Aristotle did not
attempt to write a more satisfactory transition from his ethical to his
political theory.

The difficulties which he had to face are easy to see. In earlier phases of
his development, he had dealt with ethics and politics as strictly
separate disciplines.[22] The main subject of his ethical theory is the question of
the happiness of the individual. According to his theory, this happiness
culminates in pure contemplation. But this is avowedly something that
47   transgresses ordinary human nature (*EN* 1177b26-1178a2).[23] It is realised
or realisable to the degree in which an individual succeeds in developing the
'divine' in human nature. Furthermore, the more an individual approaches
this end, which he can never fully attain, the less he is dependent on
association with other human beings.

On the other hand, a human being would not be a human being if he did
not live in a community with other human beings; this is necessary for him
in order to live a human life (*EN* 1178b5-7). It is primarily this latter aspect
of human life with which political science in its original sense is concerned.
Here, then, in a way, the 'end' is the state (*Pol.* 1252b30-4, 1253a18-30).
After Aristotle had decided to deal with both disciplines as part of one

21. Notice that in the Greek text the *tach'an* of 1181b12 is continued in the *tach'an*
1181b21.

22. The comparatively early *Eudemian Ethics* does not claim to be part of political
science, and in the likewise comparatively early first chapter of Book VII of the *Politics*
it is directly stated that a detailed discussion of the question of the best life is 'the
business of another science' (1323b39).

23. But notice that Aristotle is quite aware that within the context of this part of
the *EN* the opposite use of the term 'human being' would make even better sense:
1178a2-7.

comprehensive 'philosophy of human affairs' (cf. *EN* 1181b15) and to call ethics, too, 'political science' (*EN* 1094a27-b11), a discussion of the relation of the two 'ends', namely, human happiness and the state, to one another must have appeared theoretically desirable. But to engage in such a discussion on the occasion of the transition from the first to the second part, that is, from ethical theory in the narrower sense to political theory in the narrower sense, was hardly feasible. For, though Aristotle had now the advantage of being able simply to presuppose the result of his ethics concerning the question of human happiness – an advantage which he did not have when he wrote the first chapter of Book VII of his *Politics*[24] – he would have had to anticipate a large part of the work toward which he made his transition if he wished to make the relation between the two 'ends' perfectly clear. What is worse, the final results of his ethical theory, as summed up in the chapters immediately preceding the transition, almost preclude an unprejudiced approach to the theory of the state.

When dealing separately, either with theoretical knowledge as the aim of   48
the philosopher or with the normal human life in a political community, Aristotle could, in either case, begin with 'nature'. The first chapter of Aristotle's *Metaphysics* derives the development of theoretical wisdom from the alleged fact that 'all human beings by nature desire to know', even regardless of practical results (*Meta.* 980a21ff.), and similarly, the first book of the *Politics* argues that 'by nature all [human beings] have an impulse toward [life in] a political community' (*Pol.* 1253a29ff.), even regardless of practical results.[25] But in the tenth book of the *Nicomachean Ethics*, it is so strongly emphasised that a life devoted to theory is something beyond common human nature, and on the other hand, 'living a human life' (*anthrôpeuesthai*), applying the social virtues, is so definitely characterised as second-rate (*EN* 1178b7) that it would have been extremely difficult to proceed from here in continuous argument to Aristotle's theory that 'the state is by nature clearly prior to the family and to the individual, since the whole is of necessity prior to the part' (*Pol.* 1253a19ff., Oxford translation), and again, 'the state is a creation of nature and prior to the individual' (1253a25).

Under these circumstances, the precarious way in which Aristotle's transition from his ethics to his politics reaches its aim ceases to be puzzling. For the intention was clearly to start the course itself with laying down the proper theoretical foundations, which the transition could not and was not meant to do. Still, the main advantage of the final arrangement, in which the first book of the *Politics* is linked with the last book of the *Nicomachean Ethics*,[26] was not lost. For although the specifically Aristotelian thesis that   49
'perfect happiness is a theoretical activity' (*EN* 1178b7) cannot easily enter the discussion of the state as a whole, this thesis was, in Aristotle's view,

---

24. The whole chapter would have been superfluous; cf. also n. 22 above.

25. This is expressly added in Book III, 1278b20ff.; cf *EE* 1242a8.

26. Although the 'announcement' at the end of the *EN* seems to point forward immediately to Book II of the *Politics*, it seems that the last three words found in the manuscripts of the *EN*, *legômen oun arxamenoi* ('Let us then speak making a beginning;) were intended to introduce 'another' (or: 'fresh') beginning; cf. the first words of Book II of the *EE*: 'After this, we must make another beginning and then speak about what is to follow', and similar phrases (e.g. *EN* 1145a15).

absolutely consistent with the assumption that *in so far as* we are human beings and have to live with others, happiness or the 'good life' (*to eu zên*) can be determined only by a theory of the social virtues and closely related subjects, a task to which the largest portion of Aristotle's ethical work was devoted. The results of this part of his ethical theory are, of course, properly considered at the proper place even in the tenth book of the *Nicomachean Ethics* (1178a9ff.) After this the political theory in the narrower sense could introduce the concept of the 'good life' wherever it was needed and so far as it was needed, without special discussion.

According to the introductory paragraph of the first book of the *Politics*, the state as an association of human beings (who always act for the sake of some good, real or imaginary) has come into being for some good; but, being the highest and most comprehensive form of human association, it is aiming at the highest good. This is an appropriate start for a course in political science; but it is no coincidence that it is made up, with due alterations of arrangement, of the same conceptual ingredients which occur in the much more explicit introduction to the *Nicomachean Ethics*.[27] Aristotle certainly would have had to be more explicit at the beginning of the *Politics*, unless the whole of the *Nicomachean Ethics* was presupposed; but, since this is obviously the case, it is not even necessary to say expressly that the 'highest good' is, of course, happiness or the 'good life'.

We are not going to analyse the first book of the *Politics* as a whole and may, therefore, neglect the rest of the first chapter. The theoretical foundations for dealing with the state as such are laid in the second chapter (1252a14-1253a39). The best way, we are told, of speculating about the state is to look at things as they grow (*pragmata ... phuomena*). Since individual human beings are not self-sufficient, there will, of necessity, be associations from the very beginning. Genetically, then, the associations between male and female on the one hand, and between master and slave on the other hand, come first; both associations are based on natural differentiation and, at least in the first case, on purely natural instinct (1252a26ff.) The next step toward self-sufficiency is the combination of these two associations in family and household, 'established by nature for the supply of men's everyday wants' (1252b13). What follows is a combination of several families in the village, a higher form of association, which most naturally may be compared to a colony and which is the first to aim not only at the day's needs. When finally several villages combine to form a state, the limit of possible self-sufficiency is reached; and so the state is the perfect association (*koinônia teleios*): 'it comes into being for the sake of bare existence, but when it has come into being, it *is* for the sake of the good life (1252b29ff.)'

At this point Aristotle draws the conclusion that *every* state exists 'by nature', taking now for granted that the earlier forms of association are 'by nature', and assuming that complete self-sufficiency is the final cause of the whole progress toward it. Thus he is able to identify self-sufficiency (and the

50

---

27. Chapters 1 and 2 of the *EN* (1094a1-b11), plus Chapter 4, in which the highest practical good is identified with happiness and the 'good life'.

state in which it is realised) with the 'end' at which nature was aiming from the beginning.[28]

The rest of the chapter, in which Aristotle draws the further conclusion that it is by nature that man is a political being (more than any gregarious animal), but that the state is by nature prior to the individual, etc., is now comparatively easy to understand. But there seems to remain one difficulty. It is clear that the discussion concerns the state in general and that the conclusions drawn claim to be valid for any state as such. Yet, while it could be said of the state in general that it 'has, so to speak, reached the limit of all self-sufficiency' (1252b28ff.), it certainly would not make sense to contend that the state as such 'has reached the limit of all good life'; besides, from the contents of the second chapter, it is not at all clear how the 'good life' suddenly enters the argument.

In order to understand this, one has to go back to the introductory paragraph at the beginning of the book, part of which may be quoted in an accurate translation: 'If all communities aim at some good, the state or political community, which is the highest of all, and which embraces all the rest, aims at a good in a greater degree than any other, and at the highest good' (1252a4-6). For the purpose of following Aristotle's intentions, it does not matter whether or not we approve of the way in which the thesis that the state aims at the highest good is here presented to us; at any rate, the fact that this thesis had been proposed from the very beginning explains the only seemingly unwarranted assertion within the second chapter. For we have already seen (above, p. 124 and n. 27) that the 'highest good' is happiness or the 'good life', and we cannot fail to realise now that in Aristotle's theory the assertion, 'the state is for the sake of the good life', has exactly the same meaning as the thesis, 'the state aims at the highest good'; and this can, of course, be generally true, even if the 'good life' is actually not reached or reached only to a small extent.[29]

We cannot go into a more detailed interpretation of the second chapter of the *Politics*; so much should be clear by now that Aristotle's general theory of the state, as displayed in this chapter, cannot be fully understood without going back to the introductory paragraph at the beginning of the *Politics*, which, in turn, as we have stated earlier (above, p. 124), is closely related to the first chapter of the *Nicomachean Ethics*. But if we now compare the second chapter of the *Politics* directly with the introduction to the *Nicomachean Ethics*, an interesting change in the philosopher's orientation can be observed. In the introduction to the *Nicomachean Ethics*, it is not 'nature' that appears to be concerned with the state and the good life, but rather political art and science; the word 'nature' does not even occur. In the second chapter of the *Politics*, the political art is not entirely forgotten, as its last section (1253a30-4)

51

52

28. In order to make this plausible, Aristotle appeals to his general philosophy of nature and for once must use the word 'nature' as directly equivalent to 'end': 'now nature is an end; for what a thing is like when the development has come to its end, that we say is its nature, as in the case of "man", "horse", "house"' (*oikia* is here 'house', not 'family', cf. *PA* 646a17, b4).

29. A passage in Book III of the *Politics* (1278b24-30) shows that Aristotle was inclined to interpret even the striving for bare existence (which in 1252b29f. is opposed to the good life) as a striving for happiness.

proves, but, with this exception, the importance of 'nature', and what nature is aiming at, as the basis for an understanding of the state, is so strongly emphasised[30] that the state itself and the task of dealing theoretically with political communities is seen in a new light. So long as not only ethics but political theory, too, is dominated by the concept of the best life, the attitude toward the actually existing states is necessarily more or less critical; but, if 'nature' pervades political life in all its forms, and if, consequently, *any* state 'is' (after it has come into being) for the sake of the good life, a much more positive attitude toward all these forms appears to be possible and theoretically justified.

It is in this way that Aristotle's political theory finally attempted to become completely free from those remnants of Plato's theory of ideas[31] which could be discovered in his *Protrepticus*. Still, the theory lends itself to the construction of an ideal state, that is, the state in which the good life is realised as far as humanly possible; and, in fact, the end of the *Nicomachean Ethics* does promise another discussion of the best state. But there is now a shift of emphasis. The very sentence in which Aristotle promises the new

53   discussion of the best state shows that the 'ideal' state is no longer the sole or even the principal subject of political philosophy. At least of equal importance seems now the question of what rules, laws, regulations, and institutions are most suitable to any given kind of constitution. This change of emphasis as against the *Protrepticus* becomes still clearer if one looks at the *Politics* itself. It is, of course, not possible within the present space to analyse in detail the origin and composition of the whole work as it has come to us. But modern scholars have proved beyond reasonable doubt that its last two books, which contain an obviously uncompleted sketch of the best constitution, were written considerably earlier than the rest of the work.[32] It is possible that Aristotle intended to replace these books later by a more elaborate discussion of the same subject. But it is hardly a mere coincidence that he never did replace them and that by far the most important sections in the work as we now have it are the first book, in which he discusses the anthropological, sociological and economic foundations of political life, and Books IV to VI and parts of Book III, in which he discusses the various possible forms of government and the question of how they can be made to function well and to be as stable as possible. It is also significant that in the second book he analyses and criticises Plato's ideal state and the earlier utopias of Phaleas of Chalcedon and Hippodamus of Miletus on the same level as the actually existing constitutions which had evoked special admiration.

It is interesting to observe that the considerations which seem to have led to this change of emphasis in some way go back to Plato himself; not so much to his theoretical writings, to be sure, as to his actual attitude when he came in contact with practical politics. For in the few cases in his life in which Plato had an opportunity to exercise his influence in practical

30. Notice that the noun 'nature' occurs twenty times.

31. Already the *EE* had replaced the 'idea' of the good by the highest practical good, and so does, of course, the *EN*.

32. cf. W. Jaeger [25], pp. 259ff. Quite recently some attempts have been made to refute Jaeger's theory in this respect. But the arguments are not convincing.

politics, as in the case of his friend Dion in Sicily, in the case of his former students Erastus and Coriscus in Scepsis, and in the case of the latters' political friend Hermias of Atarneus, he did not advocate the introduction of his ideal state, whether it be the ideal state of his *Republic* or that of his *Laws*, but a much more modest change and adjustment of existing political institutions. In his *Republic* and his *Laws*, on the other hand, Plato describes not only the political and social institutions of his best and his second-best state, respectively, but also their geographical location in regard to climate, distance from the sea, distance from other political communities, the upper and lower limits of their population, etc., conditions which obviously cannot all be met by an existing state but only by a state which is to be newly founded by a certain number of selected colonists in a specifically selected location. The evident conclusion from this, stated to some extent by Plato himself in his *Laws* (V, 746A-C), is that in existing states the political and social institutions must, at least to some extent, be adapted to those existing conditions which cannot be altered.

There is another factor of equal importance. This is the question whether and how far a change toward the good may be brought about by force. Again one must distinguish, to some extent, between Plato's theoretical and his practical attitude. It is very well known that Plato did not have a very high opinion of Athenian democracy, though, after he had seen the 'happy life' in the cities of southern Italy, he was forced to admit that, at least comparatively speaking, Athenian democracy was not quite as bad as he had thought it was when he had not known anything but Athens. In any case, he never advocated or participated in an attempt to bring about a change in the Athenian constitution by force, but, on the contrary, expressed the conviction that, for the citizens of a state, resort to force in order to change its constitution was as great a crime as it was for the son to do violence to his parents. This aversion to violent change or revolution is also revealed by the fact that, wherever he did make an attempt to bring about a change of political institutions in the direction of his political ideals, he addressed himself to men already in power who could make such a change in a legal way and without the use of force and violence. This is also the reason for his association with the younger Dionysius. There is, indeed, the one important exception that he finally did give his blessing to his friend Dion, when the latter set out to overthrow the tyranny of the younger Dionysius by force, and that he supported him by his moral authority. But even in this case, where the object of the revolution was a man who at one time had aroused some hope but later had turned into a real tyrant, according to Plato the worst possible type of ruler, and where the leader of the revolution, Plato's most intimate friend, had been personally wronged by the ruler, it is obvious that Plato for a long time was very hesitant and reluctant to give his approval.

Again Plato's attitude in theory was somewhat different, that is, very characteristically for Plato, somewhat less mild and moderate than his practical attitude. Yet the difference is not a fundamental one. Rather one may say that two opposite tendencies stand out very clearly. On the one hand, there is the conviction, most definitely stated in the *Politicus* 293A, that the truly wise statesman is entitled to do what he knows to be just and good, whether his action be sanctioned by law or not and whether he can bring about what is just and good by persuasion or whether he has to do it by force. Yet, on the other hand, in the *Laws* the superiority of persuasion to force is firmly upheld, and Plato establishes the principle that no law should merely set down a rule that has to be obeyed, but that, on the contrary, every law should have a long introduction which explains to the citizen why such a rule has been set down and why the rule is just (722Dff.). The reason is that even the justest law cannot function properly if it is not understood and if its application, therefore, causes resentment among the citizens.

Though Aristotle does not discuss the question of the application of force in political life so frequently and in such definite terms as Plato does, it is quite clear from his emphasis on the *stability* of constitutions and government, which is a characteristic of his whole *Politics*, that he was even more averse to violent political changes than Plato was. For 'stability' of a constitution or a government to Aristotle does not mean unchangeability, but it does mean that a government is of such a nature that it is not likely to be overthrown or even to be attacked by a rebellious or revolutionary movement from within.

If these principles are accepted, it is clear that in a theory which wishes to provide guidance to the practical statesman under variable conditions, the problem of the ideally best state must recede into the background.[33] The construction of such an ideal state may then still serve a useful purpose, inasmuch as it helps to clarify the general direction in which the true good of a political community is to be found. But, for all practical purposes, it will be much more important to find an answer to the question of what specific form this ideal will assume under particular geographic, social, economic, and generally historical circumstances. There will also be the question of what means can or may be used to bring a state, even if it were by only a little, nearer to this specific goal. For it is now acknowledged that, with the exception of the case of absolute tyranny, which, according to Aristotle and Plato, is no government and no real political community at all, a violent overthrow of the existing form of government produces more harm than good.

It was after the discussion of these problems had become a main interest of Aristotle's political theory that the historical study of a large variety of

---

33. The new conception of a generally applicable political theory is discussed at length in the first chapter of Book IV of the *Politics*. Although it is true that, toward the end of Aristotle's life, it must have become more and more clear that those men who were to dominate Greek political life from now on would pay little attention to his political theory, and although the transition from ethics to politics at the end of the *Nicomachean Ethics* contains one passage in which Aristotle seems to concede defeat with regard to 'most of the (existing) states' (1180a26ff., cf. p. 119 above), he was far from changing his theory, as this same passage shows. It is also true that Aristotle's political theory, even though many centuries later and through indirect channels, has had a much more far-reaching influence on actual political institutions than Plato's. That Aristotle's own disciples believed in the practical applicability of their master's political philosophy is attested by the fact that his disciple Demetrius of Phaleron under Macedonian domination officially assumed the title of lawgiver (*nomothetês*) in Athens and attempted to reform the Athenian state in agreement with Aristotle's principles (cf. Sterling Dow and A.H. Trevis, 'Demetrius of Phaleron and his lawgiving', *Hesperia* 12 (1943), pp. 144ff.).

actual political institutions acquired an infinitely broader significance than it could have had for him when he wrote the *Protrepticus*. At that time, Aristotle had had only contempt for legislators who, unlike Plato, found their political ideal in existing constitutions, such as the Spartan or Cretan, and who tried to form their laws after such models. In contrast, Books IV to VI and parts of Book III of the *Politics* could never have been written without the help of the enormous enterprise of a collection of all political constitutions which, as far as could still be found out, had existed anywhere in the Greek and in some of the most important non-Greek political communities.

When Aristotle wrote the history of the Athenian constitution as an integral part of this undertaking, two different courses were open to him. He could either insert his positive and negative evaluations of the political institutions and actions into the history itself, whenever an occasion presented itself, or merely give an account of the historical facts, reserving the critical discussion of these facts for his systematic and theoretical work. It is clear that, for the most part, he followed the second course. Yet value judgments are not altogether absent from his historical treatise. They are found in Chapters 22-41[34] and become more and more frequent toward the end of that section, which deals with the development of radical democracy and the oligarchic reactions against this development down to the restoration of democracy in 403 B.C.

Aristotle was not an Athenian citizen. He could not make and did not think of making an attempt to take an active part in Athenian political life. All direct value judgments in the *Constitution of Athens* refer to a period preceding his first stay in Athens. Most of them concern a period in which Plato, according to his own testimony in the *Seventh Epistle*, 324Bff., took a passionate interest in Athenian politics, while the remainder refers to the most important steps that led to the political conditions prevailing in Plato's youth. Therefore, the question may be asked how far these value judgments were influenced by Plato's experiences with, and his attitude toward, the Athenian democracy, and how far they are the natural application of Aristotle's own political theory to the various phases of the development of Athenian institutions.

There can be no doubt that neither Plato nor Aristotle had a favourable opinion of Athenian democracy as it existed in the latter part of the fifth century. This unfavourable judgment applies not only to the development of the Athenian democracy after the death of Pericles, that is, that period which is also condemned by the historian Thucydides, but extends also, though in a somewhat milder form (*Gorg.* 515Eff., *Ath. Resp.* 27-8), to Pericles' own leadership, which is greatly admired by Thucydides. If, on the whole, Aristotle's judgment of Athenian democracy may appear less severe than Plato's, one must not forget that if Plato in the *Politicus* (303A) considers good democracy the least good of the good, he at the same time considers bad democracy the least bad of the depraved forms of government. What is more, we learn from Plato's *Seventh Epistle* that, before

58

---

34. Aristotle's defence of Solon's personal integrity and his evaluation of the personal character of Peisistratus and his sons are intended to establish factual truth and do not belong to the kind of value judgments mentioned above.

he went to Sicily, Plato despised Athenian democracy and considered it hopeless. But when he had seen the 'so-called happy life' of the Greek cities of southern Italy, he had to admit that Athenian life and Athenian democracy were far from being the worst of the forms of human, political, and social life (326Bff.). In spite of the differences in their general political theory, Plato and Aristotle, therefore, seem largely to agree in their evaluation of Athenian democracy as it existed in the last quarter of the fifth century. But Aristotle, in the *Constitution of Athens*, is more specific in regard to the historical details and the various phases of the development.

59   It is certainly significant that Aristotle does not criticise the democratic reforms of Solon, whom, on the contrary, he seems to admire very much, nor even the much more radical reforms of Cleisthenes, though there can be hardly any doubt that these reforms opened the way for the development toward an ever less restricted majority rule, the latter phases of which Aristotle greatly deplores. The first note of criticism is struck in Chapter 25, where Aristotle says that, for seventeen years after the Persian Wars, under the supervision of the Areopagus, the political order remained essentially the same, though the situation was slowly degenerating. What he has in mind becomes clear from what follows. He deplores the reduction of the powers of the Areopagus, which had been a conservative and aristocratic element in the state.[35] He also obviously looks with disfavour on the conversion of the Athenian Sea Confederacy into an Empire ruled by Athens and on the change in the political attitude of the 'people' which resulted from this political act. He attributes the responsibility for these unfortunate innovations to Ephialtes and Pericles, and also, to a considerable extent, to Aristeides, though the latter, in ancient literature in general, was rather considered a conservative and at the same time was admired for his personal integrity and disinterestedness which made him die a poor man after he had been a leader of his country for many years. Even Plato, who, in the *Gorgias*, attacks so many other great men of Athens, has only praise for Aristeides. The case of Aristeides seems to indicate that in his historical judgments Aristotle is not entirely dependent on Plato.

60   Aristotle admits in Chapter 28 that, in spite of these unfortunate steps, the state was still in a 'fairly' good condition as long as Pericles was the leader of the democratic party. But after his death, things went rapidly from bad to worse, owing to the rise of demagogues who were not gentlemen, as all the political leaders of the earlier time had been, but men of bad manners, who shouted on the public platform, who reviled their opponents, who, in their speeches, played on the emotions of their audience instead of appealing to their intellect and understanding, and who, generally speaking, catered to the wishes of the masses in order to promote their own

35. Since the Areopagus consisted of the former Archons and since until 487/6 the Archons had been selected *ek prokritôn*, i.e. from candidates previously selected by vote, and not by lot, it is possible that at the time when its prerogatives were abolished, there were still some members of the Areopagus who had been selected by this older procedure. Above all, it was only some years after the reduction of the power of the Areopagus that the archonship became accessible to the Zeugitae. In 462, therefore, the members of the Areopagus probably still belonged to the two highest property classes.

selfish interests rather than the good of the community. He praises the leaders of the conservative or anti-democratic party of the time of Pericles and the earlier part of the Peloponnesian War, Thucydides, the son of Melesias, and Nicias (Ch. 28). He also praises the initiators of the oligarchic constitution of 411, but not the way in which the men who had come to power in 411 postponed the actual application of the moderate oligarchic constitution in order to keep control of the government in their own hands (Ch. 32-3). Of the outstanding men of the last decade of the Peloponnesian War, his favourite is Theramenes, the leader of the moderate wing of the anti-democratic party. He defends (Ch. 28) Theramenes against the accusations of his enemies, who called him a turncoat,[36] a man who belonged to all parties and tried to overthrow all constitutions, by pointing out that, on the contrary, Theramenes worked for the good of any established government as long as it did not transgress the fundamental laws, but was always willing to incur the enmity of those in power in defending the law of the country against their encroachments upon it.

To sum up, then, one may say that Aristotle admired the democratic reforms of Solon and did not criticise the further democratisation of the Athenian constitution by Cleisthenes and his immediate successors, but that, in regard to the period from the end of the Persian Wars to the beginning of the Decelean War, he favoured the leaders of the conservative or oligarchic party as against the leaders of the democratic party and, in regard to the last phase of the Peloponnesian War, the leaders of the moderate wing of the conservative party as against the radicals on both sides. The shift of his preference from the democratic leaders of the period before the Persian Wars to the conservative leaders of the succeeding period can be easily explained on the assumption that he shared to some extent the opinion of the men quoted by him in Chapter 29, namely, that the constitution of Cleisthenes was not yet fully democratic. It must, however, also be pointed out that, in spite of his opposition to unrestricted democracy, Aristotle, on several occasions,[37] praises the leniency of the Athenian *dêmos* and extols especially the moderation of the democratic leaders who restored democracy after the overthrow of the Thirty, in contrast to the violence, cruelty, and disregard of the laws of their oligarchic predecessors.

In order to see all this in the correct perspective, one must be aware of the characteristic features of the Athenian democracy of the second half of the fifth century, by which it differed from all the various and again widely differing political forms which are currently designated by this name. One of the most striking features of the Athenian democracy consisted in the fact that since the early eighties of the fifth century practically all public functionaries of the state, with the exception of the military commanders, were selected, not by vote, but by lot. It must further be observed that Aristotle, though he does not consider a state in which the public functionaries are elected by vote an oligarchy, does regard election by vote as an aristocratic feature in a constitution, because in such an election naturally only those men who are known through some distinctive qualities

61

---

36. 'Cothurnus', a shoe that could be worn on either foot.
37. Chapters 22, 4 and 40, 2-3; cf. also *Politics* 1281a39ff. and 1282a15ff.

have a chance of being elected, so that the chances are not exactly the same for everybody. It was a natural consequence of the institution of selection by lot that the official civil magistrates who were responsible to the people for the administration of affairs were not the actual political leaders, but that the political leadership was in the hands either of one of the commanding

62 generals or of orators who succeeded in gaining the decisive influence in the assembly of the people but had no official responsibility at all.

The second decisive peculiarity of Athenian democracy in the same period is the almost completely unrestricted power to decide absolutely everything by a simple majority of votes, a power which the assembly of the people seems to have claimed toward the end of the fifth century. It is true that there must have existed at that time the so-called *graphê paranomôn*, which made it possible to try and to punish a speaker who had proposed a measure which was in conflict with the laws of the country. But there is also evidence to show that occasionally the assembly claimed it as part of the sovereignty of the people, not only to usurp the functions of the law courts, but even to violate established rules of procedure, if the majority of the assembly expressed the will to do so.[38]

A third point was the custom of the law courts, which consisted exclusively of laymen, not only to interpret the law very freely and to decide the cases brought before them more according to the general impression produced by the conflicting parties than on the basis of a careful investigation of the facts, but also to mete out punishment according to their arbitrary judgment in cases for which no provision had been made in the established law.

Under a system like this, a clearly conceived, steady, and consistent policy of any kind was possible only if, and only as long as, there existed a political leader of such personal influence and authority that the assembly in most cases would follow his advice and leadership. During the lifetime of Pericles, therefore, the natural consequences of the system did not become completely visible, though even Pericles not infrequently had to struggle

63 very hard to retain his leadership, and though it is not certain whether Pericles did not, in order to retain his hold on the majority of the people, sometimes make political decisions which he would not have made otherwise and which he did not like to make.

After the death of Pericles, Cleon tried for some time to continue the policy of Pericles, especially in regard to the war and the relation to the other members of the Sea Confederacy who were now considered as little, if anything, more than 'subjects' of Athens. But he continued this policy with much cruder and more violent methods. When Cleon also had died, there followed a period of complete political irresponsibility. For if a decision which had been taken turned out to have bad consequences, those who had

---

38. The outstanding example is, of course, the condemnation of the generals of the battle of the Arginusae by the assembly of the people. On this occasion, as Xenophon, *Hellenica* I 7, 11ff., informs us, several people protested that the procedure was illegal, and Socrates, who happened to be president of the Council on that day, refused to put the question to a vote. But the people shouted that 'it would be a terrible if anyone should try to prevent the people from doing what it wished to do', and the generals were actually condemned and executed.

voted for it could always claim that they had been misled or deceived by the orators who had spoken in favour of the measure while the orators could claim that they had no responsibility because they had no authority. They had merely expressed their opinion, and nobody had been compelled to follow it. There can be no doubt that this government by irresponsible advisers and chance majorities contributed largely to the crushing defeat which Athens suffered at the end of the Peloponnesian War, although at the end of the first part of that war the advantages had been all on the Athenian side in spite of the terrible and unforeseeable losses that Athens had suffered through the plague of the years 430, 429, and 426.

In the fourth century, the absolute sovereignty of the people was somewhat restricted through the introduction of a more elaborate law code and the prescription of a very strict and complicated procedure for the repeal of old, and the creation of new, laws. At the same time, the *graphê paranomôn* was now used ruthlessly against those who made proposals for decrees of the assembly which, if accepted, would have violated an established law. Nevertheless, the tendency of demagogues to win favour with the masses 'by giving the people presents out of the people's own pockets' and to cater to the immediate desires of the people rather than to promote the long-range interests of the community was still very prevalent; and again the people had finally to pay for it by succumbing to a foreign power, this time to Macedonia. 64

In view of all this, one can hardly say that Aristotle is wrong when he says (*Pol.* IV, 1292a11ff.) that in a democracy like this the people are a monarch – a composite monarch to be sure, but still a monarch whose rule may be just as arbitrary as that of a tyrant – the demagogues playing the same role with the people as the flatterers and courtiers with the king or tyrant, since by their advice they mean above all to serve their own personal interests and not those of their master whom they advise. Against the evils of such a system, Aristotle advocates in the first place a rule of law, that is, of long-range law which cannot be changed by arbitrary decision of single-chance majorities. Secondly, he wishes a democracy to be tempered by aristocratic or oligarchic elements. In this connexion, however, it must again be pointed out that election by vote, instead of selection by lot, of representatives of the people (in the Council) and of public functionaries was, in ancient tradition, considered as something not purely democratic and that, likewise, any kind of checks and balances, the like of which form the very foundation of what in modern times is mostly called democracy – though not, of course, by the totalitarian tyrannies, which also call themselves democracies – is not democratic in the sense of the absolute sovereignty of the majority of the people as conceived in the last decades of the fifth century. Apart from this Aristotle himself makes the very judicious observation that those institutions and measures might, in a truer sense, be called democratic which make a democracy stable and lasting, than those which are more democratic in the sense of an abstract ideal of democracy but which, by their very nature, will inevitably lead to the downfall of the democratic state itself (*Pol.* VI, 1320a2ff.).

There are also in Aristotle's works some other observations on various forms of less 'democratic' but more stable democracy which are obviously based, at least in part, on a study of Athenian democracy; for instance, the

observation that democracy functions best in a preponderantly rural and
65 agricultural community. For, Aristotle says (*Pol.* VI, 1318b9ff.), in such a
community people will not have the time to meddle as a body in all political
affairs. They will, by necessity, leave the conduct of ordinary political affairs
to the elected magistrates and will assemble only for the purpose of
elections, for the checking of the magistrates, and for major decisions. At the
same time, in a mainly agricultural community, there will be but few people
without property, a situation which also makes for stability in a state. This
theory is certainly connected with the observation, made in the *Constitution of
Athens* (Ch. 24), that the evils of Athenian democracy began with the influx
of a large part of the rural population of Attica into the city, in consequence
of the conversion of the Athenian Sea Confederacy into an empire. The
observation in itself seems true enough, although, under somewhat different
circumstances, the consequences of a change of this kind may not always be
exactly the same.

That, on the other hand, Aristotle in his analysis of the democratic form
of government was not exclusively dependent on Athenian history is
demonstrated by the fact that he compares the 'customary' leniency of the
Athenian *dêmos* with the rougher and more cruel methods of other
democracies, and, likewise, by the fact that he makes direct reference to the
democratic regimes in Rhodes, Cymae, Heracleia, Megara, etc., in the
Politics.

Aristotle's analysis of the general anthropological, psychological,
economic, and political foundations of the state, the most magnificent part
of his political theory, rests on a much broader basis than a study of
Athenian history could have provided; only very faint traces of the influence
of this particular study can be found in his general theory. In those
chapters, however, especially of Books III, IV, V, and VI of the *Politics*, in
which Aristotle deals with the problems of democracy – the advantages and
disadvantages of different forms of democracy, the ways and means of
making a democracy more stable, and the causes which may lead to its
decay and destruction – the influence of Athenian history on his criticism
66 and suggestions and, above all, also on his terminology is very strong, much
stronger obviously than that of other historical studies which he has made.
For a full understanding, therefore, of these sections of Aristotle's *Politics*,
and, likewise, of those sections of Plato's works in which Plato deals with the
problems of democracy, a careful study of Aristotle's *Constitution of Athens* is
indispensable.

12

W.W. Fortenbaugh

Aristotle on Slaves and Women

In an earlier article, 'Aristotle's *Rhetoric* on the Emotions', I discussed Aristotle's investigation of emotional response and pointed out how this investigation had important consequences for rhetorical and ethical theory.[1] In particular I indicated how analysing emotions as cognitive phenomena open to reasoned persuasion led Aristotle not only to assign emotional appeal a dignified position within rhetorical theory but also to formulate a new bipartite psychology which replaced Plato's tripartite psychology within the sphere of political and ethical investigation. However, I did not consider the way in which Aristotle's investigation of emotional response led to a new and more thoughtful explanation of the subordinate position of slaves and women within the Greek city-state. This omission I want now to make good. For properly understood, Aristotle's view of slaves and women is neither the sophistry of a prejudiced Greek male enjoying a privileged position nor simply the product of a misguided biologist who assumes uncritically that nature's way is identical with the *status quo*.[2] Rather it is also and even primarily a political application of what was unquestionably an important advance in philosophical psychology. Having made clear the relationship between emotion and reason and having built this relationship into a new political and ethical psychology, Aristotle was able to accept the demand of Plato that a difference in role or pursuit be tied to a relevant difference in nature (*Rep.* 454B4-E4; cf. *Pol.* 1259b36-8) and at the same time to reassert the claim of Gorgias that the virtues of slaves and women are different from those of free men because their activities or roles are different (*Meno* 71D4-72A5; cf. *Pol.* 1260a15-17, 27-8). Only this reassertion was not a case of mere retrogression. It was in fact a new development that not only recognised a difference in roles but also explained this difference by reference to recent insights into the relationship between emotion and reason.

Aristotle's remarks on slavery are admittedly difficult and controversial. He seems not only to be on the wrong side of a *nomos-phusis* (convention *versus* nature) controversy (cf. 1253b20-2) but also to express himself in a way that threatens the very humanity of slaves. He emphasises their capacity for bodily labour (1252a33, 1254b18, 25, 1258b38, 1259b26),

---

1. *Archiv für Geschichte der Philosophie* 52 (1970), pp. 40-70, reprinted in vol. IV of the present series.

2. See the recent, polemical remarks of Dorothea Wender ('Plato: misogynist, paedophile, and feminist', *Arethusa* 6 (1973), pp. 88-9) who groups Aristotle with Dr. Spock and faults both for being biologically oriented thinkers. For a more sympathetic statement see J. Randall [17], pp. 243-50.

compares their utility to that of tame animals (1254b24-6) and says that slaves differ from masters to the same extent that bodies differ from souls and beasts from men (1254b16-17). Such remarks closely relate slaves to animals, so that it is at least understandable why difficulties have been felt as to whether Aristotle classes them as human.[3] But Aristotle is quite explicit in classifying slaves as men (1254b16, 1259b27-8) and if we understand that Aristotle's idea of the natural slave is based upon his newly developed political and ethical psychology, we can see quite easily how slaves qualify as human beings. Aristotle denies slaves the capacity to deliberate (1260a12), but he never denies them the capacity of emotional response. In more technical language, Aristotle denies them the logical or reasoning half of the bipartite soul but not the alogical or emotional half. This means that slaves can make the judgments involved in emotional responses and therefore have at least a minimum share in the cognitive capacity peculiar to men in relation to other animals (cf. 1253a16).[4]

In denying slaves the capacity to deliberate (1260a12) Aristotle is not robbing them of their humanity. Rather he is meeting Plato's demand for relevant differences and so explaining and justifying Gorgias' idea of a peculiarly servile activity and virtue (*Meno* 71E9-72A4). Slaves lack the ability to deliberate, that is to say the ability to act with forethought (1252a31-2). When this deficiency is combined with bodily strength suitable for necessary tasks (1254b28-9), then a role of obedient service seems proper. And since virtue is related to role or function (1260a16-17) it also seems proper to assign slaves a virtue limited by the demands of their subordinate role. Natural slaves must have a measure of temperance and courage and in general be properly disposed toward their masters (cf. 1260a33-6). But they are not expected to have practical wisdom or in general the virtue demanded of a master.

Aristotle's psychological account of the natural slave does more than provide a way of supporting Gorgias' view of servile virtue. It also provides a reason for criticising persons including Plato (*Laws* 777E5-778A1) who would give slaves orders unaccompanied by reason (*logos*) and in particular by reasoned admonition (*nouthetêsis*) – 1260b5-7. This is an important point for it well illustrates how an advance in philosophical psychology can not only affect but also improve political theory. Having thoroughly investigated emotional response, Aristotle is quite clear that while emotions are different from *logos* (reason), they are at least open to *logos* (reasoned explanation). He applies this insight to slaves, denying them reason but allowing that they can perceive it (1254b22-3). Despite certain scholarly grumbles there is nothing inconsistent or precarious in this thesis.[5] Aristotle

---

3. On this difficulty see F. Susemihl and R. Hicks [174], pp. 160-1, E. Barker [184], pp. 364-5; O. Gigon, 'Die Sklaverei bei Aristoteles', in [186], pp. 247-83 and A.W.H. Adkins, *From the Many to the One* (Ithaca 1970), pp. 211-12.

4. To deny slaves the logical half of the bipartite soul is not to deny slaves some share in the biological faculty of cognition. At *EN* 1098a4-5 Aristotle makes clear that the alogical half overlaps with the biological faculty of cognition. See my papers [143], pp. 174-5, and 'Zu der Darstellung der Seele in der Nikomachischen Ethik I 13', *Philologus* 114 (1970), pp. 289-91.

5. *Pace* Susemihl-Hicks (above, n. 3), p. 161, Gigon (above, n. 3), p. 258, and R. Schlaifer [218], pp. 192-9.

simply recognises that while slaves tend to behave emotionally and without reflection, they are like children in being amenable to reasoned admonition (*nouthetêsis*, *EN* 1102b34). Furthermore, Aristotle not only recognises the capacity of slaves to perceive reason. He also honours it and protests against withholding reasoned admonition and reason in general (1260b5-7). Of course, one reason for Aristotle's protest is purely pragmatic. Reason influences emotions and makes slaves more tractable. Hence a master should not punish a slave without offering a reason which prevents anger by justifying the punishment inflicted (*Rhet.* 1380b16-20). But offering a reason may be more than pragmatic and self-serving. It may also be giving a slave his due. For offering a reason involves acknowledging that slaves can follow reasoned admonition and judge for themselves whether or not a particular course of action is appropriate.[6] In other words, to offer slaves reasoned admonition is to invite them to make the sort of decision they are capable of making. Slaves cannot put together reasoned arguments and cannot offer their master reasoned advice. But they can perceive their masters' reasons and can decide to follow them. To this extent they can partake of reason, so that Aristotle is on firm moral as well as psychological ground when he protests against refusing slaves reasoned admonition. To offer reasoned explanation is to respect a slave's cognitive capacity and to allow him to partake of reason as best he can.

We may conclude that Aristotle's view of slavery is neither psychologically foolish nor morally repulsive. Of course, there are no natural slaves in the world, so that the view remains theoretical. But as theory it has the merit of running a middle course between the opposing views recognised by Plato in the *Laws*. It neither allows the possibility of slaves excelling in regard to all virtue (776D9) nor despises them as if they were animals (777A4). Instead it seems to take a hint from Homer (*Od.* XVII 322) or rather Plato's misquotation to the effect that slaves lack half their wits (777A1). They lack the capacity to deliberate but are in other respects cognitive creatures. Such a view may not be altogether novel. At least in the *Laws* Klinias is prepared to equate an inability to demonstrate by reasoning (*logos*) with the condition of a slave (966B1-3). But it seems to be Aristotle who formulated this deficiency in terms of the bipartition of the soul and made it the basis of natural slavery.

In discussing women Aristotle leaves no doubt about their subordinate and domestic role. He states clearly that men are better fitted to command than women (1259b2) and that the role of women is not the bodily service characteristic of slaves but rather the preservation of goods procured by men (1252a33-b5, 1277b4-5). Moreover, since Aristotle relates virtue to function (1260a16-17), he demands of women a virtue which reflects their domestic role. They will need, Aristotle tells us, less courage than men (1277b20-2), and not the courage of command but rather the courage of subordination (1260a23-4). Similarly women must be temperate but not in the manner of men (1260a21), for were women modest in the way that good men are, they would be chatterers (1277b23).

So far Aristotle's account of women is based upon his conception of their

---

6. When we admonish (*nouthetein*) a man, he decides whether he should obey. cf. *Rhet.* 1391b10-11, where the admonished man is described as a judge (*kritês*).

role within the household. But his account goes deeper than this. It also relates women to the distinction between logical and alogical halves of the soul (1260a6-7) and contrasts the psychic capacities of women with those of both slaves and children. Slaves are said to possess the deliberate faculty not at all; women are said to possess it, but without authority (akuron); and children are said to possess it imperfectly (1260a12-14). What Aristotle means in regard to slaves has been stated in the preceding section and what he means in regard to children is clear enough. The alogical or emotional half of the soul is prior in generation to the logical or reasoning half (1334b21-2). Children will develop the capacity to deliberate, but during their immaturity they live emotionally and without reflection. However, the case of women is more obscure. At first glance it may appear that Aristotle is simply referring to the subordinate position of women (1259b2, 1260a23). He may seem to be saying that while women possess reason, it does not prevail in the society of men. This would be, of course, true enough. In comparison with men, women lacked authority both in actual Greek city-states and in the society recommended by Aristotle. But this truth does not do justice to Aristotle's point. In this portion of the *Politics* Aristotle is concerned with the virtues appropriate to different kinds of persons including women. On one level this is not a problem. Gorgias had already suggested that virtue is related to function (*Meno* 72A2-4). Aristotle accepts this principle and applies it to women (1260a16-24). The problem is on a more fundamental level – namely, why different kinds of people have different functions or roles in society. Here a reference to the newly developed bipartite psychology and to the capacity of deliberation is useful. When Aristotle says that slaves do not possess the deliberative capacity, he is not drawing a conclusion based upon the menial role of slaves. Rather he is indicating why slaves have the role they do. Similarly in the case of women a reference to their psychological make-up combined with their bodily condition explains their role within the household and therefore ultimately their peculiar kind of virtue. In comparison with man's bodily condition the bodily condition of women is one of weakness, and this comparative weakness points toward a retiring domestic role within the home. Further, their deliberative capacity is akuron, that is to say it lacks authority and is overruled easily. In stating this lack of authority Aristotle is not referring to inter-personal relationships but rather to an intra-personal relationship. Just as he looks within the slave to explain his social position, so he looks within the woman to explain her role and virtues. Her deliberative capacity lacks authority, because it is often overruled by her emotions or alogical side. Her decisions and actions are too often guided by pleasures and pains, so that she is unfitted for leadership and very much in need of temperance.

It is important to emphasise that in calling the deliberative capacity of a woman akuron, Aristotle is not impugning the cleverness of women. He recognises that women can think things through and even give reasoned advice. He would see no absurdity, for example, in Ajax praising the forethought of Tecmessa (Sophocles, *Ajax* 536)[7] or Creon fearing the

7. Tecmessa is an interesting case, for she is not only a wife but also a slave captured in battle (Sophocles, *Ajax* 211, 489). In the *Politics* Aristotle focuses on the

cleverness of Medea (Euripides, *Medea* 285). His point is not that women deliberate only in some vague and illogical way, but that their deliberations and reflections are likely not to control their emotions. This view is, of course, not an Aristotelian creation *ex nihilo*. It is a common view of women and one that is illustrated often in Greek literature. Medea is a celebrated case. Deserted by Jason for another woman, she is angered and plans to take revenge by killing the children born to her and Jason. Reflection tells Medea that such an act of revenge is excessive and against her own interests. She hesitates, but ultimately her anger (*thumos*) is stronger than her deliberations (*bouleumata*) (Euripides, *Medea* 1079). In Aristotelian terminology her *bouleutikon* is *akuron*, i.e. her deliberative faculty cannot control her anger so that she acts emotionally and unreasonably, but not without considerable cleverness. Women are most clever contrivers of every evil (Euripides, *Medea* 409). In the service of emotion their deliberative faculties are most effective at discovering means to achieve a desired goal. But in controlling and altering unreasonable desires, their deliberative faculties lack authority. Medea understands that she is about to do something terrible (Euripides, *Medea* 1078), but she is not deterred by this understanding. For in the case of Medea and other women reasoned consideration tends to be *akuron*.

Aristotle's view of women may be false. Certainly the exceptional behaviour of a tragic heroine cannot be said to decide what is in the end an empirical issue. But it would be a mistake to think that Aristotle's view is simply the creation of a prejudiced male or, more charitably, the product of an overly keen biologist.[8] On the contrary, it is a thoughtful view that well illustrates how investigations within one sphere of philosophical enquiry can determine developments within another. Aristotle investigated emotional response and drew a fundamental distinction between reason and emotion. He then applied this distinction to the field of political theory, formulated a bipartite psychology and used this psychology to explain the role of women within society. He credited women with reason and therefore distinguished them from natural slaves who lack reason altogether and from children who have not yet acquired reason. Aristotle recognised that women merit a role that is neither servile nor puerile, but he was prepared to assign them a subordinate role on the grounds that their reason or logical side is *akuron* in relation to their emotional or alogical side.

---

household and offers an account of woman as wife (1253b7) in her marriage relationship (1253b9-11, 1259a39) to a free man. His remarks do not cover the case of a female slave. Presumably Aristotle would say that Tecmessa is by birth (Sophocles, *Ajax* 487) and also naturally free. Only women lacking deliberative capacity are natural slaves and suitable mates for natural male slaves (cf. 1252b5-7).

8. It is striking that in the *Politics* Aristotle all but ignores biological explanations of female inferiority. On one occasion he does mention a connexion between parental age and female offspring (1335a12-15), but he does not develop this point. In a different context Aristotle was prepared to talk biology (cf. the *GA* where Aristotle explains that a deficiency in heat may affect the working of semen (766a18-22) and result in a female or deficient offspring (767b23)), but within his political writings he is guided by recent advances in philosophical psychology and in particular by his newly developed distinction between reasoning and emotional halves of the soul.

13

M.I. Finley

Aristotle and Economic Analysis*

3 For the argument of this paper it is essential to distinguish, no matter how crudely, between economic analysis and the observation or description of specific economic activities, and between both and a concept of 'the economy' (with which only the final section will be concerned). By 'economic analysis', wrote Joseph Schumpeter, 'I mean ... the intellectual efforts that men have made in order to *understand* economic phenomena or, which comes to the same thing, ... the analytic or scientific aspects of economic thought'. And later, drawing on a suggestion of Gerhard Colm's, he added: 'economic analysis deals with the questions how people behave at any time and what the economic effects are they produce by so behaving; economic sociology deals with the question how they came to behave as they do.'[1]

Whether one is wholly satisfied with Schumpeter's definitions or not,[2] they will serve our present purposes. To illustrate the difference between analysis and observation, I quote the most familiar ancient text on the division of labour, written by Xenophon before the middle of the fourth century B.C. The context – and this should not be ignored – is the superiority of the meals provided in the Persian palace with its staff of kitchen specialists.

> That this should be the case [Xenophon explains] is not remarkable.
> For just as the various trades are most highly developed in the large
> cities, in the same way the food at the palace is prepared in a far
> superior manner. In small towns the same man makes couches,
> doors, ploughs and tables, and often he even builds houses, and still
> he is thankful if only he can find enough work to support himself. And
> it is impossible for a man of many trades to do all of them well. In
> large cities, however, because many make demands on each trade,
> one alone is enough to support a man, and often less than one: for

---

* This essay was prepared for the *Festschrift* for Professor E. Ch. Welskopf on her seventieth birthday, and has appeared in German translation in the *Jahrbuch für Wirtschaftsgeschichte* 2 (1971), pp. 87-105. An earlier draft was presented to the Social History Group in Oxford on 3 December 1969. I have benefited from the advice of a number of friends, A. Andrewes, F.H. Hahn, R.M. Hartwell, G.E.R. Lloyd, G.E.M. de Ste. Croix.

1. J. Schumpeter, *History of Economic Analysis*, ed. E.B. Schumpeter (New York, 1954), pp. 1, 21.

2. See the review by I.M.D. Little in *Econ. Hist. Rev.*, 2nd ser., 8 (1955-6), pp. 91-8.

instance, one man makes shoes for men, another for women, there are places even where one man earns a living just by mending shoes, another by cutting them out, another just by sewing the uppers together, while there is another who performs none of these operations but assembles the parts. Of necessity he who pursues a very specialised task will do it best (*Cyropaedia*, 8.2.5).

This text contains importance evidence for the economic historian – but 4 not on division of labour for which it is so often cited. In the first place, Xenophon is interested in specialisation of crafts rather than in the division of labour. In the second place, the virtues of both are, in his mind, improvement of quality, not increase in productivity. He says this explicitly and it is anyway implicit in the context, the meals served at the Persian court. Nor is Xenophon untypical: division of labour is not often discussed by ancient writers, but when it is, the interest is regularly in craftsmanship, in quality.[3] One need only glance at the model of the pin factory at the beginning of Adam Smith's *Wealth of Nations* to appreciate the leap taken by the latter, from observation to genuine economic analysis.

Even as observation, furthermore, Xenophon's remarks do not merit the accolades they have received. As Schumpeter pointed out, economics 'constitutes a particularly difficult case' in any study of the origins of a 'science' because

> common-sense knowledge goes in this field much farther relatively to such scientific knowledge as we have been able to achieve, than does common-sense knowledge in almost any other field. The layman's knowledge that rich harvests are associated with low prices of foodstuffs or that division of labour increases the efficiency of the productive process are obviously prescientific and it is absurd to point to such statements in old writings as if they embodied discoveries.[4]

The key for antiquity rests not with Xenophon or Plato but with Aristotle. It is agreed on all sides that only Aristotle offered the rudiments of analysis; hence histories of economic doctrine regularly feature him at the beginning. 'The essential difference' between Plato and Aristotle in this respect, writes Schumpeter, 'is that an analytic *intention*, which may be said (in a sense) to have been absent from Plato's mind, was the prime mover of Aristotle's. This is clear from the logical structure of his arguments.'[5]
Aristotle then becomes doubly troublesome. In the first place, his supposed efforts at economic analysis were fragmentary, wholly out of scale with his monumental contributions to physics, metaphysics, logic, 5

3. See Eric Roll, *A History of Economic Thought*, 3rd edn. (London, 1954), pp. 27-8.
4. *op. cit.*, p. 9. Even if one grants Xenophon the insight that division of labour is a consequence of greater demand, the observation led to no analysis. To quote Schumpeter again: 'Classical scholars as well as economists . . . are prone to fall into the error of hailing as a discovery everything that suggests later developments, and of forgetting that, in economics as elsewhere, most statements of fundamental facts acquire importance only by the superstructures they are made to bear and are commonplace in the absence of such superstructures' (p. 54).
5. *op. cit.*, p. 57. Cf. e.g. Roll, *op. cit.*, pp. 31-5.

meteorology, biology, political science, rhetoric, aesthetics and ethics. Second, and still more puzzling, his efforts produced nothing better than 'decorous, pedestrian, slightly mediocre, and more than slightly pompous common sense' (*op. cit.*, p. 57). This judgment of Schumpeter's, shared by many, is so wide of the universal judgment of Aristotle's other work, that it demands a serious explanation.

1.

There are only two sections in the whole Aristotelian corpus that permit systematic consideration, one in Book V of the *Nicomachean Ethics*, the other in Book I of the *Politics*.[6] In both, the 'economic analysis' is only a sub-section within an enquiry into other, more essential subject-matters. Insufficient attention to the contexts has been responsible for much misconception of what Aristotle is talking about.

The subject of the fifth book of the *Ethics* is justice. Aristotle first differentiates universal from particular justice, and then proceeds to a systematic analysis of the latter. It, too, is of two kinds: distributive and corrective.

Distributive (*dianemêtikos*) justice is a concern when honours, goods, or other 'possessions' of the community are to be distributed. Here justice is the same as 'equality', but equality understood as a geometrical proportion (we say 'progression'), not as an arithmetical one.[7] The distribution of equal shares among unequal persons, or of unequal shares among equal persons, would be unjust. The principle of distributive justice is therefore to balance the share with the worth of the person. All are agreed on this, Aristotle adds, although all do not agree on the standard of value (*axia*) to be employed where the *polis* itself is concerned. 'For democrats it is the status of freedom, for some oligarchs wealth, for others good birth, for aristocrats it is excellence (*aretê*)' (*EN* 1131a24-9). That Aristotle himself favoured the last-named is not important for us, and indeed he does not himself make the point in this particular context, which is concerned only to explain and defend the principle of geometric proportion.[8]

In corrective justice (*diorthôtikos*, literally 'straightening out'), however, the issue is not one of distribution from a pool, but of direct, private

6. The first part of Book II of the pseudo-Aristotelian *Oeconomica* is without value on any issue relevant to the present discussion, as I have indicated briefly in a review of the Budé edition in *CR* n.s. 20 (1970), pp. 315-19. (See also note 32).

7. This difficult idea of a mathematical formulation of equality and justice was Pythagorean, probably first introduced by Archytas of Tarentum at the beginning of the fourth century B.C., and then popularised by Plato (first in *Gorgias*, 508A). See F.D. Harvey, 'Two Kinds of Equality', *Classica et Mediaevalia* 26 (1965), pp. 101-46 with corrigenda in vol. 27 (1966), pp. 99-100, who rightly stresses the point that the mathematical formulation is employed solely to argue against democracy. (My translations from the *Ethics* are based on H. Rackham's in the Loeb Classical Library, 1926.)

8. It is probable that for Aristotle distributive justice is also operative in a variety of private associations, permanent or temporary: see Joachim's commentary [39], pp. 138-40, though I see neither necessity nor warrant for his attempt to link distributive justice with the private law suit known as *diadikasia*.

relations between individuals in which it may be necessary to 'straighten out' a situation, to rectify an injustice by removing the (unjust) gain and restoring the loss. Here the relative nature and worth of the persons is irrelevant, 'for it makes no difference whether a good man has defrauded a bad man or a bad one a good one, nor whether it is a good or bad man that has committed adultery; the law looks only at the nature of the damage, treating the parties as equal . . .' (*EN* 1131b32-1132a6).

Corrective justice also has two subdivisions, depending on whether the 'transactions' (*sunallagmata*) are voluntary or involuntary. Among the former Aristotle lists sales, loans, pledges, deposits and leases; among the latter, theft, adultery, poisoning, procuring, assault, robbery, murder (*EN* 1131a3-9). There is a fundamental difficulty for us here in trying to comprehend Aristotle's categories – and no translation of *sunallagmata* by a single English word eases it – but I need not enter into the controversy except to make one point relevant to some of the discussion that will follow. Under what conditions did Aristotle envisage an injustice, an unjust gain, in a voluntary transaction, especially in a sale? The answer is, I think, beyond dispute that he had in mind fraud or breach of contract, but not an 'unjust' price. An agreement over the price was part of the agreement or 'transaction' itself, and there could be no subsequent claim by the buyer of unjust gain merely because of the price. As Joachim says, 'the law gives the better bargainer *adeia* (security)'[9]. It is necessary to insist on this (leaving aside the unfortunate injection of bargaining) because efforts have been made to drag this section of the *Ethics* into the argument about economic analysis, for example by Soudek, who offers as an illustration of corrective justice the hypothetical case of a house-buyer who brought suit on a claim that he had been overcharged and who was awarded a refund equal to half the difference between the seller's price and his own proposed 'just price' ([222], pp. 51-2). Nothing in this or any other text of Aristotle warrants this, nor does anything we know about Greek legal practice. Both argue decisively the other way. Commenting on the famous passage in the *Iliad* (VI 234-6), 'But then Zeus son of Cronus took from Glaucus his wits, in that he exchanged golden armour with Diomedes son of Tydeus for one of bronze, the worth of a hundred oxen for the worth of nine oxen', Aristotle says tersely, 'one who gives away what is his own cannot be said to suffer injustice' (*EN* 1136b9-13). We shall meet 'what is his own' again in a surprising context.

Having completed his analysis of the two kinds of particular justice, Aristotle abruptly launches into a digression (1132b21-1133b29), introducing it polemically: 'The view is held by some that justice is reciprocity (*antipeponthos*) without any qualification, by the Pythagoreans for example'. *Antipeponthos* is a term that has a technical mathematical sense, but it also has a general sense which, in this context, amounts to the *lex*

7

---

talionis, an eye for an eye.[10] On the contrary, replies Aristotle, 'in many cases reciprocity is at variance with justice', since it *'does not coincide either with distributive or with corrective justice'*. However, in the 'interchange of services' the Pythagorean definition of justice is appropriate, provided the reciprocity *'is on the basis of proportion, not on the basis of equality'*.

'Interchange of services' is Rackham's inadequate translation of Aristotle's *en tais koinôniais tais allaktikais,* losing the force of the word *koinônia,* and I am compelled to digress. *Koinônia* is a central concept in Aristotle's *Ethics* and *Politics.* Its range of meanings extends from the *polis* itself, the highest form of *koinônia,* to temporary associations such as sailors on a voyage, soldiers in a campaign, or the parties in an exchange of goods. It is a 'natural' form of association – man is by nature a *zôon koinônikon* as well as a *zôon oikonomikon* (household-being) and a *zôon politikon* (*polis*-being). Several conditions are requisite if there is to be a genuine *koinônia:* (1) the members must be free men; (2) they must have a common purpose, major or minor, temporary or of long duration; (3) they must have something in common, share something, such as place, goods, cult, meals, desire for a good life, burdens, suffering; (4) there must be *philia* (conventionally but inadequately translated 'friendship'), mutuality in other words, and *to dikaion,* which for simplicity we may reduce to 'fairness' in their mutual relations. Obviously no single word will render the spectrum of *koinôniai.* At the higher levels, 'community' is usually suitable, at the lower perhaps 'association' provided the elements of fairness, mutuality and common purpose are kept in mind.

The point to my digression is to underscore the overtones of the section in the *Ethics* on exchange: *koinônia* is as integral to the analysis as the act of exchanging. Edouard Will caught the right nuance when he replaced such translations of the opening phrase as 'interchange of services' by a paraphrase, 'exchange relations within the framework of the community' (*les relations d'échange qui ont pour cadre le communauté*).[11] Lest there be any doubt, Aristotle himself promptly dispels it. Immediately following the sentences I quoted before digressing, he goes on to say that the *polis* itself depends on proportional reciprocity. If men cannot requite evil with evil, good with good, there can be no sharing. 'That is why we set up a shrine to the Charites [Graces] in a public place, to remind men to make a return. For that is integral to grace, since it is a duty not only to return a service done one, but another time to take the initiative in doing a service oneself' (*EN* 1133a3-5).

And at long last we come to our problem. The example of proportional requital which follows is the exchange of a house for shoes.[12] How is that to be accomplished? There is no *koinônia* in this context between two doctors, but only between, say, a doctor and a farmer, who are not equals but who

10. cf. *MM* 1194a29ff.; see Joachim [39], pp. 147-8, and the commentary by R.A. Gauthier and J.Y. Jolif (the best commentary in so far as close reading of the text is concerned), [35], vol. 2, pp. 372-3.

11. E. Will, 'De l'aspect éthique des origines grecques de la monnaie', *Rev. Hist.* 212 (1954), pp. 209-31, at p. 215, n. 1.

12. Aristotle shifts from example to example and I have followed him, despite the superficial inconsistency that entails.

must somehow he equalised. 'As a builder is to a shoemaker, so must so many pairs of shoes be to a house'. The latter must be 'equalised somehow', by some common measure, and that is need (*chreia*),[13] now commonly expressed in money. 'There will therefore be reciprocity when (the products) have been equalised, so that as farmer is to shoemaker, so is the shoemaker's product to that of the farmer'. In that way, there will be no excess but 'each will have his own'. If one party has no need there will be no exchange, and again money comes to the rescue: it permits a delayed exchange (*EN* 1133b6-12).[14]

9

There follows a short repetitive section and the digression on 'this outwork of particular justice' ends.[15] Aristotle has been thinking aloud, so to speak, as he often does in his writings as they have come down to us, about a particular nuance or a tangential question that is troublesome; he is indulging in a highly abstract exercise, analogous to the passages in the *Politics* on the application of geometric proportion to public affairs; here, as often, his reflections are introduced by a polemical statement, and soon dropped as he returns to his main theme, his systematic analysis. Exchange of goods does not again appear in the *Ethics* except in two or three casual remarks.

That this is not one of Aristotle's more transparent discussions is painfully apparent, and we must look at what the most important modern commentators have made of it. Joachim, exceptionally, accepted that Aristotle really meant it when he wrote 'as a builder is to a shoemaker', and he promptly added, 'How exactly the values of the producers are to be determined, and what the ratio between them can mean, is, I must confess, in the end unintelligible to me' ([39], p. 150). Gauthier and Jolif make an ingenious effort to get round the difficulty by asserting that the builder and shoemaker are meant to be considered equal 'as persons' but different (only) in their products. However, I cannot believe that Aristotle went out of his way to insist on *proportional* reciprocity as necessary for justice in this one field, only to conclude that one pair of ratios does not in fact exist, and to make that point in the most ambiguous way possible.[16] Max Salomon

---

13. I have refrained from the common rendition, 'demand', to avoid the subconscious injection of the modern economic concept; so also Soudek [222], p. 60. The semantic cluster around *chreia* in Greek writers, including Aristotle, includes 'use', 'advantage', 'service', taking us even further from 'demand'.

14. In the *Politics*, 1257a31ff., Aristotle explains that delayed exchange became necessary when needs were satisfied by imports from foreign sources, and 'all the naturally necessary things were not easily portable'. (My translations from the *Politics* are based on Ernest Barker's, Oxford, 1946.)

15. The phrase quoted is that of Harrison, *op. cit.*, p. 45.

16. [35], p. 377. They cite in support *MM* 1194a7-27, but those lines are only a simplified and more confusing statement of the argument in the *Ethics*. For future reference, it should be noted that *MM* says explicitly that 'Plato also seems to employ proportional justice in his *Republic*'. St. George Stock, in the Oxford translation (1915), cites *Rep.* 369D, but it requires clairvoyance to see the *MM* reference there, since Plato is not discussing at all how the exchange between builder and shoemaker is to be equated, and soon goes on to introduce the trader as a middleman (significantly absent in the Aristotelian account). In general, however, this section of Book II of the *Republic* was obviously influential on Aristotle (including the stress on need and the explanation of money). For what it is worth, in reply to the commentary

10   achieves the same result by more ruthless methods: the mathematics, he
      says, is a mere 'interpolation', a 'marginal note, so to speak, for listeners
      interested in mathematics', and the whole concept of reciprocal proportion
      must be omitted, leaving Aristotle to say simply that goods are exchanged
      according to their values, and nothing more. That then leads Salomon to a
      series of grotesque translations in order to get out of the text what is not
      there.[17]
          Salomon's drastic surgery was not mere wilful caprice. Economics, he
      writes, cannot be turned into 'a kind of wergeld system on a mercantile
      base' (*op. cit.*, p. 146). The first principle of a market economy is, of course,
      indifference to the *persons* of the buyer and seller: that is what troubles most
      commentators on Aristotle. Soudek therefore suggests that 'as a builder is to
      a shoemaker' must be read 'as the skill of the builder is to the skill of the
      shoemaker'.[18] From there it is no great step to Schumpeter's interpretation.
      The key passage in the *Ethics*, he writes, 'I interpret like this: "As the
      farmer's labour compares with the shoemaker's labour, so the product of
      the farmer compares with the product of the shoemaker". At least, I cannot
      get any other sense out of this passage. If I am right, then Aristotle was
      groping for some labour-cost theory of price which he was unable to state
      explicitly' (*op. cit.*, p. 60, n. 1). A few pages later Schumpeter refers to the
      'just price' of the artisan's 'labour', still later he asserts that the 'relevant
      part' of Aquinas's 'argument on just price . . . is strictly Aristotelian and
      should be interpreted exactly as we have interpreted Aristotle's'.[19] However,
      Aristotle does not once refer to labour costs or costs of production. The
      medieval theologians were the first to introduce this consideration into the

11   discussion, as the foundation for *their* doctrine of just price, and their alleged
      Aristotelianism in this respect rested on the ambiguity of the Latin
      translations of Aristotle made available to them in the middle of the
      thirteenth century.[20]
          Anyway, none of these interpretations of what Aristotle 'really meant'
      answers the question, How are prices, just or otherwise, established in the
      market? More specifically, how are needs, on which Aristotle insists as

---

by Gauthier and Jolif cited above (note 10), I note that Plato says (370A-B), to justify
specialisation of crafts, that 'no two people are born exactly alike. There are innate
differences which fit them for different occupations' (Cornford's translation, Oxford,
1941).
    17. Max Salomon, *Der Begriff der Gerechtigkeit bei Aristoteles* (Leiden, 1937), in a
lengthy appendix, 'Der Begriff des Tauschgeschäftes bei Aristoteles'. My quotation
appears on p. 161. Salomon is not alone in dismissing the mathematics as irrelevant:
see most recently W.F.R. Hardie [58], pp. 198-201.
    18. Soudek [222], pp. 45-6, 60. The same suggestion is made by J.J. Spengler,
'Aristotle on economic imputation and related matters', *Southern Econ. Jl.* 21 (1955),
pp. 371-89.
    19. *ibid.*, pp. 64, 93. Hardie [58], p. 196, simply asserts without serious discussion
that 'the comparative values of producers must in Aristotle's view here mean the
comparative values of their work *done in the same time*' (my italics).
    20. See Soudek [222], pp. 64-5; J.W. Baldwin, 'The medieval theories of the just
price', *Trans. Amer. Philos. Soc.*, new ser. 49, part 4 (1959), pp. 62, 74-5; E. Genzmer,
'Die antiken Grundlagen der Lehre vom gerechten Preis und der laesio enormis', *Z.f.
ausländisches u. internat. Privatrecht* 11 (1937), pp. 25-64, at pp. 27-8.

basic, equated with the parties or their skills or their labour or their labour costs, whichever one prefers? Obviously Aristotle does not say, or at least does not say clearly, otherwise the modern efforts to discover his concealed meaning would all be unnecessary. For Karl Marx the answer is that, though Aristotle was the first to identify the central problem of exchange value, he then admits defeat 'and gives up the further analysis of the form of value' when he concedes (*EN* 1133b18-20) that 'it is impossible for things so different to become commensurable *in reality*'.[21] Soudek repeats his error on corrective justice, already discussed, then grasps at the word 'bargain' which W.D. Ross falsely injects into his translation in one passage (and Rackham in several), and concludes that the price is determined, and justice satisfied, by mutual bargaining until agreement is reached.[22] That is not a very good way to describe what happens in a real market situation, and Soudek suggests that Aristotle's trouble was that 'he was preoccupied with the isolated exchange between individuals and not with the exchange of goods by many sellers and buyers competing with each other' ([222], p. 46) – a strange criticism of a discussion that explicitly sets out to look at exchanges 'within the framework of the community'.

12

Schumpeter takes the opposite line. Starting from the erroneous idea that Aristotle 'condemned [monopoly] as "unjust"' he went on to reason in this way:

It is not farfetched to equate, for Aristotle's purpose, monopoly prices with prices that some individual or group of individuals have set to their own advantage. Prices that are given to the individual and with which he cannot tamper, that is to say, the *competitive* prices that emerge in free market under normal conditions, do not come within the ban. And there is nothing strange in the conjecture that Aristotle

---

21. Marx, *Capital*, transl. S. Moore and E. Aveling, i (Chicago, 1906), p. 68. cf. Roll. *op. cit.*, p. 35. 'What begins with the promise of being a theory of value ends up with a mere statement of the accounting function of money'.

22. [222], pp. 61-4. Both Ross (Oxford, 1925) and Rackham have 'bargain' in 1133a12, Rackham also in 1164a20, 30. (It is worth noting here another mistranslation by Rackham, at 1133b15: 'Hence the proper thing is for all commodities to have their prices fixed'. What Aristotle actually says is 'Therefore it is necessary for everything to be expressed in money, *tetimêsthai*'.) Furthermore, I cannot accept Soudek's use of passages from the beginning of Book IX, continuing the analysis of friendship, as relevant. There Aristotle's examples are drawn from promises to pay for services by musicians, doctors and teachers of philosophy, 'exchanges' in a sense perhaps, but in a sense that is different in quality from those Book V is concerned with. That should be clear from a number of passages. In the opening statement (1163b32-5), Aristotle distinguishes 'dissimilar friendships' (which he is about to discuss) from exchange relations among craftsmen, and he soon says explicitly that the value of a philosopher's services 'is not measurable in money' (1164b3-4). Protagoras, he writes, accepted whatever fee his pupils thought proper (1164a24-6), and Aristotle thinks that is on the whole the right procedure (1164b6-8), though he cannot refrain from the sneer (1164a30-2) that Sophists had better take their payment in advance. All this seems to me to belong to the spirit of gift and counter-gift, of the Charites. There must be reciproçity and proportion here, too, as in all human relations, but I see no other link to the digression on the exchange between builder and shoemaker.

may have taken normal competitive prices as standards of commutative justice or, more precisely, that he was prepared to accept as 'just' *any* transaction between individuals that was carried out at such prices – which is in fact what the scholastic doctors were to do explicitly.[23]

We need not discuss whether or not it is 'farfetched' to conjecture that all this was in Aristotle's mind, though not expressed in his text; it surely takes us away completely from the starting-point stated in the introduction, with its reference to Pythagorean reciprocity and its consequent mathematics.

Schumpeter further observed that the analysis was restricted to the artisan, while the 'chiefly agrarian income of the gentleman' was ignored, the free labourer, 'an anomaly in his slave economy', was 'disposed of perfunctorily', the trader, shipowner, shopkeeper and moneylender judged only in ethical and political terms, their 'gains' not submitted to 'explanatory analysis' (*op.cit.*, pp. 64-5). No wonder Schumpeter dismissed the whole performance as 'decorous, pedestrian, slightly mediocre, and more than slightly pompous common sense' (*ibid.*, p. 57). An analysis that focuses so exclusively on a minor sector of the economy deserves no more complimentary evaluation. Indeed, the time has come to ask whether it is, or was intended to be, *economic* analysis at all.

Before I proceed to give a negative answer, I must confess that, like Joachim, I do not understand what the ratios between the producers can mean, but I do not rule out that 'as a builder is to a shoemaker' is somehow to be taken literally. Marx believed that there was 'an important fact which prevented Aristotle from seeing that, to attribute value to commodities, is merely a mode of expressing all labour as equal human labour, and consequently as labour of equal quality. Greek society was founded upon slavery, and had, therefore, for its natural basis, the inequality of men and of their labour power'.[24] That natural inequality is fundamental to Aristotle's thinking is beyond argument: it permeates his analysis of friendship in the *Ethics* and of slavery in the *Politics*. True, his builder and shoemaker in the exchange paradigm are free men, not slaves,[25] but the concurrent existence of slave labour would still bar his way to a conception of 'equal human labour'.[26]

Schumpeter noticed, but brushed aside, what seems to me to be central in

---

23. *op. cit.*, p. 61. Both references to monopoly which he adduces are incorrect. *Pol.* 1259a5-36 has no condemnation but rather an implied defence of *public* monopoly, whereas the *Ethics*, 1132b21-1134a16, makes no mention of monopoly at all (nor does the *Ethics* anywhere else). Schumpeter is here also repeating his error about the scholastic theologians, from whom he takes the unfortunate word 'commutative'. Soudek, *op. cit.*, p. 64, also drags in a condemnation of monopoly, on the untenable (and irrelevant) ground that 'if the seller holds a monopolistic position, then what appears on the surface as a "voluntary transaction" is distorted in spirit'. For a correct analysis of the *Politics* passage on monopoly, see M. Defourny [188], pp. 21-7.

24. *op. cit.*, p. 69. On Marx's views on Aristotle, see E.C. Welskopf, *Die Produktionsverhältnisse im alten Orient und in der griechisch-römischen Antike* (Berlin, 1957), pp. 336-46.

25. That seems certain from *EN* 1163b32-5.

26. See J.-P. Vernant, *Mythe et pensée chez les grecs* (Paris, 1965), ch. 4.

any judgment, namely, that Aristotle by his silence separates the artisan from the trader, that he is talking exclusively of an exchange between two producers without the intervention of a middleman. Aristotle knew perfectly well that this was not the way a large volume of goods circulated in his world. He also knew perfectly well that prices sometimes responded to variations in supply and demand – that is the point underlying his page in the *Politics* on monopoly. In the discussion of money in the *Ethics* he remarks that money 'is also subject to change and is not always worth the same, but tends to be relatively constant'.[27] This observation is repeated in the *Politics* in a concrete application: in the section on revolutions, Aristotle warns against rigidly fixed assessments in states that have a property qualification for office, since one should allow for the impact on the assessment 'when there is an abundance of coin'.[28]

In short, price variations according to supply and demand were a commonplace in Greek life in the fourth century B.C.[29] Yet in the *Ethics* Aristotle does not use any of the normal Greek words for trade and trader (as he does ruthlessly in the *Politics*), but clings to the neutral word 'exchange'. That this is deliberate I cannot doubt: in the passage in the *Republic* on which much of this section of the *Ethics* is a kind of commentary, Plato concedes that the *polis* requires petty traders (*kapêloi*) who will give money for goods and goods for money because neither farmers nor artisans can count on finding someone with whom to exchange whenever they bring goods to the market (*Rep.* 371B-C). Aristotle, however, cannot introduce the *kapêlos*, since justice in the exchange (which is not Plato's question) is achieved when 'each has his own', when, in other words, there is no gain from someone else's loss (*EN* 1133a31-b6). As part of a theory of price this is nonsense, and Aristotle knew it to be nonsense. Therefore he was not seeking a theory of market prices.[30]

The digression on exchange, I repeat, was placed at the start 'within the framework of the community'. When the digression ends, furthermore, Aristotle resumes the main thread as follows (*EN* 1134a24-6): 'We must not

14

27. *Pol.* 1259a5-36; *EN* 1133b13-14.

28. *Pol.* 1308a36-8. Nowhere does Aristotle explain why money is 'relatively constant' compared with other commodities. The general observation, it should be noted, had already been made by so shallow a thinker as Xenophon, *Ways and Means*, 4.6.

29. I should perhaps not have bothered with these seeming platitudes, were it not that Karl Polanyi, 'Aristotle discovers the economy', in *Trade and Market in the Early Empires*, ed. K. Polanyi, C.M. Arensberg and H.W. Pearson (Glencoe, Ill., 1957), pp. 64-94, makes the strange remark (p. 87) that 'the supply-demand-price mechanism escaped Aristotle. The distribution of food in the market allowed as yet but scant room to the play of that mechanism . . . Not before the third century B.C. was the working of a supply-demand-price mechanism in international trade noticeable'. How wrong that is will be evident from Lysias' 22nd oration, *Against the Corndealers*, to be dated about 387 B.C., on which see R. Seager in *Historia* 15 (1966), pp. 172-84, or from Demosthenes 32.24-5 and Pseudo-Demosthenes 56.9-10, half a century later. (Polanyi's chapter has been reprinted in the volume cited in note 40, but my references are to the original publication.)

30. This is also the conclusion of Polanyi, *op. cit.* Although our analyses diverge, often sharply (see note 29), I must warmly acknowledge his having introduced me to' the problem nearly twenty years ago.

forget that the subject of our investigation is both justice in the absolute sense and political justice.' The phrase 'political justice' is an excessively literal rendering of the Greek, for Aristotle goes on to define it as 'justice among free and (actually or proportionately) equal men, living a community life in order to be self-sufficient [*or* for the purpose of self-sufficiency]'. Monetary gain has no place in such an investigation: 'The money-maker is someone who lives under constraint'.[31] It is in the context of self-sufficiency, not money-making, that need provides the measuring-rod of just exchange (and that the *proper* use of money also became necessary and therefore ethically acceptable). In the *Ethics*, in sum, there is strictly speaking *no* economic analysis rather than poor or inadequate economic analysis.

2.

It will have been noticed that in the *Ethics* Aristotle does not ask how farmers or shoemakers come to behave as they do in exchange. In Schumpeter's terms, then, in the *Ethics* there is no economic sociology either. For that we must turn to Book I of the *Politics*, and again begin by carefully fixing the context in which exchange is discussed. Aristotle first establishes that both the household and the *polis* are natural forms of human association, and proceeds to examine various implications such as the relations of dominance and subjection (including between masters and slaves). Then he turns to property and 'the art of acquiring it' (*chrêmatistikê*) and asks whether the latter is identical with the art of household management (*oikonomikê*, 1256a1-5). His choice of words is important and has led to much confusion and error. *Oikonomikê* (or *oikonomia*) in Greek usage normally retains the primary meaning, 'the art of household management'. Though that may involve 'economic' activity, it is misleading, and often flatly wrong, to translate it as 'economics'.[32] But *chrêmatistikê* is ambiguous. (Its root is the noun *chrêma*, 'a thing one needs or uses', in the plural *chrêmata*, 'goods, property'.) We have already met *chrêmatistikê* (and we shall soon meet it again) in the sense of 'the art of money-making', but here it has the more generic sense of acquisition, less common in ordinary Greek usage but essential to Aristotle's argument. For he soon concludes that *oikonomia* and *chrêmatistikê* (in the money-making sense) are different though overlapping species of the genus *chrêmatistikê*.[33]

31. 1096a5-6. For this translation of *ho de chrêmatistês biaios tis estin*, see Gauthier and Jolif [35], 2, pp. 33-4, whose commentary cuts through all the unnecessary emendation and elaborate interpretation the text has been subjected to.

32. Occasionally the word *oikonomia* was extended to the public sphere, and even then it usually refers to administration in general, as when Dinarchus (1.97) calls Demosthenes 'useless in the affairs (*oikonomiai*) of the city' (note the plural). The furthest extension is to be found in a brief section at the beginning of Book II of the pseudo-Aristotelian *Oeconomica* (1345b7-1346a25), in which four types of 'economy' are said to exist: royal, satrapic, city-state and private. There follow six short paragraphs of excruciating banality about the sources of revenue in each of the types, and that is the end of the discussion.

33. Beginning with the Sophists, philosophers were faced with the problem of creating the vocabulary for systematic analysis out of everyday words. One

Exchange again enters the discussion polemically. What is wealth, **16** Aristotle asks? Is it, as Solon had said, limitless? Or is it a means to an end and therefore limited by that end (1256b30-4)? The answer is categorical. Wealth is a means, necessary for the maintenance of the household and the *polis* (with self-sufficiency a principle in the background), and, like all means, it is limited by its end. Of course, he continues, there is the second, money-making sense of *chrêmatistikê*, and that is what has led to the false opinion that there is no limit to wealth and property. This attitude to wealth indeed sees it as limitless, but it is against nature and therefore not a proper subject of ethical or political discourse, on his fundamental principle that ethics has a natural basis. ('The money-maker', we remember from the *Ethics*, 'is someone who lives under constraint' (*EN* 1096a5-6)).

Although Aristotle singles out the *obolostatês*, the petty usurer living on small consumer loans, as the most unnatural of all practitioners of the art of money-making (1258b2-8) – money 'came into existence for the sake of exchange, interest makes it increase' – the type he selects as the exemplar is the *kapêlos*, just the man we noted as missing from the analysis of exchange in the *Ethics*. Again the choice of words is significant. Greek usage was not wholly consistent in selecting among the various words for 'trader', but *kapêlos* usually denoted the petty trader, the huckster, in the market-place. In the present context, however, the accent is not on the scale of his operations but on the aim, so that *kapêlikê*, the art of the *kapêlos*, must be translated 'trade for the sake of gain' or simply 'commercial trade'.[34] Like Plato before him, Aristotle now asks the historical question, how did exchange come to take place altogether. His answer is that as the *koinônia* grew beyond the individual household, there were shortages and surpluses and these were corrected by mutual exchange, 'as many barbarian tribes do to this day . . . When used in this way, the art of exchange is not contrary to **17** nature, nor in any way a species of the art of money-making. It simply served to satisfy the natural requirements of self-sufficiency' (1257a24-30).[35] But then, because of the difficulties created by foreign sources of supply (a passage I have already quoted in note 14), money was introduced, and out of that there developed *kapêlikê*. Its end is not 'the natural requirements of

---

increasingly common device was to employ the suffix -*ikos*. There are some 700 such words in Aristotle, many first employed by him. See P. Chantraine, *La Formation des noms en grec ancien* (Paris, 1933), ch. 36. Polanyi, *op. cit.*, pp. 92-3, was right to insist that failure to distinguish between the two meanings of *chrêmatistikê* is fatal to an understanding of this section of the *Politics*; cf. Defourny [188], pp. 5-7; briefly Barker, Notes E and F of his translation (pp. 22 and 27), though he adds new confusion by suggesting 'domestic economy, and 'political economy' as English equivalents.

34. Polanyi, *op. cit.*, pp. 91-2, was almost alone in seeing the point. However, I cannot accept his explanations, that 'no name had yet been given to "commercial trade"' (p. 83) and that Aristotle, with a kind of Shavian wit, was exposing the fact that 'commercial trade was no mystery . . . but huckstering written large' (p. 92). Polanyi did not take sufficient notice of the Platonic background.

35. It is worth noting the contrast with the 'simplest' model for 'an economic theory of the city state' put forward by John Hicks, *A Theory of Economic History* (Oxford and London, 1969), pp. 42-6. That starts with the exchange by merchants of oil for corn, 'and the trade is unlikely to get started unless, to begin with, it is a handsome profit'.

self-sufficiency' but the acquisition of money without limit. Such acquisition – we should say 'profit' – is made 'not according to nature but *at the expense of others*' (1258b1-2), a phrase that echoes in reverse the 'each has his own' of the *Ethics* and gives the final proof that commercial exchange was not the subject in the *Ethics*.

Aristotle was so rigorous in the ethical argument that he refused to make even Plato's concession. The *kapêlos* is not only unnatural, he is also 'unnecessary' (1258a14-18). That this was not meant as a 'practical' proposal is certain, but that is irrelevant in the present analysis.[36] What is relevant is that Aristotle extended his ethical judgments to embrace the highest form of *koinônia*, the *polis* itself. The state, like the householder, must sometimes concern itself with acquisition (1258a19-34, 1259a34-6). Hence, in the discussion of the ideal state, in Book VII of the *Politics*, he recommends that the *polis* be sited so as to have easy access to food supplies, timber and the like. That immediately plunges him into another current debate, whether connexion with the sea is a good or bad thing, and he decides that the advantages outweigh the disadvantages.

> It should be able to import those things which it does not itself produce, and to export the surplus of its own necessities. It should practise commerce for itself [Aristotle now switches from *kapêlikê* to the commonest word for foreign trade, *emporikê* or *emporia*], but not for others. States which make themselves market-places for the world only do it for the sake of revenue; and since it is not proper for a *polis* to share in such gain, it ought not have such an emporium (1327a25-31).

18   There will have to be merchants, of course, but 'any disadvantage which may threaten can easily be met by laws defining the persons who may, or may not, have dealings with one another'.[37]

Nowhere in the *Politics* does Aristotle ever consider the rules or mechanics of commercial exchange. On the contrary, his insistence on the unnaturalness of commercial gain rules out the possibility of such a discussion, and also helps explain the heavily restricted analysis in the *Ethics*. Of economic analysis there is not a trace.

3.

One could rest the argument there, perhaps adding the familiar point that Aristotle, and even more Plato before him, were in many respects resisting the social, economic, political and moral developments of fourth-century Greece. There is the famous analogy of the way Aristotle appears to ignore

---

36. Soudek [222], pp. 71-2, sees a programmatic difference between Plato and Aristotle. Basing himself on *Laws*, 918A-920C, and forgetting both *Rep.* 371B-C (which I quoted earlier) and *Pol.* 1327a25-31 (quoted later in this paragraph), Soudek writes that 'the author of the *Laws* . . . had made his peace with moneymaking and plutocracy, while Aristotle never gave up his opposition to this class'. Beneath this fundamental musunderstanding lies an equally fantastic picture of a sharp class struggle in Greece between wealthy landowners and merchants.

37. Plato of course drafted the legislation, *Laws* 919D-920D.

completely the careers of Philip and Alexander, and their consequences for the *polis*, the natural form of political association. He was therefore equally free to ignore the unnatural developments in commercial trade and money-making, despite their growth in the same period and the tensions they generated. Schumpeter was right to comment that 'preoccupation with the ethics of pricing ... is precisely one of the strongest motives a man can possibly have for analysing actual market mechanisms' (*op.cit.*, p. 60). It does not follow, however, that ethical preoccupations *must* lead to such an analysis, and I have tried to show that 'pricing' was actually not Aristotle's concern.

In the end, Schumpeter opted for a strictly 'intellectual' explanation. Although he wrote in his introduction that 'to a large extent, the economics of different epochs deal with different sets of facts and problems' (*ibid.*, p. 5), he ignored that point when he excused Aristotle for being mediocre and commonsensical.

> There is nothing surprising or blameworthy in this. It is by slow degrees that the physical and social facts of the empirical universe enter the range of the analytic searchlight. In the beginnings of scientific analysis, the mass of the phenomena is left undisturbed in the compound of commonsense knowledge, and only chips of this mass arouse scientific curiousity and thereupon become 'problems'.[38]

Yet Aristotle's scientific curiosity has rarely been paralleled, and the time has come to ask: the mass of what phenomena? Would an *economic* analysis have been possible had his (or anyone else's) interest not been deflected? Indeed, would even a description of 'the economy' have been possible?

Today we write books with such titles as *The Economics of Ancient Greece*, and the chapters are headed agriculture, mining and minerals, labour, industry, commerce, money and banking, public finance – Schumpeter's 'chips' of the 'mass of the phenomena'.[39] This learned activity presupposes the existence of 'the economy' as a concept, difficult as it has become to find a generally acceptable definition. The current debate about 'economic anthropology', largely stimulated by Karl Polanyi's insistence on a sharp distinction between what he called the 'substantive' and the 'formal' definitions of the economy,[40] is a debate about definitions and their implications for (historical) analysis, not about the existence of 'the economy'. As Polanyi himself said, even in early societies 'only the concept of the economy, not the economy itself, is in abeyance' (*op.cit.*, p. 86). No one could disagree with his substantive definition; in one of his varied

19

38. *ibid.*, p. 65. See the general criticism by Little (above, note 2).

39. The title and chapter headings are those of H. Michell's book, 2nd edn. (Cambridge, 1957).

40. Polanyi's theoretical essays have been conveniently assembled under the title, *Primitive, Archaic, and Modern Economies*, ed. G. Dalton (Garden City, N.Y., 1968). For a commentary on the debate, with extensive bibliography, see M. Godelier, 'Objet et méthode de l'anthropologie économique', *L'Homme* 5, no. 2 (1965), pp. 32-91, reprinted in his *Rationalité et irrationalité en économie* (Paris, 1966), pp. 232-93; S.C. Humphreys, 'History, economics and anthropology: the work of Karl Polanyi', *History and Theory* 8 (1969), pp. 165-212.

formulations it is 'an instituted process of interaction between man and his environment, which results in a continuous supply of want-satisfying material means' (*ibid.*, p. 145); his opponents merely deny that this is a sufficient operational definition. 'Modern economists make even Robinson Crusoe speculate upon the implications of choice which they regard as the essence of economy'.[41]

Nor were the Greeks themselves unaware that men procure their want-satisfactions by social (Polanyi's 'instituted') arrangements, or that there were things to be said about agriculture, mining, money, or commerce. Aristotle refers readers who may be interested to existing books on the practical side. He mentions by name the authors of two agronomic treatises (*Pol.* 1258b39ff.), and much practical information is scattered in the surviving botanical writings of his pupil Theophrastus. Greeks who thought about the matter were also aware that their want-satisfying arrangements were technologically and socially more complex than had been the case in the past. The Homeric poems and the witness of contemporary 'barbarians' were proof enough. Greek 'historical' accounts of the development from early times were largely speculative. One should not attribute to them too much accurate knowledge of the past on such subjects; they were, for example, ignorant of the complex palace-centred organisation of the late Bronze Age. The significance of the speculation lies rather in its testimony to the values of the classical era, the fifth and fourth centuries B.C. On this two points are significant for us.

The first is that growth of population, increasing specialisation and technological advances, the increase in material resources were all judged positively. They were the necessary conditions for civilisation, for the 'natural', that is, the highest, form of social organisation, the *polis*. This was no discovery of Plato and Aristotle; it was implicit in the Prometheus myth, it became more explicit in the 'prehistory' with which Thucydides opens his *History* (1.2-19) and in other fifth-century writers known to us only from fragments.[42] 'The ancient Greek world', writes Thucydides, 'lived like the barbarians of today' (1.6.6). However, progress was not an unmixed blessing. It led to bitter class struggles, imperial conquest, and the ethical dangers we have already noticed. Furthermore, there is an implication that technological and material progress has come to an end. At least I am unaware of any text which suggests that continued growth in this sphere of human behaviour was either possible or desirable, and the whole tenor of the literature argues against such a notion.[43] There can and will be progress in certain cultural spheres, such as mathematics or astronomy; there can, some thought, be improvements in ethical, social and political behaviour (more often than not put in terms of a return to older virtues); there can be

41. Roll, *op. cit.*, p. 21.

42. On the fragments, see T. Cole, *Democritus and the Sources of Greek Anthropology* (Amer. Philological Assn., Monograph 25, 1967).

43. I have examined some aspects of this theme in 'Technical innovation and economic progress in the ancient world', *Econ. Hist. Rev.*, 2nd ser. 18 (1965), pp. 29-45; cf. H.W. Pleket, 'Technology and society in the Graeco-Roman world', *Acta Historiae Neerlandica* 2 (1967), pp. 1-25, originally published in Dutch in *Tijd. v. Geschiedenis* 78 (1965), pp. 1-22.

better (truer) understanding of life and society. But none of that adds up to the idea of progress which, in my judgment, has been in the background of all modern economic analyses at least since the late eighteenth century.[44]

For Thucydides one of the driving forces in 'prehistoric' progress was the rise and growth of maritime commerce – and that is the second point. Given his grand theme, the Athenian empire and the Peloponnesian War, he was more concerned with the corollary, the navy and the maritime empire, a polemical subject both in his day and later. But interwoven with this aspect was always the other, on which I quoted Aristotle earlier, overseas trade as an indispensable supplement to home production, for foodstuffs, timber, metals and slaves.[45] And 'in Athens facts had a way of becoming spiritual problems'.[46] That is precisely how the discussion turned. I have in mind not maritime power but the 'problem' of trade and markets. Herodotus (1.152-3) reveals its existence a century before Aristotle. When a Spartan embassy came to warn the Persian king not to harm any Greek city, he tells us, Cyrus replied: 'I have never yet feared men of this kind, who set up a place in the centre of their city where they assemble and cheat each other with oaths'. This was addressed to all Greeks, Herodotus explains, 'because they have established market-places for buying and selling', whereas the Persians have neither the practice nor the market-place. Xenophon (*Cyropaedia*, 1.2.3) offers partial support in his statement that the Persians exclude all hucksters and peddlers from the 'free *agora*' (here to be translated in its original sense, 'assembly-place'). Whatever the truth may be about Persia, the *Greek* attitude reflected by Herodotus and Xenophon is evident. Aristotle used the same terminology as Xenophon when he proposed that 'provision should be made for an *agora* of the sort called "free" in Thessaly [a district in north-central Greece]. This should be clear of all merchandise, and neither a workingman nor a farmer nor any other such person should be permitted to enter unless summoned by the magistrates' (*Pol.* 1331a30-5). As a final example, there was Aristotle's contemporary, Aristoxenus, who thought it reasonable to claim that the half-legendary Pythagoras had 'extolled and promoted the study of numbers more than anyone, diverting it from the business of merchants' (Frag. 58B2 Diels-Kranz).

However, neither speculation about the origins of trade nor doubts about market ethics led to the elevation of 'the economy' (which cannot be translated into Greek) to independent status as a subject of discussion or

---

44. The faith of some Hippocratic writers, notably the author of *On Ancient Medicine* (sect. 2), that 'the rest [of medical knowledge] will be discovered eventually', is no exception, though admittedly such progress would bring 'practical' benefits to mankind. Neglect of the fundamental ,distinction between material and cultural progress in my view vitiates the much-praised polemic by L. Edelstein, *The Idea of Progress in Classical Antiquity* (Baltimore, 1967), against the 'orthodox' view, summed up by J.B. Bury, *The Idea of Progress* (New York, 1932 edn.), p. 7: '... the Greeks, who were so fertile in their speculations on human life, did not hit upon an idea which seems so simple and obvious to us as the idea of Progress'. On Thucydides, see J. de Romilly, 'Thucydide et l'idée de progrès', *Ann. Scuola norm. Pisa* 35 (1966), pp. 143-91.

45. On all this see A. Momigliano, 'Sea-power in Greek thought', *Class. Rev.,* 58 (1944), pp. 1-7, reprinted in his *Secondo contributo alla storia degli studi classici* (Rome, 1960), pp. 57-67.

46. *ibid.,* p. 58.

study, at least not beyond Aristotle's division of the art of acquisition into *oikonomia* and money-making, and that was a dead end. The model that survived and was imitated was Xenophon's *Oikonomikos*, a manual covering all the human relations and activities in the household (*oikos*), the relations between husband and wife, between master and slaves, between householder and his land and goods. It was not from *Hausvaterliteratur* that modern economic thinking and writing arose in the late eighteenth century, but from the radical discovery that there were 'laws' of circulation, of market exchange, of value and prices (to which the theory of ground rent was linked).[47] It is at least of symbolic interest that in precisely that era David Hume made the brilliant (and still too often neglected) observation: 'I do not remember a passage in any ancient author, where the growth of a city is ascribed to the establishment of a manufacture. The commerce, which is said to flourish, is chiefly the exchange of those commodities, for which different soils and climates were suited.'[48]

I would be prepared to argue that without the concept of relevant 'laws' (or 'statistical uniformities' if one prefers) it is not possible to have a concept of 'the economy'. However, I shall be content here merely to insist that the ancients did not (rather than could not) have the concept, and to suggest where the explanation lies. One consequence of the idea of the *koinônia* was a heavy encroachment by political and status demands on the behaviour or ordinary Greeks, not just in writings of a few doctrinaire intellectuals. If we consider investment, for example, we immediately come up against a
23   political division of the population that was unbridgeable. All Greek states, so far as we know, restricted the right of land ownership to their citizens (save for exceptional individuals who received the right as a personal privilege). They thereby, in effect, erected a wall between the land, from which the great majority of the population received their livelihood, and that very substantial proportion of the money available for investment which was in the hands of non-citizens.[49] Among the most obvious practical consequences was a narrowing of choice of investment (whether by purchase or by loan) for the potential investors on the one hand, and a tendency on the part of money-holding citizens to turn to the land from considerations of status, not of maximisation of profits.[50] The absence in our sources of any evidence of investment (including loans) for improvements on land or in manufacture is noteworthy, especially against the considerable evidence of relatively large-scale borrowing for conspicuous consumption

47. See O. Brunner, 'Das "ganze Haus" und die alteuropäische Ökonomik', in his *Neue Wege der Sozialgeschichte* (Göttingen, 1956), Ch. 2, originally published in *Z.f. Nationalök.* 13 (1950), pp. 114-39.

48. 'Of the Populousness of Ancient Nations', *Essays* (London, World's Classics edn., 1903), p. 415. How widely and carefully Hume had read ancient authors is demonstrated not only in this essay but also in his notebooks.

49. The important economic role of the metic (the free resident 'alien'), which underlies this point, will be considered immediately below.

50. I have discussed the evidence briefly in *Studies in Land and Credit in Ancient Athens* (New Brunswick, N.J., 1952), pp. 74-8; again in 'Land, debt, and the man of property in classical Athens', *Pol. Sci. Quart.* 68 (1953), pp. 249-68. Detailed research into the whole question of 'investments' is urgently needed.

and for expensive political obligations.[51] No doubt a modern economist could construct a sophisticated investment model to account for these Greek conditions of choice. But first the usefulness, indeed the possibility, of such a model has to be envisaged, as it was not in antiquity.[52]

Kept off the land, the non-citizens of necessity lived by manufacture, trade and moneylending. That would be of little interest were it not for the capital fact that this metic activity was not a matter of their being tolerated by the *koinônia* but of their being indispensable. They were *sought after*, precisely because the citizens could not carry on all the activities necessary for the survival of the community.[53] (Whether or not they could not 'only' 24 because they would not is a historically meaningless 'psychological' question that seems to me to divert attention from the central issue.) Slaves were the sole labour force in all manufacturing establishments exceeding the immediate family circle, right to the managerial level. Without the many thousands of free non-citizens, mostly Greeks themselves, some transient, others permanently resident (metics), maritime commerce in the more complex urbanised communities would have fallen below the essential minimum for vital supplies, not to mention luxury goods. Hence fourth-century Athens omitted one piece from its network of laws designed to guarantee a sufficient annual import of corn – it made no effort to restrict or specify the personnel engaged in the trade.[54]

The position is neatly symbolised by a single pamphlet, the *Ways and Means* (or *Revenues*) written by Xenophon in the period when Aristotle was worrying about *oikonomikê* and *chrêmatistikê*. His proposals for raising the revenues of Athens are concentrated on two groups of people. First he suggests measures to increase the number of metics, 'one of the best sources of revenue': they pay taxes, they are self-supporting, and they receive no pay

51. C. Mossé, *La Fin de la démocratie athénienne* (Paris, 1962), pt. 1, ch. 1, has argued in great detail that the fourth century B.C. witnessed more fluidity than my sketch (cited in the previous note) allowed. Even so, she agrees with the point at issue here, e.g. pp. 66-7: 'certainly such profits [from accumulation of land holdings] were rarely reinvested in production . . . That is why, if there was a concentration of landholding, it did not bring about any profound transformation in the mode of agricultural production'.

52. Political and status 'interference' was equally significant in other aspects, for example, on prices and wages whenever the state was a party, which was often the case. To enter into details would protract this discussion unnecessarily, I believe.

53. This was openly acknowledged by an anonymous fifth-century oligarchic pamphleteer, Pseudo-Xenophon, *Constitution of Athens*, 1.11-12; Plato, *Laws* 919D-920C, made a virtue of the fact; Aristotle was troubled in the *Politics* by his inability to get round this obtrusive element in the *koinônia*, as J. Pečírka showed in a short but important article, 'A note on Aristotle's conception of citizenship and the role of foreigners in fourth century Athens', *Eirene* 6 (1967), pp. 23-6. On metics generally in fourth-century Athens, see Mossé, *op. cit.*, pp. 167-79. Hicks, *op. cit.*, p. 48, seems to me to have placed the accent exactly in the wrong place when he writes of the metics, 'what is remarkable is that there should have been a phase in which their *competition* is tolerated, or even welcomed, by those already established' (my italics).

54. To avoid misunderstanding, I will say explicitly that a count of heads would probably show that even in Athens the citizens who did work of some kind, including agriculture, outnumbered the others. The point at issue is the location within the economy of the vital minority.

from the state for their services. The steps he proposes are (1) release metics from the burdensome obligation of service in the infantry; (2) admit them to the cavalry (an honorific service); (3) permit them to buy land in the city on which to build residences; (4) offer prizes to the market officials for just and speedy settlement of disputes; (5) give reserved seats in the theatre and other forms of hospitality to worthy foreign merchants; (6) build more lodging-houses and hotels in the harbour and increase the number of market-places. Hesitantly he adds the possibility that the state should build its own merchant fleet and lease the vessels out, and immediately turns to his second group, slaves. Starting from the observation that large private fortunes have been made by men who invested in slaves and let them to
25   holders of concessions in the Athenian silver mines, Xenophon proposes that the state embark on this activity itself, ploughing back the profits into the purchase of more and more slaves. After some rough calculations and various counter-arguments against possible objections, he writes, 'I have now explained what measures should be taken by the state *in order that every Athenian may be maintained at public expense*' (*Ways and Means*, 4.33).

We need not waste time examining the practicality of these schemes. Many harsh things have been said about them by modern scholars – all from the wrong point of view, that of modern economic institutions and ideas. What matters is the mentality revealed in this unique document, a mentality which pushed to the extreme the notion that what we call the economy was properly the exclusive business of outsiders.[55]

55. I have discussed the matter raised in this final section (and elsewhere) more fully in *The Ancient Economy* (London, 1973).

14

Marcus Wheeler

Aristotle's Analysis of the Nature of Political Struggle

1.

This essay is a study of the notion of *stasis* in the light of Aristotle's   145
treatment of the subject in the *Politics* and in the form of an examination of
the analysis made by him of that notion. It seems hardly necessary to defend
at length the view that this topic is one of considerable interest and
importance. Two reasons for holding the view, however, are the following.
First, our historical texts make it clear that *stasis* is a fundamental and
persistent feature of Greek politics of the classical period. It follows,
therefore, that we cannot expect to acquire an adequate grasp of the nature
of Greek public life without first understanding the phenomenon which we
call *stasis*. Second, it appears to be the case that the meaning of the word
stasis, in so far as it can be at all precisely delimited, contains an element
which is not adequately represented by any of the English equivalents
which have been suggested. This is not so small a point as it might seem.
The use of the word 'revolution', as in Jowett's translation, for instance, and
in most translations of Thucydides, is, I believe, thoroughly misleading. The
connotation of *stasis* is distinctly narrower than that of social and economic
disintegration which has been acquired in modern times by the word
'revolution'. If we say that 'revolution' is a correct description of the events
known collectively as the French Revolution and as the Russian Revolution, I
do not think we can apply the term to the kind of events referred to by the
Greeks as *stasis*, even though such events were frequently due, as Aristotle
saw, to conflicts of an economic and social rather than of a purely political
character.

It may be claimed, in conclusion, that, if translators have failed
adequately to represent the meaning of the word, commentators have failed
sufficiently to stress the importance of the notion of *stasis* as discussed by
Aristotle. The majority[1] confine themselves to bare exposition of Aristotle's   146
doctrine and leave little or no space for criticism. What comment is to be
found is seldom more than an uncritical reference to the 'ripe political
wisdom'[2] displayed by Aristotle in Book V of the *Politics*. Newman and
Barker have more to say, proportionately to the size of their works. The

---

1. e.g. F. Susemihl and R.D. Hicks [174], pp. 56-66. E. Zeller, *Aristotle and the
Earlier Peripatetics* (trans. by B.F.C. Costelloe and J.H. Muirhead, London, 1897), Ch.
8. T. Gomperz, *Greek Thinkers*, IV, Ch. 31. W. Jaeger [25], Ch. 10. G.H. Sabine, *A
History of Political Theory* (New York, 1937), Ch. 6.

2. Susemihl, p. 60. W.D. Ross [15], Ch. 8.

former's commentary is, however, largely expository rather than critical, although he does note the important distinction of *stasis* and *metabolai* in the subject-matter of Book V, also the fact that the English word 'revolution' does not exactly correspond to either.[3] Barker, unfortunately, does not include a discussion of the meaning of *stasis* in his excellent introduction to the vocabulary of the *Politics*, and relegates comment on the word to a footnote.[4]

The historical data on which Aristotle bases his treatment of the subject are sufficiently known not to require much discussion. He himself takes the greater part of his collection of case-histories of *stasis* from events of the fourth century, but we can trace the phenomenon in our extant authorities from at least the beginning of the sixth century. Not to pursue the enquiry further, we find the word *stasis* already used in the technical sense which we are considering in Solon (4.19) and Theognis (43-52; 781). The former is described as observing his city 'often engaged in *stasis*', and the assignment to him of a law requiring all citizens to take sides in times of *stasis* may be further evidence that this was already an established feature of Athenian politics (Aristotle, *Ath. Resp.* 8.4). Perhaps the *locus classicus* for the meaning of the word *stasis* and for the usage of it and its derivatives is Herodotus, I. 59.

147 3, describing the rise to power of Peisistratus: 'When the Athenian coast-dwellers and those from the plain were engaged in *stasis* ... [Peisistratus], aiming at tyranny, raised a third *stasis*, and, collecting *stasiôtai* ... contrived the following plan.' We shall have later to consider the evidence of sixth-century history in deciding to what extent it is permissible to analyse the notion of *stasis* in economic terms. The passage of Herodotus just quoted, however, is also interesting as illustrating a causal connexion which, I believe, can be shown to hold between an element in the meaning of *stasis* which is lost in renderings like 'revolution' and 'sedition' and what may be called a characteristic method of classical Greek politics. This method is one by no means invariably, but with considerable regularity employed, and its principal features are a greater or less recourse to force or fraud, and a greater or less degree of 'unconstitutional' behaviour. It is outside the scope of this essay to consider whether there is any sense in which the concept of 'parties' can be successfully applied to Greek city-states, but in so far as it will be conceded that nothing existed approximating to the modern conception of a political party, the prevalence and distinctive character of *stasis* may be explained as arising from the fact that, if an influential or an organised 'opposition' group does come into being, its aim cannot be, as it often is under a modern party-system, merely to substitute its policy for that of the group in power: it must be to capture power and, wholly or partially, modify the constitution.[5] This latter point requires more emphasis than it has previously received. It is probable that the notion of 'constitution', at any rate in its modern usage, is no more applicable to the majority of Greek city-states than that of 'party'. We are inclined to think of a constitution as sovereign and

3. Newman, [172], I 522.
4. E. Barker [176], p. 204, n.
5. For example, compare the rise to power of Cleisthenes and the 'revolution' of the Four Hundred at Athens. The former needed to acquire influential support (Herodotus, V. 66. 2). The oligarchical 'clubs' were evidently highly organised.

immutable, set up above the tendencies of a particular government or piece of legislation – 'all the rules which govern the government'. But Aristotle, although he has a glimpse of the ideal of the 'Rule of Law', sees that the goodness or badness of laws varies of necessity with the constitutions of states, and that constitutions are governed by and do not govern the group in power.[6] It is no doubt the flexibility and mutability of the *politeia* (constitution) in Greek cities which account for the interest taken by Plato, Aristotle, and others in the classification of constitutions and for the pains which Aristotle takes in elaborating in detail the varieties of each form.

148

2.

The principal criticism of the analysis of *stasis* in the *Politics* to be made in this essay is that Aristotle exaggerates the importance of exhaustiveness of treatment at the expense of lucidity, and that in consequence he obscures the distinction between the different types of phenomena which are his subject-matter, frequently confuses symptom and cause, and fails to make sufficiently precise his evaluation of the various factors involved in *stasis*. In the first place, it is important not to confuse *stasis* with *metabolê politeias* (change of constitution). It has been suggested that it is difficult to change the constitution through any medium but that of *stasis*, but it is not necessarily impossible to achieve a change by other means (V.3.8). Instances might be taken from early Greek history of the employment of a *nomothetês* or legislator who devised a new constitution with 'general consent' (see II.11), although it should be noted that the legislation of Solon at Athens, for instance, was followed immediately by a further period of *stasis*. Similarly *stasis* may occur completely divorced from the desire for *metabolê*. Thus Thucydides says of the *stasis* at Corcyra that 'the members of the factions had not in view the blessings derivable from established institutions, but were formed by ambition for their overthrow' (III.82). Possibly *metabolê* is a more comprehensive term than *stasis*: we may suggest tentatively the following distinction. *Metabolê* describes a completed act, the establishment or revision of a constitution: *stasis* describes a situation, the essential feature of which is the use of violence or 'illegal' behaviour by two or more groups.[7]

149

We wish, therefore, to discover the nature of this characteristic situation. It is perhaps unwise to speak of seeking the cause of *stasis* rather than of discovering some fundamental conflict or conflicts of which everything that is properly described as *stasis* is a manifestation. Aristotle does not use the word *aitia*, but distinguishes three factors (V.2.1). (1) psychological motive or principle; (2) concrete objectives; (3) *archai*. We may consider briefly each of these. Aristotle makes the generalisation (1) that *stasis* is everywhere

6. III, 1282b1-13. Plato has the same idea in suggesting that 'the worst of all enemies to the whole state is he who enslaves the laws ... and makes the State subject to a faction' (*Laws* 856B; cf. also Aristotle, *Politics*, III.10.5).

7. The word 'illegal' is apostrophised in view of what has been said about the connotation of *politeia* as contrasted with that of 'constitution'. In Aristotle's view, a *politeia* may be said to be 'illegal' in the same sense in which a group of revolutionaries are thought to act illegally. See IV 4, 1292a4-20; 5, 1292b5; cf. the comment on Theramenes in *Ath. Resp.* 28.5.

due to inequality (V.1.11). Not all, however, are prompted by a desire for literal equality, but they seek a share in the *politeia* compatible with their due 'in their own estimation' (V.1.5). Thus oligarchs will not in fact be content with equality, but demand superiority for the few. This aspiration is probably misrepresented if thought of as the desire for equality as an abstract principle and in fact is closely bound up with (2), the concrete objectives of *stasis*, namely political privilege (*timê*) and profit (*kerdos*). That the latter is used in a comparatively narrow sense to refer to profit accruing directly from the holding of office is suggested by the statement in a later chapter that 'the most important precaution in every type of state' is that office be not made profitable.[8] If this interpretation of *kerdos* is correct, the objectives at any rate of *stasis*, or some of them, appear to be of a purely

150   political character. We come now to (3) the *archai*. Newman remarks that 'Aristotle perhaps rates rather too highly the share of these "occasions" in causing constitutional change'. This is not an entirely justified criticism, since Aristotle does see that, if the issues of *stasis* are great, the occasions of it are small (V.4.1). A juster objection is that he does not discriminate between the occasions with which he deals, although in fact they are of very varying importance. The eleven *archai* enumerated by him in *Politics* V 2 are adequately grouped by Newman under three heads (vol. IV, p. 275):

(a) Some emotional state of the minds of the citizens, e.g. resentment of the political power and profits of others, fear or contempt of rulers[9] (*hubris*, which is especially a source of dissension in monarchies (V.10.13), is presumably an emotional state of the ruler).

(b) Social causes. The most important of these is in fact a deep-rooted economic cause of *stasis*, namely the disproportionate increase in size or power of one class in the state. In view of the charge made against Aristotle and other ancient political theorists that they ignore economic forces, it is important to notice the statement that disproportionate increase occurs 'sometimes also through chance, as due to wars, or to an increase in the prosperity of a state' (V.3.7). It is clearly not the case that Aristotle fails to recognise such forces, but simply that he uses unfamiliar language in designating them. It is perfectly plain, moreover, how it is that a modification of the *politeia* resulting from a rapid alteration of the value of currency seems to be the work of 'chance' when contrasted with production of the same modification as a result of the struggle of the underprivileged.

(c) Negligence on the part of the authorities of the State, etc., e.g. *oligôria*[10] and *mikrotês* (possibly *hubris* would be thus classified by Newman) (cf. V.11.23).

151   Consideration of these *archai* leaves the conviction that the kind of incitements to *stasis* classed under heads (a) and (c) at any rate might, as

8. V.8.15. Barker's note (p. 230) that Aristotle here anticipates Marx in saying that political power tends to be used to secure economic advantage surely confuses some such observation as this with the far more important Marxian doctrine that political power is itself a manifestation of economic advantage (e.g. *Communist Manifesto*, 1948 ed., p. 128).

9. See the view of Ephorus that *dichostasia* arises 'through excess and luxury' which causes *phthonos* (envy), *hubris,* and *misos* (hatred) (*FGrH* 70F149); cf. also Thucydides, III.82.16.

10. V, 2, 4. Barker translates 'neglect of duty'. Cf. Decret. *ap.* Dem., 18, 74.

Newman suggests, be eliminated with the aid of the precautions proposed by Aristotle in V 8-9 without really eradicating the basic conflict or conflicts which constitute *stasis*.

3.

The remark that 'the occasions of *stasis* are small, but the issues are great' has already been mentioned. We have now to enquire what are the 'great issues'. It has been suggested that in part *stasis* is a political procedure resulting from the absence in Greek city-states of anything approximating to the modern party-government system: we have also seen that, in Aristotle's view, the rewards to be gained from *stasis* are of a political nature. Nevertheless a plausible case has been made out for holding that the underlying conflict is in fact an economic one and that the phenomenon *stasis* should be analysed in terms of an economic and social class-struggle. It is further held that Aristotle himself saw the necessity of an analysis of this kind. Professor Lerner, for instance, says: 'Aristotle was interested in the rise and fall of political systems, but he did not make the mistake of tracing that rise and fall to autonomous factors within politics. His view on the economic basis of revolutions had to be rediscovered by later thinkers – by Harrington, Sir Thomas More, James Madison, Karl Marx' (in his introduction to Jowett's translation, p. 24). What is there to support this view?

The most relevant piece of evidence from Book V is the assertion that every division tends to produce *diastasis* and the most fundamental *diastasis* is that of virtue and vice, the next that of wealth and poverty (V.3.16). This statement, if it is representative of Aristotle's opinion, indicates that he conceived *stasis* to be a complex phenomenon, comprising, first, certain distinctively moral or political issues, and, secondly, a social and economic struggle. I propose to consider first some evidence for the economic element in *stasis*. It is not necessary to dilate on certain historical examples. The fact that the *stasis* with which Solon, for instance, was confronted was derived from predominantly economic causes is generally recognised (cf. *Ath. Resp.*   152 12.1). The connexion, again, between the rise of tyrannies in the sixth and seventh centuries B.C. and the introduction of coinage with the consequent increase in financial power has been sufficiently heavily stressed already[11] not to require further elaboration. That the influence on the political association of the property system was appreciated by Solon and others 'of the ancients' is observed by Aristotle, who notes regulations laid down by *nomothetai* (i) prohibiting possession of more than a fixed maximum of land, (ii) prohibiting sale of property, (iii) enforcing preservation of original lots (II.7.6). The chapter which Aristotle devotes to criticism of the scheme proposed by Phaleas of Chalcedon contains other information of the utmost value. Some theorists, he tells us, adopted in its entirety an analysis of *stasis* in terms of economic class-struggle: 'all *stasis* is about the regulation of property' (II.7.2). The implication is that Aristotle does not regard this as the sole cause, and this is made explicit in his detailed criticism of Phaleas' 'socialistic' recommendation that property in land should be equalised. In the first place, 'it is not the possessions but the desires of mankind which

11. By esp. P.N. Ure, *The Origin of Tyranny* (Cambridge, 1922), *passim.*

require to be equalised, and this is impossible, unless a sufficient education is provided' (II.7.8). This is to modify the economic interpretation of the causes of *stasis* by reference to what may for convenience be called the virtue-vice analysis. In criticising the community of property advocated for the Guardians in the *Republic*, Aristotle makes still plainer his rejection of anything like a thoroughgoing economic interpretation. Of all the evils attributed to the possession of private property, he says, none in fact occurs because of lack of community but because of vice.[12] Secondly, Aristotle thinks, although equalisation of property is part of the remedy for *stasis*, it is not a very large part (II.7.18). Once again the economic element is relegated to second place. 'For,' he continues, 'the nobles[13] would resent this arrangement since they think that they are entitled to more than an equal share.' (cf. V 1, 1301a32). Again 'the wickedness of mankind is insatiable' (II.7.19). It is to be noted that Aristotle totally fails to remark the possibility that, if the radical proposals of Phaleas were to be implemented, the term 'noble' might become obsolete. This fact in turn raises the question, strictly outside the subject-matter of this essay, to what extent Greek writers thought of the aristocracies which developed in the seventh and sixth centuries as resting on economic power.[14] In this connexion Aristotle provides a definition of the term 'nobility' (*eugeneia*) which is interesting because it is given in terms of the same combination of ideas as that we are examining in his analysis of *stasis*. It is, he says, ancient wealth and virtue (IV 8, 1294a22). Are we to suppose that, in the event of a scheme like that of Phaleas being practicable, a stratified society could still be made possible by means of the application of the criterion of virtue? Phaleas, it is true, prescribed equality of land only, but Aristotle's comment shows that he can envisage the extension of the principle to slaves, cattle, and money (II.7.21).

On the other hand it may be argued that the analysis of *stasis* in terms of economic class-struggle is vindicated by Aristotle's view as to the essential characteristics of oligarchy and democracy respectively and as to what distinguishes them. And this argument does carry much weight: Aristotle states categorically that 'the real difference between democracy and oligarchy is poverty and wealth. Wherever men rule by reason of their wealth, whether they be few or many, that is an oligarchy, and where the poor rule, that is a democracy' (III.8.7). This unmixed economic interpretation, however, is, I believe, misleading, particularly in the light of the connotation which Aristotle attaches to the word 'democracy'. We are accustomed to mean by 'the class-struggle theory' the theory according to which there is a struggle between two classes, one of which is animated by the desire to achieve a form of society in which classes, or at any rate the existing class-division, will have been abolished. We might, to be more precise, say that those who hold this theory to be a valid account of 'the

---

12. II 5, 1263b23; cf. Plato, *Rep.* 416C5ff., 422Aff., 464C5.

13. *Hoi charientes.* The translation is Jowett's.

14. It is suggested that where 'rich' and 'noble' are distinguished, the distinction is in fact one of two forms of wealth, money and land. Solon's revised constitution perhaps recognised 'wealth' in the narrower sense as the basis of political privilege. *Ath. Resp.* 7.2.

facts' believe that one possible solution of the struggle which it describes is the achievement of a society of this form. To some of those who maintain the theory it seems possible that a society of the form envisaged might be achieved by means of the equalisation of either all or some kinds of possession. It further seems possible that some such society as this might, in the current usage of the word, properly be described as a democracy. This way of thinking, however, is alien to that of Aristotle. In Greek political thought, equality of some kind – perhaps the notion of 'equality before the law'[15] – had come to seem characteristic of democracy, but not equality in the sense of abolition of economic distinctions. 'Redistribution of Land' was the slogan of tyrants (Plato, *Rep.* 566A), not the practice of democracies. Solon, who was recognised as the founder of the ancestral democracy (1273b37; cf. *Ath. Resp.* 6.1), had expressly refused to countenance any scheme for land distribution in Attica. It was not his pleasure that 'the good should have an equal share with the bad in the country's rich land' (*Ath. Resp.* 12.1). In the light of this tradition[16] concerning the conception of 'democracy' the statement made by Aristotle does not appear as paradoxical as at first sight, namely that a democracy cannot exist any more than an oligarchy unless it preserves the division of the rich and the masses. If equality of property is introduced, there is at once 'some different form of *politeia*' (V. 9. 9). Barker well points out that 'democracy, in Aristotle's sense of the word, is the government of one of the social sections, as oligarchy is that of another. If all social sections disappear, both of these forms of government will also disappear' (p. 232, n. 3). The same belief, that democracy must preserve the framework of class distinction, is expressed in the exhortation to 'spare the rich',[17] by refraining, for instance, from making confiscations or from imposing superfluous and wasteful public services (*leitourgiai*).

We may sum up this discussion by saying that Aristotle's analysis of *stasis* may well be less correct than that suggested by Phaleas and others, that the conflict underlying *stasis* is unquestionably an economic conflict to some considerable extent in the sense that it is one of classes mutually antagonised by the possession of divergent economic interests and that it arises from the structure of property-relations peculiar to the Greek *polis*, but that to apply to the phenomenon *stasis* certain modern theories about the nature of social conflicts or, in particular, to identify it with 'the class-struggle' in the Marxian usage of that term, is, for reasons which have been suggested, unwise. The idea of a radical redirection of the economic basis of society was conceivable to Plato, Phaleas, and perhaps other theorists, but was discounted in practice. Aristotle was able to imagine a *politeia* in which the experiment of 'equal shares' was made: but such a State fits none of the recognised categories (V 9, 1309b40). In practice what the groups of

155

15. Herodotus, III. 80. 6; cf. 142, 3. Thucydides, IV.78.3. On the significance of Solon's establishment of the Heliaea, see II 12, 1274a2. On the equality of democracy, Plato, *Rep.*, 558C4.

16. The striking similarity of political outlook of Solon (as portrayed in the fragments) and Aristotle is noticed below.

17. V.8.20. For evidence that this advice was not in practice considered sound see pseudo-Xenophon, *Ath. Resp.* 1.4, etc.

stasiôtai, whether oligarchs or democrats, organise themselves to obtain is concrete *timê* and *kerdos* (V.3.1), dignified by the name of 'justice' (III.9.1). Thucydides has a case which almost exactly fits this specification: 'Corcyra gave the first example of . . . the reprisals exacted by the governed who have never experienced equitable treatment . . . of the iniquitous resolves of those who desired to get rid of their accustomed poverty' (III.84.1).

4.

156   We come now to the second part or aspect of Aristotle's analysis of *stasis*. We saw that there is reason to believe that Aristotle held that there was more than one, and more than one kind of conflict underlying the phenomenon, and that in fact what he called the primary *diastasis* was that of virtue and vice (V.3.16). Judgment of political phenomena in normative terms is peculiarly difficult to criticise. It is easy to see, for instance, that what I have called Aristotle's virtue-vice analysis might well be superimposed on a thoroughgoing economic interpretation of *stasis* without modifying the latter by the addition of any description of fact. Before considering this analysis, however, I wish briefly to refer to the use by some early Greek writers of normative ethical words in a meaning which is held to be descriptive and non-ethical. Thus *agathos, esthlos* or *eslos* ('good') clearly often mean 'belonging to the party approved by me'; *kakos* ('bad') often 'belonging to the party of which I disapprove'. There is, moreover, a more than incidental connexion between *agathoi* and wealth, and between *kakoi* and poverty. Thus Alcaeus says that no poor man was ever '*eslos* or honourable' (fr. 81). So Theognis too says that 'need teacheth all evil' (389) and that 'with the aid of wealth even a *kakos* may become an *esthlos*' (1117-18). It is interesting, moreover, in the light of Aristotle's definition of nobility and the suggestion made as to the meaning of 'the good' when contrasted with 'the rich', to note a remark of Theognis about virtue: 'for the majority of men there is this one virtue – being rich.'[18]

Consideration of this usage is relevant to the subject of this essay in that it might seem to support, though it will be maintained that it does not, the view that the virtue-vice analysis is wholly reducible to the economic analysis as a result simply of elucidation of the meaning of terms like virtue. One such term

157   is *hubris*. According to Solon, *hubris* is generated by great wealth (*Ath. Resp.* 12.2). But to argue that, where *hubris* is alleged by Aristotle to be the *archê* or occasion of *stasis* (e.g. V. 2.4; 10.13) it is correct to speak of its cause as being an economic one, is, I think, plainly mistaken. Here Aristotle's usage appears to have diverged from the earlier one.

But, with regard to the fundamental analysis of *stasis*, comparison of Solon with Aristotle shows a remarkable similarity of approach. Solon combines the economic and the 'ethical' interpretations of *stasis* in the same way as Aristotle: the latter approach, moreover, clearly limits the scope of the former and does not just add to it a normative comment. Thus, according to Aristotle, Solon attached the entire responsibility for the *stasis* which he was called upon to remedy, to the rich (*Ath. Resp.* 5.3). But his economic analysis is limited by ethical considerations. He did not take the view that the conflict

18. 699; cf. Hesiod, *Works and Days* 313: 'virtue and glory accompany wealth'.

underlying the outbreak of *stasis* was in any way inherent in the economic structure of Attic society: he held simply that the *agathoi* had abused their position.[19] Solon's response to the demand for redistribution of land, again, is dictated by precisely the beliefs which animate Aristotle's criticisms of Plato and Phaleas.[20]

If we look in the *Politics* for a particular example to illustrate the modification of the economic by the 'ethical' analysis of *stasis*, the most outstanding is found to be the idea, only twice referred to in Book V but developed at length in Book IV 11, of the importance to cities of having a strong 'middle' class. This idea is not, I believe, derived by Aristotle, as it might seem to be, from the economic analysis. That it belongs to the economic analysis is suggested by the statements that 'where there is a 'strong middle class, there least of all are *staseis* and *diastaseis*' (IV.11.12) and that *stasis* arises when the two classes, the rich and the people, are equally balanced and there is no middle class (V.4.11). Possibly attention to the   **158** economic structure of the *polis* might by itself have persuaded Aristotle that the remedy for *stasis* lay in the balance which might be secured by the development of a middle class in Greek states, but it seems much more probable that considerations of this kind only reinforced what in fact was primarily the application to politics of the ethical doctrine of the desirability of achieving the Mean. The question is, moreover, decided by Aristotle's explicit reference to the doctrine of the Mean: 'If what was said in the *Ethics*[21] is true, that the happy life is the life according to virtue without impediment, and that virtue is a mean, then the life which is in a mean must be the best' (IV.11.3). And, he continues, since it is agreed that what is moderate and the mean is the best, it is clear that as regards the possession of goods also the mean is the best state: for in that state it is easiest to obey rational principle (IV.11.5). It must be obvious that Aristotle has here quite deserted his empirical method and that, to justify his assertion that the provision of a strong middle class is an important precaution against *stasis*, he is resorting to a psychological argument, namely the argument derived from the analogy of state and soul which Plato employs in the *Republic* (544D6). This conclusion is confirmed by Aristotle's assertion that a Mean *politeia* is not only a provision against *stasis* but is less likely than a state in which some possess much and others nothing to give rise to either extreme democracy, or pure oligarchy, or tyranny (IV.11.11). It is, finally, perhaps an argument in favour of the view that Aristotle is here more concerned with ethical doctrine than with economic analysis that he speaks indifferently of the Mean *politeia* as being one in which the middle class is large (IV 11, 1296a8) and as one in which (all) the citizens have 'a moderate and sufficient property',[22] although it is obvious that these two conceptions, if   **159**

---

19. *Ath. Resp.* 5.3, e.g. 'rest your great minds in things of moderation'.

20. It is possible that Aristotle in the *Ath. Resp.* projected on to Solon certain views which he felt he should have held. But the evidence of the extant fragments seems sufficient to refute this.

21. e.g. *EN* I, 1098a16; VII, 1153b10; X, 1177a12.

22. IV 11, 1295b40; cf. V 8, 14 where Aristotle gives the obscure injunction 'either to mix the mass of the poor and that of the rich, or to increase the mean'. See Newman [172], IV, p. 276.

put into effect, would produce two very different types of society.[23]

5.

The results of this examination of the notion of *stasis* are as follows. First, as to Aristotle's treatment of the subject: it is important, for the understanding of *stasis*, to distinguish it from the notion of *metabolê politeias*. Aristotle treats both these subjects together in the *Politics*, not unnaturally, since they are intimately connected. It is possible, however, that he could have distinguished the two more clearly than he does in a number of contexts. A more serious charge with regard to his treatment of *stasis* is that Aristotle does not make at all plain the distinction between the 'occasion' of the phenomenon and what I have called the underlying conflict. The implication, that he does not in his own mind always distinguish the two correctly, seems a justifiable one. It must not, on the other hand, be forgotten that Aristotle has the merit of being the first thinker, as far as our knowledge goes, to undertake anything approaching a scientific analysis of this important and peculiar feature of Greek city-state politics.

Secondly, as to rendering of the word *stasis*. I conclude that none of the habitual English translations such as 'revolution', 'sedition', 'class-warfare', etc. conveys adequately the full meaning of the Greek word.[24] The reason for the difficulty is the obvious one that the class of situations which constitute the meaning of the word is one with which in our public life there is nothing strictly comparable.

Finally, as to the analysis of the phenomenon *stasis*: I suggested that, superficially, *stasis* is a situation occurring in the public life of the greater number of the Greek city-states at larger or smaller intervals of time, that it results from the collision of temporarily organised groups of citizens, and that its characteristic feature is 'illegality' of behaviour, which may range from minor infringements of the 'constitution' to wholesale massacre of opponents. Its aims seem usually to be of a political nature, either office (*timê*) or profits from office (*kerdos*) or undefined powers (*dunamis*).[25] This use of *stasis* as what I called a 'method' in politics has, unfortunately, received comparatively scanty attention from Aristotle.

In discussing Aristotle's twofold analysis of *stasis* in terms of the divisions of wealth and poverty on the one hand, and of virtue and vice on the other hand, I further suggested that it would be more convenient to attempt to relate the phenomenon to one or more underlying conflicts than to speak of seeking its 'cause'. That a fundamental conflict of economic interest was an important contributing factor in very many instances of *stasis* seems to me absolutely certain: *stasis* in the majority of cases is a conflict of 'oligarchs'

23. *The Mean*; it is worth noticing that Solon was of 'the middle men' (*Ath. Resp.* 5. 3). cf. also the judgment of Thucydides on the 'hoplite' constitution of 411 B.C. (VIII.97).

24. I think that 'sedition', which is Barker's translation, comes nearest to doing so, as far as descriptive content is concerned, but that its emotive colouring in modern English bears little resemblance to that of *stasis*. The Irish 'troubles', in both form and matter, corresponds remarkably closely to 'political disruption' (*hê politikê tarachê*).

25. cf. *Ath. Resp.* 13.2; Herodotus, V.66.2.

and 'democrats' and Aristotle is emphatic that these groups are to be defined in terms of an economic class-division. But I think that to attempt to equate *stasis* with the Marxian notion of the class-struggle is to make a grave misinterpretation, for three reasons: first, the terminology of the 'class-struggle' hypothesis is incompatible with the fact, essential to *stasis*, that the objective in the struggle is almost always purely political power. Second, the 'class-struggle' doctrine is closely associated with the view that there may or must be achieved a society in which the distinction between economic and social classes, as at present understood, will become obsolete. No Greek of the classical period thought seriously of the possibility of such a society being achieved and not more than one or two ever regarded the existence of such a society as even in principle desirable. Finally, we have, I think, to distinguish carefully two views about the nature of *stasis*, one that it always involves a struggle between 'haves' and 'have-nots', the other that it involves a struggle between 'haves' and 'have-nots' *and* that such a conflict is inherent in the economic structure of the society. I think that both these views have some claim to be described as 'economic' interpretations of *stasis*. Aristotle, however, like Solon assents only to the first or weak form of the economic interpretion. His dual analysis seems to me partly unsound, partly sound: unsound, inasmuch as it is meaningless to postulate an underlying moral conflict in the way in which it makes sense to postulate an underlying economic conflict: sound, in that not every phenomenon which may legitimately be described as *stasis* can be related to a conflict of economic interests.[26]

161

[26. Most references to the *Politics* of the form IV.16.3 are identified by Bekker numbers in the Index of Aristotelian passages (Eds).]

15

H. Kelsen

Aristotle and Hellenic-Macedonian Policy

16   The *Politics* of Aristotle is essentially a doctrine of the constitutions, of which
the broad lines, at least, have been sketched in the *Nicomachean Ethics*. The
central theme is the celebrated six-forms scheme of constitutions, which
distinguishes three true forms of state rule – monarchy, aristocracy, and
polity. With these there are associated three perverted forms. Thus tyranny
is a perverted form of monarchy, oligarchy a perverted form of aristocracy,
and democracy a perverted form of polity. This scheme provides at the same
time for a fixed order of rank, in which monarchy appears as the best
constitution, aristocracy comes next, then polity. After these, in reverse
order, follow the perverted forms of constitution, such that democracy,
though worse than any of the three true forms, is nevertheless classed as the
best of the deviations. Tyranny is the worst of all forms. Monarchy,
17   especially unlimited hereditary monarchy, is from the very outset declared
to be the best form of all state rulerships. Thus the Aristotelian scheme
emphatically opposes monarchy to that form which would seem most nearly
to resemble it – namely, tyranny. And this opposition is chiefly effected by
representing the rule of the monarch as analogous to that of the father over
his sons, the rule of the tyrant as that of the master over his slaves. The
former is a rulership which benefits the subjects; the latter benefits only the
ruler. And this distinction is also declared to be decisive as between the true
and the perverted forms, so that democracy, which is classed in the
Nicomachean Ethics as a perverted constitution, is also characterised as a kind
of despotism, i.e. as a rule over slaves.[1]

This is very unusual teaching. For in Aristotle's time royal rule was
considered by the Hellenes as a barbarous form of government, a rulership
over slaves, to which the republican *polis*, the self-government of free men,
the special constitution of the Greek nation, stood in startling contrast. He
who in Hellas, and especially in Athens, declared kingly rule to be the best
was faced with a prevalent opinion which regarded monarchy as a
barbarian dominion over slaves. If the true significance of the Aristotelian
teaching as to forms of government is to be grasped, the political and
historical situation in which it was evolved and which it sought to influence
must be kept in mind.

The historical situation is Athens, republican Athens, in which the proud
recollection of that great epoch of Periclean democracy is still living, where

---

1. cf. *EN* 1160b-1161b; *Pol.* 1278b-1279b, 1289a-1289b, and esp. 1312b5: 'The
extreme form of democracy is tyranny.'

the word of Euripides is still the expression of public opinion. 'Nothing is more pernicious to a state than a one-man rule where that which is of first importance – a common law – is non-existent. A master there is who is a law unto himself – so that equality of right there is none' (*Supplices*, 442ff.). The heroic days of the monarchy of antiquity, it is true, are still piously held in historical remembrance. But nothing is more significant than that their mythical representative, King Theseus, is honoured as the founder of the democratic form of government. Euripides puts into his mouth the words: 'The city is not governed by one man, but is free. And the people rule by turn in annual succession' (*ibid.*, 417ff.).² Writing about Athens Isocrates says that it 'hates monarchy most of all things' (*Nicocles*, 6). The *polis* democracy had passed its culminating point when Aristotle was living in Athens. But it was in the bitterest phase of its struggle against the Macedonian hereditary monarchy. Those were the years in which Demosthenes, one of the leaders of the national democratic party, in his passionate orations against Philip and Alexander, called on the Athenians to vindicate their political freedom. In these orations the Macedonian monarchy is charged with precisely those distinctive qualities, those terrifying characteristics, from which monarchy, in the Aristotelian doctrine of government, was supposed to be exempt. The Aristotelian doctrine most emphatically repudiates those very accusations which Demosthenes, in his orations, levels against the king. If the philosopher again and again declares that kingly rule is essentially different from a rule of force – that it is not a rulership over slaves as is a tyranny – the orator on the other hand warns his country against the Macedonian hereditary monarchy by stigmatising it again and again as a form of government fit only for slaves. Thus he says in his first Olynthian oration, with reference to Macedonia, that he believes 'a state ruled by force is generally an object of suspicion to free states, especially when both are neighbours'; further, it is to be presumed that 'the Paeonians and the Illyrians and generally all those peoples would much prefer to be free and independent than to be slaves; for they are not accustomed to obey and he [King Philip] is reported to be an imperious master'. To be governed by a king is for Demosthenes synonymous with being a slave. Only in a democracy can one live as a free citizen; and therefore he represents the struggle against the Macedonian monarchy again and again, and especially in his second oration against Philip, as the defence of 'free states against the encroachments of the tyrant'. ' "What do you desire?" I said. "Freedom. And you do not see that even Philip's title means just the contrary? For every king and tyrant is an opponent of freedom and an enemy to order according to law." ' King and tyrant are for Demosthenes one and the same, not, as Aristotle declares, 'distinct and different'. The struggle, therefore, of Athens against Philip and Alexander is a struggle of democracy against monarchy.

18

19

2. cf. Kaerst, *Studien zur Entwicklung und theoretischen Begründung der Monarchie im Altertum* (1898), pp. 5-9: 'Nothing is more characteristic of the development of the two great nations of antiquity from a political standpoint than the fact that their constitutions and their conceptions of state at the time of their most flourishing periods were in direct antagonism to monarchy'.

While Aristotle is never tired of proclaiming that kingly rule guarantees the most complete community of interests between the ruler and the ruled, as the king like a father seeks only the good of his subjects, Demosthenes adjures the Athenians in his second Olynthian oration as follows: 'Believe not, Oh ye men of Athens, that he [King Philip] and his subjects have a common interest. He, on his side, thirsts for glory, they, on their side, have no part in this kind of glory, rather are they harassed being exhausted by the continual and diverse campaigns.' While Aristotle teaches that not monarchy but tyranny is the rule over slaves, and therefore suitable for barbarians, who are by nature slaves, Demosthenes does not cease to stigmatise the Macedonian monarchy as a barbarous form of government. 'Is not Philip our enemy?' he exclaims in the third Olynthian oration. 'Is he not the robber of our property, is he not a barbarian, the epitome of all thinkable evil?' He reminds Athens that Macedonia had formerly been subject to her. Nor does he omit at this point to emphasise the natural subjection of the barbarian monarchy to the Hellenic democracy.[3]

This is the political atmosphere in which Aristotle presents his theory of constitutions. It is true he never expressly says, nor even suggests, that the monarchy which he holds up as the best form of government is the Macedonian monarchy and that the democracy to which he assigns an inferior place is the Athenian democracy. But was it possible, considering the circumstances of the town in which he lived and the time in which he wrote, to speak of the comparative values of monarchy and democracy without every word being understood as either for or against the Macedonian monarchy, for or against the Athenian democracy? Is it possible to mistake the connexion between the political attitude of the greatest and most popular orator who, with all the convincing rhetoric at his disposal, hammered into the Greek brain and heart again and again the thesis: royal rule is slavery, only democracy is freedom; and the theory of government of the leading philosopher of the time, who maintained royal rule to be diametrically opposed to a rulership over slaves, the latter to be rather – as all perverted constitutions are – democracy. Aristotle's doctrine of government is not without its political background. It can be understood only by remembering the direct opposition in which it stood to the political system, which obtained its living expression in the orations of Demosthenes.

This is shown by an analysis of the chief work of the Aristotelian theory of state – the *Politics*. A complete analysis of this work would not here be possible. We shall call attention only to those points which bear directly on the historical context.

Book I of the *Politics* contains an examination of the different relationships of rule, in which a parallel is established between rule of a state and that of a family. This parallel is designed chiefly to show the principal difference between the rule of the master over his slaves and the rule of the father over his children – the mastery of the king being that of the latter, not that of the

---

3. cf. in this connexion Kaerst, *Geschichte des hellenistischen Zeitalters*, I (1901), pp. 162ff. The same author, in *Studien zur Entwicklung und theoretischen Begründung der Monarchie im Altertum*, p. 7, writes: 'The struggle of the Macedonian monarchy against the Hellenic free states, especially against Athens, must be regarded above all as the antagonism of two totally different political developments'.

former type. Thus the whole presentation of the slave problem in this first book of the *Politics* is rather of a political than of an economic character. Aristotle is here, it is true, concerned with the justification of slavery an an economic institution, but this is certainly not his chief concern, as is generally believed. His aim above all is to vindicate monarchy against its opponents who love to identify it with slavery. Therefore he does not omit, especially in this connexion, to insist on the fact that the oldest and most naturally organised community amongst men had a monarchical character and that even the community of the Olympian gods was a kingly rule.[4] The decisive passage is the following:

> Of household management we have seen that there are three parts –
> one is the rule of a master over slaves, which has been discussed
> already, another of a father, and the third of a husband. A husband
> and father, we saw, rules over wife and children, both free – but the
> rule differs – the rule over his children being a royal, over his wife a
> constitutional [that is a republican] rule ... But in most
> constitutional [republican] states the citizens rule and are ruled by
> turns, for the idea of a constitutional state implies that the natures of
> the citizens are equal, and do not differ at all. Nevertheless, when one
> rules and the other is ruled we endeavour to create a difference of
> outward forms and names and titles of respect, which may be
> illustrated by the saying of Amasis about his footpan. (1259a37-b9)

22

4. *Pol.* 1252b. Isocrates says much the same in his praise of monarchy (*Nicocles*, 6): 'The Gods are also under the royal rule of Zeus ... we would not say the Gods make use of monarchy, if we did not believe it to be superior to other constitutions'.

The text of Book I contains not only an examination of the different relationships of rule in the family and in the state, but also a discussion on the 'so-called art of getting wealth', which has no material connexion with the first problems. Attention was already drawn to this subject in *Pol.* 1253b, where it may be seen how artificially the connexion is established between the sociological-political analysis of the relationship of rule and the discussions on economy. The three kinds of rule, of the father over the children, of the husband over the wife, and of the master over the slave, are represented from the point of view of household management. And now it runs as follows: 'And there is another element of a household, the so-called art of getting wealth, which according to some is identical with household management, according to others a principal part of it; the nature of this art will also have to be considered by us.' But this has nothing to do with the real subject matter of politics, with relationships of rule, of which Book I of the *Politics* treats. And next, nothing more is said about this art of getting wealth, but the subject of the different forms of government is immediately taken up. 'Let us first speak of master and slave', it continues. So that it is hard to understand why this reference should have been made at all. For in what follows – that is, the celebrated justification of slavery – the relationship between master and slave is represented essentially as one of rulership and therefore rather from a political than from an economic standpoint. In the foreground is set the question whether the mastery over slaves is according to nature and therefore just. And this question is answered by an analysis of the relationship of the ruler to the ruled, of which the most important conclusions are: that rulership – and not only that of master over slave – is inherent in the very nature of man, not of the ruler and of the ruled, and that slavery is not similar, as some believe, to state rulership but essentially different from it, the latter being a rulership over free men;

23   This is not a very flattering allusion. Herodotus relates of Amasis who, although of modest origin, had risen to the throne, that he was rather despised on account of his humble birth. Amasis, however, ordered the statue of a god to be made out of a golden basin which his guests used for washing their feet and other like purposes and thus compelled the Egyptians to pay homage to what they had been wont to despise. Whoever has read carefully the foregoing passages in which Aristotle endeavours to show that the distinction between the ruler and those who are ruled is according to nature, cannot help noticing the subtle thrust directed against the democratic republic, in which he who yesterday had to obey, today commands, and where the natural distinction between such as are born to command and such as are born to obey is ignored. Nor is it proper to compare the rule of the husband over the wife to the republican form of constitution. In this connexion it is said that 'the male is by nature fitter for command than the female'. And in fact the relationship between husband and wife never changes, for it is always the husband who rules over the wife. 'Now the relation of the male to the female is of this kind [rulership] but there the inequality is permanent'. After this covert disparagement of the republican-democratic form of government Aristotle continues, expressing a thought already developed in the *Nicomachean Ethics*:

> The rule of a father over his children is royal, for he rules by virtue both of love and of the respect due to age, exercising a kind of royal

---

that consequently the rulership of the king over his subjects must be totally different from that of the master over slaves. The latter is not yet directly expressed but follows as a logical consequence of *Pol.* 1255b20, in connexion with 1242a7-17.

The treatise about the art of getting wealth only begins with the preceding passage, 1255b40. Here too the connexion is quite superficial. 1255b30ff. runs thus: '. . . for the master as such is concerned, not with the acquisition but with the use [of slaves]'. Then a little farther, 'The art of acquiring slaves, I mean of justly acquiring them, differs both from the art of the master and the art of the slave, being a species of hunting or war'. And now 1255b40: 'Enough of the distinction between master and slave. Let us now enquire into property generally; and into the art of getting wealth in accordance with our usual method, for a slave has been shown to be a part of property'. But slaves have been less considered as a special part of property, i.e. in the economic sense, than as members of a relationship of rule, and therefore in a political sense. From the standpoint of an analysis of the subject-matter the whole of the following discussion has no place within the plan of Book I. After the conclusion of the economic treatise, the examination of the rulerships of government is again taken up (1259a37) with the words: 'Of household management we have seen that there are three parts, one is the rule of a master over slaves, which has been discussed already, another of a father, and the third of a husband', as if a fourth element, 1253b12-14, had not been stated, namely, that which represented no rulership – the getting of wealth. And although the chapter immediately preceding the treatise about the art of getting wealth concludes with these words: 'Enough of the distinction between masters and slaves', as if this chapter were at an end, nevertheless a new one begins about the art of getting wealth and the examination is again taken up of the relation between masters and slaves. I therefore venture the supposition, based merely on the consideration of the subject-matter, that 1255b40-1259a36 was interpolated from another of Aristotle's works and that the interpolator, in order to prepare this incorporation, first introduced the passage 1253b12-14.

power. And therefore Homer has appropriately called Zeus 'father of Gods and men' because he is the King of them all. For a King is the natural superior of his subjects, but he should be of the same kin or kind with them, and such is the relation of elder and younger, of father and son.

The preference given already in the first book of the *Politics* to monarchy as being that form of government most conforming to nature, in opposition to the republican and therefore democratic form, is unmistakable.[5]   24

The train of thought pursued in Book I, which seeks by examining the different forms of government to lay the foundation for a doctrine of constitutions, is continued only in Book III. Book II, as also the greater part of Books VII and VIII, is devoted to the problem of the ideal state. They are evidently to be attributed to a youthful production of Aristotle, and were only later incorporated into his doctrine of constitutions which has been handed down to us under the name of *Politics*. And this work was certainly produced during the period of the philosopher's second stay in Athens, while the writing about the ideal state was done at the time when Aristotle was still the pupil of Plato and a member of the latter's Academy. This work is openly under the influence of Plato's *Republic*. Therefore we cannot find in it Aristotle's real and definitive opinions about the state and the value of the constitutions. These are contained in the theory of state of Books I, III-VI, of   25
the so-called *Politics*, which is a very contradictory compilation of two quite different works of Aristotle.[6] Book III, which continues the train of thought of the first, opens with the discussion of certain preliminary questions

---

5. This is expressed still more clearly than in Book I of the *Politics* in the paragraph of the *Nicomachean Ethics* devoted to the problem of constitutions (1160a31ff.). 'There are three kinds of constitution, and an equal number of deviation-forms – perversions, as it were, of them. The constitutions are monarchy, aristocracy, and thirdly that which is based on a property qualification, which it seems appropriate to call timocratic, though most people are wont to call it polity. The best of these is monarchy, the worst timocracy. The deviation from monarchy is tyranny; for both are forms of one-man rule, but *there is the greatest difference between them;* the tyrant looks to his own advantage, the King to that of his subjects . . . One may find resemblances to the constitutions and, as it were, patterns of them even in households. For the association of a father with his sons bears the form of monarchy, since the father cares for his children; and this is why Homer calls Zeus "father"; it is the ideal of monarchy to be paternal rule . . . The association of man and wife seems to be aristocratic; for the man rules in accordance with his worth, and in those matters in which a man should rule, but the matters that befit a woman he hands over to her. [This is a different notion from that of the *Politics*: Divided rule, not rule of turns.] . . . The friendship between a King and his subjects depends on an excess of benefits conferred: for he confers benefits on his subjects, if being a good man he cares for them with a view to their well-being, as a shepherd does for his sheep [whence Homer called Agamemnon "shepherd of the peoples"]. Such too is the friendship of a father, though this exceeds the other in the greatness of the benefits conferred; for he is responsible for the existence of his children, which is thought the greatest good, and for their nurture and upbringing. These things are ascribed to ancestors as well. Further, *by nature a father tends to rule over his sons, ancestors over descendants, a King over his subjects.'*

6. See *Additional Note,* below, pp. 191-4.

concerning the doctrine of constitutions, especially of that problem which lay at the basis of all the political theory of the ancient city-state, namely,

26   the description of the citizen. Who is the citizen? And the further question: Is the virtue of the good man and the virtue of the good citizen one and the same? This may be said to be the core of the democratic *polis* ideology, according to which man attains his full, i.e. his moral, personality in participation in government, wherefore the slave, who had no political rights, was not considered to be a full man, and therefore virtue can be

27   developed only in political activity. Consequently the virtue of the good citizen and of the good man must be regarded, according to the official conception, as identical. But as Aristotle's object is to show by his teaching that monarchy, under which the subject is excluded from all share in government, is the best form, he must above all try to overthrow this fundamental doctrine of the democratic *polis* ideology. The utmost

28   caution, of course, had to be observed in an attack directed against a sacred political dogma. Accordingly, Aristotle first of all maintains that the conception of what constitutes the citizen must vary according to the form of government and that the usual conception of the citizen which takes its initial idea from the extent to which he shares in government is, in the main, applicable only to democracy which, as his later arguments are intended to

29   prove, is not a true state form. 'For in some states the people are not acknowledged, nor have they any regular assembly, but only extraordinary ones' (1275b7). He is evidently thinking here of monarchy; he does not say so, however, nor does he dare to draw the final conclusion from his recognition of the connexion between forms of government and the definition of a citizen. He is contented with showing the relative significance of the prevailing conception of what constitutes the citizen. But nevertheless there is no ambiguity in such statements as that 'the subject is a citizen as well as the ruler' (1277a21). Thus the conception of citizen is no longer limited exclusively to the active political qualification, but is extended to the passive condition of being ruled, and in this way adapted to the passive condition of being ruled, and in this way adapted to the monarchical form of government. And a like tendency is perceptible in the answer to the question whether the virtue of the man is identical with that of the citizen. Aristotle was obliged to answer in the negative. Again he insists on the dependence of the ideal of virtue on the form of government:

> The virtue of the citizen must therefore be relative to the constitution of which he is a member. If then, there are many forms of government, it is evident that there is not one single virtue of the good citizen which is perfect virtue. But we say that the good man is he who has one single virtue which is perfect virtue. Hence it is evident that the good citizen need not of necessity possess the virtue which makes a good man. (1276b30-5)

30   Thus the virtue of a good man and the virtue of a good citizen need not be identical. 'But will there then be no case in which the virtue of the good citizen and the virtue of the good man coincide? To this we answer that the good ruler is a good and wise man' (1277a13-15). And after calling attention to the necessity of a special education for the ruler, he arrives at

the conclusion that both virtues, the virtue of the good man and the virtue of a good citizen, are really united only in the person of the ruler, not in that of the subject. For the 'virtue of a ruler differs from that of a citizen' (that is, he who is only ruled) (1277a23). The subject 'may be compared to the maker of the flute, while the ruler is like the flute player' (1277b29). The reference to the monarchy is unmistakable.

The theory of government in the true sense of the word begins with the question 'whether there is only one form of government or many, and if many, what they are, and how many, and what are the differences between them' (1278b7). And from this in the further development of his thesis the question arises: 'What is to be the supreme power in the state: Is it the multitude? Or the wealthy? Or the good? Or the one best man? Or a tyrant?' (1281a12) Although to put the question thus is to answer it, since no disagreement is possible that the one best man, if such there be (which is assumed in this question), should have the supreme power in the state, nevertheless the advantages and the disadvantages of the different forms of government, and particularly of democracy and of monarchy, which obviously are in the foreground, are most carefully weighed one against the other. The very certainty of the conclusion (in favour of monarchy) compels objectivity in the discussion. And such objectivity was imperative in the political conditions then prevailing in Athens, on the soil of a democracy defending itself desperately against the encroachments of a monarchy. Aristotle shows himself extremely anxious to consider sympathetically the arguments generally advanced in defence of democracy, as opposed to aristocracy and monarchy. But finally he reaches the conclusion: 31

> If, however, there be some one person, or more than one, although not enough to make up the full complement of a state, whose virtue is so pre-eminent that the virtues or the political capacity of all the rest admit of no comparison with his or theirs, he or they can no longer be regarded as part of a state; for justice will not be done to the superior, if he is reckoned only as the equal of those who are so far inferior to him in virtue and in political capacity. Such an one may truly be deemed a God among men. (1284a3-11)

What does the cautious condition stipulated in this formula mean, since to all those to whom it is of importance it may be asserted that the condition is fulfilled? To whom else, if not to Philip or to Alexander, should these words refer? The former was worshipped almost as a god. A statue had been erected to him in Athens, and Isocrates had written of him – 'when Philip has subdued the kingdom of Persia nothing will remain for him to do, except to become a God.'[7] Theopompus had said of him that it was believed nature herself was in union with him, as with her favourite, because during his Grecian campaigns in Macedonia she caused the fig trees and the vine to bear fruit even in the middle of spring (fr. 265). This contemporary historian had declared Philip to be the greatest statesman Europe had yet

---

7. Isocrates III (letter). It is true that Wilamowitz ([204], II 395) declares this spurious, but Beloch (*Griechische Geschichte*, II 574) remarks aptly that if it is false it is nevertheless written in the spirit of Isocrates.

produced, in any case the greatest who had ever sat upon a throne (fr. 27).
Alexander too was given a place among the Olympian gods and an altar
was erected to him as to a god. Callisthenes, the nephew and disciple of
Aristotle, as the official historian of Alexander, maintained his divine
origin.[8] Can one seriously doubt, then, the intention, when in a work on
politics appearing in Athens under the reign of Alexander a monarch is
spoken of who by virtue of his pre-eminent capacity and incomparable
political gifts 'may truly be deemed a god among men'? Can a general
doctrine of state, such as the Aristotelian *Politics* claims to be, express this
intention in plainer terms; can it set forth other than hypothetical
assertions? Is it not sufficient to develop a theory – i.e. theses generally
applicable and therefore necessarily formulated in hypothetical terms – a
theory which may then be used as an apology applicable directly to a
concrete case, that is, to a certain definite person? Are they not the most
effective ideologies that employ this method?

It is very interesting to note the extreme skill with which Aristotle leads
up cautiously yet persistently to his fundamental thesis – the demonstration
of the superiority of hereditary monarchy over democracy. After obtaining,
in the first place, the general recognition of the possible supremacy of
hereditary monarchy as the best form of state government, the important
point now is to deepen and strengthen this position. This cannot be
achieved better than by using the proved method of producing the desired
effect by contrast. Monarchy glowing in the halo of its own virtue, in which
the best man exercises his rightful rule, is placed in relief against democracy
as the background, painted in sombre colours – democracy in which there is
no room for the one best man. Democracy is attacked on one of its worst
defects, on one of its worst abuses, namely, ostracism, and compared with
monarchy just on this its weakest side, not without recognising beforehand
the claim of the monarch, by reason of his pre-eminent virtue, to be exempt
from all legal control. 'Hence we see that legislation is necessarily concerned
only with those who are equal in birth and capacity; and that for men of
pre-eminent virtue there is no law, they are themselves a law. Anyone would
be ridiculous who attempted to make laws for them' (1284a11-15). The king
is himself the law, for he is the incarnation of the highest virtue. Ostracism
means the elimination of the most capable. It is recognised as a necessary
consequence of democracy, and therefore in a certain sense justifiable. But
this concession is made only with a view to justifying monarchy more
effectively and to raising it above democracy.

> It would certainly be better that the legislator should from the first so
> order his state as to have no need of such a remedy [as ostracism]. But
> if the need arise, the next best thing is that he should endeavour to
> correct the evil by this or some similar measure ... It is true that,
> under perverted forms of government and from their special point of
> view, such a measure is just and expedient; but it is also clear that it is
> not absolutely just. In the perfect state [and by this, in Book III of the
> *Politics*, is meant the monarchy of the six-forms scheme of

8. Callisthenes, frags. 36 and 37 (*Script. rer. Alex.*, pp. 26 f.); cf. Beloch, *op. cit.*,
III 1, 49.

constitutions] there would be great doubts about the use of it; not when applied to excessive strength, wealth, popularity, or the like, but when used against some one who is pre-eminent in virtue. What is to be done with such a man? Mankind will not allow him to be banished and exiled. On the other hand, he ought not to be a subject – that would be as if mankind should claim to rule over Zeus, dividing his offices among them. The only alternative is that all should joyfully obey such a ruler, according to what seems to be the order of nature, and that men like him [the born to rule] should be kings in their state for life. (1284b17-34)

The superiority of monarchy having been thus established, it is asserted:

The preceding discussion by a natural transition, leads to the consideration of royalty, which we admit to be one of the true forms of government. Let us see whether in order to be well governed a state or country should be under the rule of a king or under some other form of government. (1284b35-7)

All this as if the question had not already been decided, as if any other possibility were open except that of recognising that monarchy alone was the best form of government. But the same answer to the question is to be obtained a second time and thus it is to be rendered still more affirmative and convincing. And every effort is made in this second demonstration to avoid all appearance of prejudice and to be as just as possible to democracy. But the final conclusion, which characteristically starts from the supposition that there exists in a state a family pre-eminent in capacity, runs as follows:

But when a whole family, or some individual, happens to be so pre-eminent in virtue as to surpass all others, then it is just that they should be of the royal family and supreme over all, or that this one citizen should be king of the whole nation. For, as I said before, to give them authority is not only agreeable to that ground of right which the founders of all states, whether aristocratical, or oligarchical, or again democratical, are accustomed to put forward [for these all recognise the claim of excellence, although not the same excellence], but accords with the principle already laid down. For surely it would not be right to kill, or ostracise, or exile such a person, or require that he should take his turn in being governed. The whole is naturally superior to the part, and he who has this pre-eminence [that all others together have less virtue and political capacity than he alone] is in the relation of a whole to a part. But if so, the only alternative is that he should have the supreme power, and that mankind should obey him, not in turn, but always. (1288a15-29).

The scales so long in the balance are now definitely weighed down in favour of monarchy and against democracy. But the arguments that have led up to this result are marked by an extraordinary measure of prudence and an obvious endeavour to avoid hurting democratic sensibilities. After all

34

this is a state which is proud of its republican democracy; there is at least one powerful party which has not given up the struggle for Athenian political self-determination.

Book III having closed with an examination of the monarchical form of government and its cautious hypothetical justification, Book IV opens with an explanatory development of the thesis that not only an absolute, but also a relative good exists, and that therefore the doctrine of state has to propound not only the absolutely best form, but also the relatively best. Here the order of rank of the values corresponding to the six-forms scheme
35 of constitutions comes in a general manner under discussion, and it is just in this connexion that the opinion is unequivocally expressed that monarchy is the absolutely best form of government. At the beginning of chapter 2 attention is called to the distinction made between the three true and the three perverted forms, and to the discussion which has already taken place of monarchy and aristocracy, 'for the enquiry into the perfect state is the same thing with the discussion of the two forms thus named'. Aristotle here treats monarchy as a kind of aristocracy, that is, as the name implies, government by the one best man, or by the best. To speak of monarchy (or aristocracy) means to speak of the best form of government. And then in conclusion he lays down most emphatically that tyranny is the worst form; that royalty, of which tyranny must be considered a perversion, is 'the first and the most divine', therefore the absolutely best form of consititution.[9]

Of the further developments which, whether directly or indirectly are intended to glorify hereditary monarchy, only two passages will be especially noted here. In Book V we find:

> The appointment of a king is the resource of the better classes against the people, and he is elected by them out of their own number, because either he himself or his family excel in virtue and virtuous actions; whereas a tyrant is chosen from the people to be their protector against the notables, and in order to prevent them from being injured. (1310b9-14).

Royalty is the protection afforded to good citizens by an intellectually and morally pre-eminent man; nor in defining it thus does Aristotle neglect to associate with the praise of the king his family, for his object is the glorification of hereditary monarchy. But tyranny is the protection of the
36 multitude, whose inferiority, even worthlessness, is sufficiently set forth.[10] It

9. 1289a. Book IV is the immediate continuation of Book III. The former expressly refers to the latter. Their connexion and relation to the later teaching is evident from the standpoint of an analysis of the contents. In Book III the general theory of constitutions and the absolutely best form of state, monarchy, are presented. To these, in Book IV, the discussions of the others in order of excellence are added. Here in the beginning of Book IV 'best constitution' means, just as in III, best state *form*, not as in II, VII, and VIII, best essence of state in the sense of an ideal state in the manner of Plato's *Republic*.

10. Especially in the *EN*; cf. 1179b. Arguments 'are not able to encourage the many to nobility and goodness. For these do not by nature obey the sense of shame, but only fear, and do not abstain from bad acts because of their baseness but through fear of punishment; living by passion they pursue their own pleasures and the means

would appear, however, that tyranny, in so far as it may be a protection for the people – safeguarding them from the notables – cannot be totally condemned. But we are reminded that most of the ancient tyrants were originally demagogues. Of these demagogues it is said:

> Sometimes the demagogues, in order to curry favour with the people, wrong the notables and so force them to combine; – either they make a division of their property, or diminish their incomes by the imposition of public services, and sometimes they bring accusations against the rich that they may have their wealth to confiscate. Of old, the demagogue was also a general, and then democracies changed into tyrannies. Most of the ancient tyrants were originally demagogues. They are not so now, but they were then; and the reason is that they were generals and not orators, for oratory had not yet come into fashion. Whereas in our day, when the art of rhetoric has made such progress, the orators lead the people, but their ignorance of military matters prevents them from usurping power; at any rate instances to the contrary are few and slight. (1305a2-15)

This passage seems to be an allusion to Demosthenes who is here, though not expressly named, stigmatised as a demagogue, and to the king of Macedonia, to whose military capacity special attention is called. The following is very important:

> And so, as I was saying, royalty ranks with aristocracy [i.e. with the rule of the best], for it is based upon merit, whether of the individual or of his family, or on benefits conferred, or on these claims with power added to them. For all who have obtained this honour have benefited, or had in their power to benefit, states and nations; some, like Codrus, have prevented the state from being enslaved in war; others, like Cyrus, have given their country freedom, or have settled or gained a territory, like the Lacedaemonian Macedonian and Molossian kings. (1310b31-40)

If it were still possible to entertain any doubt that this apology for royalty 37 was intended to be the ideology of one definite hereditary monarchy, this passage must remove all such doubt. For it shows clearly that Aristotle applies his theoretically established category of hereditary royalty as the absolutely best constitution to real states existing in history and organised as hereditary monarchies. If he credits his reader with discerning not only in the Lacedaemonian and Molossian reigning dynasties, but even in the Persian monarchy founded by Cyrus – therefore in a barbarian rule – the realisation of the highest form of virtue, or at least the most perfect statesmanship, this sacrifice to intelligence can obviously only have its foundation in the intention to combine discreetly and naturally the Macedonian with the Persian, Lacedaemonian and Molossian kings. He

---

to them, and avoid the opposite pains, and have not even a conception of what is noble and truly pleasant, since they have never tasted it.'

who offers the crown to the latter, can scarcely refuse it to the former. A witness of extraordinary significance to an ideological critical analysis of the *Politics* is furnished here. In no other passage does the extremely cautious Aristotle venture so far. Only he who is blind or shuts his eyes to the political reality can believe that Aristotle, the contemporary of Demosthenes, was not conscious of the political import of his teaching.

And it is only by keeping in view the historical situation, of which we shall have to speak later, that the full significance of the ensuing line of argument can be understood, by which Aristotle pleads the cause of hereditary monarchy in the Athenian democracy, appealing to the propertied class, to whom hereditary royalty alone can offer security.

> The idea of a king is to be a protector of the rich against unjust treatment, of the people against insult and oppression. Whereas a tyrant, as has often been repeated, has no regard to any public interest, except as conducive to his private ends. His aim is pleasure, the aim of a king, honour. Wherefore also in their desires they differ; the tyrant is desirous of riches, the king of what brings honour. (1311a1-7)

38   But what is urged in favour of monarchy, as against tyranny, is also skilfully used against democracy. For in this same passage we are reminded that 'tyranny has all the vices both of democracy and oligarchy'. From oligarchy tyranny, the perversion of monarchy, borrows the principle that the end of government is wealth, but 'from democracy tyrants have borrowed the art of making war upon the notables and destroying them secretly or openly or of exiling them' (1311a15-17). The 'notables' are evidently the persons who possess any property; these are always attacked by democracy, which is the rule of those who possess nothing. To the propertied classes no better form of government could be proposed than one which guaranteed ownership. And it is especially as such that monarchy is represented.

The second passage is still more significant. At the opening of Book VII of the *Politics* Aristotle expressed the opinion that the best form of government is that which conduces by its organisation to a happy life for the individual. In what does this happy life consist? The answer is the same as in his *Ethics*: in virtue. Some general reflections precede the assertion that happiness consists in an interior subjective attitude of man. God himself is called to witness that true happiness consists in virtue 'for He is happy and blessed, not by reason of any external good, but in Himself and by reason of His own nature' (1323b24-6.) The problem of virtue is then put in the form of an alternative: 'which is the more eligible life, that of a citizen who is a member of a state', i.e. one who takes a share in the government and public administration, 'or that of an alien, who has no political ties' (1324a14-17), i.e. one who holds aloof from all political activity. This is the distinction already developed in the *Ethics* and fundamental for Aristotle's dual morality – the distinction between the contemplative and the active life. The relevance of this problem to the question of the form of government is obvious. The opposition between autocracy and democracy which dominates Aristotle's

39   whole doctrine of government corresponds to a hair to the opposition between the two ideals of virtue. The question as to which of the two manners of life is

to be preferred from a moral point of view is almost identical with the question as to which of the two forms of government should have the preference. For the ideal of democracy presupposes that virtue is to be found in the life 'of a citizen, who is a member of a state', i.e. of one who takes a share in the government and public administration. The teaching of the autocratic ideal is that the individual, because he has no 'political ties', is as 'an alien in the state', i.e. he holds aloof from all political activity, and that this attitude must be ideologically honoured as being virtue. As the ethics of the Greek *polis* – at least in its official representatives – still continued to maintain the former standpoint – namely, that virtue is to be found in the active sharing in the government and that therefore democracy has the preference – extreme caution was naturally to be observed in the enunciation of the contrary opinion. The reasoning at this point, therefore, is by no means direct. To express his meaning Aristotle makes use of a parallel between the individual and the state, similar to that established by Plato in the *Republic* to illustrate the nature of justice. The happiness and therefore the virtue of the individual is 'the same as that of the state' (1324a8). And since that state is not the best organised, whose chief aim is to gain despotic power over its neighbours, but rather that which limits its action to establishing interior order (1324b-1325a), so also that individual life is not the best, of which the aim is directed outwardly toward others, that is, to master them, which is the aim of active political life. Indeed, it must be allowed that only an active life can be happy in the sense of being virtuous, 'for happiness is activity' (1325a32).

> But perhaps someone, accepting these premises, may still maintain that supreme power is the best of all things, because the possessors of it are able to perform the greatest number of noble actions. If so, the man who is able to rule, instead of giving up anything to his neighbour, ought rather to take away his power; and the father should make no account of his son, nor the son of his father, nor friend of friend . . . There might be some truth in such a view if we assume that robbers and plunderers attain the chief good! (1325a34-b2)

40

Aristotle's design in propounding this strange opinion is to present the principle of the active political life, i.e. the principle of mastery over others, as highly problematical, and he does so by showing how, if generalised and pushed to its extreme limit, it would inevitably lead to the struggle of all against all. Some form of restraint, at least, is necessary and this is the state, where only some rule and the others are ruled. And here the two forms, democracy and monarchy, are opposed. 'For equals the honourable and the just consist in sharing alike, as is just and equal', i.e. governing in turns, because it is impossible for all to govern at the same time, and Aristotle continues:

> But that the unequal should be given to equals, and the unlike to those who are like, is contrary to nature, and nothing which is contrary to nature is good. If, therefore, there is anyone superior in virtue and in the power of performing the best actions, him we ought

to follow and obey, but he must have the capacity for action as well as virtue. (1325b8-14)

Aristotle's mention here of the problem of democracy and monarchy would be absolutely incomprehensible did we not suppose a connexion with the question whether the virtue of the individual should consist in political activity or not. If men were equal, the question would be answered in favour of political activity, that is, of democracy. But if they are not equal, and if one is pre-eminent over all the others, then monarchy, which means that from all – with the exception of the monarch – a non-political life is demanded. That such is the sense of the preceding passage, the following shows: 'If we are right in our view, and happiness is assumed to be virtuous activity, the active life will be the best, both for every city collectively, and for individuals.' But, Aristotle adds, 'not that a life of action must necessarily have relation to others, as some persons think' (1325b16). Judging by all that has preceded this pronouncement, no doubt is possible but that the life 'directed outwardly, towards others' is the active political life; participation in the government and public administration is the activity which every citizen of a democracy must, and in the fullest measure only a democracy can, exercise. Above this ideal of political activity Aristotle places here in the *Politics*, as he does also in the *Ethics*, the ideal of the contemplative life. 'Nor are those ideas only to be regarded as practical which are pursued for the sake of practical results, but much more the thoughts and contemplations which are independent and complete in themselves.' Also by the activity directed wholly inwardly man can attain to virtue. 'Neither, again, is it necessary that states which are cut off from others and choose to live alone should be inactive; for activity, as well as other things, may take place by sections; there are many ways in which the sections of a state act upon one another.' Thus Aristotle characterises the internal activity of the state. And he adds: 'The same thing is equally true of every individual' (1325b28). Just as the state should not strive for the mastery over other states, neither ought men to seek dominion over their fellow men. Just as the state should restrict itself to an internal activity, so ought men to renounce all activity having relation to others, i.e. all political activity. To the question, Which of the two ways of life is to be preferred, the life of active sharing in the government of the state, or that deprived of all such sharing? Aristotle finally gives the answer in favour of the second alternative[11] without, it is true, totally rejecting the first. The possibility of

11. That the first three chapters of Book VII do not belong to the rest of this book is shown by the standpoint taken in these to the question of the ideal of virtue, and the consequences involved for the constitution, a standpoint quite different from that taken in Book III. Already the senseless repetition of the same problem, proposed within a relatively narrow space, is striking. The first chapter begins by laying down that, 'He who would duly enquire about the best form of a state ought first to determine which is the most eligible life', i.e. what is necessary for happiness; which leads to the statement that happiness consists in virtue, and that the best constitution is that which enables the individual to live virtuously. But, in Ch. 13, as if no mention had yet been made of the subject, it is declared that 'Since our object is to discover the best form of government, that namely under which a city will be best governed, and since the city is best governed which has the greatest opportunity of obtaining

allowing the latter as an ideal of secondary value is left open. But, nevertheless, what a contrast to the traditional ethics of the *polis* democracy, according to which morality can only be realised by active sharing in the affairs of state and by which he who has no such share is considered as useless (Thucydides, II.49.2).

This whole question as to the best life for the individual is of secondary importance, and this Aristotle, from time to time, conveys (1324a23). The important question is: Which is that form of government whose organisation conduces most effectively to the happy life of the individual? But this question is left here without a direct answer. For the answer has been already practically given in that given to the question alleged as secondary. The political ideal of a virtue remote from all active share in political life corresponds to monarchy alone. But for an ideal so foreign to that of the Hellenic city-state, Aristotle deems an absolutely unassailable justification necessary. As he had appealed to the Godhead in the beginning of the paragraph, so he repeats his appeal at its close. There is no need of human activity directed to others. For 'if this were otherwise, God and the universe, who have no external actions over and above their own energies, would be far enough from perfection' (1325b28-30). God himself justifies the ideal of a non-political life. Only here, where ethics and metaphysics meet in politics, do their central ideas, the pre-eminence of theoretical over

43

happiness, it is evident that we must clearly ascertain the nature of happiness' (1332a5ff.). To which the statement is added that happiness consists in virtue, and further it is said that a state can be virtuous only 'when the citizens who have a share in the government are virtuous' (1332a33). It may be that an editor, guided only by superficial resemblances, on account of the parallelism in the putting of the problem added the first three chapters to the rest of the contents of Book VII, overlooking completely the total difference in the solutions of the problem. For the answer given to the decisive question of the ideal of virtue in the first three chapters is totally different from that given in the thirteenth. There Aristotle's aim is the contemplative life as opposed to one directed outwardly, especially to political activity; here, on the contrary, the latter is set up as a moral ideal. It is asserted that 'happiness is the realisation and perfect exercise of virtue', by which the practical virtues, the virtue of deeds, not of knowledge, is meant. Thus attention is directed especially to the most important of these practical virtues: justice – e.g. 'just actions ... just punishments and chastisements do indeed spring from a good principle' (1332a12ff.). This virtue consists essentially in external activity, that is, the virtue of the statesman. And in accordance with this a correspondingly useful application for the constitution of the best state is evolved: 'all the citizens share in the government.' Here Aristotle decides, as though it were self-evident, in favour of that ideal which he has described in the first three chapters of Book VII as '*the life of active sharing in the direction and affairs of the state*', but to which he there prefers the other life in which one lives 'as an alien who has no political ties'. In contrast to this, in Ch. 13, there is no question whatever about the ideal of non-political contemplation. And thus his ideal state, the picture of which he sketches in the second half of Book VII, is a democracy – even if a limited one. The reflections about the ideal state in Books VII and VIII cannot be accepted as forming part of the same work as the first three chapters of Book VII, Book I, and Books III-VI. Between the time in which Aristotle composed his work treating of the ideal state and that in which the work was produced from which the principal part extant of the *Politics* was taken, a very essential change must have taken place in his political conceptions, especially in his attitude to monarchy.

practical virtue and the self-regarding Godhead resting in himself, show
their real, i.e. their political, significance.

A distinctive peculiarity of the Aristotelian theory of government, which
has not hitherto been sufficiently remarked, is that it starts, in principle,
from two different standpoints and consequently answers the question as to
the best form of government according to two methods, each exclusive of the
other. The line of argument which leads to the glorification of hereditary
monarchy is carried from the premiss that there exists an absolutely best
form of government, which is monarchy, from which a strict rank order of
constitutions follows: aristocracy, polity, democracy, oligarchy, and
tyranny. This scale of values proceeding from the absolutely best to the
absolutely worst form is at the foundation of the six-forms scheme,
according to which the forms of government are divided into three true and
three perverted forms. But already in the representation of this scheme
another point of view appears. Each of the three true forms of government is
only true under certain quite definite conditions, but these conditions being
present, then anyone of them will be the best. Thus monarchy will be best
when any one individual is pre-eminent over all the others, when he is more
virtuous than all the others together; aristocracy when a minority fulfils the
same conditions; and democracy or polity when all the citizens are equally
virtuous and all together possessed of greater capacity than any one citizen
or than a minority group (1279a; 1281a). This is an altogether relativist
principle of values which cannot be associated methodically with the
apodictic thesis that royalty is always the best form of government. It is just
this relativist principle that Aristotle takes up again in Book IV, after
having, in Book III, represented royalty as being always the best form of
government. Here he develops in the introduction the notion that the true
legislator and statesman 'ought to be acquainted, not only with that which
is best in the abstract, but also with that which is best relative to
circumstances', and it is not sufficient to lay down the always best, it is
rather necessary 'to know the form of government which is best suited to
states in general' (1288b26), which is obviously the same as that described
in another passage as 'the best constitution for most states' (1295a25). The
conception of such a constitution, relatively, because only in certain
circumstances best, is not clearly expressed in the beginning of Book IV,
where it is confused with other problems, e.g. how such a constitution is to
be founded, how upheld, or which is the nearest attainable constitution. But
in the further course of his arguments Aristotle places this principle of
relative value more and more in the foreground. Thus we read: 'All these
forms of government have a kind of justice, but, tried by an absolute
standard, they are faulty' (1301a36); or, in another passage: 'I say relative
to given conditions, since a particular government may be preferable, but
another form may be better for some people' (1296b9-12). In the same line
of thought with this relativity, the rigid relation between oligarchy and
democracy, according to the six-forms scheme, is relinquished in the
admission of the question as to forms of governments 'to which each is
suited. For democracy may meet the needs of some better than oligarchy,
and conversely' (1289b16-19). And then it is said, too, that 'that which most
contributes to the permanence of constitutions is the adaptation of
education to the form of government', and therefore it is necessary that 'the

young are trained by habit and education in the spirit of the constitution, if the laws are oligarchical' (1310a16-18). And right in the middle of the discussion as to the cause of the change and decay of democratic and oligarchical constitutions Aristotle speaks of 'virtue and justice of the kind proper to each form of government' and adds in explanation, 'for, if what is just is not the same in all governments, the quality of justice must also differ' (1309a37-9). This is the classical formula of a fundamental relativist principle of constitutional justice.

It is from this standpoint that Aristotle can be relatively just to democracy. That in the rigid scale of values of the six-forms scheme a more favourable place has been assigned to democracy than is its due – as a perversion of the worst of the three true forms – is clear. In the reflections contained in Books IV-VI a markedly indulgent criticism of popular government is evident. It is spoken of not as a rulership of the poor, but of a free people, or at least of a constitution 'when the free who are also poor govern' (1290b18). Different kinds of democracies are distinguished, but only so as to attribute to the most extreme form of this constitution – to that, namely, 'in which not the law but the multitude have the supreme power and supersede the law by their decrees' (1292a5) – the place which, according to the original six-forms scheme, should fall expressly to democracy in general as a perversion, being a despotic, a tyrannical form of government. 'This sort of democracy being relative to other democracies what tyranny is to other forms of monarchy, the spirit of both is the same, and they alike exercise a despotic rule over the better citizens' (1292a18). Only of this extreme form of democracy it is said that 'such a democracy is fairly open to the objection that it is not a constitution at all; for where the laws have no authority there is no constitution . . . So that, if democracy be a real form of government, the sort of system in which all things are regulated by decrees is clearly not even a democracy in the true sense of the word . . .' (1292a30-6). The effort is clearly evident to draw a sharp line between moderate and extreme democracy, admitting the former as a constitution and having, therefore, at least a relative political value. This is a totally different attitude from that which led Aristotle to invent the form of polity, with a view to contrasting it with democracy as its perversion.[12] Now Aristotle goes so far as to declare that in certain circumstances, namely, 'where the number of the poor is more than proportioned to the wealth of the rich, there will naturally be a democracy, varying in form with the sort of people who compose it in each case' (1296b24-7). And in speaking of a democracy in which all 'elect to offices and conduct scrutinies and sit in the law-courts' but where 'the great offices should be filled up by election and from persons having a qualification, the greater requiring a greater qualification, or, if there be no offices for which a qualification is required, then those who are marked out by special ability should be appointed', Aristotle declares: 'Under such a form of government the citizens are sure to be governed well [for the offices will always be held by the best persons; the people are willing enough to elect them and are not jealous of the good].

46

12. Usually, that is for theorists taking their stand on the republican *polis* democracy was considered as polity, i.e. as a constitutional state par excellence. Cf. Henkel, *Studien zur Geschichte der Griechischen Lehre vom Staat* (1872), p. 40.

The good and the notables will then be satisfied . . .' (1318b33). Democracy, this unnatural rule over slaves, has been promoted to the rank of a well-governed state, in harmony with the will of the people, always supposing, of course, that it is a moderate democracy.

And this is the constitution which under the name of polity is declared to be the best for most states. It can, obviously, only be this for the reason that the conditions under which the constitution must be considered as the best are, as a rule, most frequently given. Aristotle characterises this polity again and again as a fusion of democracy and oligarchy (cf. esp. 1293b). He remarks occasionally, it is true, that it approximates very nearly to the so-called aristocratic form (1295a). But everything he says about polity – and his remarks are mostly of a very general character – shows that the democratic element in it is predominant. 'The government should be confined to those who carry arms'. There is also a property qualification. 'As to the property qualification, we must see what is the highest qualification sufficiently comprehensive to secure that the number of those who have the rights of citizens exceeds the number of those excluded' (1297b5). By this is emphatically laid down that when speaking of polity it is to be understood as a fusion of oligarchical and democratic elements, in which the latter prevail. Should the government incline rather toward oligarchy, then aristocracy is spoken of (1293b; cf. 1307a). If the differentiation in terminology between oligarchy and aristocracy resulting from certain political tendencies be disregarded, then what Aristotle calls a polity may be denominated as a democracy with a certain aristocratic element. Aristotle also finally allows that 'polity more nearly approximates to democracy than to oligarchy' (1302a14). He says that according to the generally accepted doctrine which distinguishes only 'two principal forms', namely, oligarchy and democracy (obviously monarchy is not here in question), 'aristocracy is considered to be a kind of oligarchy, as being the rule of a few, and the so-called constitutional government' – that is polity – 'to be really a democracy', (1290a16-18) and that 'the states which we call constitutional governments have been hitherto called democracies' (1297b24). Besides, Aristotle himself uses indifferently in speaking of one and the same form, at one time the term 'polity', at another the term 'democracy'; thus he speaks of the form of government which succeeded the Gelo's tyranny as democracy (1316a33), although in a former passage he had denominated it polity (constitutional government; 1304a28).

The characteristic feature of this moderate democracy is that the supreme power is vested in the middle class. 'Now in all states there are three elements: one class is very rich, another very poor, and a third is a mean. It is admitted that moderation and the mean are best, and therefore it will clearly be best to possess the gifts of fortune in moderation' (1295b1-5). The mean being the best and the most useful for the state leads to the conclusion that

> the best political community is formed by citizens of the middle class, and that those states are likely to be well-administered, in which the middle class is large, and stronger if possible than both the other classes, or at any rate than either singly. Great then is the good fortune of a state in which the citizens have a moderate and sufficient

property ... The mean condition of states is clearly best, for no other
is free from faction; and where the middle class is large, there are
least likely to be factions and dissensions. (1295b35-1296a7)

This mean condition of states is polity, for 'where the middle class is large
and stronger if possible than both the other classes, or at any rate than
either singly, a lasting polity is possible'. It is a democracy guaranteed by
the moderate fortune and therefore itself a guaranty for the same, in modern
language a property class democracy, not a proletarian democracy. This is
just what distinguishes it essentially from extreme democracy, which is the
rule of the poorer classes over the richer, which Aristotle always reproaches
with injuring the latter by confiscating their property in favour of the
former. Very appropriately has Oncken remarked: 'The rule of the middle-   49
class with Aristotle is only another word for the rule of the propertied
class'.[13] Aristotle earnestly urges that 'those who have the welfare of the
state at heart' must above all counteract the demagogic confiscation of
property in the law courts by making a law that 'the property of the
condemned should not be public and go into the treasury, but be sacred'
(1320a6-9). It is from democracy that he requires that

the rich should be spared; not only should their property not be
divided, but their incomes, also, which in some states are taken from
them imperceptibly, should be protected. It is a good thing to prevent
the wealthy citizens, even if they are willing, from undertaking
expensive and useless public services, such as the giving of choruses,
torch-races, and the like. (1309a14-20)

This requirement polity fulfils, and it is one of the chief reasons why
Aristotle deems it, generally, 'the best constitution for most states'.

It is the *mesotês* (mean) formula, according to which polity is declared to
be the best form of government (1294a; 1294b). It appears therefore –
although in no wise in harmony with the six-forms scheme of constitutions –
that polity as a true form of state is the mean, or in other words the result of
the fusion of two perverted forms of government. But such a fusion should
produce a still worse constitution. And, indeed, if Aristotle speaks of
tyranny as the worst form of government, he describes it as follows: 'A
compound of Oligarchy and Democracy in their most extreme forms; it is
therefore most injurious to its subjects, being made up of two evil forms of
government, and having the perversions and errors of both' (i.e. of the most
faulty; 1310b3-7). To tyranny he does not apply the *mesotês* formula. He
does so only as regards polity. According to this formula, it must be the
mean between two evils. In answering the enquiry 'What is the best
constitution for most states, and the best life for most men?', Aristotle   50
declares:

If what was said in the *Ethics* is true, that the happy life is the life
according to virtue lived without impediment, and that virtue is a
mean, then the life which is in a mean, and in a mean attainable by

13. Oncken, *Die Staatslehre des Aristoteles*, II (1875), p. 272.

everyone, must be the best. And the same principles of virtue and vice are characteristic of cities and of constitutions, for the constitution is in a figure the life of the city. (1295a35-40)

And thus polity, instead of being a kind of aristocracy, as it would be according to the six-forms scheme, is characterised as a mean between oligarchy and democracy, two perverted constitutions according to the six-forms scheme. But what is good or right in the meaning of the *mesotês* formula is so not relatively but absolutely, representing the highest grade in moral and political value. If polity is, as Aristotle here declares, a *meson*, a mean form of constitution, it follows that in the meaning of the *mesotês* formula it is the best of all constitutions, just as monarchy, according to the six-forms scheme of constitutions, is pre-eminent among all others. According, therefore, to the one formula, the order of constitutions would be quite different from the order according to the other. In fact, it appears in one passage as if Aristotle were inclined to draw this conclusion from the application of his *mesotês* formula to his doctrine of government. He says, with reference to polity as a mean:

> What then is the best form of government and what makes it the best, is evident; and of other constitutions, since we say that there are many kinds of democracy and many of oligarchy, it is not difficult to see which has the first and which the second, or any other place in the order of excellency, now that we have determined which is the best. For that which is nearest to the best must of necessity be better, and that which is furthest from its worst. (1296b3-9)

But from this passage it may be seen that the scale of excellence descending from polity as the best constitution does not include all constitutions. Monarchy obviously is here not included because Aristotle wishes to make monarchy also appear as always the best form of government. But this appreciation of monarchy corresponds to a totally different scheme incompatible with the *mesotês* formula. Thus he either drops at once his estimation of constitutions, determined according to the *mesotês* formula, or he limits it considerably, adding the remark already quoted in another place: it may be that the value of a constitution is to be estimated according to existing conditions, i.e. on the principle that any form of government in certain circumstances, especially in respect to the nature of the people, may be the best. This means that he falls back on the principle of relative constitutional justice. This teaching, however, is not in harmony with the doctrine that in a fixed hierarchy of excellence royal rule must be assigned the first place.

All these inconsistencies, however, are the result of Aristotle's effort on the one hand to present hereditary monarchy as the highest ideal of constitution, and especially to contrast it with democracy. On the other hand, he desires, but less urgently, to assign to democracy – that is, of course, to a moderate form, protecting property, a form designated under the name of polity – a place with the best constitution. Therefore, he utilises at one time the conception of the citizen whose essential qualification is his sharing in government, at another time that of the subject distinguished as such by his aptness to be ruled. And this dual structure of his politics, according to which on the one hand hereditary monarchy is best, on the other moderate democracy, corresponds exactly to the dual morality of his ethics, which alongside the practical virtue of deeds sets up as an ideal theoretical contemplative knowledge. It corresponds likewise to the discord in his metaphysics which, far from questioning the many gods of the official state religion, with Zeus at their head governing the word, seeks to confirm this belief, yet seeks to elevate the self-contemplating, inactive godhead above the world, a sole godhead, who by his very nature is irreconcilable with the polytheism of the Greek religion.

Additional Note

Wilamowitz (*Aristoteles und Athen*, I 356) has already expressed the opinion that layers of different ages have been deposited in the *Politics*. But Jaeger [25] deserves the credit for having been the first in his penetrating analysis to discover that the subject-matter of the *Politics*, as we have it, is for the most part to be attributed to two distinct successive writings of Aristotle, one written in youth, while still under the influence of Plato's *Republic*, the nucleus of which is a plan of an ideal state, the other containing a realistic empirical doctrine of state, probably written by the philosopher during the last ten years of his life. This thesis is supported only by an examination of the subject-matter of the *Politics*, considered as a theory of state. But I cannot, however, wholly follow Jaeger in his answer to the question, Which part of the *Politics* is to be ascribed to the earlier and which to the later work of Aristotle? Jaeger would place the plan of the ideal state in Books II, III, VII, and VIII, and the later doctrine of state in Books IV-VI. He supposes that Aristotle composed Book I later, as an introduction to the compilation undertaken by himself. But Book III, by its subject-matter, belongs plainly to the later doctrine of state and not to the youthful plan of an ideal state. The former is essentially characterised by the six-forms scheme of constitutions: monarchy, aristocracy, polity, tyranny, oligarchy, democracy, and by the trend already manifested in this scheme to make hereditary monarchy appear as the absolutely best form of state. In Book III, this scheme of government is developed for the first time, and in Book IV it is again expressly referred to. Likewise, Book III contains already very significant if cautiously formulated contributions to the apology for monarchy, in which again only one line of thought is followed, that which is begun already in Book I, which, with its examination of the types of government, represented the general sociological foundation of a doctrine of state, the nucleus of which is a theory of constitutions. Book III, which offers the fundamental conception of a theory of constitutions, is the natural continuation of the first. Moreover, Jaeger himself must allow ([25], p. 291, n. 1) that the development of the multiplicity of forms of royal rule in the latter part of Book III probably does not belong to the earlier plan for an ideal state. Now, these remarks form nearly a third part of the whole of Book III and are in close organic connexion with the preceding examination of the different types of government, which begin with *Pol.* 1278b6.

The scheme of the six forms of constitutions, which is the basis of Aristotle's doctrine of state, is first presented in Book III. This doctrine gives decided direction to Book IV and cannot be ascribed to the productions of Aristotle's early youth, written under Platonic influence. For apart from the fact that it is also found in the *Nicomachean Ethics*, which is certainly not a production of youth, it is essentially different from the Platonic division of forms of state. Two points of difference only will be noticed here. Plato considered all real forms of state as mere imitations of his ideal state. Within these he distinguishes – following the usual division – monarchy, aristocracy, democracy, and within these again respectively a better and a worse form. Aristotle considers only those forms designated by Plato as mere 'imitations', declaring hereditary monarchy as absolutely the best, which Plato by no means allows. But Aristotle classes democracy in the perverted forms, whilst Plato, distinguishing a good lawful democracy from a bad lawless one, classes it amongst the true forms. To the constitution corresponding to Plato's lawless democracy Aristotle refuses the name of democracy. He calls it polity, although Plato expressly says 'As concerns democracy [whether good or bad] everybody calls it by this name' (*Politicus* 292).

The six-forms scheme of constitutions is not mentioned by a single word in Books II, VII, and VIII, although here, where the discussion turns on the form of the ideal state, its introduction might be thought imperative. The constitution of the ideal state is in no wise entitled 'polity', which it practically is according to the scheme formulated in Book III. The conception of 'polity' does not appear in Books II, VII, VIII, with the exception of a single passage, 1265b27, which is probably an interpolation of the compiler. It introduces the remarks which are devoted to the criticism of that constitution for the ideal state which Plato develops in the *Laws*. It runs as follows: 'The whole system of government tends to be neither democracy nor oligarchy, but something in a mean between them, which is usually called a polity'. Then follows an explanation of this type of constitution, which closes Ch. 6. But the constitution of the ideal state in the *Laws* has already been discussed much earlier, namely, 1265a1ff., and here it is only remarked that the *Laws* said very little about forms of constitutions, and if the part treating of the community of women and property be excepted, the discussion differs very little from the constitution of the ideal state in the *Republic*. The manner of treatment gives the impression that Aristotle saw no special reason why he should discuss the constitution of the *Laws* state. If he had intended to do so, he must have done it in this place. The detailed criticism of the constitution of the *Laws* found at the close of Ch. 6 has no connexion whatsoever with the context. Moreover, it is advanced in this criticism of Plato that 'In the *Laws* it is maintained that the best constitution is made up of democracy and tyranny, which are either not constitutions at all, or are the worst of all' (1266a1ff.), Now this attitude to democracy is in direct contradiction to the manner in which, in the same Book II, Aristotle speaks of democracy. Thus in Ch. 2 (1261b1ff.) democracy, that is, a form of government in which 'all should share in the government', is declared to be, under certain conditions, even just. In *Pol.* II, 1264b6, the objection is raised to Plato's *Republic* that 'he makes the same person always rule. And if this is often cause of disturbance among the meaner sort, how much more among high-spirited warriors?' Thus the advantage afforded by the interchange of rulers under a democratic system is recognised. Then Book II (1273b36ff.) contains a very appreciative presentation of the constitution of Solon who 'emancipated the people, established the ancient Athenian democracy and harmonised the different elements of the state'; but in any case, the chief reason for recognising this state form as democratic is that 'Solon appears to have given the Athenians that power of electing to offices and calling to account the magistrates which was absolutely necessary; for without it they would have been in a state of slavery and enmity to the government'. And finally, the criticism of the constitution of the 'Laws' concludes (1266a25ff.) with the reflection, 'These considerations, and others which will be adduced when the time comes for examining similar polities, tend to show that states like Plato's should not be composed of democracy and monarchy'. This is a reference to *Pol.* 1292a39ff., and also to a part of the *Politics* which, and this is Jaeger's opinion too, does not belong to the plan for an ideal state contained in the youthful plan but to the later doctrine of state. To this group probably belongs the criticism of the 'Laws' constitution, added by the compiler to the conclusion of chap. 6 of Book II. That particularly Books II and III are not connected with each other may be clearly discerned in the fact that Book III tends to show conclusively that monarchy is the best state form, while Book II is very sceptical as to this state form. Thus, in speaking of hereditary monarchy amongst the Spartans, he says: 'They should at any rate be chosen, not as they are now, but with regard to their personal life and conduct. The legislator himself obviously did not suppose that he could make them really good men; at least he shows a great distrust of their virtue. For this reason the Spartans used to join enemies with them in the same embassy, and the quarrels between the Kings were held to be conservative of the state' (II 1271a20ff.). This reveals unmistakably a distinct dislike for hereditary monarchy. But contrasting with this we read in Book III (1285a3ff.): 'Of royalties according to law, the Lacedaemonian is thought to answer best to the true pattern; but there the royal power is not absolute, except ...' This is quite different from the appreciation of the Spartan monarchy found in Book II. The reflections on monarchy amongst the Carthaginians (II 1272b38ff.) show the same character. And the constitution of the ideal state developed in Book VII is in no wise a monarchy (in the sense of the scheme of constitutions in Book III, according to which hereditary monarchy is the best form) but a moderate democracy.

It is reasonable to suppose that Aristotle, at the time when he was Plato's young pupil, did not appreciate the value of monarchy, and that it was only after his stay at Assos, after he had lived at the court of a monarch, as the confidant of King Philip and the tutor of the heir-apparent, in his riper years, that he realised the value of this form of government. If the attitude towards the question of the form of state be recognised as decisive, then Book III cannot belong to the same line of thought as Books II, VII, and VIII. It contains, more probably, with Books I and IV-VI the doctrine of state, which owed its origin to the philosopher's second stay in Athens.

The division of the *Politics* into the two complexes, Books II, III, VII; VIII on the one side, and Books I, IV-VI on the other side, Jaeger, amongst others, explains (*op. cit.*, p. 270) by pointing out that the ideal state, which is the nucleus of the first group, is not the leading norm in the second. This is correct. But this is true not only for Books IV-VI but also for Book III, which from this standpoint certainly belongs to the later realistic doctrine of state, not to the writing concerning the ideal state. The decisive norm for Books IV-VI is the six-forms scheme of constitution. But this is first drawn up in Book III, and even with the tendency to make monarchy appear as the absolutely best form of government. Opposing this connexion between Books III and IV, Jaeger argues that in Book III democracy and oligarchy are qualified, unreservedly, as bad forms, whereas in Book IV we read 'In these two types almost all real constitutions have their foundations'. Only 'almost' all, for IV, like III, is under the six-forms scheme, with monarchy on the top! And Jaeger establishes beyond all doubt that Aristotle adheres to this scheme also in Book IV. The explanation of the contradiction in the treatment of democracy and oligarchy – it concerns rather democracy than oligarchy – may be seen in the foregoing text.

The thesis that Books II, III, VII,' and VIII form the so-called *Ur-Politik* is supported by Jaeger on the ground that these books contain a number of references one to the other, while the intervening Books IV-VI are not mentioned in the books belonging to the first group. But it is quite possible that the references in Book III to Books II, VII, and VIII may have been incorporated by the compiler. Jaeger himself is obliged to have recourse to a similar supposition to explain references which do not agree with his hypothesis (e.g. that Book I is quoted in Books III and VII). Moreover, many passages which Jaeger considers as a reference to the ideal state of Book VII may be explained otherwise, i.e. as a reference to hereditary monarchy, which was declared to be the best form of government in Books IV-VI. Thus, for example, III 1284b25, where monarchy is clearly intended, and not the moderate democracy representing the ideal state of Book VII. It must not be overlooked that there is not only one best state in the sense of the plan of an ideal state, contained in Books II, VII, and VIII, but also a best constitution totally different from and independent of the ideal state of Book VII, a best constitution in the sense of the six-forms scheme of Books III-VI, i.e. Aristotle's later doctrine of state. In the ideal state of Books II, VII, and VII the question is: What is the best substance of state, what is the best manner of forming the contents of an ideal state-order? Here the question of the type of constitution is not in the foreground, just as in Plato's ideal state. Books III-VI examine the best form of state, that is, the constitution in the narrower sense of the word. The constitution of the best state of Books II, VII, and VIII is a limited democracy; the absolutely best constitution of Books III-VI is a hereditary monarchy. That the best state described in Book III cannot be identical with that of the last two, and that Book IV is most closely connected with Book III, Bendixen has already shown in his remarkable essay, 'Über die Reihenfolge der zur Politik des Aristoteles gehörigen Bücher', *Philologus* 13 (1858), pp. 264ff. Concerning the place to be assigned to the first three chapters of Book VII see above, n. 11.

One further remark. In face of the enormous difference in the political attitude at the basis of the plan for an ideal state and the later realistic doctrine of state, it is extremely improbable that Aristotle himself compiled together in one work these two writings so totally different, without even making an effort to reconcile the contradictions arising out of their contents. The existing text of the *Politics*, from the stand-point of an analysis of its subject-matter, gives the impression of a much too superficial compilation – I am thinking here of the treatise on the art of getting wealth embedded in Book I – to be one for which the philosopher can be held responsible.

16

Maurice Defourny

The Aim of the State: Peace

In the case of substances, form is the principle of unity; it is also the final 475
cause. Sovereignty is the form of political unity, uniting the many diverse
elements that make up society and guiding their activities towards one end.
This end is happiness and virtue, in a word *to eu zên*, the happy and virtuous
life. Aristotle reiterates this principle *ad nauseam*: 'But a state exists for the
sake of a good life, and not for the sake of life only' (*Pol.* III 9, 1280a31); 'It 476
is plain that a city worthy the name must have virtue as its aim' (*ibid.*
1280b6-8); 'A state . . . a community of families and aggregations of families
in wellbeing, for the sake of a perfect and self-sufficing life' (*ibid.* 1280b33-
5); 'A state is the union of families and villages in a perfect and self-sufficing
life, by which we mean a happy and honourable life' (*ibid.* 1281a1). 'A state
is . . . a community of equals who are seeking the best possible life . . .
Happiness is the highest good, being a realisation and perfect practice of
virtue' (VII 8, 1328a35-8). Happiness is therefore the supreme aim of the
state and virtue is the road to happiness.

What is happiness in the state? The state is happy when it is made up of
happy people. Happiness is the aim both of the individual and of the state:
'It remains to say whether happiness is the same for the private individual
as for the state, or not the same. This too is evident; for everyone would
agree that they are the same.' If riches make men happy, they will also make
a political society happy. If the individual finds happiness in dominating 477
others, the political society will be happy by conquering other states. If a
man finds that virtue is his greatest joy, so will the political society (VII 2,
1324a4ff.).

What then constitutes happiness? Happiness is the possession of the
various goods that correspond to our faculties: knowledge for
understanding, self-control for the will, health for the body. To these three
we must add exterior goods: an adequate income, a varied and carefully
chosen circle of friends, many distinguished children. Through these goods
there runs a hierarchy mirrored in the hierarchy of the faculties: the goods
of the soul are supreme, and among these the goods of understanding rank
above the goods of the will; the goods of the body are less important; and
external goods come at the bottom of the ladder. Happiness results from the
simultaneous possession of all these goods, provided that the established
hierarchy is observed. Knowledge should be acquired for its own sake, and
the rest according to the demands of understanding. Happiness may be
attained by concentrating the entire personality on the higher spiritual life;
virtue lies in applying each faculty to its object as far as the spiritual life
demands. Virtue leads to happiness. The state's aim is therefore to help its

members to attain happiness by practising virtue.[1] Men should convince themselves that the aim in life, for the private individual as well as for the state as a whole, should be the supremacy of virtue, to the exclusion of everything except virtuous actions. 'Let us assume, then, that the best life, both for individuals and states, is the life of virtue, when virtue has external goods enough for the performance of good actions' (VII 1, 1323b40-1324a1). And 'It is evident that the form of government is best in which every man, whoever he is, can act best and live happily' (1324a24-5).

A happy and virtuous life is thus an intellectual one (*ho kata ton noun bios*). The intellect is the highest part of man; the intellect, Aristotle wrote in the *Nicomachean Ethics*, is something divine in men, and the life of the mind is divine in relation to the rest of human life. As far as possible, we should look to immortality and exert ourselves to live according to the noblest part of us; and we shall succeed when our whole existence is controlled and dominated by this part. Then we shall live a life proper to us, indisputably our own. Such a life can fall, in this world, only to us men, and it raises us above our animal and material nature; surely it would be madness to prefer some other life led by lower beings? 'That which is proper to each thing is by nature best and most pleasant to each thing; for man, therefore, the life according to reason is best and pleasantest, since reason more than anything else *is* man. This life therefore is also the happiest' (*EN* X 7, 1177b30-5; 1178a1-8). In order to promote men's happiness, the state should encourage its members in a speculative life, and in the purest, the profoundest, and the most exalted intellectual operations within that life. The highest ambition of the state should be to lead men towards the calm wisdom and beauty of philosophy, and to attend to the rest – goods of the will, goods of the body, and exterior goods – as far as they are necessary for this end. This is the concept that will form the basis of Aristotle's theory of the peaceful state; and the theory (which incidentally owes something to Plato) will become, by its systematic rigour, the philosophical innovation of the age.

Plato says that what is best in the state is neither war nor revolution – on the contrary, it would be better to do without them altogether – but mutual peace and concord (*Laws* I, 628C). War is to the body politic as medicine is to the body human: it is a means of restoring peace, as the remedy is the means of restoring health. This principle should form the basis of all sensible politics, and anyone who does not subscribe to it will never rise to the top of the legislative profession; preoccupied only with external battles, far from organising the war with an eye to peace, he will subject peace to war (*ibid.* 628D). War for the sake of peace and not peace for the sake of war! This formula – as I intend to show – is Aristotelian: plainly, it was inspired by Plato. Yet once he has stated his ideal of peace, Plato speedily casts it aside. He constructs a state in which the wording of every law and the structure of every institution are stamped with the imprint of extreme militarism. His city is a city of soldiers, and civil life – except for a favoured few – is one long training camp. Certainly he could never be accused of

---

1. I have described this theory of happiness, and cited supporting texts, in [188], part I, pp. 130, 147; part II, pp. 272ff.; I refer the reader there for additional details and a complete discussion.

today's 'bleating pacifism'. He bases peace on a full-scale military organisation.[2]

On one occasion, however, Plato does remember his stipulation that in principle war should be subordinate to peace: that is when he examines the rules of military conduct. In a war against barbarians, any atrocity is permissible; but in a war between Greeks, the combatants should behave like gentlemen. The Greek soul is sickly when the Greek states are split in a struggle. Armed conflict between them is not a true war, but internecine strife. The Greek states together form a kind of great republic, of which they are all members (*Republic* V, 470C). Friends, temporarily estranged though they may be, do not try to destroy each other, do not indulge in campaigns of total destruction, and above all do not take slaves; they limit punishment to the sowers of discord, and spare the masses – all this to preserve valuable fighting men in good order for future use against the barbarians (*Republic* V, 469B). Yet it this not a second contradiction? Plato is limiting humanitarian principles to a war between Greeks, and has no thought of limiting the ravages of a war outside Greek borders. **481**

Aristotle picks up this point; and as a general rule of military conduct, whether in a war against barbarians or among Greeks, he prescribes humanity as an inviolable law. 'Nor is it right to say that the guardians should be fierce towards those whom they do not know; for we ought not to be out of temper with anyone; and a lofty spirit is not fierce by nature, but only when excited against evil-doers' (*Pol.* VII 7, 1328a7-10). Furthermore, once we have accepted the principle that war should be subordinate to peace, mercy becomes a rule that should apply to every victory. If we infuriate the enemy by extraordinary ill-treatment, we shall only poison his mind and instil in him a desire for revenge at the moment of his defeat, and we shall eliminate any hope of a genuine submission or a lasting peace.

It is certainly Aristotle's view that war should be subordinate to peace. Not only does he lay claim to such a view, he accepts its material consequences. He approaches the problem of war with a depth and thoroughness foreign both to the *Republic* and to the *Laws*.

For him the roar of battle, camp life, gruelling drill sessions, the exhaustion of active service, the continual watchfulness and bustle – all these are only obstacles to calm intellectual meditation. The speculative life that leads to happiness demands peace and quiet (*EN* X 7, 1177b4). It is **482** clearly wrong to present war and conquest as desirable state policy, though it is a policy espoused by many nations. Examples tumble from Aristotle's pen: Sparta and Crete, where education and the legal system are almost entirely military in character; the Scythians, the Persians, the Thracians, and the Celts, who hold war in too high regard, as do all other nations who think themselves powerful enough to succeed in a bid for foreign victory. It is indeed a fatal misconception that seems sanctioned by habit and the established institutions of society. The Carthaginians wear as many bracelets as they have campaigns to their credit; the Macedonians put a halter on the neck of anyone who has failed to kill an enemy; the Scythians forbid any man who has not slain an adversary in battle to touch the cup that is passed round during celebrations; the Iberians, a warlike nation,

2. On the rules of war in Plato, see Diès, *Platon*, pp. 167 and 169.

adorn the tombs of the dead with as many swords as they slew warriors in battle. All such practices – and the list need not stop here – are absurd. They impel men relentlessly towards war, as if war were legitimate in itself. Yet it is not, because injustice cannot be legitimate. Is it not unjust to subjugate your neighbours, who neither want nor deserve it? Subjugation and domination are conditions of natural law, and nobody has the right to tailor them to his own desires: 'such behaviour is irrational – unless the one party is, and the other is not, born to serve' (VII 2, 1324b36-7).

Here is another proof that war is not the be-all and end-all of the state. States, like people, find happiness in perfect activity, conforming to the nature of the subject and to the hierarchy of its faculties. But let us not imagine that activity, let alone perfect activity, is the acting of one being on **483** another, so that, supposing the universe consisted of only one being or of several beings without access to each other, no form of activity could exist. Quite the contrary is true. Doubtless action *ad extra* is real and not uncommon; but this is neither the only possible nor the most exalted activity. Purely internal actions, like thinking and meditating, are far more sublime. We measure the dignity and worth of a man by the depth and degree of introspection of his thoughts. This entirely intellectual and intimate stream of life, of which external life is after all only a tributary, is a far better realisation of the concept of activity.

> Not that a life of action must necessarily have relation to others, as some persons think, nor are those ideas only to be regarded as practical which are pursued for the sake of practical results, but much more the thoughts and contemplations which are independent and complete in themselves: since virtuous activity, and therefore a certain kind of action, is an end, and even in the case of external actions the directing mind is most truly said to act. (1325b16-23)

God and the universe, who perform no action *ad extra*, whose whole life is **484** centred on themselves,[3] would hardly exist if activity were necessarily the action of one being on another; they would be dormant substances. Thus an isolated state, having no relations with any other, either good or bad, or even a state without neighbours, surrounded by desert as far as the eye can see, would not necessarily be an inactive state. On the contrary, following the universal rule, it might indulge in a sublime form of activity resulting from the interaction of the multiple elements of which it is composed (1325b24-30). If such an exclusively internal activity of the isolated state is

---

3. This point is argued for in *EN* X 8, 1178b. This is how the argument goes: 'We all allow that the gods are happy. So they act, since happiness is the result of activity. They are, indeed, supremely active since their happiness is the greatest of all. With what actions should we credit them? No external action fits their nature. Not justice, because justice presupposes exchanges, conventions, rewards, and finance. Not courage, because courage presupposes fear, adventures, and anger which would ruffle their happiness. Not liberality, for they have no money and no one to give it to. Not evil passions, which are unworthy of them. And yet the gods do not spend their time asleep: they act – for they are happy. If we eliminate from activity any external elements, we are left with purely introspective activity: contemplation. Therefore the activity of God, which surpasses all others in blessedness, must be contemplative'.

well ordered under a good legislative plan, the city will be happy, even very happy. And yet it is plain that any idea of conflict and domination will be foreign to it: 'such a city would not be constituted with any view to war or the conquest of enemies – all that sort of thing must be excluded' (1325a1-5). War cannot be the final end of the state.

Aristotle says that the nurture of military institutions is fine and noble but that it is not the supreme goal of the state but only a means to achieve it (VII 2, 1325a5-7). The supreme goal is happiness, intellectual development in the citizens, and peace, which will provide a serene calm to encourage the ripening of a speculative life. Peace and tranquillity are goods preferable to war and disruption. Of course, a man must be able to stir from his armchair   485 when he is needed on the battlefield; but he must prize peace more highly. He must turn his hand to war as something that has its occasional uses and fulfills an occasonal need; but his devotion to peace should dominate his warlike spirit just as the good and the beautiful should dominate the useful (VII 14, 1333a41-b2).

Of course, we must know how to enjoy peace. Peace is far from idleness, indolence, and debauch. We must use the leisure peace provides in an intelligent way – that is to say, in a way consonant with the nature of man, by the enriching and expansion of the intellectual life. The way of peace, so understood, cannot be trodden *extempore*: it needs careful thought. Aristotle outlined a programme of education which was crowned by the study of literature, below which stood music, then gymnastics, and finally drawing. Such an education will guarantee that the personality, guided by the mind, enjoys a harmonious balance of all the faculties. This done, men may lie in the arms of peace and gently cultivate their understanding, with breaks for making and listening to music, and for gymnastics, so as to dispel any conceivable monotony in the uninterruptedly speculative life and to exercise the lower talents in the service of thought. Thus thought becomes the centre of existence, the meeting-point for all activities. Peace enjoyed in this way is a virtuous and happy one, in which men truly realise their nature.

Here, fact comes to the aid of reasoning. Happiness flees those cities which are only concerned with war, in which institutions are founded on purely military ideals, and which neglect the teaching of those virtues   486 necessary to the true enjoyment of peace. These cities survive as long as war lasts, but perish with the signing of peace, whether it is a peace of victory or a peace of defeat. Look at Sparta, deep in the slough of despair since the fortunes of war were its undoing and Thebes trampled on all its might: 'but surely they are not a happy people now that their empire has passed away' (VII 14, 1333b22). Even if flushed with victory and power, Sparta would hardly have been happier: as steel eventually loses its edge, so too do military cities when condemned to years of inaction for lack of foes (1334a6-8). In short, whether warriors win or lose, they are doomed to forfeit all contentment. How should it be otherwise? Once peace is signed, warlike virtues are useless, and in any case, peace without the knowledge how to use it cannot lead to happiness. War is not the supreme goal of the state, since it must culminate in victory or defeat, and both possibilities, equally ruinous, involve misery and decay.

War can only play a subordinate role in the state. It is only good if its aim is peace: 'the aim of war is peace' (1334a14-15); 'of necessity war is for the sake of peace' (1333a35); and Aristotle had already said in the *Ethics* that 'we make war that we may live in peace' (*EN* X 7, 1177b5-6). Although this statement may appear paradoxical, it is profoundly true. Those who want war for its own sake and for the slaughter it involves are indeed murderers (*miaiphonoi*) (1177b10). War can only be justified if its aim is to establish and preserve order, to repel aggression and to protect justice. The state's aim is not peace at any price; peace with vassaldom or anarchy are by no means desirable, but a controlled and ordered peace is infinitely precious. To achieve and guarantee such a peace, war is legitimate. Three situations arise where it is permissible; here is Aristotle's text:

> Neither should men study war with a view to the enslavement of those who do not deserve to be enslaved; but first of all they should provide against their own enslavement, and in the second place obtain empire for the good of the governed, and not for the sake of exercising a general despotism, and in the third place they should seek to be masters only over those who deserve to be slaves. (VII 14, 1333b39-1334a2)

A defensive war that aims to preserve the nation's independence is thus legitimate. A nation under attack must defend itself; and if it surrendered without resisting the aggressor, it would imperil all future peace and justice, and encourage the predator's ambition and greed. Next, a war that is waged in the interest and for the happiness of the enemy is also legitimate. An armed intervention in the internal affairs of another nation is legitimate in itself, provided that the goal is to rescue it from disorder and oppression and to bless it with peace and justice. Finally, wars of conquest are legitimate if their goal is the subjugation of inferior races, doomed by nature to obedience and vassaldom. Such a war also aims to establish order and keep the peace, respecting the conditions of natural law. Aristotle tells us that some men, the *phusei douloi*, are formed by nature for obedience and that others are formed to command. It is in the best interest of the former to be slaves, of the latter to be masters; and when they both live according to the dictates of nature, happiness comes their way. In theory, the Greeks are made to command, the barbarians to obey.[4] War of conquest is never permissible among the Greeks; only when waged by Greeks against a foreign nation does it thereby become a just war. This adumbrates that modern view which condemned conquest among civilised nations but was quick to commend it against savage tribes.

In short, war is just when waged on behalf of a civilised nation, when waged as a justifiable intervention in the affairs of another nation, civilised or not, and when waged to conquer less civilised nations. Apart from these three situations, just war does not exist. War for war's sake, war for conquest's sake, are a moral disgrace and a legal prevarication; those who condone it are no better than murderers. It is perfectly permissible for a country to hold itself in readiness and to maintain military institutions, but

---

4. See [188], part I, pp. 27 ff.

it should never forget that its aim is to nurture the general peace and tranquillity (1334a2-5).

This theory of a peace-making war was destined to survive. Patristic literature, canon law, and the Scholastics, without following it slavishly, found it a rich source of inspiration. Peace is the aim of war; a striking slogan that was to remain at the heart of history. Saint Augustine, Gratian of Bologna, Saint Thomas, and Victoria – to mention only the most important – repeat it incessantly and use it as the foundation-stone of their theory of international law.

489

17

Raymond Weil

Aristotle's View of History

161   Aristotle's historical works have already received some attention here during the proceedings of 1956 on *Histoire et historiens dans l'antiquité*, when a masterly article by Kurt von Fritz demonstrated Aristotle's influence on Greek historiography and recalled the importance in his own writings of what may be called in a broad sense 'historical' research. In the narrowest sense of 'historical', the modern one, only a small number of historical works have survived: the *Athenian Constitution*; certain passages of the *corpus* and especially of the *Politics*; and finally a few fragments, interesting, but of mixed provenance and disappointing brevity. Working from the two most substantial texts, the *Athenian Constitution* and the *Politics*, we may investigate the relationship between history and philosophy, and in particular the way in which history, as presented by Aristotle, shows itself when surveyed and interpreted by a philosopher. On the other hand, there are also occasions when, as I have suggested elsewhere [185], Aristotle's political philosophy develops from his historical knowledge – or at least is subject to and shaped by it. The contrary is also true: Aristotle the historian remembers that he is a philosopher. And without doubt these two propositions should be linked – or better still synthesised – if we wish to understand this aspect of Aristotle's personality.

    If we embark on this attempt, our way is endangered by many reefs; the ideal explorer would be a philosopher, a philologist, and a historian: a demanding role. Fortunately, detailed studies now proliferate that will help us to launch the enterprise. There are other, more objective, difficulties: Aristotle's personal contribution can only be precisely assessed if we have

162   access to his sources; and indeed it would be desirable to have an exact knowledge of the relevant historical facts. But Aristotle is often our chief source for them, or even the source from which all others flow – the only indication that there were others to draw from, the source of sources. This difficulty can be overcome, however, in as far as comparisons may be made among the internal and the external elements of Aristotle's work – the internal in particular. Such comparisons have long aroused doubts about the authenticity of the *Athenian Constitution*; since even an opponent of authenticity now admits that this opuscule was written by a contemporary writer who was well acquainted with Aristotle's ideas (Hignett [195], pp. 29, 390), the comparisons are endowed with a deeper significance.

    Aristotle himself sets us on our way when, in a famous passage in the *Poetics* (9, 1451b5ff.) he states that poetry is more philosophical and more interesting than history, since the former deals with the general but the latter only with the particular. This text, which should be accepted for what it is, namely a piece of polemic aimed chiefly at Plato, makes no more than a superficial contrast between the two genres of poetry and history; it offers no more than a hint: if Aristotle the philosopher took an interest in history, it was because it could reward him with satisfaction of a 'philosophic' character which he appreciated by reason of his true profession. He does not make an outright and general attack upon history; nor does he absolutely deny either that it is philosophical or that it is interesting. This hypothesis is confirmed in the twenty-third chapter of the *Poetics*, 1459a17ff., which refers to histories which are 'ordinary' or 'vulgar' (*sunêtheis* – a manuscript reading which there is no reason to amend) and this implies that certain histories are not 'vulgar', or, as the context reveals, that they are not merely annals and chronicles. These 'extraordinary' accounts must have some unity, some bearing on the general: here we may detect traces of Thucydides and of Aristotle's personal preferences – he is not happy with the 'vulgar'. If, setting the example himself, he urges us to collect material for reflection, it is because reflection is used in this very process. (See perhaps *EN* X 9, 1181a.) And the form in which we now have some of this material is in fact the result of reflection, in the *Politics* and even in the *Athenian Constitution*. 163

Another text, this time from the *Politics*, illustrates Aristotle's desire to interpret history and to discover its most important lessons. He tells us that Sardanapalus was the victim of an assassination because he was despised; his murderer had seen him carding wool with his womenfolk (V 10, 1312a1ff.). Aristotle adds: 'If the storytellers say truly; and the tale may be true, if not of him, of someone else.' This is a remarkable comment, first because it implies a precise realisation of the problem this event raises. Sardanapalus-Assurbanipal is by no means a straightforward character; according to Callisthenes there were two princes of this name. At least two versions of his death were current: according to one, Sardanapalus was assassinated; according to the other, he was driven to suicide (Newman, *ad loc.*; Jacoby, *FGrH* II B 124, fr. 34). Aristotle seems *au fait* with these doubts and uncertainties, and advances with caution. And this attitude, which forces him to remain uncommited (our sources are story-tellers, he says: *hoi muthologountes*), also allows him to raise the philosophy of history above its factual details: a fig for the prince himself, since the moral remains the same.

Such Aristotelian passages should encourage us to grasp at once the lure which history offers the philosopher: the search for its laws. It is true that in Aristotle's explanation of historical facts, there emerges the scheme of the four causes. In the city, for example, we can observe a material cause (the different estates), a formal cause (the form of the constitution), an efficient cause (the legislator), and a final cause (a good life). (See Day and Chambers [196], pp. 54ff.). But this is superficial. It is more tempting to track down essence and accident in Aristotle's history (*ibid.*, pp. 42 ff.); this is however a delicate manoeuvre since the verb *sumbainein*, which officially expresses the notion of the accidental (*ta sumbebêkota*), is frequently used by writers who give it no precise philosophical overtones or at least who are in no way Aristotelians: Thucydides, Demosthenes, Isocrates, Plato, Xenophon. It is impossible to tell if the twenty-five occurrences of this verb in the *Athenian Constitution* indicate the precise philosophical notion of 164 'accident', or are nothing more than a manner of speaking. In short, we must approach the question on a lower level.

Even at this level, I do not claim that Aristotle invented what he wrote. Although he says somewhere that as he grew older he grew fonder of myths, he does not deserve to be classed with the *muthologountes*; he made it abundantly clear that he was no friend of theirs. What he does do is to accept more willingly (as is only natural) those traditions which fit his own conceptions and which he could have entertained in his imagination. At the beginning of the *Athenian Constitution*, according to one fragment, he wrote that before Cleisthenes the Athenians 'were divided into four tribes, like the seasons of the year; each tribe was divided into three sections, so that in all they should be twelve, like the months of the year; and these sections were called trittyes and phratries. In each phratry were thirty families, like the days of the month, and the family comprised thirty people' (fr. 3; cf. fr. 4). The artificial or theoretical character of this text has often been remarked upon; in its context, it reminds us of Plato's *Laws*, of the famous number five thousand and forty, and of similar speculations (Aymard, *Les Premières Civilisations* (Paris 1950²), p. 534; Hignett [195], pp. 47 ff.; P. Lévêque and P. Vidal-Naquet, *Clisthène l'Athénien* (Paris 1964), p. 145). Such speculation was attacked by Aristotle himself in the *Politics* (II 6, 1265a38ff.). If this fragment is a true reflection of his opinion, and not of a theory that he quotes without accepting, it may be that Athenian history seemed to him to show the uselessness and instability of such over-rigid divisions, destined to an early death once the population increased, in a city where such increase went unchecked.

The story of Solon is more characteristic because the texts are more reliable. We know that the Solon of the *Politics* and the Solon of the *Athenian Constitution* are more or less one and the same: the principal disparity concerns the archons, who, according to the *Politics*, were elected and controlled by the people (II 12, 1274a15ff.; III 11, 1281b32ff.), whereas according to the *Constitution* they were picked out by lot from a list drawn up in advance by the Areopagus (8.1,4). This inconsistency is probably only the remains of a much more widespread disagreement, which Aristotle noticed and attempted to reconcile: namely, the discrepancy between Solon as depicted by the authors of the fourth century and the Solon of the older writers, Herodotus, for example. As was often the case, the story of Solon was the object of discussion, of invective, and of propaganda; among others, there were at least a democratic version and an oligarchic version of the event. Slowly, Solon assumed the role of the founder of democracy, where Herodotus had seen him as a scholar and poet, the creator of a legal code, but not the instigator of constitutional reform and still less the father of democracy; in Herodotus' opinion, the Athenian democracy dated from Cleisthenes, from the end and not the beginning of the sixth century (Jacoby, *Atthis*, quoted by Hignett [195], pp. 2ff.; Herodotus, I 30, 2; II 177, 2; V 113, 2; VI 131, 1). Aristotle took a stand in this argument, and, as Hignett observes (p. 89), he reacted against the tradition. In the *Politics* (II 12, 1273b35ff.) he lists the bouquets and the brickbats Solon has received, and comes to the conclusion that if radical democracy has its roots in Solon's activities, it was by force of circumstance and was not his aim.

'Solon, himself, appears to have given the Athenians only that power ... which was absolutely necessary.' The *Athenian Constitution* is stamped with the same virtues of objectivity and justice, whether it is dealing with the conditions that achieved the abolition of debts, with the drafting of laws, or with the right to intervene in judicial matters; and its author shows how Solon did not hesitate to dupe both the noble and the democratic parties in order to save his country (6ff.).

Beyond doubt, Athens under Solon retained many characteristics of the preceding aristocratic regime: indeed, Aristotle sees Solon's Athens as the '*origin* of democracy' (*archê dêmokratias*) – but as nothing more (41, 2). When he refers to Solon as the 'first leader of the popular party' (2, 2), that is obviously only a manner of speaking, or is over-influenced by its sources: the context explains the phrase, in which the word 'first' is really the most important. For in the *Politics* as well as the *Constitution*, Aristotle emphasises more heavily this idea of beginning than the heritage from the previous regime. He is seeking a 'point of departure,' an *archê* – a habit incidentally of Herodotus, that devotee of the *archaios*. It is therefore natural to compare 167 this portrait of Solon's achievements with the definition Aristotle gives elsewhere of the first type of democracy: this regime, under which suffrage is restricted and which is legally governed by the middle classes – usually the yeomen – is indeed the oldest of the democracies he describes (1292b25ff.; cf. 1291b39ff., 1318b6ff.; see Day and Chambers). More important, however, Solon's rule is a moderate and well-balanced one (*metrios, mesos*): it evokes the ideal and the reality of the 'mixed' or 'mean' constitution praised by Aristotle. It is 'constitutional' rather than 'democratic' (G. Mondrup, *Aristoteles Athenaeernes Statsforfatning* (Copenhagen, 1938), p. 20). This is why people have wondered if Aristotle was referring to Solon when he says that only one man really encouraged the spread of such a government (1296a30ff.; Andrews draws up a list of interpretations of this passage in *Class. Rev.* 66, n.s. 2 (1952), pp. 141ff.). Aristotle also wrote that the ancient Greeks called some regimes 'democracies' which did not strictly qualify (IV 13, 1297b24ff.).

This ancient dilemma confronts even such eminent modern scholars as Glotz (*La Cité grècque*, Paris 1953). What Aristotle rejoiced to discover in Solon (and was obliged to discover in one of the Seven Sages) is the political embodiment of 'nothing in excess', of the mean (*mesotês*). When the Solon of the *Athenian Constitution* introduced lottery of the archons from a prearranged list, he was adopting a system which, according to the *Politics*, is appropriate in a *politeia* or even in an aristocracy. Notice also how assiduously Aristotle attempts to prove that Solon was a member of the middle classes; on this point as on many others, he strives to reconcile diverse traditions, and does so with enormous care, indicating the interest he took in his proof. 'Solon was by birth and reputation among the first of the city; but by fortune and 168 by rank he was a man of the middle classes' (*Ath. Resp.* 5, 3; in 28, 2 one of the two traditions is boldly paraded; it states that Solon, like Peisistratus, was among the 'nobles and the notables'). The *Politics* cite Solon, along with Lycurgus and Charondas, as examples of middle-class citizens, men who have proved to be the best legislators (IV 11, 1296a18ff., cf. Plutarch, *Solon* 1;14). It is amusing to observe with Newman (ad 1296a19) that Solon's poems, referred to in the *Politics* and quoted in the *Constitution* in order to

prove that Solon was a member of the middle class, do not by any means do
so; they at most hint at it in as much as they reveal that Solon was not a rich
man. In Aristotle's eyes, however, Solon took the middle road, as Lycurgus
did in certain respects; and his constitution was mixed as was that of
Lacedaemonia in certain respects.

Let us go further back in time. The *Athenian Constitution* provides us with
unique information on the government before Solon's: in about 620 the
archon Dracon organised a constitution ignored by all other sources,
including Aristotle's *Politics* (which goes so far as to deny it altogether:
1274b15). This denial is justified; it is generally agreed that such a
constitution never existed. It is also generally accepted that the text of the
Athenian Constitution reveals traces of patching and stitching which indicate
that this passage (Chapter 4; cf. 41, 2) was added to an earlier version. It is
not quite clear why Aristotle was impelled to correct his own work – the
early version and the *Politics* – by accepting a document that was probably
forged at the end of the fifth century. Aristotle's predilection for precise
documents, as it were fragments from the archives, has misled him. Why?
This is a fault we must lay at the door of political philosophy: the content
and the historical place of Dracon's false constitution were bound to tempt

169   Aristotle. Its content must have tempted him, because its putative forger
projected into the past an oligarchic ideal of a 'mean' constitution; and such
an ideal contained an implicit criticism of fifth-century Athenian
democracy: political rights reserved for men rich enough to arm themselves
as hoplites; magistrates elected from these same hoplites, with the highest
positions going to the richest; fines levied on those counsellors who
neglected their political duties – fines, moreover, proportionate to their
income; and the predominance of the Areopagus. These characteristics
define a type of *politeia* (see Mondrup, *op. cit.*, p. 20) which even includes the
balancing factor of a lottery based on a wisely controlled suffrage.

Unfortunately for him and perhaps for his plan, the author of this false
constitution perpetrated errors and anachronisms, in particular in
reckoning fortune in terms of money. Aristotle would be all the less likely to
notice this because this *politeia* of Dracon's slipped into place just where
book IV of the *Politics* allows for such a regime in history (1297b16): after
monarchy and oligarchy, when the expansion of the cities gave the hoplites
the edge over the cavalry, in both military and political affairs. This
coincidence is the more curious because Aristotle hesitated between at least
two orders of succession. In Book III (1286b8ff.) he puts what he calls
politeia after monarchy but before oligarchy: in this context, the word
appears to mean a government akin to aristocracy and still more to the
'mean' constitution; in this sequence, at any rate, *politeia* does not occur in
any of the subsequent stages and we therefore pass on to oligarchy, then to
tyranny and finally to democracy. It looks as though, from one book of the
Politics to the other, from one lecture to the next, the author's views had
changed. At any rate, he decided to consider another aspect of his problem;
and, in the same way, he accepted the 'Draconian constitution' as a *politeia*
in which the democratic element is even less marked than under Solon.

170   We might now pass on in time to the events of 411 and the ensuing years,
which are linked to the constitution of Dracon and which Aristotle
portrayed in a vague and complicated way, in keeping with the events

themselves. But whether we are dealing with the rule of the 400, of the 5,000, or of the 30, these apparently precise numbers hide a mass of uncertainty; and we should have to examine a vast number of sources, inspired by Theramenes or by his opponents. (This has been done from another point of view by Georges Mathieu in his *Essai sur la méthode suivie par Aristote dans la discussion des textes*.) It seems probable that Theramenes, nicknamed 'the buskin' because this shoe fits both feet, accepted any constitution that was legal and inclined towards the mean favoured by Aristotle. But this is a question of instinct rather than theory, and Thucydides holds an opinion on the government of the 5,000 which is very similar to Aristotle's own (*Ath. Resp.* 33, 2; Thuc. VIII 97, 2).

It is more interesting to go still further back in time, before Dracon, to the very first chapters of what survives of the *Athenian Constitution*, where Aristotle sometimes opines that Athens had a single constitution before the seventh century (Chs. 3 and 4), and sometimes that this constitution was modified by the successive creation of distinct magistracies (3, 2ff.). Besides, the fragments of the first chapters, and Chapter 41, mention at least two separate organisations, by Ion and by Theseus: we might believe that these were earlier stages if Chapter 3 (2-3) did not show that the monarchy did survive but gradually weakened until it disappeared altogether. Theseus' government was monarchic but 'inclining a little away from royalty' (41, 2). The government before Dracon is described as an exaggerated oligarchy (2, 1), or as based both on nobility and on wealth (*aristindên kai ploutindên*: 3, 1; 6); these two definitions are identical only from our point of view; for 171 Aristotle there was no question of an oligarchy here but only of a type of aristocracy (as was the case in Carthage, *Pol.* II 11, 1273a21ff.; cf. IV 7, 1293b7ff.). These passages give a general impression of vacillation, which is not simply due to the textual condition of the *Constitution*: what we are offered does not correspond to any strict definition, or perhaps the definitions are too tenuous to be clear. Further, Aristotle realises that governments may change gradually, and so move from one category into another (see, for example, 1303a20, 1306b9, 1307b3, 30, etc.). He is working here in a historical landscape that is devoid of landmarks and whose chronology was probably uncertain in his own mind. So the very facts conform to no clear pattern. It is not clear in what order they occur, nor even how they fit in with each other. Having adopted a scheme that was both chronological and systematic, Aristotle could not, under such conditions, be more precise – and perhaps he had no need to be.

One last example, perhaps more typical, is provided by the government known as that of the Areopagus, which followed the Persian wars (*Ath. Resp.* 23). Aristotle tells us that the Areopagus, whose role before Salamis had increased its prestige, put an end, or at least a limit, to the democratic government that originated with Cleisthenes: its power rested on its authority; and it was, says Aristotle, a good government, lasting roughly eighteen years till 462 – though it did not preserve its virtue unimpaired to the end.

This would not be remarkable in itself – wars bring many changes – if Aristotle were not working so systematically that, in the recapitulation of chapter 41, he classes the event as one of the eleven constitutional alterations of the Athenian state. This remark is unique; unparalleled in any other author, it contains various Aristotelian anachronisms which render it suspect: Aristotle shows us the Athenians of this period deploying resources that they did not possess till later and enjoying a hegemony of an extent and nature proper to a later age. It is possible that Aristotle invented none of this, and that he is drawing on one of the Atthidographers. The latter were convinced that Cleisthenes' and even Solon's democracies were a very advanced form of government in which the Areopagus was demoted to a secondary status, and they were thus unable to understand Ephialtes' action against the Areopagus in 462; they had to suppose that the council had enjoyed a resurgence of power before this date, in order to give Ephialtes something to deprive them of (see Hignett [195], pp. 147ff.; Day and Chambers [196]).

However that may be, Aristotle did not have the same reason for accepting this version, which was unknown to Herodotus; for Aristotle does not credit Cleisthenes with a radical democracy: he accepts that Cleisthenes broadened the citizenship (*Pol.* 1275b35), even though a moderate democracy is restricted to citizens of respectable birth (e.g. 1292a1ff.); and he makes a logical connexion between Cleisthenes' action and the creation of an extreme democracy (1319b19ff.); nevertheless, he is very much aware that the expansion of democracy was gradual at the end of the sixth century and the beginning of the fifth (*Ath. Resp.* 23, 1); he shows that democracy did not become extreme until 462 (26ff.); and finally in his recapitulation he remarks simply that Cleisthenes' reform 'was more democratic than Solon's' (41, 2). If, then, the so-called constitution of the Areopagus appeared a genuine constitution to Aristotle, it was due to the political preoccupations of the fourth century and to the demands of his own theory. These political preoccupations are well known, in particular from Isocrates' *Areopagiticus* and from an inscription dating from after the defeat of Chaeronea, which urges the Areopagus not to sit in the event of a tyrannical revolution (Meritt, *Hesperia*, 21 (1952), pp. 355ff.; Pouilloux, *Choix d'inscriptions grecques* (Paris 1960)). Various texts prove that when times were hard the Athenians turned to the Areopagus (Lysias, *Eratosth.* 69; Lycurgus, *Leocr.* 52; Aeschines *Ctes.* 252; Plutarch, *Phoc.* 16); it had its adherents and its enemies. And when Plato, in the *Laws*, attributes the Athenian victory in the Persian wars to the 'traditional' government of the city, with its magistracies based on four distinct census classes (III, 698B), he anticipates the spirit if not the letter of Aristotle's account. Aristotle was thus siding with orthodoxy when he ascribed to the Areopagus a constitution that may be called reactionary, in as much as it was concerned to preserve the order and morality of the primitive constitution (*Ath. Resp.* 3, 6; cf. 4, 4; 8, 4; Mathieu, *Essai sur la méthode* ..., p. 9). A fuller explanation is to be found in the *Politics*, the only other text to allude to this event. Aristotle says: 'Governments also change into oligarchy or into democracy or into a constitutional government because the magistrates, or some other section of the state, increase in power or renown. Thus at Athens the reputation gained by the court of the Areopagus in the Persian war seemed to tighten the reins of government' (1304a17). This may have been no more than a reaffirmation of the Areopagus' authority, still amost intact, in hard times when the nation pulled together for victory and reconstruction; but in Aristotle's eyes it assumed the aspect of a distinct constitution. He took sides in the complicated discussion on the relative merits of the parties during the Persian wars (see 1274a12ff.). And he opted for this sort of constitutional reform all the more readily in that his theory of progressive change found itself on friendly soil; this is shown, in particular, by chapters 22ff. of the *Constitution*, where the expression *kata mikron* ('gradually') occurs twice (23, 1; 25, 1). (See Pokrowsky, *Neue Jahrb. für Philologie* 151 (1895), p.   174 469; an interesting article to which Day and Chambers [196] have called attention). Aristotle thus categorises the Areopagus' regime as an oligarchy (the text of the *Politics* does not allow Day and Chambers' hypothesis of a 'democracy'), and a moderate oligarchy at that (*suntonôteron* is only a comparative). The *Athenian Constitution* also says that this government was a step backwards (*palin ischusen*), but not a giant step; the expression *epoliteuthêsan kalôs* ('they were well governed'), which qualifies it at 23, 2 recurs a little further on when Aristotle is assessing the hoplite government of 410 (33, 2: as we have seen, Thucydides uses almost the same terms, *eu politeusantes*, VIII 97, 2); in the *Politics* the same words are applied to an aristocracy which can also pass for a *politeia* or for a moderate form of democracy (1304a27ff; 1312b6ff.; 1316a32ff.), namely the aristocracy in Syracuse in the middle of the fifth century, which lasted from the expulsion of the tyrants up to the Athenian invasion. In short, the so-called government of the Areopagus is an oligarchy having certain characteristics of an aristocracy (Mondrup, *op. cit.*, p. 21), or of a *politeia* (1295a33ff.; 1298a35ff.; 1305b10ff., etc.). We should not attempt to be more specific than Aristotle and, like him, should simply register the tendency. In any case, Busolt has already shown the influence of an oligarchic source on these chapters of the *Athenian Constitution* (*Gr. Gesch.* III 1, p. 27, quoted by Mathieu, p. 61).

Thus, the constitutions that Aristotle disinters from the graveyard of history correspond in part to his own political categories. Further, the succession of these constitutions demonstrates a twofold Aristotelian theory: on the one hand, there was once, long ago, an established order of political and constitutional evolution; on the other hand, any constitution, in general, can rise from any other (V, 1316al ff.). Although, according to the *Politics*,   175 there are four or five types of democracy, only two, or three at the most, can be traced in the *Athenian Constitution*; it is unlikely that the *Constitution* of any other country could have better illustrated the symmetrical forms of oligarchy and their succession (see Glotz *op. cit.*; Richard Robinson's denial is over-hasty – [175], p. 52; Newman manages to unearth twelve types of oligarchy – [172], IV, pp. xxiv ff). Oligarchy succeeds democracy, democracy oligarchy; there is room for *politeiai*, and also of course for a kind of monarchy such as the rule of Peisistratus.

The question arises: does this evolution have any meaning? It must clearly be linked to the Aristotelian notion of teleology; however, the word that leaps to mind in this connexion, progress, proves in the event to be somewhat awkward.

If we speak here of progress, we may fall into paradox: Aristotle is both a lover of order and a teleological philosopher. Yet the concept of order does not always exclude that of progress (as the Positivists were aware; and perhaps Aristotle deserves to be known as an enlightened conservative); nor

is teleology anything more than a general framework, within which both
progress and decline are possible. If it is true that the end already contains
in itself those degrees of perfections whose gradual maturing we can
observe, it is no less true that man retains the right to assess progress or
decline in the way Aristotle does himself – relatively (see Delvaille, *Essai sur
l'histoire de l'idée de progrès* (Paris 1910), pp. 54ff.). This is also valid in the
cyclic approach that Aristotle adopts when he shows that inventions have
been made, forgotten, and rediscovered several times (examples proliferate:
Pol.   1264a1ff.;   1329b25ff.;   *Meteor.*   339b27ff.;   *Meta.*   1074b10ff.;
Cael. 270b19ff.): in the time between a generation and a subsequent
corruption, progress will find a place. Furthermore, we should discover the
176   principles of what actually happens (Day and Chambers [196], p. 45). As
Robinson says ([175], pp. xix ff.) the doctrine of the ends of the city is
prescriptive rather than descriptive.

Progress also proves a difficult notion because Aristotle has no special
word for it: *prokoptein* only crops up once in the *corpus* with a different
meaning; *prokopē* naturally does not appear at all; as for *epididonai* and
epidosis, they rarely appear in a political context; and Aristotle has recourse
to *kinein*, an equivocal word which can describe various changes, in
particular revolutionary ones (see Newman at 1268b27, and Bonitz, [9]
s.v.). But the vocabulary of a Protagoras appears to have been no more
exact, and the idea is victor over the word. We find the idea of technical
progress, with many references to inventions; the idea of intellectual
progress, enhanced by experience; the idea even of moral and political
progress: the art of politics is compared to technical skills which develop
gradually (1268b25 ff.); the reservations that Aristotle makes about
changes, and the prudence that he recommends, both have an effect on the
type and the degrees of change, but they do not destroy the basic principle.
He shows us civilisation as the work of men who invent, organise, and
improve (here again, there are many examples, among others: *EN* 1098a24,
1175a35; *Cat.* 13a24; *Pol.* 1271b20ff.; 1282b14ff.; cf. Zeller, *Die Philosophie der
Griechen*, II 2³, pp. 507 ff.; Robin, '*La conception épicurienne du progrès*', in his *La
Pensée hellénique*, pp. 540ff; Aubenque, *Le Problème de l'être*, pp. 72ff.; etc.). If the
general problem of progress, mooted by Plato and before him by the sophists,
is not explicitly treated in Aristotle's *Politics* (as Gigon notes in the
introduction to his edition (Zurich 1955), pp. 14 ff.), it is only because the
doctrine of teleology relegates it to second place, and because Aristotle wants
no dreams of the Golden Age; but the problem still lurks under all this.

177   This explains Aristotle's attention to chronology: he is not just concerned
to establish the order of facts or events, or to pinpoint, as Herodotus did,
various starting-points, for example to judge between the Cretans and the
Egyptians and any others who claim any priorities (1271b20ff.; 1274a25ff.;
1329b22ff.). He distinguishes two main historical periods, past and present,
ancient times and modern times, describing the latter by *nun*, sometimes by
ēdē or *neōsti*, the former usually by *archaiōs, palaiōs*, or *palai*. The break seems
to be the Persian Wars (except that Dionysius I is at 1286b37ff. grouped
with the *archaioi*; but perhaps he does not really belong with them, and he is in
any case an exception). The *archaioi* are, for example, Homer's times
(1285a9), the oligarchies of the knights (1289b36, 1297b21), the periods of
the *aisumnētes* – 'elected tyrants' – (1295a12), of the Gamori of Syracuse

(1303b19). *Palai* refers to Solon's times (1266b16); *palaiôs*, to the period prior to the radical democracy (1277b2). In the *Athenian Constitution* (28, 5), three men of the fifth century are distinguished from the *archaioi*: Nicias, Thucydides, and Theramenes. And although each city may have its key dates – Leuctra in 371, for Sparta – the importance of the Persian Wars is abundantly clear; they asserted the personality of the people and of the Areopagus in Athens (1274a13; 1304a21), and they heralded an era – an era of burning ambition, of general intellectual curiosity, or, better, of intellectual freedom (1341a30ff.); in short, the opening of an age of enlightenment.

Further, the 'ancient' period may be subdivided; it consists first of the 'heroic' times (1285b3ff., 13, 20ff.; *EN* I 10, 1100a8; *Prob.* XXX 1, 953a13ff.), which includes the Trojan War but apparently not the Dorian invasion (Newman). When, in the *Rhetoric* (1396a14), the example of the Heraclidae is quoted along with Marathon and Salamis, there is one   178 important reservation: the participle *dokountôn*: 'all praise is based upon actions which are fine and true, or which *seem* so.'

This past is distinguished as a whole by characteristics foreign to the Greece of *nun*. These are varied, and touch on everyday life as well as on legislation and government: certain oligarchies (1289b35ff.), and above all monarchy (III 14; V 1305a15; 1310b14; 1313a3) appear to be linked to the conditions then prevalent, to the political situation, military resources, and even to the cultural climate: the advance of rhetoric, according to Aristotle, means that the demagogues are no longer, as formerly, military leaders but orators, and that they rarely aspire to tyranny (1305a7ff.). On the other hand, the inclination towards moderate liberty and the feeling for true discipline tended, according to Aristotle, to encourage the spawning of governments that were balanced, aristocratic *politeiai*; and this too has vanished (1296a36ff.). These general trends, bringing with them advantages and disadvantages, are confirmed by comparison with those parts of Greece which we might call under-developed (the examples of the 'peoples', as at 1261a27ff.), and above all with the Barbarians (1268b39ff.; 1295a11ff.). Here we find echoes of Thucydides' so-called 'archaeology' (I.5ff.).

But Aristotle's account of human evolution is not ordered in the same way as that of Thucydides: Thucydides thinks in terms of power – for he is explaining the origin of the most important war in the fifth century, when Athens and Sparta were at the height of their powers. Aristotle's position is not quite coherent; this development does not fit exactly with his chronology, and its stages are not all well established. We can pick out at least two periods.

The first marks the formation of the city. This appears to be clear-cut;   179 there is progress, because the city is the 'end' of this process. The various stages are mapped in the *Politics*; and they were doubtless described after its own fashion in *On Philosophy* which as far as we can tell is more Platonic. Like the primitives of Plato's *Laws* (Book III), who are neither very good nor very bad, but who are unhappy, the men of *On Philosophy* only gradually discover how to exist first without suffering and then with wisdom. The *Politics* are even more definite; the exceedingly elementary life of the Cyclops and his family is by no means desirable, and Aristotle is no more drawn to the 'sons of the earth', if they ever existed, or to the primitives (1268b39ff.);

in this, he is close to Protagoras (Plato, *Prot.* 327Cff.). The different modes of life men may invent (I 8) have no utility or pleasure unless they are combined; and that does not happen at first (1256b2ff.). Besides, even in the village stage, men only gathered together in order to stay alive; only in the city do they congregate for the sake of 'living well'.

This tidy chart of development, from the couple to the household (*oikia*), then to the village (*kômê*), then to the city (*polis*), clearly does not fit the facts (Robinson [175], pp. xivff.). If it is true, as Defourny remarks, that Aristotle saw 'villages' around him transformed into 'cities', and even new villages springing up, he has no proof that this change always happened in the past; the notion of a primitive scattering is at least controversial (Defourny [188], pp. 379ff., who cites the Arcadians as an example of a scattered community; Aristotle's text (1261a27) quotes them rather as an example of a federal organisation or a confederation of people; see Newman *ad loc.*). In Greek history, and in particular during the fourth century, cities broke up into 'dioecisms'; and that contradicts Aristotle's conception of teleology.
180 Aristotle is well aware of these difficulties, because he suggests another approach, where there is a transition from the 'people' to the city. This means people on the move, not 'people' spread among villages. Aristotle is conscious of migrations and invasions, of the instability of population that Thucydides describes at the beginning of his history. There are traces of it in fragments of the *Constitution*, and in the *Politics*, which tell of the nomadic life, of the migrations of the Italian races, and of the settlement of peoples by their kinds (1256a31ff.; 1329b14 ff.; 1310b34ff.). Similarly, Plato says in the *Laws* that after every catastrophe annihilating the previous civilisation, settlements moved gradually down the mountain-side to the valleys. This is scarcely compatible with the history of the Dorians: they were a people on the move who then settled in cities (see my *Archéologie de Platon*, p. 86). This incongruity is more striking in Aristotle's case because he is more systematic. The relationship between the transition from 'family' to 'village' and these nomad tribes remains unfathomable. History is framed by theory; the very word *kômê* (village), unknown in epic poetry, rare in Plato if not in Attic as a whole (Glotz, *op. cit.*, pp. 39ff.), is used to give a superficial consistency to Aristotle's account; but it does not give complete satisfaction.

The city, once established, fulfils basic needs: it provides security, and it is diversified enough to be self-sufficient. Aristotle will not commit himself to a firm date for this decisive stage, when Greeks can for the first time be properly distinct from barbarians – it occured 'in ancient times'.

This archaic city, its laws still primitive, is clearly far from perfect. In particular, the middle class is still weak, numerically and organisationally speaking (1297b27ff. in the manuscript reading; Newman's interpretation
181 seems the most natural). The relative sparsity of virtuous citizens simplifies legislation: there is less competition for government posts, and patriarchal monarchy is easily maintained. And the first development of the city only improves matters, because it remains small and readily patrolled. Foreigners are rare birds; sometimes, like slaves, they are restricted to jobs repugnant to the citizens (1278a6ff.). Barter only takes place when strictly necessary, and 'business' (*chrêmastikê*) stays within reasonable proportions. In many states, the citizens are peaceful country-folk; and their life, whether they are Athenians or Spartans, implies in any case that they show a certain

form of virtue. This is what Lycurgus and Solon wanted. The government, be it known as aristocracy or *politeia* or moderate democracy, is in the hands of soldiers, old soldiers. This happy balance may last a long time; it may even be established by a reasonable monarch: the Athenians said, and Aristotle happily repeats it, that Peisistratus' tyranny was the time of Cronos (*Ath. Resp.* 16, 7). Like Isocrates and many others, Aristotle is seduced by the delightful mirage of the so-called 'traditional' constitution, the *patrios politeia*, the Athenian *belle époque*. The Golden Age, they said, is not beginning; it lies in the past, in ancient times.

None the less, Aristotle only saw this Golden Age in the past in his system, because he credits Solon and Dracon with his own theory of *mesotês*, of a balanced constitution. He freely admits that such a balance was rarely a stable one (1296a36ff.); that tyrannies, in particular, arose quickly with all the concomitant perils; and that a purely aristocratic regime never existed. 182 The great development which, after the Persian Wars, hastened the states to what he calls their present condition – the great split of Greece into democracies and oligarchies – had its roots in the period before the Persian invasion. If Aristotle wants a return to the past, it is to the theoretical past and not to the real Dracon, under whom the question of debts, as Aristotle knew, was never solved, nor to Solon, who gazed helplessly on the destruction of his labours. Aristotle may praise this past, as do Isocrates and even Plato; but as far as he can, he exposes its faults: it is part of his theory rather than an embodiment of his ideal.

The next stage might be simple. Since a certain constitution suits each country, soil, and population, it might be enough for such a constitution to come about in fact, or for men to work towards it. This would be progress, or the direction in which progress is moving, predetermined by its 'end' as that notion implies. But Aristotle arrives at a more delicate postiion. Evolution, it seems to him, is inevitable, because material conditions themselves inevitably change. All forms of activity, agricultural, industrial, and commercial, must improve; Aristotle does not seek to conceal the interest he feels in such activities and improvements, as long as they pursue their goal (I 11); and he stresses that politics, or rather the politician, must take all these factors into account (e.g. 1259a33 ff.). If love of money is encouraged by such easy material progress, Aristotle will urge that virtue treads in the footsteps of riches, since riches bring leisure (1341a28ff). This affects political life, not necessarily adversely. Techniques change and are perfected, whether in the field of arms or in daily life; cities expand; and governments feel the repercussions (1289b35ff.; 1297b15ff.; VI 7). Under such conditions, two types of government arise, democracy and oligarchy 183 (1296b24ff.), while tyranny is uncommon (1305a7ff., especially 14ff.) and the most prolonged tyrannies happened in ancient times (V 11 and 12). (Plato, on the other hand, in the *Republic*, puts forward the idea of an extension of tyrannies.) Democracy triumphs, because it was born of the expansion of the cities; in the *Politics*, this expansion seems an accepted fact (1286b20ff.) Furthermore, democracy is buttressed by the very conditions it is founded on; its safety is assured by its large population (1321a1ff.). It is in the great cities that the middle class flourishes, and the political balance is steadfast in the democracies (1296a9ff.). Aristotle's verdict on this government is in the main favourable, as long as it involves a moderate democracy. (He sees the value of public opinion – e.g. *Politics* 1286a30ff., and also *Athenian Constitution*, 41, 2.)

In as much as the ideal goal is stability, and not any super-human virtue, Aristotle thinks that his own times have made some progress and can make more. He realises the value of material improvements, which are mirrored by political advances: the most 'common', *koinotatê*, constitution becomes generally more accessible. If in his system he seems to date the Golden Age sometime in the past, his moderation and objectivity lure him gradually towards the present and the future. Since the very nature of things has changed, he anticipates changes in the law.

For this reason, he wrote two books about the best constitution, a third solution, as it were, after Plato's *Republic* and his *deuteros plous* the *Laws* (cf. V, 739E). Not only does he insist that his ideal state must be 'possible' (1265a17ff.; 1325b38ff.) – Plato does that in the *Republic* (V, 456C) – but he goes so far as to place his two books right at the close of his work, as though they were a manifesto. He also keeps as close to reality as possible; for example, he requires that the city be able to defend itself – a constant necessity – and above all he admits that certain contemporary conditions are inevitable and may have happy outcomes: the ideal city would enjoy a 'political' life, forging relations with other cities; it would not be too self-contained; and it would embark on trade, and even, in certain cases, on conquest (1327a11ff., b1; 1333b38ff.). Its organisation should take into account all modern inventions, all developing techniques. When Aristotle tells us that we must look to the ideas of our predecessors, he is not just referring to abstract ideas. For example, he would like us to combine two methods of urban construction, ancient and modern, to preserve both security and pleasure (1330b21ff.); we should, he says, be careful to check on water supplies, profiting from the use of that happy invention, the reservoir (1330b5ff.); when we fortify the city, we should bear in mind the advances made in the art of war, especially as regards ballistics and sieges (1331a1). This model city will be in the forefront of progress, because its creators and its inhabitants consider all past discoveries and themselves strive to progress further (1329b33; 1331a14; cf. 1264a1). In this connexion Aristotle even uses the verb *philosophein* (1331a16), thus laying heavy stress on the intellectual character of their investigations; such improvements are a kind of wisdom.

It is therefore scarcely to be wondered at if the ideal city's constitution reminds us not only of Plato's *Laws* but also of a 'modified' democracy which is close to a *politieia* – a 'democracy' in which the citizens have the same advantages as they do in an oligarchy but are more numerous, a regime where all participate in government, but successively (1332a34, b12ff.); a 'democracy' in which virtue can reign supreme as it does in an aristocracy; in short, a contemporary city centred round virtue. It is a theoretical city that Aristotle sketches for us, and yet it suggests that he had not altogether despaired of his own times. Perhaps we can even glimpse, beneath the hints of a union of Greek cities, a desire to match political life to material reality: if the march of progress took the Greeks beyond the stage of the city-state, then Aristotle must discover the conditions under which such an evolution would be a good. At all events, in the context of the city-state itself there was a clear tendency to advance; if the city 'to be prayed for', *kat' euchên*, in 330 or 320 was different from the ideal city before such and such a recent invention, then what might not happen as a result of further technological improvements?

Thus we observe two contradictory or complementary tendencies in Aristotle's view of history: optimism combined with pessimism. The fifth book of the *Politics*, for example, draws up a gloomy register of revolution and disaster, but it does suggest remedies – indeed, a fundamental remedy: governments may achieve so perfect a balance that they all become alike; the tyrant himself, if he wants to stay on his throne, will emulate virtuous men till he comes to resemble them (V 11, 1315a41ff). The fiction of decadence and of progress, separate or combined, is to be found in Plato; but Aristotle spurns fiction and grounds it in fact.

His presentation of the different stages of the past is subject to two tendencies: on the one hand, he does the best he can to uncover the truth, sifting an immense amount of evidence; none the less he collects and interprets this according to his own theories. Doubtless such a propensity appears in the work of any historian who is concerned with probabilities, as   186 Herodotus already knew and as Thucydides taught. Further, historical objectivity, and even the concept of historical truth, were not faultless: for orators like Isocrates, Aeschines, and Demosthenes, history was a series of examples, to be exploited as the occasion demanded; Plato himself juggled with history. Aristotle never juggles with the facts, even if he juggles with the ideas.

What is more, he tailors his ideas to fit the facts. This happens when he is considering particular historical events – the constitution of Syracuse or the election of magistrates under Solon; and it is also evident when he examines the evolution of history. On one side he notes down the elements of continuity (1286b8ff., 1297b16ff.), a continuity that does not necessarily inhibit respect for the past, all the more since it is part of a cyclical system (another idea common to both Aristotle and Plato). On the other hand, observance of the facts coupled with reasoning restores the primitives to their proper place. Above all, continuity is replaced by a line that is either broken or multiple: Aristotle concedes that there are several ways of achieving the aim of the city, according to where and when it exists. Basically, he forges an alliance between the traditional concept of degeneration – principally degeneration of *mores* – and the idea of material progress as we see it in Thucydides. Progress is the victor, in a struggle in which the vanquished does not lose all.

The personal and involved tone of many of these texts helps us to realise how difficult it must have been for Aristotle to make this intellectual journey. When he is describing the development of extremes (e.g. 1296a21ff.), he seems deeply discouraged. Of course, this type of pessimism was the fashion among historians (it occurs in Thucydides, for example, in his description of the moral effects of the war (III 82), and the Roman historians, in particular Sallust and Tacitus, followed his lead). Again, a strong but controlled passion runs through the lines that tell of the enthusiasm and energy that inspired the Greeks during the Persian Wars   187 (1341a28ff.), the passage criticising Plato's theory of the nuptial number and the regular succession of constitutions (1316a1ff.), and the paragraphs in the seventh book that list various new inventions. In these last passages, indeed, Aristotle's personal tastes poke through, that love of the pleasures of life – we might even say of 'mod. cons.' – for which he has been so firmly rebuked; here we see an Aristotle who is, in the vulgar sense, an epicurean, and it is not surprising that he aired views on progress not dissimilar to those advanced by the Epicureans themselves; nor is it surprising that this superficial resemblance, linked with so many disagreements, resulted in clashes.

Aristotle has no theory of progress. These last points alone would suffice to discourage us from even referring to the idea of progress in his political philosophy: we are dealing with tendencies, hopes, inclinations, which crop up here and there but which it would be unwise to systematise. Yet this attitude finds history attractive because it is guided and supported by two notions. First, the notion of balance, around which constitutions must revolve and which Aristotle takes as the centre of his portrait of real constitutions: it is a fact and a value, a value that may be won with time. This is the second of the fundamental notions: while one stream of ancient thought saw time as the enemy of humanity, as Bury remarks in his book on *The Idea of Progress* (p. 11), with Aristotle it becomes beneficent and kindly. The Erinyes have become the Eumenides. Nor is this the looser, vaguer, conception of a man like Herodotus, who thought that 'everything can happen in the fulness of time' (V 9). Time the agent, filled with energy, imbued with the vital force that Gerber has recently perceived in some of Pindar's verse (*Trans. Am. Philol. Ass.* 1962, pp. 30ff.), is able to work transformations of every kind: in the configuration of the earth (*Meteor. passim*, e.g. I 14, 351bff.), in the lives of men and in their communities; finally, time may be an 'inventor' or a 'useful auxiliary' of human action (*EN* I 7, 1098a24). For 'one swallow doesn't make a summer'.

When Aristotle shows us, in the *Parts of Animals*, that man is, of all living creatures, the best equipped for technical advances, his opinion corrects Protagoras', and yet, strangely enough, it strengthens the theory of progress (IV 10, 687a19ff): Plato's Protagoras asserted that man was the least well-endowed of living beings, until he received the gift of fire, and then of conscience and justice. Aristotle believes that the human hand is worth all animal endowments, whether defensive or offensive: it is adaptable; it becomes 'claw, talon, horn, sword, or spear'; and man, equipped with hands, the most intelligent of creatures, succeeded in inventing the arts and in organising the social life that his nature demands; and he is still able to perfect all this. When Aristotle wavers between hope and pessimism, he probably had in mind (although he does not quote it) the famous chorus from Sophocles' *Antigone* (331ff.). This chorus contains the realisation that men can be both good and evil. But Aristotle, even more than Sophocles, stresses man's enormous resources. One subtle interpretation would have Sophocles say that man is *pantoporos aporos*, a being the richer in resources as he is deprived of them. As Aubenque noted (*Le Problème de l'être chez Aristote* (Paris 1962), p. 489), this formula would fit well with the Aristotelian idea of a philosopher. But it does not fit with Aristotle's idea of man; for that we must return to the standard interpretation of Sophocles: one man is rich in resources, *pantoporos*, and *aporos ep'ouden* etc. (see Jebb *ad loc.*). This man of unlimited resources must, however, limit his desires and must understand that his situation is limited. Yet what he has is free: just as the art of medicine constantly seeks health, so the art of politics relentlessly pursues its goal, according to circumstances, the more so since it is constantly fanned by the winds of technical progress.

BIBLIOGRAPHY

1. TEXTS

The classic edition of the Greek text of Aristotle was prepared by Immanuel Bekker for the Berlin Academy, and published in 1831; references to Aristotle's works are standardly given by page, column, and line of this edition. As a text, however, Bekker's edition has been largely superseded: most of Aristotle's works can be found in the Oxford Classical Text, Teubner, Budé, and Loeb series.

The standard English translation of Aristotle is
[1] J.A. Smith and W.D. Ross (edd.), *The Works of Aristotle translated into English* (Oxford, 1910-52).
There is an extremely useful abridgement of this, the 'Oxford Translation', in
[2] R. McKeon (ed.), *The Basic Works of Aristotle* (New York, 1941).
The volumes in
[3] the Clarendon Aristotle Series (ed. J.L. Ackrill)
contain translations and notes tailored for the Greekless reader. The commentaries by Sir David Ross are invaluable, not least on account of the comprehensive and accurate English analyses of the texts which they provide:
[4] W.D. Ross (ed.), *Aristotle's Metaphysics* (Oxford, 1924);
[5] *id.*, *Aristotle's Physics* (Oxford, 1936);
[6] *id.*, *Aristotle's Prior and Posterior Analytics* (Oxford, 1949);
[7] *id.*, *Aristotle's Parva Naturalia* (Oxford, 1955).
Many of the ancient Greek commentaries were published under the auspices of the Prussian Academy in the series
[8] *Commentaria in Aristotelem Graeca* (*CIAG*) (Berlin, 1882-1909).
None of these is available in English. Several of Aquinas' Latin commentaries on Aristotle can be read in English translation.

An indispensable aid to the study of Aristotle is
[9] H. Bonitz, *Index Aristotelicus* (Berlin, 1870).
There is an English concordance, based on the Oxford Translation,
[10] T.W. Organ, *An Index to Aristotle in English Translation* (Princeton, 1949).
A comprehensive bibliography of writings on Aristotle up to 1896 can be found in
[11] H. Schwab, *Bibliographie d' Aristote* (Paris, 1896).
See also
[12] M.D. Philippe, *Aristoteles*, Bibliographische Einführungen in das Studium der Philosophie 8 (Berne, 1948),
[13] *Isis Cumulative Bibliography* 1913-65.

Many of the books mentioned in this list contain their own bibliographies; the Archivum Aristotelicum of Berlin will eventually produce a comprehensive continuation of Schwab.

2. GENERAL

There is a magisterial guide to all aspects of Aristotle's life and thought in
[14] I. Düring, *Aristoteles* (Heidelberg, 1966).
Of several shorter English studies giving a general account of Aristotle's thought, the following are especially good:
[15] W.D. Ross, *Aristotle* (London, 1923),
[16] D.J. Allan, *The Philosophy of Aristotle* (London, 1952),
[17] J. Randall, *Aristotle* (New York, 1960),
[18] M. Grene, *A Portrait of Aristotle* (Chicago, 1963),
[19] G.E.R. Lloyd, *Aristotle* (London, 1968).
It is still worth consulting
[20] G. Grote, *Aristotle* (London, 1883).
The surviving evidence about Aristotle's life is collected in
[21] I. Düring, *Aristotle in the Ancient Biographical Tradition*, Studia Graeca et Latina Gothoburgensia 5 (Göteborg, 1957).
See also volume I of
[22] A.H. Chroust, *Aristotle* (London, 1973).

All questions about Aristotle's writings are exhaustively discussed by
[23] P. Moraux, *Les Listes anciennes des ouvrages d'Aristote* (Louvain, 1951).
There is an amusing reconstruction of Aristotle's lecture room in
[24] H. Jackson, 'Aristotle's lecture-room and lectures', *Journal of Philology* 35 (1920) pp. 191-200.
A major portion of the scholarly work done on Aristotle during the last half century has taken its start from
[25] W.W. Jaeger, *Aristotle*, trans. R. Robinson (Oxford, 1948).
The first, German, edition of Jaeger's book appeared in 1923. Two of the most ambitious contributions to this line of scholarship are
[26] F. Solmsen, *Die Entwicklung der aristotelischen Logik und Rhetorik*, Neue Philologische Untersuchungen 4 (Berlin, 1929),
[27] F.J. Nuyens: *L'Evolution de la psychologie d'Aristote* (Louvain, 1948).
Nuyens' book first appeared in 1939, in Flemish. Solmsen's views are conveniently expounded in
[28] J.L. Stocks, 'The composition of Aristotle's logical works', *Classical Quarterly* 27 (1933), pp. 114-24,
and Nuyens's in the introduction to Ross's edition of the *Parva Naturalia*. This tradition of scholarship is surveyed by
[29] A.H. Chroust, 'The first thirty years of modern Aristotelian scholarship', *Classica et Mediaevalia* 24 (1963/4), pp. 27-57.
The papers by Ross and Owen which form Chapters 1 and 2 of our first volume offer two appreciations of the state of play in this field.

Since 1957 triennial Symposia Aristotelica have been held in Europe; their published proceedings provide excellent samples of modern Aristotelian scholarship:

[30] I. Düring and G.E.L. Owen (edd.), *Aristotle and Plato in the Mid-fourth Century*, Studia Graeca et Latina Gothoburgensia 11 (Göteborg, 1960),

[31] S. Mansion (ed.), *Aristote et les problèmes de méthode* (Louvain, 1961),

[32] G.E.L. Owen (ed.), *Aristotle on Dialectic* (Oxford, 1968),

[33] I. Düring (ed.), *Naturforschung bei Aristoteles und Theophrast* (Heidelberg, 1969),

[34] P. Moraux and D. Harlfinger (edd.), *Untersuchungen zur Eudemischen Ethik*, Peripatoi I (Berlin, 1970).

3. ETHICS

The fullest, and in many respects most helpful, commentary on the *Nicomachean Ethics* is in French:

[35] R.A. Gauthier and J.Y. Jolif, *Aristote: l'Ethique à Nicomaque* (Louvain, 1970).

English readers will still find much of value in three older commentaries:

[36] A. Grant, *The Ethics of Aristotle* (London, 1885),

[37] J.A. Stewart, *Notes on the Nicomachean Ethics of Aristotle* (Oxford, 1892),

[38] J. Burnet, *The Ethics of Aristotle* (London, 1900).

See also

[39] H.H. Joachim, *Aristotle – the Nicomachean Ethics* (Oxford, 1955)

and the notes to

[40] J.L. Ackrill, *Aristotle's Ethics* (London, 1973).

There is a modern German commentary by

[41] F. Dirlmeier: *Aristoteles – Nikomachische Ethik* (Berlin, 1966).

Aquinas' commentary has been translated by C.L. Litzinger. Three special commentaries are listed below: [104], [138], [169].

There is at present no English commentary on the *Eudemian Ethics*; but see, in addition to [34],

[42] F. Dirlmeier, *Aristoteles – Eudemische Ethik* (Berlin, 1962).

On the *Magna Moralia* see

[43] F. Dirlmeier, *Aristoteles – Magna Moralia* (Berlin, 1958).

In this commentary Dirlmeier defends the authenticity of the work, as does

[44] J.M. Cooper, 'The Magna Moralia and Aristotle's moral philosophy', *American Journal of Philology* 94 (1973), pp. 327-49; the opposite view is argued by

[45] F. Dirlmeier, 'Die Zeit der "Grossen Ethik"', *Rheinisches Museum* 88 (1939), pp. 214-43;

[46] D.J. Allan, 'Magna Moralia and Nicomachean Ethics', *Journal of Hellenic Studies* 77 (1957), pp. 7-11.

[47] C.J. Rowe, 'A reply to John Cooper on the Magna Moralia', *American Journal of Philology* 96 (1975), pp. 160-72.

For the *Protrepticus* see

[48] I. Düring, *Aristotle's Protrepticus*, Studia Graeca et Latina Gothoburgensia 12 (Göteborg, 1957),

[49] A.H. Chroust, *Aristotle's Protrepticus* (Notre Dame, 1964) and Chapters 7-10 in volume 2 of [22].

On the evolution and chronology of Aristotle's ethical thought see, in addition to Flashar (Chapter 1 of this volume), Chapters 4 and 9 of [25], Chapters 1 and 2 of our volume 1, G. Lieberg [159], A.J. Festugière [158], H. Jackson [104], F. Dirlmeier [42], pp. 361-5, A. Grant [36] and °

[50] A. von Fragstein, *Studien zur Ethik des Aristoteles* (Amsterdam 1974),

[51] J.D. Monan, *Moral Knowledge and its Methodology in Aristotle* (Oxford, 1968),

[52] C.J. Rowe, *The Eudemian and Nicomachean Ethics – a Study in the Development of Aristotle's Thought, Proceedings of the Cambridge Philological Society*, Suppl. 3 (Cambridge, 1971),

[53] D.J. Allan, 'Quasi-mathematical method in the *Eudemian Ethics*', in [31],

[54] D. Harlfinger, 'Die Überlieferungsgeschichte der Eudemischen Ethik', [34], pp. 1-50,

[55] A. Mansion, 'La genèse de l'oeuvre d'Aristote d'après les travaux récents', *Revue Néoscolastique de Philosophie* 29 (1927), pp. 307-41 and 423-66.

On Aristotle's method in ethics see [51], [53], and

[56] G.E.R. Lloyd, 'The role of medical and biological analogies in Aristotle's ethics', *Phronesis* 13 (1968), pp. 68-83,

[57] W.W. Jaeger, 'Aristotle's use of medicine as a model of method in his ethics', *Journal of Hellenic Studies* 77 (1957), pp. 54-61.

See also Owen's paper, Chapter 7 of our volume 1.

A helpful companion to the *Nicomachean Ethics* is provided by

[58] W.F.R. Hardie, *Aristotle's Ethical Theory* (Oxford, 1968).

See also

[59] R.A. Gauthier, *La Morale d' Aristote* (Paris, 1963),

[60] J.J. Walsh and H.L. Shapiro, *Aristotle's Ethics* (Belmont, Cal., 1967),

[61] R. Loening, *Die Zurechnungslehre des Aristoteles* (Jena, 1903),

[62] M. Wittmann, *Die Ethik des Aristoteles* (Regensburg, 1921),

[63] R. Stark, *Aristotelesstudien*, Zetemata 8 (Munich, 1972),

[64] J.M. Cooper, *Reason and Human Good in Aristotle* (Cambridge, Mass., 1975).

Aristotle's criticism of Plato's Form of the Good, and his own remarks about the different ways in which things are called good, have occasioned a quantity of comment. See, in addition to Flashar (Chapter 1) and Ackrill (Chapter 2),

[65] D.J. Allan, 'Aristotle's criticism of Platonic doctrine concerning goodness and the good', *Proceedings of the Aristotelian Society* 64 (1963/4), pp. 273-86,

[66] L.A. Kosman, 'Predicating the good', *Phronesis* 13 (1968), pp. 171-4,

[67] G.E.L. Owen, 'Logic and metaphysics in some earlier works of Aristotle', in [30],

[68] W.W. Fortenbaugh, '*Nicomachean Ethics* I, 1096b 26-9', *Phronesis* 11 (1966), pp. 185-94,

[69] E. Berti, 'Unité et multiplicité du bien selon *EE* I 8', in [34],

[70] D. Wiggins, 'Sentence-sense, word-sense, and difference of word-sense', in *Semantics of Natural Languages*, edd. D.D. Steinberg and L.A. Jakobvits (London, 1971).

See also von Fragstein [50], pp. 45-53; and compare in general Chapters 1-4 of [74].

On Aristotle's positive suggestions about goodness and happiness see Kenny (Chapter 3) and Defourny (Chapter 10). See also
[71] J.L. Ackrill, 'Aristotle on *Eudaimonia*', *Proceedings of the British Academy* 60 (1974), pp. 3-23,
[72] G. Müller, 'Probleme der aristotelischen Eudaimonielehre', *Museum Helveticum* 17 (1960), pp. 121-43,
[73] W.F.R. Hardie, 'The final good in Aristotle's *Ethics*', *Philosophy* 40 (1965), pp. 277-95,
and Chapter 5 of
[74] G.H. von Wright, *The Varieties of Goodness* (London, 1963).
Aristotle's notion of goodness is defended by
[75] S.Hampshire, 'Ethics – a defense of Aristotle', in his *Freedom of Mind* (Oxford, 1972),
and it is given a formal analysis by
[76] B.A.O. Williams, 'Aristotle on the Good – a formal sketch', *Philosophical Quarterly* 12 (1962), pp. 289-96,
[77] C.A. Kirwan, 'Logic and the Good in Aristotle', *Philosophical Quarterly* 17 (1967), pp. 97-114.
Aristotle was made into a hedonist by
[78] H.A. Prichard, 'The meaning of *agathon* in the *Ethics* of Aristotle', *Philosophy* 10 (1935), 27-39.
Against this see
[79] J.L. Austin, '*Agathon* and *Eudaimonia* in the *Ethics* of Aristotle', in *Aristotle*, ed. J.M.E. Moravcsik (New York, 1967).
See also
[80] F.A. Siegler, 'Reason, happiness and goodness', in [60],
[81] J. Léonard, *Le Bonheur chez Aristote*, Mémoires de l'Académie de Belgique (Brussels, 1948),
[82] T. Nagel, 'Aristotle on *Eudaimonia*', *Phronesis* 17 (1972), pp. 252-9,
[82a] R.C. Solomon, 'Is there happiness after death?', *Philosophy* 51 (1976), pp. 189-93.

On ethics and the function of man see
[83] M. Ringbom, 'Aristotle's Notion of Virtue', *Ajatus* 29 (1967), pp. 51-61,
[84] S. Clark, *Aristotle's Man* (Oxford, 1975),
[85] P. Glassen 'A fallacy in Aristotle's argument about the Good', *Philosophical Quarterly* 7 (1957), pp. 319-22,
[86] R. Sorabji, 'Function', *Philosophical Quarterly* 14 (1964), pp. 289-302,
[87] P.T. Geach, 'Good and evil', *Analysis* 17 (1956/7), pp. 33-42,
[88] R.M. Hare, 'Geach, good and evil', *Analysis* 17, (1956/7), pp. 101-11,
[89] A.M. MacIver, 'Good and evil and Mr. Geach', *Analysis* 18 (1957/8), pp. 7-13,
[90] B. Suits, 'Aristotle on the function of man', *Canadian Journal of Philosophy* 4 (1974), pp. 23-40.

With Hardie's discussion (Chapter 4) of the doctrine that moral virtue is a 'mean' compare Chapter 6 of

[91] H.W.B. Joseph, *Essays in Ancient and Modern Philosophy* (Oxford, 1935), and see S. Clark [84]; also

[92] E.H. Olmsted, 'The "moral sense" aspect of Aristotle's ethical theory', *American Journal of Philology* 69 (1948), pp. 42-61,

[93] J.O. Urmson, 'Aristotle's doctrine of the mean', *American Philosophical Quarterly* 10 (1973), pp. 223-30.

[94] W.W. Fortenbaugh, 'Aristotle and the questionable mean-dispositions', *Transactions of the American Philological Association* 99 (1968), pp. 203-31.

On the historical background to the doctrine of the mean see [57] and

[95] H.J. Krämer, *Aretê bei Platon und Aristoteles,* Abhandlungen der Heidelberger Akademie der Wissenschaft, philos.-hist. Kl. 6 (Heidelberg, 1959), Chapter 6,

and see

[96] F. Wehrli, 'Ethik und Medizin: zur Vorgeschichte der aristotelischen Mesonlehre', *Museum Helveticum* 8 (1951), pp. 36-62,

[97] T. Tracy, *Physiological Theory and the Doctrine of the Mean in Plato and Aristotle* (The Hague 1969).

On the acquisition of moral virtue see, Sorabji [145],

[98] E. des Places, 'L' éducation des tendances chez Platon et Aristote', *Archives de Philosophie* 21 (1958), pp. 410-22,

[99] R.S. Peters, 'Reason and habit – the paradox of moral education', in *Moral Education in a Changing Society,* ed. W.R. Niblett (London, 1963),

[100] W.K. Frankena, *Three Historical Philosophies of Education* (Glenview, Ill., 1965),

[101] R.S. Peters, 'Moral development – a plea for pluralism', in *Cognitive Development and Epistemology,* ed. T. Mischel (New York, 1971).

On the various moral virtues see

[102] R.A. Gauthier, *Magnanimité,* Bibliothèque Thomiste 28 (Paris, 1951),

[103] D.A. Rees, ' "Magnanimity" in the Eudemian and Nicomachean Ethics', in [34].

The special virtue of justice is analysed in *EN* V; there are useful notes on this in

[104] H. Jackson, *Peri Dikaiosunês – the Fifth Book of the Nicomachean Ethics of Aristotle* (London, 1879).

Aristotle's analysis is discussed by J.O. Urmson in [93] and by

[105] R. Bambrough, 'Aristotle on justice, a paradigm of philosophy', in *New Essays on Plato and Aristotle,* ed. R. Bambrough (London, 1965),

[106] H. Kelsen, 'Aristotle's doctrine of justice', in [60],

[107] K. Marc-Wogau: 'Aristotle's theory of corrective justice and reciprocity', in his *Philosophical Essays,* Library of Theoria (Lund, 1967).

For a treatment from a legal point of view, one may consult

[108] P. Vinogradoff, *Outlines of Historical Jurisprudence,* vol. II (Oxford, 1922),

[109] A.R.W. Harrison, 'Aristotle's Nicomachean Ethics, Book V, and the law of Athens', *Journal of Hellenic Studies* 77 (1957), pp. 42-7,

[110] M. Hamburger, *Morals and Law – The Growth of Aristotle's Legal Theory* (Newhaven, Conn. 1951).

See also Chapter 10 of [58], and Finley (Chapter 14), and references below on the legal background to Aristotle's treatment of voluntariness.

On the special virtue of friendship see

[111] E. Hoffmann, 'Aristoteles' Philosophie der Freundschaft', in *Festgabe für H. Rickert*, ed. A. Faust (Bühl-Baden, 1933),

[112] A.W.H. Adkins, 'Friendship and self-sufficiency in Homer and Aristotle', *Classical Quarterly* 13 (1963), pp. 30-45,

[113] E. Telfer, 'Friendship', *Proceedings of the Aristotelian Society* 71 (1970/1), pp. 223-41,

[114] J.C. Fraisse, '*Autarkeia* et *Philia* en *EE* VII 12, 1244b1-1245b19', in [34],

[115] W.W. Fortenbaugh, 'Aristotle's analysis of friendship: Function and analogy, resemblance, and focal meaning', *Phronesis* 20 (1975), pp. 51-62,

[116] G. Vlastos, 'The individual as object of love in Plato', in his *Platonic Studies* (Princeton, 1973).

Virtuous and vicious action demand a certain state of mind in the agent; Aristotle's subtle remarks on the mental preconditions of action are found in *EN* III, VI and VII, and *EE* II. Modern discussions of this topic tend to circle about the problem of free will; for Aristotle's attitude to this issue see Furley (Chapter 5), Loening [61], and

[117] T. Gomperz, *Greek Thinkers*, vol. 4, Chapters 10 and 16 (London, 1912),

[118] P.M. Huby, 'The first discovery of the freewill problem', *Philosophy* 42 (1967), pp. 353-62,

[119] W.F.R. Hardie: 'Aristotle and the freewill problem', *Philosophy* 43 (1968), pp. 274-8.

(On Aristotle's attitude to determinism see also the Bibliography to our Volume 3, where there will be further reading on voluntariness.)

Aristotle's account of voluntariness is placed in its historical setting by

[120] A.W.H. Adkins, *Merit and Responsibility* (Oxford, 1960).

The legal background is discussed by

[121] H.D.P. Lee, 'The legal background of two passages in the *Nicomachean Ethics*', *Classical Quarterly* 31 (1937), pp. 129-40,

[122] R. Maschke, *Die Willenslehre im griechischen Recht* (Berlin 1926),

[123] D. Daube, *Roman Law: Linguistic, Social and Philosophical Aspects* (Edinburgh 1969), Part III: 1A,

[124] M. Schofield, 'Aristotelian mistakes', *Proceedings of the Cambridge Philological Society* 19 (1973), pp. 66-70,

[125] G. Glotz, *La Solidarité de la famille dans le droit criminal en Grèce* (Paris, 1904), pp. 413-19.

See also

[126] F.A. Siegler, 'Voluntary and involuntary,' *Monist* 52 (1968), pp. 268-87,

[127] J.L. Austin, 'A plea for excuses', in his *Philosophical Papers* (Oxford, 1961), reprinted from *Proceedings of the Aristotelian Society* 57 (1956/7), pp. 1-30,

[128] V. Haksar, 'Aristotle and the punishment of psychopaths', *Philosophy* 39 (1964), pp. 323-40,

On choice of *prohairesis* see, in addition to Anscombe (Chapter 6), Chapter 7 of [91], Wiggins [129], Sorabji [145], and

[128a] W.W. Fortenbaugh, '*Ta pros to telos* and syllogistic vocabulary in Aristotle's Ethics', *Phronesis* 10 (1965), pp. 191-201.

Intentional action is in some sense governed by the 'practical syllogism'; on the difficult passages in which Aristotle describes this sort of reasoning, see, besides Furley (Chapter 5) and Robinson (Chapter 8),

[129] D. Wiggins, 'Deliberation and practical reason', *Proceedings of the Aristotelian Society* 76 (1975/6), pp. 29-51,

[130] D.J. Allan, 'The practical syllogism', in *Autour d' Aristote* (Louvain, 1955),

[131] T. Ando, *Aristotle's Theory of Practical Cognition* (Kyoto, 1958),

[132] S.G. Etheridge, 'Aristotle's Practical Syllogism and Necessity', *Philologus* 112 (1968), pp. 20-42.

See also [128a], and the papers on weakness of will listed below. Aristotle's discussion of practical reasoning has sparked off some exciting modern studies; see especially

[133] G.E.M. Anscombe, *Intention* (Oxford, 1963),

[134] G.E.M. Anscombe, 'Two kinds of error in action', *Journal of Philosophy* 60 (1963), pp. 393-401,

[135] M. Mothersill, 'Anscombe's account of the practical syllogism', *Philosophical Review* 70 (1962), pp. 448-61,

[136] A.J.P. Kenny, 'Practical inference', *Analysis* 26 (1965/6), pp. 65-75,

[137] R.M. Hare, 'Practical inferences', in his *Practical Inferences* (London, 1971).

Many of the difficulties in *EN* VI are eased by

[138] L.H.G. Greenwood, *Aristotle – Nicomachean Ethics Book Six* (Cambridge, 1909).

The 'intellectual virtues' which this book dissects have received scanty attention, with the exception of 'practical wisdom' or *phronêsis*. Some of the problems surrounding this notion are examined by Allan (Chapter 7). Allan adopts Loening's view [61] and is strongly supported by Gauthier [35], vol. 1, pp. 267-83. On the other side see

[139] J. Walter, *Die Lehre von der praktischen Vernunft in der griechischen Philosophie* (Jena, 1874),

[140] P. Aubenque, *La Prudence chez Aristote* (Paris, 1963),

[141] P. Aubenque, 'La prudence aristotélicienne, porte-t-elle sur la fin ou sur les moyens?', *Revue des Études Grecques* 78 (1965), pp. 40-51,

[142] W.W. Fortenbaugh, 'Aristotle's conception of moral virtue and its perceptive role', *Transactions and proceedings of the American Philological Association* 95 (1964), pp. 77-87,

[143] W.W. Fortenbaugh, 'Aristotle: emotion and moral virtue', *Arethusa* 2 (1969), pp. 163-85,

[144] W.W. Fortenbaugh, *Aristotle on Emotion* (London, 1975).

For a rival view see

[145] R. Sorabji, 'Aristotle on the rôle of intellect in virtue', *Proceedings of the Aristotelian Society* 74 (1973/4), pp. 107-29.

On *phronêsis* see further

[146] R. Jackson, 'Rationalism and intellectualism in the Ethics of Aristotle', *Mind* 51 (1942), pp. 343-60,

[147] R. Demos, 'Some remarks on Aristotle's doctrine of practical reason', *Philosophy and Phenomenological Research* 22 (1961/2), pp. 153-62,

[148] C.J. Rowe, 'The meaning of *phronêsis* in the *Eudemian Ethics*', in [34],

[149] E.M. Michelakis, *Aristotle's Theory of Practical Principles* (Athens, 1961).

On a related topic see

[150] G. Ryle, 'On forgetting the difference between right and wrong', in *Essays in Moral Philosophy*, ed. A.I. Melden (Seattle, 1958).

On the puzzles surrounding Aristotle's discussion of moral weakness or *akrasia* see, in addition to Robinson (Chapter 8),

[151] J. Cook Wilson, *On the Structure of Book Seven of the Nicomachean Ethics* (Oxford, 1912),

[152] J.J. Walsh, *Aristotle's Conception of Moral Weakness* (New York, 1963),

[153] R.D. Milo, *Aristotle on Practical Knowledge and Weakness of Will* (The Hague, 1966),

[154] A.J.P. Kenny, 'The practical syllogism and incontinence', *Phronesis* 11 (1966), pp. 163-84,

[155] G. Santas, 'Aristotle on practical inference, the explanation of action, and akrasia', *Phronesis* 14 (1969), pp. 162-89.

See also Chapter V of

[156] R.M. Hare, *Freedom and Reason* (Oxford, 1963),

and

[157] D. Davidson, 'How is weakness of the will possible?' in *Moral Concepts*, ed. J. Feinberg (Oxford, 1969).

Various reasons make pleasure a central concern of the moral philosopher. Most of the problems raised by the dual accounts of pleasure in *EN* VII and X are dealt with by

[158] A.J. Festugière, *Aristote: Le plaisir* (Paris, 1946),

[159] G. Lieberg, *Die Lehre von der Lust in den Ethiken des Aristoteles*, Zetemata 19 (Munich, 1958).

Issues of a more philosophical nature are raised by

[160] J.O. Urmson, 'Aristotle on pleasure', in *Aristotle*, ed. J.M.E. Moravcsik (New York, 1967),

[161] A.J.P. Kenny, *Action, Emotion and Will* (London, 1963), Chapter 6,

[162] P. Merlan, *Studies in Aristotle and Epicurus* (Wiesbaden, 1960), Ch. 1.

Owen's challenging suggestions (Chapter 9) have been examined by

[163] J.C.B. Gosling, 'More Aristotelian pleasures', *Proceedings of the Aristotelian Society* 74 (1973/4), pp. 15-34.

On the distinction between change (*kinêsis*) and activity (*energeia*) see Chapter 8 of [161], and

[164] J.L. Ackrill, 'Aristotle's distinction between *energeia* and *kinêsis*', in *New Essays on Plato and Aristotle*, ed. R. Bambrough (London, 1965),

[165] C.C.W. Taylor, 'States, activities and performances', *Proceedings of the Aristotelian Society* Suppl. 39 (1965), pp. 85-102,

[166] T. Penner, 'Verbs and the identity of actions', in *Ryle*, edd. O.P. Wood and G. Pitcher (London, 1971),

[167] L.A. Kosman, 'Aristotle's definition of motion', *Phronesis* (1969) pp. 40-62.

Some of these studies are indebted to

[168] Z. Vendler, 'Verbs and times', *Philosophical Review* 66 (1957), pp. 143-60.
(See further the bibliography to our Volume 3.)

There is a commentary on *EN* X by
[169] G. Rodier, *Aristote: Éthique à Nicomaque, livre X* (Paris, 1897).
For the last book of the *EE* see
[170] P. Moraux, 'Das Fragment VIII. 1 – Text und Interpretation', in [34],
[171] W.J. Verdenius, 'Human reason and God in the Eudemian Ethics', in [34].
See also Defourny (Chapter 10), and the papers on happiness cited earlier.

4. POLITICS

The classic commentary on the *Politics* is
[172] W.L. Newman, *The Politics of Aristotle*, 4 vols. (Oxford, 1887-1902).
This contains essays, copious notes, and appendices of great value. See also
[173] F. Susemihl, *Aristotelis Politica* (Leipzig, 1879).
For Books I-V there is
[174] F. Susemihl and R.D. Hicks, *The Politics of Aristotle* (London, 1894).
For Books III and V there is
[175] R. Robinson, *Aristotle's Politics Books III and IV*, in [3] (Oxford, 1962).
There are informative introductions in
[176] E. Barker, *The Politics of Aristotle* (Oxford, 1946),
[177] J. Aubonnet, *Aristote-Politique,* I-II (Paris, 1960), III-IV (Paris, 1971), V-VI (Paris, 1973),
and
[178] Kurt von Fritz and Ernst Kapp, *Aristotle's Constitution of Athens and Related Texts* (New York, 1950), from which our Chapter 11 is taken.
For background reading, see
[179] T.A. Sinclair, *A History of Greek Political Thought* (London, 1951),
[180] K.J. Dover, *Greek Popular Morality in the Time of Plato and Aristotle* (Oxford, 1974),
[181] M.I. Finley, *Democracy Ancient and Modern* (London, 1973),
the sharp attack on Aristotle by
[182] K.R. Popper, *The Open Society and its Enemies*, vol. 2, (London, 1945),
and the account of Greek culture and education in
[183] W. Jaeger, *Paideia* (New York, 1943-4).
Plato's *Laws*, as well as his *Republic* and *Statesman*, may profitably be read in conjunction with Aristotle's *Politics*.

The following are general works bearing on Aristotle's *Politics*:
[184] E. Barker, *The Political Thought of Plato and Aristotle* (London, 1906),
[185] R. Weil, *Aristote et l'histoire: Essai sur la 'Politique'* (Paris, 1960),
[186] Fondation Hardt, *Entretiens XI, La 'Politique' d'Aristote* (Geneva, 1964)
contains seven addresses by leading scholars on the *Politics*.
For a full discussion of *Politics* Book III see
[187] E. Braun, *Das dritte Buch der aristotelischen Politik: Interpretation,* in

Sitzungsberichte der Österreichischen Akademie der Wissenschaften, Philos.-hist. Klasse, Band 247.4, (1965).

There is still much of value in
[188] M. Defourny, *Aristote: Études sur la Politique* (Paris, 1932),
from which our Chapter 16 is taken. See also
[189] G. Bien, *Die Grundlegung der politischen Philosophie bei Aristoteles* (Munich, 1973).

Some of Aristotle's concepts are discussed in
[190] K.J.J. Hintikka, 'Conceptual presuppositions of Greek political theory', *Scandinavian Political Studies* 2 (1967), pp. 11-25.

Aristotle's *Constitution of Athens* was discovered in Egypt in 1890. It is a contribution by him to the set of 158 constitutions whose collection he organised. On this enterprise, see Jaeger [25], Chapter 13. Fragments of other constitutions collected by Aristotle or his associates can be found in
[191] V. Rose, *Aristotelis qui ferebantur Librorum Fragmenta* (Leipzig, 1886).

The fragments are discussed by
[192] H. Bloch, 'Studies in the historical literature of the fourth century: Theophrastus' *Nomoi* and Aristotle', in *Athenian Studies presented to W.S. Ferguson, Harvard Studies in Classical Philology*, Suppl. I (1940), pp. 355-76,
[193] *id.*, 'Herakleides Lembos and his *Epitome* of Aristotle's *Politeiai*', *Transactions of the American Philological Association* 71 (1940), pp. 27-39.

For a translation of the *Constitution of Athens*, with illuminating introduction and notes, see von Fritz and Kapp [178]. A more recent translation, with full historical commentary, is
[194] J.M. Moore, *Aristotle and Xenophon on Democracy and Oligarchy* (London, 1975).

See also R. Weil [185], and
[195] C. Hignett, *A History of the Athenian Constitution* (Oxford, 1952),
[196] J. Day and M. Chambers, *Aristotle's History of Athenian Democracy*, University of California Publications in History 73 (Berkeley and Los Angeles, 1962),
[197] J.J. Keaney, 'The structure of Aristotle's *Athenaion Politeia*', *Harvard Studies in Classical Philology* 67 (1963), pp. 115-46,
[198] J.J. Keaney, 'The date of Aristotle's *Athenaion Politeia*', *Historia* 19 (1970), pp. 326-36.

Aristotle's method of collecting data is discussed in
[199] L. Bourgey, *Observation et expérience chez Aristote* (Paris, 1955),
from which an extract bearing on science is translated in our vol. 1. Aristotle as a historian is discussed by R. Weil in the present volume, and in [185], by Jaeger [25], Chapter 13, and by
[200] G. Huxley, 'On Aristotle's historical methods', *Greek, Roman and Byzantine Studies* 13 (1972), pp. 157-9,
[201] G. Huxley, 'Aristotle as antiquary', *Greek, Roman and Byzantine Studies* 14.3 (1973), pp. 271-86,
[202] K. von Fritz, 'Die Bedeutung des Aristoteles für die Geschichtschreibung', in Fondation Hardt, *Entretiens* IV (Geneva, 1956), pp. 83-145, and
[203] G. de Ste Croix, 'Aristotle on history and poetry (*Poetics* 9. 1451a36-

b11)', in *The Ancient Historian and his Materials*, Essays in honour of C.E. Stevens (Farnborough, 1975)
who is also concerned with his attitude to historians. A disparaging view of his powers as a historian is taken by Day and Chambers [196], and by
[204] U. von Wilamowitz-Moellendorf, *Aristoteles und Athen* (Berlin 1893).

The only early political work of Aristotle, of which substantial fragments survive, is the *Protrepticus*, for which see the editions of I. Düring [48] and A.H. Chroust [49], and
[205] P. von der Mühll, 'Isocrates und der Protreptikos des Aristoteles', *Philologus* 94 (1941), pp. 259-65,
[206] B. Einarson, 'Aristotle's Protrepticus and the structure of the Epinomis', *Transactions of the American Philological Association* 67 (1936), pp. 261-72,
[207] W.G. Rabinowitz, 'Aristotle's Protrepticus and the sources of its reconstruction', *University of California Publications in Classical Philology* 16 (1957), pp. 1-96.
For other more fragmentary early works, see
[208] P. Moraux, *'A la recherche de l'Aristote perdu: le Dialogue Sur la Justice'* (Louvain, 1957),
[209] A.H. Chroust, 'Aristotle's *Politicus*: a lost dialogue', *Rheinisches Museum für Philologie* 108.4 (1965), pp. 346-53, reprinted in [29].

W. Jaeger's attempt in [25] (1923) to established a chronology for the political writings was opposed by the different scheme of
[210] H. von Arnim, 'Zur Entstehungsgeschichte der aristotelischen Politik', *Sitzungsberichte der Österreichischen Akademie der Wissenschaft in Wien*, Philos.-hist. Klasse 200.1 (1924),
Von Fritz and Kapp [178] have some interesting things to say on Aristotle's development, which modify the views of Jaeger. And there is further comment in
[211] W.D. Ross, 'The development of Aristotle's thought', *Proceedings of the British Academy* 43 (1957), pp. 63-78, reprinted in our volume 1.
Developmental hypotheses have been called into question, e.g. by Barker in [176], pp. xli-xlvi, who is there recanting some of his earlier views. But such hypotheses appear in Kelsen's article in the present volume, and in
[212] J.L. Stocks, 'The composition of Aristotle's politics', *Classical Quarterly* 31 (1937), pp. 177-8.
There is further controversy about the proper order of the books of the *Politics*. Bekker's edition, and the Oxford translation, follow the order found in all the MSS. But Reiz, followed by Susemihl and many other scholars, placed the books which are VII and VIII of the Ms. order immediately after Book III. On this controversy, see again Ross [211], and
[213] W. Theiler, 'Bau und Zeit der aristotelischen Politik', *Museum Helveticum* 9 (1952), pp. 65-78,
[214] E. Braun, 'Zu einem Zusammenhang zwischen dem III und dem VII Buch der Politika des Aristoteles', *Jahreshefte der Österreichischen Archäologischen Instituts, Wien* 41 (1954), Beiblatt, pp. 169-72,
[215] R. Stark, 'Der Gesamtaufbau der aristotelischen "Politik" ', in [186], pp. 1-35.

Much of the first book of the *Politics* is concerned with *nature*. The state is based on nature, not on contract. The subject of *nature* is illuminatingly discussed by von Fritz and Kapp in Chapter 11 of the present volume. See also Day and Chambers [196], Chapter 3. Aristotle's theory of the nature of man is discussed by S. Clark [84], and by

[216] E. Weil, 'L'Anthropologie d'EE', in his *Essais et conférences*, I (Paris, 1970), reprinted from *Revue de Métaphysique et de Morale* 51 (1946).

Slavery is said to be suited to the *nature* of certain persons. Fortenbaugh's clarification of this doctrine in the present volume may be read as a reply to

[217] O. Gigon, 'Die Sklaverei bei Aristoteles', in [186], pp. 245-76, and to

[218] R.O. Schaifer, 'Greek theories of slavery from Homer to Aristotle', *Harvard Studies in Classical Philology* 47 (1936), pp. 165-204, reprinted in M.I. Finley (ed.), *Slavery in Classical Antiquity* (Cambridge, 1960).

See also

[219] A. Baruzzi, 'Der Freie und der Sklave in Ethik und Politik des Aristoteles', *Philosophisches Jahrbuch* 77 (1970), pp. 15-28.

J. Ritter discusses the basis of natural law in human *nature* in

[220] J. Ritter, 'Le droit natural chez Aristote – Contribution au renouveau de droit naturel', *Archives de Philosophie* n.s. 32 (1969), pp. 416-57.

Retail trade is declared *unnatural*. This is explained not only by M.I. Finley in the present volume, but also by

[221] K. Polanyi, 'Aristotle discovers the economy', in *Trade and Market in the Early Empires*, edd. K. Polanyi, C.M. Arensberg and H.W. Pearson (Glencoe, Ill., 1957), pp. 64-94. See also

[222] J. Soudek, 'Aristotle's theory of exchange', *Proc. Amer. Philos. Soc.* 96 (1952), pp. 45-75.

Karl Marx's views on Aristotle's economic theory are reported by

[223] E.C. Welskopf, *Die Produktionsverhältnisse im alten Orient und in der griechisch-römischen Antike* (Berlin, 1957), pp. 336-46.

Aristotle's conception of the state as a natural growth is discussed by

[224] A.C. Bradley, 'Aristotle's conception of the state,' in *Hellenica*, ed. E. Abbott (London, 1880).

For Hobbes' attitude to Aristotle on this and other matters, see

[225] J. Laird, 'Hobbes on Aristotle's Politics', *Proceedings of the Aristotelian Society* 43 (1942-3), pp. 1-20.

In Book II, Aristotle studies various constitutions, ideas and actual. For his criticism of the Spartan constitution in II 9, see

[226] E. Braun, *Die Kritik der Lakedaimonischen Verfassung in den Politika des Aristoteles, Kärtner Museumsschriften* 12 (Klagenfurt 1956),

[227] P. Cloché, 'Aristote et les institutions de Sparte,' *Les Études Classiques* 11 (1942), pp. 289-313,

[228] R.A. de Laix, 'Aristotle's conception of the Spartan constitution,' *Journal of the History of Philosophy*, 12 (1974), pp. 21-30.

For his criticism of the Cretan constitution in II 10, see

[229] G. Huxley, 'Crete in Aristotle's Politics,' *Greek, Roman and Byzantine Studies* 12 (1971), pp. 505-15.

Aristotle's criticisms of Plato are discussed by

[230] E. Bornemann, 'Aristoteles' Urteil über Platons politische Theorie,' *Philologus* 79 (1923), pp. 70-158, 234-57.

From Book III, the definition of citizenship in III 1 is discussed by

[231] C. Mossé, 'La conception du citoyen dans la *Politique* d'Aristote', *Eirene* 6 (1967), pp. 17-21,

[232] J. Pečirka, 'A note on Aristotle's definition of citizenship', *Eirene* 6 (1967), pp. 23-6.

The nature of civic virtue in III 4 is discussed by

[233] E. Braun, 'Aristoteles über Bürger – und Menschentugend', *Sitzungsberichte der Österreichischen Akademie der Wissenschaften*, Philos.-hist. Klasse 236.2 (1961),

[234] R. Develin, 'The good man and the good citizen in Aristotle's "Politics" ', *Phronesis* 18, (1973), pp. 71-9.

Different constitutions imply different conceptions of justice; Aristotle's discussion of this in III 9 ff. is treated by

[235] F.D. Harvey, 'Two kinds of equality', *Classica et Mediaevalia* 26 (1965), pp. 101-46.

The democratic idea of pooled wisdom in III 11 is treated by

[236] E. Braun, 'Die Summierungstheorie des Aristoteles', *Jahreshefte der Osterreichischen Archäologischen Instituts, Wien* 44 (1959), pp. 157-84.

Kelsen's view of the influence of Alexander the Great on Aristotle's attitude to monarchy is opposed by

[237] V. Ehrenberg, *Alexander and the Greeks*, Oxford 1938, Ch. III.

Another aspect of monarchy is treated by

[238] R.G. Mulgan, 'A note on Aristotle's absolute ruler', *Phronesis* 19 (1974), pp. 66-9.

Aristotle's kinds of democracy in Books IV and VI are discussed by

[239] M. Chambers, 'Aristotle's "Forms of Democracy" ', *Transactions of the American Philological Association* 92 (1961), pp. 20-36.

Aristotle's treatment, in Books IV and V, of the prevention of revolution is discussed by Wheeler in this volume, Chapter 14, and by

[240] E. Braun, 'Ein Maxime der Staatskunst in den Politika des Aristoteles', *Jahreshefte der Österreichischen Archäologischen Instituts, Wien* 44 (1959), pp. 386-98.

and

[241] F. Kort, 'The quantification of Aristotle's theory of revolution', *The American Political Science Review* 46, (1952), pp. 486-93,

who compares the Pareto-Davis theory of income distribution and political disturbances.

Aristotle's city planning in Book VII and elsewhere is discussed by

[242] G. Downey, 'Aristotle as an expert on urban problems', *Talanta* III (1971), pp. 56-73.

Leisure, peace, education, and the aim of the ideal state of Books VII and VIII, are the theme not only of M. Defourny in this volume, but also of

[243] F. Solmsen, 'Leisure and play in Aristotle's ideal state', *Rheinisches Museum* N.F. 107 (1964), pp. 193-220.
[244] J.L. Stocks, '*Scholē*', *Classical Quarterly* 30 (1936), pp. 177-87.
See also under *Ethics* for readings on education.

The rights of the individual *vis à vis* the state are discussed by
[245] D.J. Allan, 'Individual and state in the *Ethics* and *Politics*', in [186], pp. 53-85.
The individual and the state is the theme of some papers in Swedish in the Finnish journal *Ajatus* XXVIII, 1966. There are brief summaries in English of the contributions by K.J.J. Hintikka ('The individual and the ends of the state: some aspects of a Greek way of thinking'), and by I. Düring ('Individual and social ethics in Plato and Aristotle'). There are brief German summaries of O. Gigon ('Der Autarkiebegriff in der griechischen Philosophie') and of Sven Krohn ('Aristoteles als Gründer der Normativen Ethik').

The relation of the *Politics* to the *Ethics* is discussed by von Fritz and Kapp in their introduction to [178], by Newman in Appendix A to vol. 2 of [172], by Allan in [245]; by
[246] H. Flashar, 'Ethik und Politik in der Philosophie des Aristoteles', *Gymnasium* 78 (1971), pp. 278-93;
and by
[247] P. Betbeder, 'Éthique et Politique selon Aristote', *Revue des Sciences Philosophiques et Théologiques*, 54 (1970), pp. 453-88,
[248] S. Cashdollar, 'Aristotle's politics of morals', *Journal of the History of Philosophy* 11 (1973), pp. 145-60,
[249] E. Trépanier, 'La politique comme philosophie morale chez Aristote,' *Dialogue* 2 (1963-4), pp. 251-79.

For Aristotle's theology, see Volume III, and for the *Rhetoric*, Volume IV.

ADDENDA (ETHICS)

Voluntariness and determinism in Aristotle are the subject of R.R.K. Sorabji, *Necessity, Cause and Blame* (forthcoming, London and Ithaca, N.Y.). Two articles on Aristotle's ethics will appear in *Midwest Studies in Philosophy*, ed. P.A. French, T.E. Uehling Jr., and H.K. Wettstein (Minnesota 1978). They are D. Pears, 'Aristotle's theory of courage', and T.H. Irwin, 'First principles in Aristotle's ethics'. See also D. Charles, *Aristotle's Philosophy of Action* (forthcoming, London).

GENERAL INDEX

INDEX OF ARISTOTELIAN PASSAGES